THE MEN WHO MAKE OUR NOVELS

THE MEN WHO MAKE OUR NOVELS

BY

CHARLES C. BALDWIN

REVISED EDITION

Essay Index Reprint Series

Originally published by:

DODD, MEAD AND COMPANY

BOOKS FOR LIBRARIES PRESS, INC.

FREEPORT, NEW YORK

First published 1924
Reprinted 1967

LIBRARY OF CONGRESS CATALOG CARD NUMBER:
67-30174

PRINTED IN THE UNITED STATES OF AMERICA

TO JUDY
WHOSE SEVEREST CRITIC I AM

CONTENTS

Contents

THE MEN WHO MAKE OUR NOVELS

BILL ADAMS

Damn Conrad anyway! Even so generous a name-sake as the author of *Success* and *Siege* must ring in Conrad when he writes of Bill Adams and all because Bill writes of the sea.

The sea!

As an old beach comber once said, the sea is wide and uncertain. It belongs to no man. It is England's and it is ours. It is a fair field for the ripe endeavor of Dago and Chink and Swede. It is, humanly speaking, of limitless possibilities.

How then did Conrad, an inland Pole who had never glimpsed the blue of Channel or Mediterranean until he was well past twenty, come to preëmpt the sea? Why do we, with the Pacific on one side and the Atlantic on another, allow his claims to prior right to go unchallenged, without dispute? Have we no seamen of our own and no pleasure in the sea?

II

As a matter of fact the comparison is useful only as showing a difference, and a fundamental difference, in outlook and in philosophy. Conrad left the sea. He left the sea with few illusions and no conceit. He had not conquered the sea. He was not Byron hailing the storm as brother; he was not Lear hunted upon the heath. He simply retired in good order. He had experienced the fury of the gale and he knew that he could not long endure such torment.   It was a trial of strength beyond his poor powers.   But the sea whipped Bill Adams.   It broke his body and cast him aside, a wreck upon the shores of California.   The everlasting beat of spray upon his breast, the rush of ice cold winds upon his lips, shattered his lungs.   Bill is now a tubercular fruit grafter in the hills back of San Francisco.

And naturally this defeat rankles in Bill.   He aches to be back at his old adversary.   He has none of the resignation of Conrad.   He has not found peace. He is an outcast from his element and he is restless. He is disturbed.   He could no more write, as Conrad does in *Youth,* of the charm of the sea than he could, with Mr. Wells, fly to the moon.   He must picture the sea as terrible, with visible dangers, with threatening clouds as they rush to an encounter with some long-battered ship, icebergs looming out of the fog, waves rising high and sweeping across the deck.

There is nothing mysterious about Bill Adams' sea. It is the sea of Masefield, of the Dauber and the ships that lie at anchor in the Mersey or sail around the Horn.   Bill tells of rowdy nights in the saloons along the water-front, of painted women and huge, hard-handed sailors singing rude songs or dancing a clumsy hornpipe.

III

Bill Adams first appeared upon the literary horizon in a letter to Christopher Morley's *Bowling Green* column in the New York *Evening Post.*   The letter asked why, in this and that, the world at large did not write to Bill, a lonely prisoner on the desert's edge, far from his beloved sea—that old devil sea whose laureate is Eugene O'Neill.

Shortly thereafter, in 1921, his first story, *The Bos'n of the Goldenhorn's Yarn*, appeared in *Adventure;* to be followed, during the next twelve months, by *Amos Tregenna, Twinkle-Bright* and half a dozen other sea tales, and some verse—one poem, *Billy Peg-Leg's Fiddle*, passing by word of mouth from ship to ship clear round the globe.

These stories instantly won for Bill an ever-increasing circle of friends and admirers. "I doubt," says Sam Adams, "if Conrad could have done better." "I love sea stuff," Grant Overton said, "and I particularly love Bill Adams' sea stuff."

Quite naturally the stories were collected and published together in one volume, with the poems scattered here and there at a story's end; and that volume, *Fenceless Meadows,* has been wonderfully successful.

But do not, for this reason, think that we have here one of the great writers of the sea. We have a phase of sea-life, nothing more—the talk and work and wants of the men in the forecastle. There is here no wide vision of human folly, such as you will find in McFee; there are here no Lord Jims going steadily forward to a self-appointed doom; you will not even meet with the Hairy-Ape. Just ordinary men glimpsed and admired by an ordinary man who, in his loneliness, has done some reading and feels the urge to write of the things which he has known and seen.

IV

The Bos'n of the Goldenhorn's Yarn is an excellent
story. It is simple and it is direct. It has the pathos
of all things that are human and frail. It tells of the
second mate of the *Goldenhorn* and of the girl who
came down to kiss him good-by when his ship put out
from Liverpool to sail for 'Frisco round the Horn.

She was a little thing with sandy hair and clear
hazel eyes—a clipper-built slip of a girl.

Clegg, the mate, leaves the fo'csle head and climbs
over the rail, standing on the beading, holding with
one hand as he bends toward her.

She turns to Mick Sinclair, the boss stevedore, and
smiles up at him. Mick puts his big paws under her
and lifts her to Clegg. A bit of breeze whips the
river as they kiss good-by; and as Mick lowers her
to the dock she calls to her sweetheart, "There's luck
to you, Willie; round the Horn with your skysails set."

Mick laughs. "There's to make a bold sailor of
you, my boy," he says—"eh, what?"

Clegg climbs back to the clipper's deck. "Aye," he
answers, slowly, "a bold sailor it will be now."

V

There is about Bill Adams' stories, occasionally,
this note of gentleness—but there is nothing gentle
about his sea. Indeed there has been nothing gentle
about life, for him. Life has been, in his own
words, a queer dance. And though one may, at times,
want to forget some of those things which hurt so
much when one was little and all alone in the world,

yet it is impossible ever really to forget them—or to want to forget them. After all, they bring a fellow friends—and friends are always worth while. Then, too, even among the deepest shadows some light can be found. If we wait long enough we will see the light.

VI

Bill Adams was born in England forty-four years ago. When he was little more than a baby his mother died. As he says, that was tough; for he was left in the care of a middle-aged spinster with a stern faith in righteousness and a grim consciousness of her own abilities as a mother. She used to lick him a good deal—for nothing, so far as he could make out; and this hurt him, not physically but mentally, because he was a sensitive child and wanted to believe in the justice and beauty of living.

He was brought up with the ministry in view, and taught hymns by the dozen, hundreds of collects, prayers without end. He was taught to respect God. And he pictured God as a very tall man, a high gold crown on his head, a nightgown hanging to his feet, two large bony hands, and a face as hard as the crown he wore. For reasons unknown, lambs gamboled before him and doves flew round and round his head; while just back of him, seated on golden stools, row after row of angels, strumming harps, shouted, Hallelujah!

One evening, while he was still very young, his guardian, pointing from a high hill, showed him the sea—and immediately he wanted to go to sea. He wanted to find out what lay beyond that strange and peaceful-seeming floor of blue and gray.

Slowly he began to impress upon his guardian the hopelessness of making a minister out of him.   Finally, she consented to his being a sailor.   He was nearly eighteen at the time.   He had had the best education England afforded, but he loathed school; he wanted to be free.

Just before he went to sea his father died, a very old man, having been sixty-seven at the time of Bill's birth—at sixty, while a lawyer in New York State, he had eloped with an Irish girl engaged to marry a congregational minister.

Bill had been very fond of his father, though he had never seen very much of him.   The man was always away somewhere, in America, traveling.   He had run away from home as a boy and enlisted in the French Foreign Legion.   There he fought with distinction.   Leaving the Legion, before he was grown to manhood, he went to America and rode with Sherman to the sea.   When he lay dying he asked for Bill and about Bill, and Bill told him he was going to sea.   He smiled.   "You'll find it a hard life," he said.   And Bill has.

VII

In his writings Bill has told perhaps all there is to tell of his life at sea—how he was bitterly disappointed when the full rigged *Helenslea* put to sea without him; how he was to go with the big ship *Monarch* and didn't, and was glad afterwards because she was a ship

where men and boys were treated with damnable
brutality; how he finally got away on the *"Old Fast
and Furious"* and loved her, in spite of the vermin
with which she swarmed and the vile grub and hard
treatment.   He made four midwinter passages around
Cape Horn.

But fate was not kind to him.   In the full flush of
his young strength he was cut down and cast ashore,
a mate's ticket in his pocket and a master mariner's
career ahead of him.   The captain was afraid he
would die on his hands on the voyage home.   Bill was
a sea-broken man.   They put him ashore, hopelessly
afflicted with a bronchial affection that will go with
him to the grave.

Alone and friendless, without a trade, Bill faced
starvation.

But that's how life's music plays, fiddle and tear,
a queer jig; and Bill's been many things since those
far days.   For twenty years a day laborer—gardener,
stable-boy, muleteer, farmhand, tramp, policeman,
vineyard- and orchard-worker—for years and years
never so much as a glimpse of the sea.   Yet every
spring when the sap rises and the birds fly away to
find their mates, Bill's heart cries out and Bill longs to
be off; to China, to the Cape, to many places where
his fancy can be free.   He has never forgotten the
sunrise at sea, where the trades blow easy; he can recall the scent of little islands, the scent of fruit and
flowers, and see the out-spread wings of a ship—a ship
is still his chief delight—a ship under square sail with
the snow at her flying heels and albatrosses about her.

VIII

About the time I wrote to him, in June, 1924, Bill discovered his favorite author—Jack London. "I read him aloud," he says, "to a pal of mine who is stone blind."

Let the cultured folk say what they will, Bill knows the smell of salt water when it flows his way and for Bill there is more of the actual slap of the waves in London's *Sea Wolf* than in any other sea book he has ever read—as there is more of the slap of life ashore in *John Barleycorn*. London and London's revolt against the toadying of the upper classes—the ruling classes, as they like to call themselves—were made for Bill.

Others of Bill's favorites are Carl Sandburg, though at first he was a bit of a shock, and Walter de la Mare. "I'd sell my soul," he says, "to make the little songs jingle and sing as they do in de La Mare's *Peacock Pie*." And of course, Masefield. Masefield's *Captain Margaret* suits him to a T, and Masefield's poetry. If he were allowed but one poem out of all the literature of the world, the poem Bill would keep would be *The Everlasting Mercy*.

IX

As a boy he read Deadwood Dick, the Bible, Dumas, Dickens, Scott, Chaucer and Shakespeare; tales of slavers enthralled him; Grenville at Flores, Collingwood, Jarvis, Paul Revere. Some of his youthful heroes are heroic (or, at any rate, remembered) even yet: D'Artagnan, the Fat Boy in Pickwick, Scrooge,

Pontius Pilate, Horatius at the bridge, Caractacus dragged in a Roman triumph, Alfred with the burning cakes, Hereward, the mare Swallow, and Martin Lightfoot.

At school he learned to hate poetry. They used to make him write it—heaven knows why. But years after, his love of verse returned and he found that he could live a new life, a singing life, in poetry.

Then for years, after he came ashore, expelled from the sea, he was too poor to buy even a daily paper and too body-weary to be able to read when his day's work was done. He forgot all about books. He was a wage slave. But even slavery cannot rob a man of all the music in his soul. He used to find himself reciting lines from Keats and Milton and Shelley.

Then, with his first story sold and the first check in his pocket, he sat back and laughed till he cried. He was free! He chucked off his overalls and took a few days' rest.

X

"You writing Johnnies," he says, "amuse me a lot. I'd like to drift into your town of New York and look in on some of you. But I will never get away from this valley. I can't travel—my old lungs don't draw right. I'm jailed here for keeps—until she swings to the ebb of the tide and the Skipper sings out, 'Heave in, and set those topsails, sir. Let's go.'"

SAMUEL HOPKINS ADAMS

Fine! There is no other word for him—the picture of health, of good humor—an honest citizen.

Mark that word "citizen," for it is the key to one half his activities. It explains the frequent trips to Washington, the curiosity about Europe. It is the *Sesame* to his absorbed interest in his fellows. He takes politics seriously and really believes that our governors should truly represent the best of which we are capable.

II

"I think," he told me, "that Wells is the finest intelligence writing. Now, mind, I don't say that I know all there is to know about living writers. There may be greater writers in France—Bergson, perhaps. But from among those I know I should put Wells first."

And Wells is our most incorrigible politician. Wells is interested in world politics, a Utopia that shall unite the nations of the world.

Let Mr. Mencken say that Arnold Bennett beats Wells forty ways, that Wells is a pedagogue, a boomer, an aphorist. Mr. Mencken is a Tory whose little world is bandied about by a select circle of *Feinschmecker;* Mr. Mencken was astounded and gratified by even so easy a triumph as *The Pretty Lady*—Wells has other maids in mind. Wells wrote *Kipps* and Wells wrote that curious and wonderful history

that, for any one else, would have been a lifetime of
pedantic drudgery, conning texts and correcting
sources.

But the point is with Mr. Adams—he has faith in
Wells. He does not think (with Hergesheimer) that
the best of life can be spent in pastimes, in day-dreams
and pleasure, sipping frappées and wondering gravely
which, from twenty cravats, is the tie to match the
glow on the hills and which to wear to lunch at the
Algonquin. Mr. Adams is sturdy, and Mr. Adams is
forthright and hearty. He would never have fitted
into one of Wilde's comedies, the place, undoubtedly,
for Mr. Hergesheimer.

III

Mr. Adams is a good American. He likes American furniture, early colonial furniture; is interested in
American prints, in what the book catalogues call
Americana. He lives among Americans on a farm
near Auburn, New York. Not that he is provincial,
but that there are certain evils here that need correcting before he can feel that it is time to turn his
attention to Europe and the Japanese.

IV

"Know sir," he wrote to me, early in 1919, "that
war à la Sherman has pitchforked me into the job of
farmer's chore-boy. The farmer for whom I work
is also named Adams, and under her stern governance
I have learned much, though by no means all, of the
art of agriculture. I can now address a pig in terms
suitable to his status and value on the hoof; I can

wait on a cow with tact and decorum; I can persuade a reluctant hen to practice anti-race-suicide over a china doorknob—a dazzling life!

"Looking back, autobiographically, upon more easeful days, I recall that I was born too near 1870 to be any longer young"—at Dunkirk, N. Y., January 26, 1871—"and am therefore well along in what Mrs. Gertrude Atherton calls the splendid, idle Forties.

"My first literary effort was a critique upon the faculty of Hamilton College, so brilliant that it got me fired. Since then I have published ten books, but nothing equal in effect upon my environment to that early masterpiece. With the aid of *Collier's* I once haled Peruna, Duffy's Malt, Swamp Root and other patent devices for interior decoration, before the bar of public opinion—they had previously enjoyed a conspicuous and profitable position at other bars—and gave them what their proprietors confidently asserted would be a large amount of effective and valuable free advertising. I understand they still consider the advertising to have been free and effective, but have revised their views as to its value."

v

Mr. Adams might be called the father and initiator of our Pure Food laws. He had written on tuberculosis, typhoid fever, yellow fever, the nostrum evil, the specialist humbug, preying on incurables, etc., etc. He knew the danger that lurks in a bottle, under a fancy name. He thought the name ought to be less fancy and more truthful. He became a stickler for the truth and nothing but the truth, on labels, in names, and in the advertising of those names. He fought for the truth and for a law that should make the truth compulsory. Such a law is the Pure Food law.

VI

It was out of his fight against patent medicine frauds that his campaign for honest advertising grew. He had set forth something of his theories in *The Clarion,* a novel with a newspaper as hero and villain. The editors of the New York *Tribune* read the book; they liked the theories. Mr. Adams was asked to write for them a series of articles on advertising as it existed locally in New York, in the fall of 1914. In his novel he had stressed the relationship that existed between a newspaper and its advertisers. In his articles he went further, explaining the *Tribune's* newly inaugurated policy of guaranteeing its advertising to the reader—guaranteeing satisfaction to the purchaser of any article advertised in the *Tribune's* pages.

"The articles," Mr. Adams says, "stirred up much comment and more enmity; the experiment was at the time quite new in the field of daily journalism and has not since been followed, so far as I am aware, by any other important daily in this country. They dealt with a frankness somewhat startling to the advertiser (who had always deemed himself immune from criticism on account of his heavy expenditures in the papers) with various phases of paid exploitation of merchandise, from the out-and-out swindles, medical and financial, to the exaggerations and misrepresentations indulged in by some of the largest and most representative mercantile concerns in the city.

"Before the twelve original articles were finished, we had caught so many and such large fish by the tail, and were trailing or being trailed by so many more —including two of New York's great department stores, one of the big theatrical syndicates and several rival publishers—that it was impossible to let go. The series ran on into the following spring, when I left for a trip to South America and the smaller West Indies.   The call of fiction was pulling at me again, and I dropped journalistic polemics and wrote *The Unspeakable Perk,* the scene of which is laid in one of those tropical republics which have strongly appealed to my imaginative sense since first I became acquainted with that part of the world.

"On my return, some months later, I found the advertising fight which I had started still raging, and was swiftly drawn back into it.   What with new issues cropping up, libel suits coming due (the sum total of damages from suits aggregating some three millions was a modest six cents, a discouraging result to our opponents who had held the comfortable theory that advertising, good or bad, was nobody's business but the advertiser's) and the principles of sound advertising spreading in various parts of the country, I was kept busy writing, addressing advertising and commercial organizations, and generally doing propaganda work along these lines until the war broke out.

"I had meantime cherished in my mind the idea of setting down, in a series of stories, the casual record of a quaint and lovable locality which I had known well on the east side of New York.   This book, *Our Square,* was quite aside from my main line of

interest, which has always been the American newspaper as an institution.   To that I went back in my
novel, *Common Cause,* which portrayed the newspaper
in its struggle to maintain its independence against the
forces which seek to employ it as an agency for alien,
and in this case anti-American, propaganda.   The
underlying theme is essentially the same as that of
the *Clarion;* that is, the persistent and perhaps inevitable effort to use the newspaper press for ulterior
purposes and thus divert it from its one proper function of informing public opinion.   There adheres in
this effort an intense and dramatic struggle which has
its effect upon practically every phase of our national
life."

Mr. Adams' present favorite among his novels is
Success which was published in 1921.   "I put my best
into that," he says.

VII

But if you think from all this that Mr. Adams wears
a frown down the middle of his forehead, with his
lips pressed tight in thought, it is only because you do
not know of his capacity for taking things easy when
he is on a holiday, away from the newspapers.   He
can jump into an argument with the fleetest, but he
can be out again (literally) before you know it.   Indeed, so great is his reputation for the light fantastic,
he has been everywhere acclaimed the author of the
decade's best flapper story, *Flaming Youth.*   It did
him no good to disclaim that honor, saying that he
would not have been ashamed of such a book—the
rumor persisted and still persists.   He was known for

the dialogue in *Little Miss Grouch* and the repartee of *The Unspeakable Perk*. True, his books are for the most part in the tradition of Brieux, but even Brieux can forget his thesis now and again, as *Les Hannetons* shows. But Mr. Adams has done better than merely follow Brieux—he has recreated a whole generation in *Siege,* the clash of generations, in a book that is a picture and not a parable at all.

VIII

Mr. Adams is an amateur archer, an amateur farmer, an amateur collector of curios and what-not; and a genuine lover of life, of good horses, of the smell of the woods, the salt of the sea; and he is a first-class journalist. He is utterly fearless and absolutely honest, with such a fund of information, such a wealth of experience, as is possible only to one who has been active, in present-day affairs, up to the minute, for thirty years.

Mr. Adams is the author of *The Great American Fraud,* 1906; *The Mystery* (with Stewart Edward White), 1905; *The Flying Death,* 1906; *Average Jones,* 1911; *The Secret of Lonesome Cove,* 1913; *The Clarion,* 1914; *Little Miss Grouch,* 1915; *The Unspeakable Perk,* 1916; *Our Square and the People in It,* 1917; *Common Cause,* 1918; *Wanted, A Husband,* 1919; *Success,* 1921; *Siege,* 1923.

JAMES LANE ALLEN

I have a notion that all of Mr. James Lane Allen can be put into and taken out of one sentence in *A Kentucky Cardinal*. The Adam Moss who is telling the story for Mr. Allen goes to call upon his fair neighbor Georgiana Cobb to tell her how that morning he thrashed a young poacher whom he had caught setting traps for the Kentucky warbler that nightly roosted in the cherry trees beneath his window. She listens; then, reminded of the friendships that have been celebrated between man and certain of the lower animals, launches into a long treatise on the Arab and his horse, camels, mice, etc. Such pedantry disconcerts Moss. This that he has recounted is a special case and demands immediate attention; it is a modern instance that should evoke present indignation against man's cruelty to bird and beast. Miss Cobb's detached air seems to him inhuman and unnatural. It makes him feel as though he were himself no more than one of Æsop's *Fables* or "that old schoolroom horror of 'Androclus and the Lion.'"

I have put in quotes the phrase that seems to me to contain the pith of Mr. Allen's magic wand—the wand which he has used so effectively in calling from the fairylands where they slumber the gentle creatures of his fancy.

Mr. Allen is nothing if not deliberate. And yet you will notice that Androcles has ceased to be the timid Greek whose hesitations served George Bernard

Shaw as plot for the most engaging and wise of latter-
day parables.   Androcles has deteriorated.   He is no
longer a pattern for tailors everywhere, the very spit
of the Athenian Quince, one at whom Bottom might
roar as at a nightingale.   He has become a Latin and
a classroom horror.

Yet it is no worse than might be expected, for Mr.
Allen is the professor turned prosodist; and the professor, a much abused person, is always a little ashamed
of any enthusiasm he may have felt for the nonsense
taught in schools.   He would deny that he ever saw
any beauty or humor in that nonsense.   His is an ill-
paid calling; and since, in this acquisitive country,
money is the measure of success, it is a calling one
cannot well be proud of.   So Mr. Allen tries to forget
his school-teaching days—but it is a trial that is bound
to end in failure.   We don't escape our formative
years by merely growing old.   Wisdom is not acquired
so easily.   Indeed this very acceptance of face-values,
this contempt for the familiar Androcles is in itself a
sign of immaturity.   After all Androcles' was once a
name to stir the pulses.   He embodied the helpless
courage that was to save the Christian religion which
but for such fanaticism as he exhibited and such faith
as was his in the gentleness of man and beast, in the
power of a soft answer to turn aside wrath, would
have been wiped out of existence by the persecuting
Romans.   Androcles may have been impossible
socially but his fame is secure none the less.   You cannot dismiss him on the say-so of tutors.

No, beautiful as Mr. Allen's books are, each phrase
polished to add refinement to refinement, there is about

them so strict an air of propriety that one longs for the real Androcles, for the rough fellowship of Falstaff, a slap on the back or the flip of a coin. Here, we are bound to say, is but half a world. Did these people never rattle their spoons for more? Are they always so conventional?

This is not to say that Mr. Allen has no uses. There is the portrait of the horse-breeder in *The Doctor's Christmas Eve;* and *Summer in Arcady,* his masterpiece, has at once rich passion and spare form. Here he is at his best. And to those who like Trollope he will seem well-nigh perfect. If you want words neatly strung together, if you want rhythm for rhythm's sake, you will be unable to keep back the shout that must go up when you first encounter Mr. Allen's impeccable prose. It defies description; it is so easy and so restrained, faultlessly dressed, gracious and kindly, as becomes the speech of one born near Lexington, Ky., in 1849. And he has humor.

"It made me feel so uncomfortable," he says, "to see her go tripping out of her front gate on the arm of a youth; men differ so in their virtues and are so alike in their transgressions." Mr. Allen is in a blue funk lest this forward gosling, in white duck pantaloons, with pumps flat enough to have been webbed, scenting the air with a far-reaching pestilence of bergamot and cinnamon, should try (as Mr. Allen had lately tried in the arbor) to kiss the lovely and frivolous Sylvia.

II

But enthusiastic as I may be about his prose, I cannot forget that to Mr. Allen a bad word is nothing but

a long dash preceded by a big, big D. To him
Anatole France is a sly old amorist and Renan an un-
believer.   They are naughty because so often they dig
down to fundamentals; they deal with some of the
more common aspects of life; they are forever asking,
with Pontius Pilate, "What is truth?" and they are not
satisfied with the mere gloss behind which we seek to
hide the marks made upon the spirit by the hands of
that cyclopean youth, Instinct.

The phrase, describing Instincts, is Mr. Allen's—
as are so many lovely phrases; and yet he is forever
turning away from life.   He prefers the primrose to
the orchid because the orchid requires dung that it
may grow.   In short, for all his fine manners, he is
not so much civilized as frightened.   And these in-
hibitions of his have made existence a shallow thing
for the most of his characters.   They suffer need-
lessly.   There is in every one of his books a climax of
misery.   In *The Choir Invisible,* for example, John
Gray, in love with a married woman, becomes engaged
to another only to learn too late that his love is free to
marry him; but with the silly self-sacrificing courage
which Mr. Allen admires he goes through with the
engagement and enters into a marrige which is bound
to make three people unhappy.   And in *Aftermath,*
the sequel to *A Kentucky Cardinal,* the eternal note of
sadness is brought in because Mr. Allen insists that the
heroine die to try the hero in the fires of bereavement.

Such folly has been time out of mind the curse of the
world.   We must have a truce to futile tears if we are
ever to taste the salt of life.

III

Unless we can learn to accept life we can never hope to grow up; and Mr. Allen has steadily refused to face a real world. He seeks forgetfulness. He would escape from the grave responsibilities that are our heritage into greener fields and cleaner lands. The filthy pavements of London fill him with a loathing that far surpasses the nostalgia of Kipling's soldier-man. But Suez is still worse. All the teeming life of the Orient is there, the stench of camelherds, the oaths and blasphemies of alien and fecund gods. He wants not only cleanliness but beauty.

So he dreams back upon his own youth in Kentucky —not the frantic youth that rebels against a thousand laws enchaining and thwarting us, but a poet's youth, the youth of a dreamer—a sentimental youth.

IV

Mr. Allen can number among his paternal ancestors some of the first settlers of Virginia. They came over when all gentility seemed threatened with eclipse; when the rude soldiers of Cromwell were lording it above the petty nobility; when the gentlemen of England were at a loss where to lay their heads. They found a home congenial to their leisure-loving hearts among the bays and hills of tidewater. They prospered. And awhile later one of their younger sons, Richard Allen, moved west to the pleasant valleys of Kentucky where to a ripe old age he led the easy, hospitable life of a country gentleman.

Mr. Allen's mother was descended from the Brooks family, Scotch-Irish stock that had settled in Pennsylvania. She was herself a native of Mississippi, a lover of nature and of literature; and she inspired in her son a curiosity concerning the old romances of poetry and a liking for Theocritus.

Mr. Allen has never forgotten Theocritus. As Carl Van Doren points out, he is thinking of Theocritus when he tells us that in Kentucky he has seen "the warm-eyed, bronzed, foot-stamping young bucks forsake their plowshares in the green rows, their reapers among the yellow-beards; and the bouncing laughing, round-breasted girls arrange their ribbons and their vows." This is almost pure Theocritus; but it is a Kentucky ennobled beyond recognition. Mr. Allen is manufacturing for himself a more charming youth than any he really experienced.

As a boy he passed through the wholesale horror and the suffering of the Civil War. He had been born near Lexington in 1849; and all the misery, the hopelessness of that unequal struggle was evident in the general havoc all about him. The year previous his father had lost his fortune. The family was in desperate straits. Schools were closed. There was no hope of any kind of formal education. All the schooling he could receive was that made possible by his mother's tutoring in time snatched from her other duties.

Later, however, he did attend Transylvania University, graduating in 1872 and receiving the M. A. degree in 1875.

A little before this his father had died; and Mr.
Allen (to meet expenses) spent a year as master of a
country school, walking six miles to and from his
work.   Then he moved to Missouri where he taught
for two years, coming back to Kentucky as a private
tutor.   He was next called to Transylvania University; and two years later Bethany College in West
Virginia offered him the chair of Latin and higher
English.

v

Mr. Allen was a long time making up his mind but
finally, after spending some months in graduate work
at Johns Hopkins, deciding to visit Germany, deciding
not to, hoping to take up medicine, thinking better of
it, he moved to New York.   He went to live in a
garret and started out in a very small way, sending
letters to the New York *Evening Post,* poems to
Harper's and the *Atlantic Monthly,* essays to the
Critic and the *Forum.*   He had no letters of introduction; he was quite unknown; but he had decided on
literature.

It was a review of Henry James' *Portrait of a
Lady* that first attracted attention; and soon editors
everywhere were seeking him out and asking for more
of his work.   They liked the somewhat cloying sweetness of it; they liked the local color.   The Blue Grass
region (they said) has found a lover who is also an
artist; never was daring blended with a finer sense
of chivalry; woman was never more thoroughly
idealized, the Grail was never better served; here is
the laureate of a fast disappearing South.

But it is to be noted that this laureate who so loved Kentucky was living in New York and would soon ·desert New York for Cincinnati.   There was something somewhere that Mr. Allen was seeking.   He did not know what it was but it was something.   So he moved from Cincinnati to Washington; and from Washington back to New York.

VI

He had been seven years getting established; but in 1891 his first collection of tales, *Flute and Violin,* was published, to be followed the next year by *The Blue Grass Region of Kentucky*—and immediately Mr. Allen entered his little niche.   The character of all his later work was fixed; and the character of the criticism that was to greet each new volume as it appeared.   He was an historical novelist worthy to rank with Nathaniel Hawthorne; and it was even hinted that his remarkable success was due to the fact that he had been born a seventh child.

However, of late years the general cry has been that he no longer writes as he used to—which may mean that he never did.   Androcles is typical.   Had Androcles been the creation of some major poet, Lucretius or Vergil, Mr. Allen would have taken him to his heart and loved him; his name would have been sacred to Mr. Allen.   But Androcles was the work of ignorant and credulous folk; he has no fine literary heritage; therefore he is damned.   For Mr. Allen's are literary measures; he lives in a literary world; and if, as Shaw's critic said, a man is a great writer then his is a great book; if not, why then——

VII

I wrote to Mr. Hamlin Garland and asked him to tell me something about James Lane Allen, something arresting, something jocund. I knew, of course, that Mr. Allen had never married.

"With regard to Allen," Mr. Garland replied, "I am less certain, although I know him and like him and value his work. He is to be reckoned with the 'local color' school. His stories of Kentucky are vital parts of the Southern development. He is a stately, somewhat ornate writer, always the fine professor, thoughtful, careful and high-minded. He lacks humor, the marvelous corrective insight which is in Howells, but he is a gallant figure nevertheless. Of late his health has been very poor and we see almost nothing of him. This seems to me a pity, for he is a charming and scholarly figure."

Carl Van Doren says that but for his extravagant taste for sweetness he might have achieved pastorals of an imperishable sort.

Mr. Allen is the author of *Flute and Violin,* 1891; *The Blue Grass Region and Other Sketches of Kentucky,* 1892; *John Gray,* 1893; *The Kentucky Cardinal,* 1895; *Aftermath,* 1896; *A Summer in Arcady,* 1896; *The Choir Invisible,* 1897; *The Reign of the Law,* 1909; *The Mettle of the Pasture,* 1909; *The Bride of the Mistletoe,* 1909; *The Doctor's Christmas Eve,* 1910; *The Heroine in Bronze,* 1912; *The Last Christmas Tree,* 1914; *Sword of Youth,* 1915; *The Cathedral Singer,* 1916; *Kentucky Warbler,* 1918; *Emblems of Fidelity,* 1919.

SHERWOOD ANDERSON

This world is full of a number of things. Eggs, for instance—eggs in crates, in baskets, in cartons, on the floor, on shelves, piled to the ceiling—millions of eggs. Or milk bottles—on the fire escape, the table, the window ledge, at tenement doors—row after row. Or dung—littering the ground, spread on the garden, covering the meadow, heaped at the stable door. Old maids and cripples—cowards and touts—children and sailors—clerks, stenographers, motormen. A very ordinary world. A futile world, sandy and monotonous.

It is all, of course, a matter of emphasis. It may be a globe-encircling world, signaling Mars—or just the world of Sherwood Anderson.

II

One of Anderson's first stories appeared nine years ago in *The Little Review*—the story of a young woman artist, called *Sister*. "She is my sister," Anderson said, "but long ago she has forgotten that and I have forgotten."

It was not a remarkable story, except in so far as it was Anderson's, told in his level voice, quietly, without any inappropriate gestures. It turned about the whipping the girl received when she announced to her father that she was about to take a lover. But it was not the whipping that mattered, only the meaning of that whipping. "I am the world," Anderson said, "and my sister is the young artist in the world. I am afraid the world will destroy her. So furious is my love for her that the touch of her hand makes me tremble."

III

There, in a thousand words, Anderson made ready for all his future work. He sits across the table from you as you read. You can almost hear him breathe. It is all so real. This is the way people feel and the way they think, the way a story of this kind must be told. And though this may not be all the world, the world of flowers and ships at sea, it is the frustrated world of the artist, driven back upon himself, and the repressed world of youth. And between the lines there is that something—call it symbolism, atmosphere, the mystery of being, what you will—that is in all of Anderson's stories. Rebecca West has said that it is really the emotion of poetry. To him the world is close-knit, throbbing, pulsating with one life, men and animals, trees, clouds, earth, the whole of nature. And it is that throb, the pulse of creation, that makes the rhythm of his prose. It is like the beat of the ocean along the beach. There is a very good example of it in *Marching Men:*

"All over the city McGregor talked of old Labor and how he was to be built up and put before men's eyes by the movement of the Marching Men. How our legs tingle to fall in step and go marching away with him. And all over the country men were getting the idea—the Marching Men—old Labor in one mass

marching before the eyes of men—old Labor was going to make the world see—see and feel its bigness at
last.   Men were to come to the end of strife—men
united.   Marching!   Marching!   Marching!"

IV

It is, of course, a trick; but it gets over Anderson's
idea; the drabness, the sameness, the monotony of
what we call civilization, a regimentation, everything
in its little cubbyhole, no freedom, no time for play,
millions of men in the factories, millions of eggs in
their crates, brownstone fronts and tenements, alike
as peas.   No wonder he cries out for revolution.
Any change would be for the better.   Even beauty, if
it is the same beauty over and over again, B Major
or a cerulean blue, will pall.   Imagine raising tulips,
acres and acres of tulips, year after year, and your
neighbors raising tulips, far as the eye can see, plant-
ing them, weeding them, potting and selling them,
nothing but tulips, from dawn to dark.   Or teaching
children A B C, this year and next, and looking forward to a lifetime spent teaching children A B C.   Or
opening the door on a subway and having people pour
in on you, and opening it at the next station and more
people; more people in the Bronx, at Times Square,
getting on, getting off, all day long—stupid people,
the same people, in Coney Island or Harlem, wearing
the same clothes, saying the same thing—you might
love them the first day, but in the end you would come
to despise them, as you would despise the sun if there
were no escape from its shining.

V

That is the story Anderson has to tell, in *Winesburg, Ohio* and *Horses and Men,* in *Poor White* and *Many Marriages.* We are all of us seeking an escape from the prison which is our thoroughly explored and law-abiding world. We want a thrill, excitement—as Loeb wanted a thrill. We seek it in detective stories, in perverted amours, at the gaming table. We are blasé and sophisticated; introverts. Though we walk with fifty housemaids out of Clapham to the Strand, Lord, what do they understand! Though we drink ourselves blind, quarrel, make war—there is no escape. There was always, for Kipling's soldier-man, the East a-calling, a cleaner, greener land; but there is no cleaner land for us; we know the East is filthy.

VI

It is not at all a pleasant picture, but it has its truths. We are most of us uninspired. We don't know what to do with our time, where to go on a holiday, what to plan for as a fine and spirited old age. We are, in other words, fools.

This is generalizing, of course, but that is what Mr. Anderson does. Like every other artist he talks about himself, and, like most of them, he sees himself as typical. "He who bares self," says James Oppenheim, "bares humanity." How much truth there is in such a statement, I do not know—to me humanity is a vague and infinite word—but Mr. Anderson has taken it as gospel. He talks about himself and says

that he is talking about the world.   He reasons from
himself when he is bored and says the world is bored.
Fat wenches take his eye—they have the eye of the
world.   He longs to strip off his clothes, to be free,
to stretch his arms and roll naked on the grass.
Given the chance, the world would go back to the savage and barbaric pleasures of Attila and Tamerlane;
we would deck ourselves with beads, paint our faces,
call (in full Meredithian fashion) that slaves might
make the bed for us—scratch us and you'll find the
Tartar or the Hun.

VII

"I was born," says Mr. Anderson, "in 1876 of
Scotch-Irish parents, in a little village in Ohio.   My
mother was tall and gaunt and silent, and after giving
birth to seven children—all except one now living—
died of overwork before reaching the age of forty.
By an odd coincidence, the portrait of myself painted
by Bill Hollandsworth, that I am using in publicity, is
a remarkably good portrait of my mother.   This
young artist has been able to reach down through
the rather commonplace-looking, fairly prosperous
business-man I am, and get a hold of what there is in
me of this gaunt woman whose blood is in my veins.
The portrait I am sure does not look much like me, but
the artist has caught in it the very spirit of my mother.

"In our family there were five boys and two girls.
A girl died, and when my mother died also, my sister,
who was a few years older than myself, became the
housekeeper in our house.   It was thin housekeeping.
My father, a journeyman harness-maker of the old

days, was a lovable, improvident fellow, inclined to stretch the truth in statement, loving to swagger before his fellow-townsmen, not averse to losing an occasional battle with the demon rum—on the whole, a dear, lovable, colorful, no-account, who should have been a novelist himself. Lord, but we were poor— too poor. An incident of that time will illustrate how poor we were.

"In our village the boys celebrated Hallowe'en by creeping along the street in the darkness and throwing heads of cabbages against the doors of the houses. If no one paid any attention to them, they went on their way, but if an irate housekeeper came out of the house and ran after them, they returned again and again to the charge. My mother, knowing this, took advantage of it. You get a sense of her tall, gaunt figure crouching in the darkness waiting for the boys. When they had thrown the cabbages, she pursued them. The game was sometimes kept up for hours and my mother acquired by this method twenty-five or thirty cabbages on which we were fed for the next month.

"All of this, as you may suppose, gave me an almost overweening respect for cash. As early as I can remember, I was on the streets of our town, sweeping out stores, mowing the lawns before houses, selling newspapers, taking care of horses belonging to families where there were no men, selling popcorn and peanuts to the crowds on Saturday afternoon—perpetually busy. I became known in the town as Jobby Anderson, because of my keenness for any job that presented itself. As the result of this method, I soon had money jingling in my pocket, although I had no time to go to school. What education I got was picked up in the bar-rooms, stores, and on the street, and by the grace of certain lovable characters in our place who took me in hand, loaned me books, and talked to me through the evenings about the old poets and story tellers.

"When I was sixteen or seventeen years old, I came to the city of Chicago and there made the most serious mistake of my life. For four or five years I worked as a common laborer and got myself caught in that vicious circle of things where a man cannot swagger before his fellows, is too tired to think, and too pitifully ashamed of his appearance to push out into the world. The Spanish War saved me from this. I enlisted, frankly not through patriotism—but in order to get out of my situation. To my amazement, when I went home to my home town to become a soldier, I was greeted as a hero—one who had given up a lucrative position in the city in order to fight for his country. My natural shrewdness led me to take advantage of this situation, and I enjoyed it thoroughly.

"The rest of my story is a very simple one. When I came back from the war, I got into the advertising business, and have been a writer of advertising ever since excepting for a few years when I attempted to become a manufacturer and made a failure of it. The advertising business is one that lends itself peculiarly to what I wanted to do in life. I do not understand why more novelists do not go into it. It is all quite simple. You are to write advertisements for one who puts tomatoes in cans. You imagine yourself a canner of tomatoes. You become enthusiastic about the tomato. You are an actor given a rôle to play and you play it. There is an idea abroad that to do this one must become in fact a canner of tomatoes, but it is as absurd to say this as to say that the actor who plays *King Lear* must necessarily go about choking women to death.

"The impulse that led me to write novels was the impulse for my own salvation. I did not want to become the canner of tomatoes. There was in me a good deal of my father's swagger and pretentiousness. At the time I wrote my first novel I was just failing in my manufacturing adventure, and losing a good deal of money for my personal friends. I worried about the matter. I found myself in the pitiful position of so many business-men and thought it not unlikely that at forty I would be an irritable, nervous wreck, spending my time protesting against the unfairness of life. One day I sat down and began to write a novel. I liked it. To my amazement, I found that on paper I was entirely honest and sincere—a really likeable, clear-headed decent fellow. At once, I knew that I would write novels the rest of my life, and I certainly shall. "In the beginning it was my dream that I would write during my life perhaps ten or fifteen novels without publishing any of them. I did not want to be a novelist, although I wanted to write novels. I do not want a myth built up about me. It struck me as a bully adventure to spend my life writing novels and have them published only after my death. I have changed my mind about this, only because it may be possible that my novels will make me some money and I want the money."

JOSEPH ANTHONY

Mr. Anthony was tense. He had given a copy of *The Gang* to the late W. H. Hudson, and now he was waiting the verdict of that critical and kindly man.

There was an ominous pause. A throat cleared in the distance. Feet shuffled on the pavement outside. For the rest the night came down and swallowed up the houses across the street.

Mr. Hudson raised his eyes.

"Well?" said Anthony.

"You write," said Mr. Hudson, "like Stephen Crane."

Anthony straightened. His chest swelled—ever so slightly, but still a swelling—as though he had been struck a resounding blow on the ribs. The flesh heaved around his heart, and his eyes shone bright.

But not for long. Mr. Hudson had not finished. "You write," Mr. Hudson said, "like Stephen Crane— but then I never did like Stephen Crane!"

II

Mr. Anthony is an idealist—an idealist who smiles, a little wryly, at his own preposterous fancies, his hopes, his faith in the world, his love and liking for his fellows. And Mr. Anthony is ambitious. He actually believes that your writer can accomplish something, can (by merely writing about them, pointing them out) help to correct a few of the abuses of

34

civilization—and so alleviate a little of the misery all
about him, in town and country, on lonely farms, in
crowded tenements, upstairs and down, where money
is counted and where it is squandered. I am not so
sure. Crane failed—for all his earnestness. Shaw
has failed. This is not noticeably a better world.
Lincoln is followed by Coolidge. Christ has as his
successor the Rev. Canon Chase. We have not lately
brought forth another like the gentle saint who
walked, in poverty, the hills of Umbria. Even our
snows are not so white and beautiful as were the snows
of yesteryear. We grow old but we do not improve—
we persist in admiring and preferring Barrabas. We
are second-rate—and your first-class writer is ignored.

III

But Mr. Anthony is my friend—and I am sure that
he will make his mark—not the mark of Stephen
Crane, the mark of the rebel, but a mark all his own.
I was (and am) enthusiastic about *Rekindled Fires,*
that *Cranford* of the immigrant, beginning with a
youth that revels in *The Talisman* while peddling
vegetables, ending on a note of high resolve. I recognize *The Gang*—voted the best American novel of its
year, in England—as a painstaking, honest and interesting account of boy-life in Harlem. I see *The
Golden Village* as a step forward, a long step, in the
right direction—the irony of it, the patience and
understanding, the dream-besotted old man, the half-
credulous youth, and the long adventuring towards a
pilgrim's home—Bunyan's parable retold appropri-
ately, in excellent taste, without travesty, or a mere ap-

ing, silly and sedulous.   Yet where, in all this, is the
bloody realism of Crane?   Nowhere.   This man Anthony is a teller of tales, frankly, and not a reporter at
all.   He belongs, on your shelves, next to Dickens or
Chateaubriand.

IV

Because I cannot hope to exceed it in precision or
fancy, I quote *verbatim* the report Mr. Anthony has
given me of himself:—

"Strictly speaking, my first novel was *The Tale of
the Order of Goats,* which ran serially in the Hackensack High School *Critic.*

"*Rekindled Fires* was begun when I was a student
at Columbia (I submitted the first part of it, chapter
by chapter, as my work in Professor Erskine's English class) and finished the summer after I graduated.
I was a reporter on the Newark *Evening News,* and
just turned twenty-one, when Henry Holt & Company
published it, in 1918.   Then I had seven months as
one of the land-sailors of Pelham Bay, helping win the
war by working on Larry's famous coal pile, and
shouldering a dummy gun equipped with a wicked-
looking bayonet.

"After another spell on the *News,* I got a job with
Harper & Brothers, and later with the National Association of Book Publishers.   Having been a sailor, I
concluded that I would like a taste of the sea, and
shipped out as supercargo of a collier going to Italy.
I came back, wrote *The Gang* on a farm in New Jersey,
and came to New York to deliver the manuscript and
look for another job.   A few days later—in August,

1921—I was on my way to London to open an office there for the Century Company.

"My stay as representative of the Century people lasted two years. Jonathan Cape published first *The Gang,* then *Rekindled Fires,* in London, where they didn't set the Thames aflame, but were very hospitably received. I learned to play cricket—after a fashion. And I had many delightful evenings at the Savage Club.

"Once, at the Savage, Aubrey Hammond grew reflective over his beer, and remarked: 'You know, Anthony, if all Americans were like you, there wouldn't be any Anglo-American problem. You fellows over there who are of the same blood as ourselves, we know and like. But it's those Americans who haven't a drop of Anglo-Saxon blood in them that we can't understand. They're a pack of bleary-eyed blighters.'

"When he was all through, I grinned and replied: 'That's fine! But as it happens, I haven't a drop of Anglo-Saxon blood in me.' (My parents were immigrants from Hungary.)

"There was a moment of agonized suspense, as the story-book says. And now, for the benefit of those who think the Englishman is slow with a come-back, I want to chronicle that he lifted his beer-mug gracefully, and said, 'Well, you *are* a bleary-eyed blighter!'"

REX BEACH

A huge creature, voluminous and self-consciously healthy in all he does, hunting bear on Kadiak Island and writing interminable love stories with the same energy and oneness of purpose—to accomplish something extraordinary—that is Rex Beach. There is no repose in him; and all the simple beauties of nature must be heightened and made garish if they are to win his notice. To him a tree is not a tree unless it is one of the monster redwoods of California; a man is not a man until he has attained he-manhood. His heroes are always heroic; they give their days to heroism, and their nights—they eat heroically; they laugh and make love and do business as only heroes can. His women are invariably the impossible stuffed creatures of the popular imagination—they are movie queens, Betty Blythe or Lois Wilson. Naturally his books sell and are serialized and screened until the lowliest alley is hoarded with billboards announcing his greatness and understanding. A blare of trumpets proceeds him wherever he goes. Editors flock at his heels. It is generally supposed that a dumb-bell is one who has not heard of Rex Beach, a flapper who thinks his name connotes some summer resort.

II

He was born in Atwood, Michigan—not far from the home of James Oliver Curwood—on September 1, 1877.

At eighteen, like the chap in the fairy tale, he set out for Chicago in search of fortune. He was restless, and a giant for strength. Naturally, he looked around for some sort of job where he could employ that strength. In those days the various athletic associations of the larger cities maintained professional football teams for the entertainment and delight of the public. When Beach presented himself, after seeing one game, as a possible candidate for the position of guard, he had no trouble getting on—without hesitation he was engaged to play tackle. And he helped his team to win the championship of America—that one season. After that the games were discontinued. The college teams with whom they used to play had to surrender, for, though the truck-horse professionals could not be hurt, the students, as Beach has said, were apt to tear under the wing. However, one season was played out. Then, with that insatiable appetite for food which has always distinguished him and the need of money, Beach transferred to the swimming team—and broke an indoor record at water polo.

III

All this was in the winter of 1897, the year of the Klondike gold rush; and in the course of time stories of the unbelievable rewards waiting enterprise and youth in the far valleys of the Yukon reached Chicago. They fired many a young adventurer, and among others Rex Beach. With two partners he set out for Alaska, to be dumped off the boat one rainy night at Rampart. He was broke and his partners were broke.

But they had plenty of goods; they had visions of becoming exorbitantly wealthy; they were restless; so with every rumor of a strike they stampeded all winter long.   It was a hard winter and for Beach a fruitless one—fifteen-hundred roughnecks in town, little food and plenty of scurvy.   He wasn't long in becoming discouraged with his partners.   They were lazy; they got to preferring tasty messes cooked on a cabin stove to tearing through blizzards at the tail of a dog team; they said they could wait until spring for their millions. But Beach couldn't wait; he wanted his by Christmas; and off he went alone.   Then the arctic got him; the beauty of the snowclad mountains, the toil of the winding trail, the passion and fury of a primitive society. He got to thinking about it all.   It seemed to him romantic.   He was fascinated.   Something urged him to write about it.   And he did.

IV

Pardners, his first story, was published in 1907; to be followed the next year by *The Spoilers,* the novel that gave him an instant reputation.   Here, the blurbs said, is the Victor Hugo of the North.   Indeed, it seemed likely.   There was something robust and astonishing about Mr. Beach and his stories.   But there was also something lacking—and that something was simplicity and truth.   Mr. Beach just naturally had to exaggerate.   He wanted our attention and he thought the way to get it was to bawl at the top of his lungs.   He lacked the sincerity and depth of Jack London.   It was all too blamed manly.

Two more Alaska novels followed, *The Barrier* and *The Silver Horde;* then Mr. Beach turned south and in *The Ne'er-Do-Well* wrote of the Panama Canal and of a young waster who made good there on the Isthmus as a builder. Next, the New Orleans of Mafia days, in *The Net*.

But no successful novelist can stay away from New York; and in 1914, the spell of the Yukon broken, Mr. Beach felt that the time had come when he must give us his opinion of the hothouse life our young débutants (and their mothers) lead in the metropolis. The life of our modern Babylonians had left him aghast; and no embittered roué could have imagined worse things than occurred to Mr. Beach when, seated at the typewriter, he began to put together *The Auction Block*. Girls are sold into marriage in New York! My God! the spinsters of Oskosh and the Ozarks cried with one voice; it was too awful to be true. All that remained was to sell the script to the movie people—and Mr. Beach was elected president of the Authors' League. He had done what is expected of a popular novelist.

Mr. Beach is the author of *Pardners*, 1905; *The Spoilers*, 1906; *The Barrier*, 1907; *The Silver Horde*, 1909; *Going Some*, 1910; *The Ne'er-Do-Well*, 1911; *The Net*, 1912; *The Iron Trail*, 1913; *The Auction Block*, 1914; *Heart of the Sunset*, 1915; *Rainbow's End*, 1916; *The Crimson Gardenia*, 1916; *The Winds of Chance*, 1918; *Big Brother*, 1923.

THOMAS BEER

I am enthusiastic, without reservations, about Joseph Conrad and Joseph Conrad's work. The pale and slightly neurotic idealists of our weekly journals of opinion (when they tell me that, in ten years, his novels will be forgotten) affect my hearty pleasure not at all. Sir Thomas Browne is forgotten, to all intents and purposes; I do not number among my friends a single man who has read Homer, in the original Greek, from cover to cover—but that makes me no less a reader of Sir Thomas and Homer. I am not reading with one eye on ten years hence, but solely for my present delight.

A lot of hokum is talked about posterity. We have all about us the posterity of Lincoln and Jefferson and Burr—what are they? Members of the Klan, anti-Semites, lynchers, and subscribers to Anderson's fund for invading the home.

As I write it is August the twelfth. Ninety-six years ago William Blake died in England, Blake of the innocent songs, Blake of the matchless line, Blake the mystic and the rebel, Blake who said the fool shall not enter into Paradise be he ever so righteous—and four years ago in Boston Ponzi went to jail. There's progress for you and, if they need it, a fig for posterity.

II

I am enthusiastic about Joseph Conrad. You have some notion, then, of my joy in Thomas Beer's *Stephen*

Crane when I tell you that Beer's notes on Crane are incomparably more interesting and valuable than Conrad's windy preface. Conrad was Crane's friend, but Beer is Crane's biographer—and a better biographer could not be found. The absurd and absorbing nineties are in the book, the bemused phrases of Henry James, the *bon mots* of Harold Frederic, all the characters of Du Maurier's drawings, the life of New York and London—and Crane! It is literary history and a history of manners—a book to keep on your shelves and chuckle over.

Beer has said, "My one excuse for writing a study of Stephen Crane, is, of course, my admiration for his work." It is excuse enough. A good wine needs no bush; and an excellent volume asks for nothing but itself as proof of worth.

Crane the baseball player, Crane the student, the lover, the explorer of slums, Crane the reporter, and Crane the author of *The Red Badge of Courage* and the friend of authors his peers. . . .

It's all there and told with energy and gusto.

III

The book is not perfect. Not one of Mr. Beer's books is perfect. He is too mannered. He is so afraid of being obvious and simple that he becomes labored and involved. His matter does not flow easily from a full and o'erflowing imagination. It is picked and sorted from a pile of notes accumulated on his desk. It is fitted into a pattern—like a puzzle; and you can see where one bit breaks and is separated from another. It becomes a trick; and reading one of his

books is like winning a game of solitaire: it requires
ingenuity and patience.

Mr. Beer writes self-consciously—but he writes and
that is more than most of us can do.

IV

The Fair Rewards is the first of Mr. Beer's novels.
It is the story of Mark Walling, a clodhopper from
the New Jersey foothills, become an actor and later a
successful manager, a story that deals with Clyde
Fitch, first nights and first-night audiences, with the
greenroom and the greenroom ladies, spanning the
New York stage from Frohmans' first presentation of
The Prisoner of Zenda to *The Jest* with Jack and
Lionel Barrymore and the vivid and glorious Gilda
Varesi.   It is brilliant, but I do not find it credible;
staccato rather, as Percy Hammond said—and over-
dressed.

V

Sandoval is the second and latest of Mr. Beer's
novels—a romance of bad manners, as the subtitle says
—"My lord hath taken his vanitie into the North
upon a business."

It is a tale of the generation that evolved Crane,
slight but so carefully and wonderfully well-written
that it becomes a precious thing, rare in the facile literature of America.   It shows traces of Conrad and
traces of Hergesheimer—but more, it shows plainly
the hand of Beer; and Beer alone can evoke, with a
smile, a wry and cynical and wondering smile, the van-
ished scenes of our American past with all their frills

and furbelows, the simpering and the cruelty, the deceit and the hope, and the health of our forebears.

VI

Sandoval is a satire, but it has a definite plot and a real villain in Christian Coty de Sandoval of New Orleans, a professional Southerner come North, with his bad manners and great wits, upon a mission for the Franco-American society of Louisiana. The book is the record of his undoing: the scene for the most part Dobbs Ferry, at the home of a cotton profiteer.

But it is the age, the generation following the Civil War, that matters—and the writing.

VII

Mr. Beer was born at Council Bluffs, Iowa, November 22, 1889. He was educated at Mackenzie School, at Yale and at the Columbia School of Law. His first job was that of law clerk in his father's office in New York. In May, 1917, he enlisted in the U. S. Field Artillery, becoming later a first lieutenant and serving with the 87th Division in France.

Mr. Beer is a frequent contributor to the *Century, Smart Set, Saturday Evening Post* and other magazines.

The Fair Rewards was published in 1922; *Stephen Crane*, 1923; and *Sandoval* in 1924.

LOUIS BROMFIELD

Since I am self-confessed a clown I may as well drag in Balzac—his is the first name that comes to mind on reading Mr. Bromfield's *The Green Bay Tree*. Here is the crowded canvas of *La Comédie Humaine* and here in all her glory is Balzac's *la femme de trente ans*. Chapter follows chapter; a whole family life develops; a generation passes along the way to dusty death; they wax rich and powerful; they decay and are forgotten. They have their little day, their influence, their pride; and they see that pride humbled and made a mockery. And the writing is thick and vivid, colorful. The effect is realistic, as in *Pére Goriot*, like some busy faubourg in the Paris of before the war. There is intrigue and a clash of wills. And, best of all, there is no psychoanalyzing. There is no going beneath the surface to dissect motives and peer with a microscope into emotions. Life is accepted as mysterious. The characters live by their own right; and their histories are reconstructed from bits of gossip, from confidences, gestures, tones of the voice, from things they say and do. *Gott sei dank,* Mr. Bromfield does not write with one eye peeled on the medical profession and both ears listening to the wails of suppressed desire. Mr. Bromfield is (you can shout it on the streets of Ascalon, if you will) an artist. Land knows we have waited long enough for his arrival.

II

Louis Bromfield was born in Mansfield, Ohio, twenty-seven years ago, of stock that came over the mountains into the Western Reserve from Maryland and the vicinity of Boston as early as 1817. He was educated in the public schools and at fifteen began working on the newspapers of his home town. At sixteen he went to Cornell University to the School of Agriculture, intending to follow in the steps of his grandfathers and become a farmer. His father wisely took him out of agricultural school and gave him the family farm to operate for a year. At the end of that period he decided against farming, made an about-face and went to the Columbia School of Journalism.

He was there only a year when he went to Europe to serve for two years in the war with the French Army, in one division after another, all the way from Switzerland to the North Sea. After the armistice was signed he remained abroad another year, living among the French people. He came to know them during the war and he liked them. He lived as one of them, not as a visitor or a tourist. His Paris, though a war-time Paris, was peculiarly unwarlike, since the men and women he met were bourgeoises and Bonapartists, solid as rocks, perhaps the most unemotional of the French.

Returning at last, reluctantly, to New York, he went into the newspaper field with the New York City News Association and later with the Associated Press. Contrary to the popular conception, he found the newspaper business both tedious and unromantic, and in due time escaped to the staff of *Musical America* where he served for a year as Foreign Editor.   After that, he worked for a time in the theater with one of the leading producers, and at length settled down in the publishing business, where he expects to remain until old age removes him.   Not that he will give up novel writing.   He likes it too much.   And it takes care of a vast amount of excess energy.

III

The Green Bay Tree is the first of five or six novels, all dealing with the same people, a complete picture of the American Spectacle as Mr. Bromfield sees it.   The second, *The Evolution of Lilli Barr,* is nearing completion—for Mr. Bromfield is a rapid worker; he took but six months to the writing of *The Green Bay Tree.*

IV

"I have seen the wicked," said the Psalmist, "in great power, and spreading himself like a green bay tree."

Such a state of affairs upset the Psalmist, but it does not upset Mr. Bromfield.   He goes calmly to work. He studies the wicked—or one generally accepted as wicked, the mother of a child born out of wedlock— and decides that she is just a little bit of all right; that, first-off, she is a beautiful woman, a charming woman; and that perhaps the father of her child, while all right as a lover, would not measure up to her requirements in a husband.   Perhaps she knows this?   Perhaps she has money enough so that she is not dependent upon him for support? Of course, she would have to go away; she could not remain in the town where she had grown up and allow her neighbors to stigmatize the child as a bastard. She goes away. She goes to Paris—and there she flourishes. She flourishes while the home Town decays. The Town becomes prosperous and hard. It booms. Once a farming community, steel mills are built, soiling the rivers with grease and coal, filling the air with fumes of smoke and acid, enlarging the population. Her gallant mother fights against this invasion, against the destruction of so much that was once beautiful, against the avaricious and cunning newcomers whose servants the mills are. Her sister joins in the fight, going into the homes of the mill-workers, ministering to them, undoing as best she can the neglecting and impersonal cruelty of the mills. The sister is good.

The good sister is contrasted with the wicked one. No judgment is passed; no choice is made; they are what they are, for better or worse. Each has a light to guide her. But the wicked one leads a full life, while the good sister retires to a nunnery. The good sister loses her faith in mankind; the wicked Lily Shane is forever renewing her beliefs in contact with the world. She has her son; she has a lover; she marries when the son is old enough to shift for himself and the lover is dead of a stray bullet in the war.

V

Mr. Bromfield does not speak in parables. He has no lesson to teach, no moral to bring home to us. Two things, he says, inspired the writing of *The Green*

Bay Tree, both of them reactions: one against the conventional drab presentation of the Middle West and the other against the psychoanalytical presentation of character development.   He was born in the Middle West and he knows there is a tremendous amount of romance there.   What is more romantic than the passing of one era and the rise of another, the destruction of a pleasant life by the growing-up of a monstrous industry?   This is what has been going on in many a midland city for a quarter century past; and in some cities the struggle is over, the monster triumphant.

VI

Mr. Bromfield is not fascinated by the perversities and delusions of adolescence.   He wants a full life, a good life—and it is a full life he gives to his characters.   All the humanity of the French lies between him and Nathaniel Hawthorne.   Here is no scarlet letter branded upon the breast of Hester Prynne.   He dresses his Magda in silks and satins.   She is well-bred, gentle, sympathetic; she is well-loved and true.   It is *Hindle Wakes* in terms of good sound sense.   Lily Shane will lead her own life.

VII

Of course, the war, brought on by the bullet of an assassin, flings its armies across her garden at Germigny beyond the suburbs of Paris.   Her son rides bravely off.   Her lover is listed among the missing.   And there comes at night to knock on her door the strange and fascinating captain of a troop of Uhlans.

They talk. And such talk! Read it; you will be astounded to find so complete a philosophy of revolt and negation expressed in so short a space.

VIII

Incidentally Mr. Bromfield has a great enthusiasm for the future of America in the arts. He believes that all that has gone before will be as nothing to what is to come within the next three hundred years or so. America is nearly grown up and with her coming of age she is bound to experience such a Golden Age as was never (or rarely) seen in this world. The signs are beginning to appear, slowly. He is inclined to believe, at the moment, that literature is the liveliest of the seven arts, and that the livest of all literary forms is the novel where a tremendous amount of experimenting goes on.

As to literary enthusiasms, they include roughly among the Anglo-Saxons Arnold Bennett, Joseph Conrad, (not A.-S. but writing in English), Virginia Woolf, Henry James, Thackeray and Dickens. Among the French Balzac, Flaubert (in fact almost any Frenchman down to Prevost and Bourgeois). Among the Germans Jacob Wassermann; and among the Russians Tchekov (whole-heartedly) and a little of the Tolstoi of *War and Peace*. Among Americans Hawthorne, Poe, Willa Cather—and that's about all.

HEYWOOD BROUN

"I have never been able to reconcile myself to fishing with worms," said Broun after a month at Hale Lake this last summer.

Never is, of course, a long word—but not for Broun. To Broun it seems cruel, no matter what the anglers say. And so, in his column in the New York *World,* every morning, six days in the week, through thousands of words, he recounts his attempts at reconciliation: fishing with roast chicken, with bread crumbs, with salt port and bacon—until at last Edward Goodman could restrain himself no longer.

"Your vacation," said Goodman, "has ruined your prose style and subject matter. Fish is inexhaustible only for unimaginative old fogies and orchid athletes who caress with a self-conscious avidity the traditional mysteries of angling. You, however, have become the unassuming champion of the conservatively hysterical seekers for wistfully complete individualities. Don't fail us, old man; no more fish."

II

That's the way it goes, month after month, in Broun's column. His admirers are always despairing of him, fearing that his well of inspiration has run dry, that another vacation such as the last will be the end of what style he has, and always their fears are groundless. Broun, like a bear in winter, can feed

52

for weeks on his own fat—and in summer baseball and
the revues are enough for him.

III

Most anything is grist to his mill. . . .

"If I were an artist," he says, "I would not pay
much attention to the theory of the development of
genius by promenades along the primrose path. Certainly I would not walk there through any sense of
duty. It does not seem to me that the artist in search
of educational experiences presents a very attractive
figure. No matter what he says, his words must convey the thought 'Please fly with me and be my love,
because I am planning a new novel and it must be an-
imated by fire and passion.' I should hardly think
any woman would regard it as an endearing proposal."

IV

A while ago he wrote about wistfulness. The wistful, he said, always inherit the earth; whoever looks
wistfully at any object is pretty sure eventually to get
it. And to prove his point he quoted from the
World's story of Patrick E. Crowley: "He was born
beside the line and from toddling days watched with
wistful eyes that road's marvels come from a mysterious somewhere down the track."

Mr. Crowley became president of the New York
Central.

"To-morrow," said Broun, "at 11 o'clock I am going
to begin looking wistfully at the National City Bank."

But the idea was a failure.

Mr. Crowley had gazed wistfully at the Erie tracks

only to become president of the New York Central.
Besides wistfullness worked both ways—for and
against—and that is not always desirable. . . .

"Your article on wistfulness wounded me to the
quick," Dorothy Homans said.   "I used to gaze wistfully out of a bank window.   Now I am out."

VI

Broun, however, was not to be deterred.
"Why shouldn't I be wistful?" he asked.
He had been reading about himself in Gilbert Seldes'
The Seven Lively Arts: and he needed only three
paragraphs to fill out his column.   It would have been
the same if he had asked, Why shouldn't I be coy?
The column must be filled—if not by Seldes, then by
Broun.

VII

But he made good use of what Seldes had written—
he quoted it in full:

"He has a peculiar mind, apt to find in a trifling detail the clue to too many great things; he has a sense
of the pompous and the pretentious; he is actually a
humorist when he lets go.   But a strange thing has
happened to him.   While he was acquiring a reputation as arbiter of taste in New York by putting down
his simple feelings about books and other things, he
was slowly becoming aware of the existence of the intellect.   It was borne in upon him, as I believe the
phrase is, that a work of art is the product of an intellect working upon materials provided by a sensibil-
ity.   The discovery unnerved him—I might almost

say deflowered. For Broun has lost his native innocence; he is a little frightened by the hard young men
who suddenly let loose the jargon of æsthetics, of philosophy, of the intellect in general; and, what is worse,
he thinks that they may not be bluffing. He has gone
manfully to work, but the middle distance is dangerous. . . . In the moment of hesitation he does one
thing which may save him—slowly renouncing literature, he digs into his humor and works hard. He or
it will be exhausted presently; when that happens he
will be out of the woods—on either side."

VIII

This did not altogether suit Broun. But it served
as an excuse for one of his excellent essays on the arts
of criticism and literature as practiced by himself.

"I'm sure the 'hard young men' are bluffing," he
said. "They frighten me because they bluff so well.
Something of bluff is in all criticism. The critic may
very well know that he has an intense enjoyment from
some particular form of art, but once he begins to
set down reasons he must inevitably deal with things
which are largely irrelevant. The trick, I suppose,
comes in making these vague and haphazard guesses
at causes seem altogether true and pertinent. It follows, then, that the great critic is himself a creator,
since he makes up out of his own head amusing fictional
conceits which he calls by such names as 'form' and
'technique,' and sometimes he spins these fairy tales
so well that his findings are held to be almost scientific in their accuracy. Many people act as if he
had taken the play or novel under discussion into a

laboratory to be weighed, measured and analyzed. He hasn't. All that he can ever do is to make his guess, which is just as good as the next man's."

IX

Never strike a woman, Broun once cautioned his men readers. Look at the Sheik! He raised his hand to her and immediately she fell in love, clung to him and would not leave him until they were happily married.

X

Elinor Glyn's *The Philosophy of Love,* a trite and silly collection of newspaper and magazine articles, is being advertised (to catch the timorous) as The Most Daring Book Ever Written. However, the publishers do not care to send the volume—all about parking your corsets at dances, rouging the cheeks and rolling the eyes and stockings—to any one under eighteen. Broun is over eighteen. But he decided not to send for the book because all of the test questions are ridiculously easy—and the publishers have said that if you can answer the questions you do not need the book.

For instance: Do you know how to win the one you love? To that Broun simply answers, "No"— and passes on to the next question: Do you know why husbands with devoted, virtuous wives often become slaves to creatures of another 'world'? Again Broun answers, "No." Do you know how to curb a head-strong man, or are you the victim of men's whims? A double negative and Broun has passed the examination 100% perfect.

XI

There was only one query to disturb him— What do *you* know about love? There was something menacing about that question—almost it seemed to point. Broun's inclination was to dodge a direct answer by asking, in his turn, What does Elinor Glyn know? Indeed, what does anybody know? Instead he pointed out how ridiculous such treatises as this of Elinor's are. Obviously every man and every woman cannot win the one they want. Supposing four men, all students of Elinor's, want the same girl, etc., etc.

XII

Broun was born in Brooklyn, in 1888, the son of wealthy parents, his father an importer of glass or liquor or something. Broun attended Horace Mann and then Harvard. In the summers, between terms at Harvard, he reported for the New York *Evening Sun*. Almost his first assignment, the story of a crippled boy out at Coney Island, brought him praise. There was nothing to the story as news, but as it was written by Broun it was a touching and colorful bit of life. After finishing at Harvard—if my memory serves me, he did not graduate—he went to work for the New York *Morning Telegraph,* and from there to the *Tribune* where he made a name for himself as a sporting writer. He is still, in my affections, first and easily first as a sports writer. Successively, through the years, on the *Tribune,* he became dramatic critic, literary editor, and columnist. During the war he

was one of the overseas correspondents at the front
for the *Tribune*.   Then he transferred to the *World;*
and there he still holds court.   He covers yacht races,
baseball, football, boxing, books, plays, politics and,
most often, himself, his heirs and assigns.

XIII

Three or four years ago he published his first novel,
The Boy Grew Older, a kindly and witty story of a
father (Peter Neale, a sports writer), his wife (a
singer), and their son.   The story is reminiscent of
Broun and Broun's doings—Broun even appears in
it, unshaven, as one of the celebrities to be pointed out
to young Neale—but it is charming and at least as
good, if not so dramatic, as most American novels.

Last year he published *The Sun Field,* a romancing
about Babe Ruth—Tiny Tyler, as he is called, the
home-run king—and Judith Winthrop, who is engaged
upon an article for *To-morrow,* to be called: "Sherwood Anderson, The Sublimation of the Inferiority
Complex."   Judith falls in love with Tiny because of
the beauty of his throwing arm after he sends the ball
home from a catch in center field.   But she has her
troubles—and she surmounts them. . . .

"I may not have character enough to make this man
seduce me," she says, "but I'm not such a blooming
idiot that I can't get him to marry me."

So they marry.   And their marriage makes an excellent problem for any novelist, and especially for
Broun, who treats the whole thing with just the right
mixture of humor and restraint.

XIV

"Broun," says Van Doren in *Many Minds,* "illustrates the paradox that if a writer is only personal enough he achieves impersonality as well."

XV

Broun illustrates many paradoxes—yet he is as forthright and honest a person on occasion as any occasion could demand. I hope he lives to a ripe old age and writes consistently and voluminously as suits his fancy.

ARTHUR BULLARD

As a rule we complain when some hurried Englishman, after a short visit over here, goes home to write
a book. By what right (we ask) does he presume to
pass judgment on us? His conclusions, based upon
insufficient evidence, must be, at best, circumstantial.

But the Englishman is not the only traveler. There
is also the visiting Yank.

II

The war gave a great spurt to our interest in things
European. We heard of Bessarabia and learned that
Antwerp was not in Italy. We suddenly discovered
that Portugal was an ally of ours. And naturally our
interest produced a corps of young reporters, anxious
and ready to tell us of Arabia and Lisbon and Liège.
They had visited Russia and could write books about
the Russians. They wrote about England and New
Guinea and Spain; they cabled long articles on the Caucasus. Arthur Ruhl was one of these; Ernest Poole,
Dos Passos and—the papa of them all—Arthur Bullard. Bullard can tell you about the North Coast of
Africa, the islands of the Caribbean, the foothills of
Albania; he has been on duty in Vladivostok and Mos-
cow, in Adrianople and Cologne; he has reported the
Balkan War and the Russian famine; he knows Paris
and London as well as he knows Washington. And,
believe me, he knows Washington—he lives there; it
was there, as a member of George Creel's Committee

on Public Information, that he really got down to brass
tacks and told us just as much as he (and the rest of
them) thought we ought to know about the war and
anything else. He is now one of the editors of *Our
World*.

III

Bullard was born in St. Joseph, Mo., December 8,
1879. He came East to school, graduating from the
Blair Presbyterian Academy, Blairstown, N. J., in
1899. Next he spent two years at Hamilton College,
Clinton, N. Y. When about twenty-one he became
engrossed in the problems of poverty, crime and social
justice. He went to live on the lower East Side in
New York. He was made a probation officer by the
Prison Association of New York, 1903–06. He was
also connected with the University Settlement.

At first he had no thought of writing. It was only
in rebellion against conditions as he found them in the
tenement district that he was forced to write. As a
sane and decent citizen he could not keep silence. The
world, as he found it, was rotten. He turned socialist
and has remained a socialist ever since.

His interest in socialism quite naturally took him to
Russia; and in 1905 he set sail. But first, with characteristic thoroughness, he spent a year in Switzerland
learning the Russian language; and, after that, for two
or three years, his time was mostly passed in Russia.

So far his development was not unusual or unlike
that of many another. But about fifteen years ago he
began to branch out for himself. His interest veered
more and more from the struggle between rich and

poor to the rivalry between various nations and the
possibility of that rivalry leading to war.   This interest kept him in Europe.   He was in Turkey and
Bulgaria when the Young Turk movement began.   He
visited France, England and North Africa.   He wrote
magazine articles and later a book on the workings of
the old diplomacy and the first vague signs of what
was later to be heralded, by Wilson, as the new.   Soon
after the Great War broke out he returned to this
country convinced that we too would soon become involved.   About eight months later, in June, 1917, he
returned to Russia as a correspondent, remaining there
in one capacity and another for two years until in-
valided home from Siberia.

IV

He is the author of three novels, the first two, *A
Man's World* and *Comrade Yetta,* being published
over the pen-name, Albert Edwards.   His latest novel
is *The Stranger.*

Though much has been made of his novels by those
who look up to him as a world-citizen with the interests
of the whole world dear and absorbing to him, I think
it is his personal charm and wide travel that gives them
whatever of importance they may have.   They are a
side-issue, a by-product.

Mr. Bullard is the author of *Panama,* 1911; *A
Man's World,* 1912; *Comrade Yetta,* 1913; *The Bar-
bary Coast,* 1913; *The Diplomacy of the Great War,*
1915; *Mobilizing America,* 1917; *The Russian Pen-
dulum,* 1919; *The Stranger,* 1924.

STRUTHERS BURT

The Interpreter's House is a very fine book and it
has made a great stir in the world; but to me there is
always something a little unreal in the writing of those
who go in for living in order that they may write the
better. Living, as they interpret it, made no appeal
to Keats or Shelley or Fielding; it meant nothing at
all to the blind Homer, less than nothing to Lucretius
and Dante. But living is the bane of English instructors. They grow up in the best traditions of English
prose; they are familiar with the literature of Addison
and Arnold; they listen to talk on the Restoration
drama. Then they decide that they want to write.
They begin hunting around for something to write
about. It is not easy to find that something! They
try their hand at an essay, then at a short story.
Their essays and stories are, of course, conventional.
They have a hard time selling them. They meet always the same criticism: no one is interested in that
stuff; get out and mix with people; write about America. It is Mencken's invariable advice to all newcomers. It is at once silly and futile. Is Thoreau
about American life? Is Poe? Is Whitman? Is
Shaw about England? Or Anatole France about
France? Have they not one and all of them followed
the admonition given to Sir Philip Sidney by his muse
—Look into thy Heart and write?

But your instructor, of course, suffers from atrophy
of the heart. He has a notion that the brain is of

first importance, correct grammar, an easily flowing vocabulary. (He should take a look at Hergesheimer's grammar—it is atrocious; or the hard-wrung words of Dreiser and Sherwood Anderson.)

So your instructor sets to work. He feels that he knows the language and that if he can only know life he will be another Masters or Balzac—he turns out to be Rupert Hughes.

The case of Rupert Hughes, indeed, is typical. Hughes will argue you clean off your feet and tell you all there is to tell about his kinship to the great masters of literature—but has he created one character you can remember after a moment's notice? Are we the wiser for his nineteen years spent in the study of sculpture, his devoted attention to the details of routine in Washington during the war? No. Sympathy and understanding are not something come by over the teacups or at a club dinner. They are vision. And it is still true that the writer is born, not made by a meticulous study of the demands of magazine editors.

So there remains, for me at any rate, something a little unreal, something shallow about all this writing that is done by those who want to write and in order to write go out and make believe that they are living. Is their self-conscious round of living life? Is life getting divorced two or three times? Is it running for the office of county assessor? Is it building a house in the suburbs? To me that is, at best, a form of exercise. Life is something thick and unexpected, yet inevitable. It is the endless blundering of Burns, the ministrations of Tchekoff, the slow dying of John Millington Synge. It is as possible in a convent as

on the crowded sidewalks of Broadway; and it loses
its significance the instant it becomes premeditated—
it is then a mere following of patterns.

But not everyone, of course, is capable of living—
Shaw is alive and H. G. Wells—but has Hall Caine
ever given any indications of being other than an
automaton?

II

And so, though I know that *The Interpreter's House*
is admirable, it still remains, for me, writing. It is
not spontaneous; and because it wants to deal with
life, it has none of the enchanting artistry of Mr.
Cabell at his best. Nor has it that amazing absorp-
tion in the common life which makes of *The Old
Wives' Tale* so exciting an experience, where even conversation with the slavey on the stairs is a matter
of grave importance and a wedding is a rare occasion.
After all, in most books we care very little who marries
whom.

III

Mr. Burt is, of course, more than the author of *The
Interpreter's House*. He has published two volumes
of verse and two volumes of first-rate stories; and he
is the husband of Katharine Newlin Burt, herself not
unknown to novel readers. He was born in Baltimore, October 18, 1882.

"I was born in Baltimore," he tells me, "by the
merest chance, for I am by inheritance a dyed-in-the-
wool Philadelphian, but my father was in Baltimore on
business so I happened to be born there.

"I was educated in private schools in Philadelphia and graduating before my time was for two years a reporter on the old Philadelphia *Times,* under that extraordinary type of Civil War newspaperman, Colonel Alexander McClure, who was Lincoln's private secretary. I think he gave me a good many ideas and mental pictures in my extreme youth. I was the youngest reporter in Philadelphia. Another man who had a great influence over me, and who was the first man to advise me to write, was Philip Keats Speed, for a while city editor, the great-grandnephew of John Keats. His brother, Keats Speed, is now managing editor of the New York *Telegram.*

"At eighteen I went to Princeton, where my grandfather and father had gone before me, and graduated in the class of 1904 with the degree of B. A. At Princeton I did everything I could in the way of writing, being Editor in Chief of *The Tiger,* an editor of *The Nassau Lit,* of the *Bric-A-Brac,* and for two years wrote the librettos for The Triangle Club.

"After Princeton, I went to Germany for a while and finally landed up at Merton College, Oxford, where I stayed for a year and a half. I wish I had had enough sense to stay three years and get my degree, but there was a vacancy in the English Department at Princeton and they asked me to come back and teach and I was foolish enough to do so. For three years I was an Instructor of English.

"But in my first year as an Instructor, the Far West, which I already knew well and which had always been an important part of my life, asserted itself and I obtained an interest in a ranch and went out each summer, coming back to teach in the winter.

"Pretty soon the West entirely got the better of me, and I became a citizen of Wyoming and have been one ever since. Besides being a writer, I am an official of the Bar C. B. Ranching Company, which another man and myself started.

"In 1913 I married Katharine Newlin Burt, herself a writer, some of her books, such as *The Branding Iron,* being very well known, and I have two children, a son of ten and a daughter of eight.

"My war record was short and unheroic. All my partners were in the service and had distinguished records, but I could not go until I had things in shape, and so was not able to volunteer until late. For a few months I was a private in the Air Service.

"Undoubtedly, as far as writing is concerned, I am a case of arrested development, for my Western experience has set me back at least ten years in actual production. My first short story—after years of rejection—was not accepted until I was thirty-one years old, in 1914, although I began writing when I was eight, and to date I have published only the following slim list of books: *In The High Hills,* Houghton Mifflin (verse), 1914; *John O'May* and other stories, Scribners, 1918; *Chance Encounters,* Scribners, 1921; *Songs and Portraits* (verse), Scribners, 1921; *The Interpreter's House* (novel), Scribners, 1924.

"Until after the war I was a hard-working ranchman and had only about four months in the winter when I could write at all. Now I have my company so organized that I am, thank God, entirely a non-active partner, and so am spending all my time writing.

"I realized, of course, when I went West that I would have a long and hard struggle before I would reach the point where my time would be my own, but I accepted the handicap knowingly. There is nothing I so firmly believe as the truth of the fact that writing is made of the stuff of life and that no man can write anything worth reading unless he knows something of life outside writing and publishing circles. In my humble opinion the most fatal thing any young man can do who wants to be a writer is to go to New York immediately after leaving college and announce himself as a writer. I don't have to continue the thesis, the publishers' lists are full of examples that, to me at least, seem to prove my point.

"I chose ranching, instead of the sea, or the law, or something else, because the West has always been in my blood and because my family happened to be one of those American families with a frontier tradition. My great-grandfather, when he landed in America from Ireland at the beginning of the nineteenth century, was a fur-trader in the Northwest for many years before he settled as a merchant in Philadelphia. An uncle who graduated from Princeton in 1882 was a cattleman in Arizona and California.

"The environments that have most affected my life and point of view up to the present have been Philadelphia, Wyoming, Princeton, Oxford and my grandfather's farm up in Lancaster Country, Pennsylvania, where I spent a good deal of my boyhood. I think I am what is called 'an escaped Philadelphian.' I

think it is a good thing to be a Philadelphian, or a
Princeton man, or an Oxford man, so long as you try
to pick out the gentle and sometimes beautiful things
these places can give you, and at the same time remain,
or become, in all the more essential things a rebel.
I don't give a fig for a rebel who has never experienced the things he has chosen to rebel against. Nor
do I give a fig for the radical who has no intention
to preserve what is worth while in the past. Philadelphia and Wyoming give a man, or should give a
man, a fairly catholic point of view. Moreover, especially perhaps on my grandfather's farm, I have
seen the beauty and quiet graciousness of the American tradition, so I not only know that there is an
American tradition, which a great many of my fellow-
writers apparently don't know, but I also know that
in many respects it is magnificent and can be reconstructed—in fact, imperceptibly is being reconstructed
even in this age of surface jazz.

"Henry van Dyke, Stockton Axson (Woodrow
Wilson's brother-in-law), Sir Walter Raleigh, three
men who taught me English, had an enormous effect
on my life; also President Hibben of Princeton, who
was my uncle's best friend, and whom I knew intimately
as an under-graduate. My wife (although you hate
to say this on account of the movie stars) has, of
course, influenced me more than most wives influence
their husbands, because she is not only a writer herself but a most excellent critic. Books have been too
scattered and read at random for me to say much
about them, except possibly *The Compleat Angler,
Vanity Fair,* and all of Keats.

"My hobbies are trout-fishing and camping and golf; everything in connection with mountains.

"It is a little more difficult to tell you what my enthusiasms and views of life are. Sometimes I think I'm a radical and frequently I find I'm conservative. I suppose my two deepest passions are this country, which, it seems to me, is wrong in almost every respect, but which I find myself loving better every year, and the necessity for recognizing the dignity of the individual. The latter is the reason why I hate Prohibition, cruelty, mobs, capital punishment, etc., etc., and like the fundamental ethics of the Christian religion and all other great religions. Also the reason why, a believer in democracy, I also fear it unless it is guided by wise and gentle men."

DONN BYRNE

When they went to Thomas Gray (whose *Elegy* you may remember) and told him that Boswell had written a very fine book, Gray, though slightly incredulous, merely said: "It only shows that any fool can write a good book if he will but apply himself."

I never liked Gray. He seems to me a stuffy and chuffy sort of person; and so I am not inclined to agree that Boswell's success proves anything of the kind. But it is true that good books are not necessarily written by good and wise men, but (for the most part) by rascals. Cellini is but one example—a superlative blackguard who wrote superlatively well; Burns, that honest libertine, drunkard and sot, is another, Villon a third. The list is long—perverts and nymphomaniacs, sodomists, thieves and seducers. But scarce a bishop, only now in three centuries or so a saint, few statesmen, few (as the poets believe) virgins.

There must be something evil or shameless about the Muse. We remember Rabelais—we have forgotten the popes he outraged. We read Byron—but where are those who denounced him? We delight in Shelley—can you name me one of the dons who saw to it, when he announced himself an atheist, that he should be expelled from Oxford?

II

All this, though far-fetched, is *à propos* of Donn Byrne—for I have yet to hear a good word for Donn

Byrne from any of those who know him or from his neighbors in New York or Connecticut. But he writes (so I hear) beautifully.

I say, "so I hear," because I do not find his writing beautiful. I find it thin. After the glorious, full, robust and rhythmic prose of Synge, I find it wan and repetitious. I find it cut up into short sentences, jerky sentences, the same words recurring again and again all down the page and on to the next page. But I am apparently alone in this aberration of mine. Mr. Cabell swears that he finds it hard to contain his admiration for Mr. Byrne. Professor Richard Burton, of the University of Minnesota, at the top of his lungs, proclaims Donn Byrne the ablest writer of short stories since the heyday of Kipling. Byrne's publishers are lavish of prose.

For what it is worth you have their opinion—and you have mine. I find him affected and stilted. I am not to be bowled over by pale moons and white hands or old harpists strumming in the Waverley fashion while they recite, in a dilution of Ulster English, legends that have been better told by A. E. and Yeats and Lady Gregory.

III

Mr. Byrne's full name is Brian Oswald Donn-Byrne, but he prefers the use of Donn Byrne without the hyphen.

He was born in New York, of a north of Ireland family. His father, an Irish architect, had come to this country for a brief stay to superintend a building of which he was the designer.

At the age of three young Byrne was taken back to Ireland to grow up on the family estate, where Gaelic was more spoken than English, and where he might absorb all the fanciful lore of the Irish. He received his degree from University College, Dublin (where he was, for a time, a college boxing champion), and later studied at the Sorbonne in Paris and at Leipsic University in Germany. In 1911 he returned to America, and, after an apprenticeship at editorial work, made a name for himself in the magazines as a writer of short stories.

IV

His first published volume was *Stories About Women,* 1919; his first novel, *The Strangers' Banquet,* 1919. Then followed *The Foolish Matron,* 1920; *The Woman God Changed,* 1921; and his first triumph, *Messer Marco Polo,* 1921.

It is *Messer Marco Polo* on which Byrne's laurels rest, a re-telling in Anglo-Irish idiom of the adventures of the great Venetian traveler and how, from hearing of her, he fell in love with the daughter of Khubla Khan.

In 1923 he published, *The Wind Bloweth,* and *Changelings,* a book of short stories.

This year, so far, there have been *Blind Raftery* and another, the name of which I forget.

Mr. Byrne's wife was part author, with Gilda Varesi, of that wise and witty play, *Enter Madam.*

JAMES BRANCH CABELL

In Richmond the most unpopular (and probably the loneliest) boy at school—dubbed "Sister" by the young rowdies who, with their uncouth manners and half-formed thoughts, already, so early, had permanently alienated him from our common (oh, so common) humanity—teacher's pet then, and now the pet of such critics as, in his entourage, have taken teacher's place, the pedants, professors of an interest in connotation and commentary—that is Mr. Cabell, the (I should say) most distinguished writer in America, a precious and precise reveler strayed from the narrow confines of the Eighteen-Nineties, an ironic Pound with no memories of Idaho to lend pathos to his present disilluson.

II

"I place you," I said to him, just before the publication of *Jurgen,* "a little lower than Oscar Wilde in my affections."

I was deliberate then; and I am deliberate now when I say that, with the publication of *Jurgen, Figures of Earth* and *The High Place,* I see no reason for altering that earlier estimate of mine. Praise has not helped to mellow Mr. Cabell. It has merely spoiled him. And the harrowing of smut-hounds, far from bettering his character, has served to make him self-conscious, so that he is now a martyr, posed against a phallic cross, suffering for all the dirty stories men have ever told.

74

III

Persecution has not improved his temper. He refers, in a note on why he wrote *The High Place,* to certain of his readers—readers who have failed to perfectly understand his intentions—as illiterates, as though an understanding of Mr. Cabell were the test of literacy. Such puerile damned nonsense, without humility and without a smile, could, in the present year of grace, come only from the ill-tempered and priggish.

IV

He writes, he says, or tries to write beautifully of beautiful happenings. . . .

Though there can be no doubt of the beauty of his writings, I have heard doubt expressed, by Mr. Sumner, Bob Benchley and others, concerning the beauty of the happenings which he chooses for record. They are (I am told) more often vile than not—a play on the Latin word for lance.

V

And the beauty of his writings, as he would be free to confess, is largely a remembered beauty—plagarism, as he says of *The High Place*—picked out, one word with another, from among discarded manuscripts, gleanings from the library floor, a winnowing rather than a harvest. . . .

It is the feast of the Barmecide that he spreads for us, poor food for the heart-hungry, useless to build muscle or understanding.

VI

There is no power in his prose to move us to anything but a vain regret, pity that so much loveliness should be without life and without hope—as when we look on the dead face of some once lovely girl. It is a reminder of things past and done with. The quiet and peace that enthralls us is the peace and quiet of the grave. It is English written (as Max said of the English of Walter Pater) as though it were a dead language.

VII

I had often wondered, before the publication of *Jurgen,* what might be Mr. Cabell's inspiration. To know that he invents his authorities, as he invented Poictesme and Lichfield, is no help. And the critics, so far as I knew them, Van Doren and Mencken and Rascoe, Boyd and Follet and Guy Holt, were no help. Yet it was—or so I thought—a riddle that might bear resolving. More than once I appealed to Mr. Cabell but he always put me off with an evasion. So I turned the matter over in my mind.

Then I read *Jurgen;* and on page 80 I found my answer:

"And I wonder that you who are only a king, with bleared eyes under your crown, and with a drooping belly under all your robes, should be talking of rewarding a fine young fellow of twenty-one, for there is nothing you have I need be wanting now. . . ."

I turned back to the title page to see if no credit had been given to Synge whose Maurya was speaking there and no credit to *The Playboy of the Western World*. But Mr. Cabell is not generous. There was no mention of Synge.

The scoundrel, I said to myself. Here he has been posing as a great reader of Villon, an erudite student of the lore and literature of the middle ages, and all the time (had I but known it) his matter was lifted bodily from the Irish, his rhythms from Yeats and Synge, his wit from Wilde and Swift and Moore. Lord—and I laughed—now that I am able to take notice, without George Moore there never would have been any Cabell!

And I was not sure whether I should praise or blame Moore—Mr. Cabell is at times so pale a reflection of his masters. But he can no longer fool me with his allusions to Ronsard and Clement Marot —he has them, I know, at second-hand.

VIII

This is not to say that he is without worth.

These people (as Jurgen said) may be right. Therefore I must remember always, in justice to myself, that I very probably hold traffic with madmen. Rome was a fine town, and it was geese that saved it.

IX

I would not say that he is without wisdom.

"Jurgen abode among persons to whom life was a high-hearted journey homeward. God the Father awaited you there, ready to punish at need, but eager to forgive, after the manner of all fathers: that one became a little soiled in traveling, and sometimes blundered into the wrong lane, was matter which fathers understood: meanwhile here was an ever-present reminder of His perfection incarnated in woman, the finest and noblest of His creations. Thus was every woman a symbol to be honored magnanimously and reverently."

X

The worship of women (domnei) is, of course, the chief concern of those warriors and wits and poets who are the Cabellian hero. Love is canonized. And to the beloved are ascribed all the virtues, chastity of spirit though she lay in the arms of another, beauty of form and holiness, so that she may approach in divinity to the God whose symbol of perfection she is—for Jurgen and Perion and Demetrius of Anatolia, for Charteris and Kennaston and Dom Manuel of Poictesme.

XI

But I like best the more matter of fact conclusions— as when Jurgen argues that nothingness cannot be the end of all: that would be too futile a climax to content a dramatist clever enough to have invented Jurgen.

And so, believing in immortality, Jurgen decides to do nothing that he cannot more or less plausibly excuse—in case of supernal inquiries.

XII

When Jurgen wakes to find two ghosts at the foot of his bed—one an impudent, leering phantom, in a suit of old-fashioned armor: the other a pale and lovely lady, in the customary white—he bids them good-morning, and is only sorry that he cannot truthfully say that he is glad to see them.   However, they are welcome enough if only they can manage to haunt the room quietly.

Jurgen, you see, must sleep.   He has been up half the night drinking with two of Gogyrvan's barons.

XIII

I have said that Mr. Cabell writes beautifully and I will give you an example:

"So it was that Jurgen came into Cockaigne, wherein is the bed-chamber of Time.   And Time, they report, came in with Jurgen, since Jurgen was mortal: and Time, they say, rejoiced in this respite from the slow toil of dilapidating cities stone by stone, and with his eyes tired by the finicky work of etching in wrinkles, went happily into his bedchamber, and fell asleep just after sunset on this fine evening in late June: so that the weather remained changeless, with no glaring sun-rays anywhere and with one large star shining alone in clear daylight.   This was the star of Venus Mechanitis, and Jurgen later derived considerable amusement from noting how this star was trundled about the dome of heaven by a largish beetle, named Khypre. . . ."

XIV

That the body of man is capable of much curious pleasure is an observation made over and over again in Mr. Cabell's books.   It is a discovery for which Jurgen cannot be too grateful.   It buoys up Dom

Manuel through all the tedium and hardships of war. It is with John Charteris in Lichfield——

"I have read," says John Charteris, "that the secret of gallantry is to accept the pleasures of life leisurely, and its inconveniences with a shrug; as well as that, among other requisites the gallant person will always consider the world with a smile of toleration, and his own doings with a smile of honest amusement, and Heaven with a smile which is not distrustful—being thoroughly persuaded that God is kindlier than the genteel would regard as rational."

That is the cream of the Cabellian philosophy, the *leit motif* running through all his romances, the spirit of every age with which he deals, the ages of mythology and chivalry, Congreve and the troubadours, of to-day and to-morrcw.

XV

"A man possesses nothing certainly save a brief loan of his body."

XVI

When in Rome one must be—in Mr. Cabell's terrible pun—romantic, for romance is the real demiurge, the first and loveliest daughter of human vanity, whereby mankind is duped and exalted.

"No one," says Charteris, in *Beyond Life,* "on the preferable side of Bedlam wishes to be reminded of what we are in actuality, even were it possible, by any disastrous miracle, ever to dispel the mist which romance has evoked about all human doings."

Romance creates the dynamic illusions of love and chivalry and common sense, religion, art and patriotism with which the ape, reft of his tail and grown rusty at climbing, has clothed himself for so long that he now imagines his vagaries as of some cosmic importance. Poor and naked as this ape may seem to the eye of reason, is there not (Charteris asks) something magnificent about his imaginings?

And when Charteris speaks he speaks for Mr. Cabell's—as Mr. Cabell speaks, this time at any rate, for Anatole France.

XVII

Of all Mr. Cabell's books I like best *The Rivet in Grandfather's Neck,* because I like Mr. Cabell best when he is in Lichfield, in Virginia, and not romping all over the thirteenth and fourteenth centuries, through Scandinavia, Portugal, Rome, Alexandria, Constantinople, Aquitaine, England, Paris, Navarre, and wherenot. Mr. Cabell is (to my notion) distinctly not of the Latin temperament. He cannot carry, with an air of easy familiarity, the trappings of Machiavelli's Prince, leavening his detachment with the worldly wisdom of the priest—such priests, of course, as are the *alter ego* of Monsieur France. A brush with Chesterton or Belloc, with Rabelais or Boccaccio, and all Mr. Cabell's world of faëry vanishes into thin air. These are not arch-scoundrels that he pictures, but yokels on a visit to the baths and lupanars, the chapels and bazaars of a great city.

But in Virginia Mr. Cabell is at home.

XVIII

The Rivet in Grandfather's Neck—from an expression of Hans Anderson's—is the love-story, the marriage and death story, of Colonel Rudolph Musgrave and his second cousin once removed, Patricia Vartrey. For at least a decade, before the coming of Patricia, Colonel Musgrave had been invaluable to Lichfield matrons, alike against the entertainment of an out-of-town girl, the management of a cotillion and the prevention of unpleasant pauses among incongruous dinner guests. He was, by all accounts, the social triumph of his generation.

"At worst," he said, as he reflected on Patricia's threatening visit, "I can make love to her. They, as a rule, take kindly to that, and in the exercise of hospitality a host must go to all lengths to divert his guests. Failure is not permitted. . . .

"Failure is not permitted," he was saying to himself, when he saw her coming, all in white, across the trim, cool lawn.

"You're Cousin Rudolph?" she asked. "How perfectly enchanting. You see until to-day I always thought that if I had been offered the choice between having cousins or appendicitis I would have preferred to be operated on."

It may be that he entertained her or she him—he had noted that her hair was really like the reflection of a sunset on rippling waters, and that her mouth was an inconsiderable trifle, a scrap of sanguine curves, and that her eyes were purple glimpses of infinity. At any rate they fell in love. She had been engaged to an earl, but the earl was forgotten; and they married.

And they were, to all outward seeming, quite happy. It is of their happiness that Mr. Cabell tells—and of the serpents in Eden. Also something of the Colonel's past; and of John Charteris the novelist and (with Mr. Cabell) the chief spokesman of Mr. Cabell's thoughts; and of Anne Charteris, his wife; and of the Colonel's son who was also Patricia's son; and of the death of Charteris who had hoped to be Patricia's lover; and of the death of Patricia; and the death of Colonel Musgrave.

XIX

"I question whether wickedness is possible to humanity outside of literature," says John Charteris in *Beyond Life*. "In books, of course, may be encountered any number of competently evil people who take a proper pride in their depravity. But in life men go wrong without dignity and sin, as it were, from hand to mouth."

It is so at any rate that Charteris sins—for want of something better to do, without shame and without enthusiasm.

"Let us forget," he says to Patricia, "the crudities of life and say foolish things to each other. . . . Or would you prefer that I whistle into the opening of this doorkey—to the effect that we must gather our rosebuds while we may, for time is still a-flying, fa-la?"

But she reproves him: "Don't be foolish, *mon ami!* I am unhappy."

XX

As indeed she is. We are all of us unhappy when
we love, unhappy while we live. Even desire is
futile. There remains only disillusion and the glory
that desire was while it lasted, and the comic spirit.

XXI

But I am apparently alone in liking *The Rivet in
Grandfather's Neck*. Hugh Walpole has said that
The Rivet proves that in the accepted, conventional
sense Cabell is scarcely a novelist at all. He takes too
many shocking liberties with his characters; he is not
very deeply aware of the motives that govern their
minds; he cares nothing for them, and is all too ready
to cover up the weak spots in his narrative with a
motto, a footnote or an epigram. To Walpole it is
in *Beyond Life* that Cabell is at his best—a magnificent, unequivocal, defiant testament, he calls it—and it
is as readable and amusing a book as you will find, if
you are like me, in a dog's age.

XXII

But it is *The Cream of The Jest* that those who are
confirmed Cabellians like most to cry up. Here
Poictesme and Lichfield are divided only by waking
and sleeping—and Felix Kennaston, the central character, is native to both.
Kennaston, walking in his garden at twilight, plotting the final chapters of his novel—the novel that is
to commemorate the high-hearted adventures of
Guiron and Etarre—stoops to pick up a shining bit
of metal that lays beside the path. Later by long

gazing on this bit of metal he is able to hypnotize himself and so slip out of Lichfield and into Poictesme and all the various worlds of Mr. Cabell's fancy, and hold court with Dom Manuel and make record of the doings of Melicent, of the men who loved Alison, and the Audit at Storisende.

XXIII

Mr. Cabell has been writing for twenty years and yet—as I am not the first to point out—his name, save for the scandal of *Jurgen,* is almost unknown to the ordinary reader. This state of affairs is, of course, interpreted by Mr. Cabell and his more besotted admirers as a sign of ignorance in the American public. But the success of Shaw and Hergesheimer and Conrad, of Lewis and Bromfield and Mencken, proves that such ignorance is non-existent. The fault then must be with Mr. Cabell—and it is. He is often a bore, repetitious and affected—for all that Hugh Walpole insists, over and over, that the poses are natural to the man. What if they are, they remain postures and affectations just the same. And the matter is thin. Mind you, I enjoy his books and am grateful for them—but I do not for that reason consider myself especially wise. Books are not, so far as I have been able to make out, the best that there is in life. And to judge a man by his attitude towards Cabell is certainly silly.

XXIV

Mr. Cabell was born in Richmond, Virginia, April 14, 1879, the son of Robert Gamble Cabell and his wife, Anne Branch Cabell.   He received his early education in Richmond, and, in 1898, graduated from the College of William and Mary, where he had been for some time an under-graduate instructor in French and Greek.   He then worked in the pressroom of the Richmond *Times,* and, from 1899 to 1901, on the New York *Herald,* returning to Richmond and the city staff of the *News* in the latter year.   In 1902 he quit newspaper work, and, until 1910, supported himself by writing some sixty short stories for various magazines, besides doing a number of translations, verses, essays, and historical and genealogical studies. In 1904 the first of his novels, *The Eagle's Shadow,* was published.

He has spent some time traveling in France, Ireland, England and America.   He has published three volumes of Virginian genealogy.   He was for a time Custodian of the Virginia Society of Colonial Wars and of the Virginia Society of the Sons of American Revolution.   From 1911–1913 he was coal-mining in West Virginia.   Since his marriage in 1913, he has lived (for the most part) at Dumbarton Grange, Dumbarton, Virginia.   There, though a figure of some importance in the social and intellectual life of the community, he spends his days in writing, his evenings reading.

XXV

"My books," he says, "must stand for my biography. My personality is, even to me, entirely devoid of interest.   My life has been uneventful and, to the bystander, colorless. My philosophy, such as it is, I have endeavored to voice in my books. For the rest, I would say that in *Beyond Life* you will find opinions upon pretty much any topic. I warn you, though, that I decline to endorse the views of Mr. Charteris. Such as they are, I present them: that is all."

XXVI

In *The Round Table in Poictesme,* printed by the Colophon Club of Cleveland, there is an interview with Mr. Cabell the author of *The Eagle's Shadow* by Mr. Cabell the author of *Jurgen.* It is an interview well worthy of remembrance. Says Mr. Cabell of his earlier self:—

"He was fat, remarkably fat for a lad of twenty-two or thereabouts; and he had, as I noticed first of all, most enviably thick hair, sleeked down and parted 'on the side' with some fanfaronade in the way of capillary flourishes. He was rather curiously dressed too, I considered: the lapels of his coat were so small and stiff; they were held in place, I deduced, by a coat spring: and he wore a fawn-colored waistcoat and his rigorous collar towered, incredible in height, above a sky-blue 'Ascot tie,' which was resplendently secured with a largish sword-hilt a-sparkle everywhere with diamonds. It must have been, in fine, twenty years since I had seen anybody appareled quite as he was. . . .

" 'Have just sold three stories to magazines,' he announced. 'And I was wondering, sir, if you would advise me to become a regular writer now.'

"To that I gave my customary sage and carefully considered reply. 'Of course,' I informed him, 'there is a great deal to be said upon both sides.' "

When the younger Cabell says the older is only poking fun at him, the elder replies: "I know. But I cannot help it. For you appear to me, I confess, the most ridiculous person save one that I have ever ‸wn. I am the other person."

ROBERT W. CHAMBERS

"He is shy to the point of obscurity," says Rupert Hughes, who ought to know and can, I presume, be trusted on oath. "He is the least photographed, least press-agented, least 'posey' successful author in the world."

Of course, this would not necessarily make Mr. Chambers either famous, great or interesting; but it would add to our impression of him as a man—if true. But there has poured in on my desk, from Mr. Chambers' various agents and publishers, such a mass of photographs, interviews, magazine articles, press notices—Mr. Chambers in his garden, Mr. Chambers hunting wild boar, Mr. Chambers fishing, or discussing Chinese jade, at work, at play—that were I not already doubtful of the Major's say-so, I might be forced to believe in at least two, if not three or four, R. W. Chamberses. But I know that the sentences I have quoted are just the Major's way of saying, more or less obscurely, that he is fond of Mr. Chambers. I know the Major's limitations. He cannot like you unless you are the most or the least something-or-other. To be simple, without pretense or affectation, is to be lost in that circle which, with the death of Howells, has taken to wholesaling novels in job lots to people who have no interest whatsoever in literature and very little in life—if they can escape into a world of trivial emotions and easy adventure they are happy.

II

To be shy and unphotographed is, to say the most, no proof of virtue. Shaw was never averse to speaking his mind and he towers above our little heirs to all the ages. But even so, Mr. Chambers cannot be called shy—as Willa Cather is shy, as Edwin Arlington Robinson is shy, as was W. H. Hudson. Mr. Chambers is none of the things that the Major claims for him. Why, then, did Hughes (who, at that time, was being paid to boost Chambers, among the others) write as he did? Because he could think of nothing else to say. Mr. Chambers must be made to seem astounding—and he isn't. He has facility and grace and wit; he had in him, some think, the makings of an artist; but he sold out early to ephemeral fancy and he made for himself, as he believes, a good bargain. He is well satisfied. He has not tried to do anything of enduring worth—and he never will. Forty-five volumes in the first twenty years of his writing life—short stories, novels, juveniles, verse, a play and nature studies—and not a one of them an improvement on the other. Indeed, had I my choice I'd take the first three or four and let the rest go hang. The best of Chambers was his youth, his running on wherever the notion took him, his apparently inexhaustible ingenuity, his high spirits, his admiration for beautiful but empty-headed girls, his interest in the man who is not tied down to some tiresome job. But now that he wants to discuss divorce and the failure of most marriages, the brutality of the

Germans, the God-fearing heroics of America, he is a bore.

III

Robert William Chambers was born in Brooklyn, May 26, 1865, but (as the Major says) he has tried to make amends for that early mistake. He has fought shy of the merely so-so, the commonplace, the ordinary, every-day life of our time. You have his measure when you ask him to write of the family next door. He can't do it. You would never recognize your neighbor as either possible or probable once Mr. Chambers had been commissioned to put him into a book. He would become addicted to sipping Cologne; he would speak with sudden flashes —as though Wilde were his mentor; he would inherit a lot of rugs and bric-à-brac; his body would be beautiful; and without any evil intent he would succumb to the attractions of every pretty face he saw—but his feet would be so far off the ground it would be impossible to trip him up.

Mr. Chambers is not interested in his neighbors. He lives in a Hans Anderson world, a woodland world; and it is there he shines. When he writes of gardens, of lakes in the forest, of flowers and clouds and hills, he is at his best—and that best is pretty good.

IV

He studied drawing at the Art Students' League in New York, where he had Charles Dana Gibson as a fellow-pupil. With Gibson he went to submit his first sketches to *Life*.   As might be expected, Gibson's drawings were refused, those of Chambers were accepted; so Chambers set sail for Paris and Gibson stayed home.   In Paris Chambers studied at the *École des Beaux Arts,* and at Julian's, from 1886-1893.   In 1889, at the age of twenty-four, he had his first painting accepted by the Salon—and he has been a Salon painter ever since.

If you have ever been in Paris you will know what that means.   Sentiment and anecdote set up as the noblest end of art; a catering to every taste; smooth surfaces; imbecile smiles; learn what the public wants —and give till it hurts.   Nothing of the pity of Rodin, the deep shadows of Brangwyn, the open-eyed wonder of Whistler; no excursions with Odilon Redon into the unknown; no attacking of convention with Augustus John or Jack Yeats; no freedom, no robust rebellion against an effeminate age—just something pretty, like a soap ad.

v

He returned to New York in 1893, and for a time supported himself by doing illustrations for *Life, Vogue, Truth,* etc.   Then it occurred to him, under the influence of Henri Murger's *La Vie de Bohème,* to make some use of his Latin Quarter experiences and he wrote *In The Quarter*.   It was immediately accepted.   It was successful in its way.   And Mr. Chambers (who thought nothing of devoting seven years to learning the rudiments of black and white) decided overnight that he was a writer of parts. Discipline was unnecessary, form, coherence, accent and restraint. You merely babbled on and—there's your book. How different it all might have been had he been a student of literature as he was a student of the lesser arts—had he suffered, for a while, the agonies of refusal. But his instant acceptance by the public gave him a contempt for the craft of the novelist. It was just one of a dozen things that he could do and do well enough to earn a fair living. So he set to work on *The King in Yellow;* and before the year was out his second book had been published. His facility was his undoing. He became as easygoing as his readers, as uncritical, as well-pleased with any and everything.

VI

In The Quarter describes, in a series of vivid pen pictures, the usual ups and downs in the modern art student's life, the pathos and humor of it all, the poverty, the feasts, the entanglement of an American with a Parisian model of the better sort, an estrangement brought about by the American's inheritance of a fortune, the interference of a jealous sister, and finally, with all the melodrama considered so essential, the murder of the American by the sister. In short a pretty howdy-do, without coherence or reason—but lively, moving with the lightning speed which is so characteristic of Mr. Chambers at his most exuberant.

VII

The King In Yellow clinched Mr. Chamber's decision. He would throw over illustrating and become, in deadly earnest, an author—at first of short stories,

and then, in *The Witch of Ellangowan,* with Ada
Rehan as Meg Merrilies, of a play for Augustin
Daly—dramatized from Scott's novel, so tradition
has it, in a week.

VIII

Mr. Chambers knows how to tell a story; and if
you want to have the hair raised on your head, read
The King In Yellow—or *The Maker of Moons,* for
preference, all about a band of unscrupulous counter-
feiters who have discovered the alchemist's long-
sought gold, moonshine gold that defies chemical
analysis but leaves, wherever it is found, curious,
crawling, misshapen creatures, half crab, half spider,
a-litter on the ground. And then the dream-
lady who appears to the hero, standing beside a
fairy fountain, speaking of a magic city beyond the
Seven Seas and the Great River, "the river and the
thousand bridges, the white peak beyond, the sweet-
scented gardens, the pleasant noise of the summer
wind, laden with bee music and the music of bells."

IX

Followed then, at irregular intervals, four novels
dealing with the Franco-Prussian War—*Lorraine,*
Ashes of Empire, The Red Republic and *The Maids
of Paradise*—all with their languishing heroines, and
for heroes, dashing young Americans who overcome
evil as easily as, in less proper times, Boccacio's
anchorite put the devil back into hell; situations bordering on farce, characters for the most part as wooden as
their heads, but all recounted in the accepted manner,

following the fashion set by Stanley Weyman, Max
Pemberton and that fine faker, Richard Harding
Davis.

X

Then, in an off moment, Mr. Chambers lost his
temper and blurted out some of the bitter truths he
had learned in his always heretofore guarded dissatisfaction with things as they are. He ridiculed
American culture, American architecture, American
society, the petty life of our self-styled Bohemians, the
second-rate scribblers who do our writing for us; and
he did it all so vigorously that, among his friends,
a cry went up against him—Chambers had blundered.
They wanted the *Outsiders* recalled.

But it is, for all that, a sincere and honest piece
of work.——

XI

"Far up the ravine of masonry and iron a beautiful
spire, blue in the distance, rose from a Gothic church
that seemed to close the great thoroughfare at its
northern limit.

" 'That's Grace Church,' said Oliver, with a little
catch in his voice.

"It was the first familiar landmark that he had
found in the city of his boyhood—and he had been
away only a dozen years. Suddenly he realized the
difference between a city in the Old World acceptance
of the term, and the city before his eyes—this stupen-
dous excrescence of naked iron, gaunt under its skin of
paint, flimsily colossal, ludicrously sad—this half-
begun, irrational, gaudy, dingy monstrosity—this tem-

porary fair-ground, choked with tinsel, ill-paved, ill-
lighted, stark, treeless, swarming, crawling with humanity."

XII

I hear it said that Mr. Chambers would like to
go back to the *"Outsiders"*; that he is tired of pretending that wealth and mere numbers are enough;
that beauty follows after the crowd; that when a
fat broker builds his summer home on the North Shore
it is worth a volume of extravagant prose. Mr.
Chambers is, rumor says, aweary of boosters and
boasters, of *Athalie* and *Iole,* the gilt and monotony
of Newport and Palm Beach.

Perhaps.   But it is late for him to be turning over
a new leaf.   Editors are hard put to it to fill their
gawdy magazines with just the right mixture of
daring and drivel—and Mr. Chambers knows their
formula.   Money may not be the only good, but
(time out of mind) it has made the mare go.   The
editors will keep Mr. Chambers put.   And without
much difficulty, for it is probable that if he took to
serious writing—took to imitating Mr. Bromfield—
he would fail.   He will not repeat the sarcasms of
the *Outsiders.*   He is getting on; and three-
halfpenny-worth of ease is worth sixpence to him.

WINSTON CHURCHILL

Here on a smaller stage has been played out the tragedy of Wolsey, the story of the well-intentioned man who puts his trust in others rather than himself, who talks in terms of service and judges by appearances—only to learn too late that appearances are deceitful. It is the fable of the man who wants so much to accomplish something better, who tries for something better and fails because he is incapable of going to the roots of life. He has saved the surface, but the heart—he has never reached the heart, never touched the heart; he has been a cork bobbing on the surface of life. To him the roots are rotten, or they are ugly, clogged with muck and mire. He turns away from them in disgust. They are nasty; and to him nastiness is nastiness; he will not touch nastiness. He has not the courage of the shameless Freud. He is ashamed; and shame makes cowards of us all. He is a coward. He thinks of the effect upon his friends should he announce that he believes a child's love for its mother to be, in essence, incestuous. It may be true, but he refuses to accept any such belief since such a belief would mean that he is dirty-minded; and he intends, at all costs, to keep his mind clean. He is going to be decent.

Decent! There's the word that takes his fancy; Roosevelt's word, a great clamor signifying the land only knows what—but impressing the shallow-pated. A convenient word. It has a high resounding echo; it displays that moral earnestness of which our fathers made so much. But what does it mean? Was Lincoln decent with his dirty stories? Is Hamlet with his talk of Ophelia's legs? Was Christ with his interest in the Magdalen, in sinners of all sorts, his preference for Mary over Martha? I'll gamble neither Roosevelt nor Mr. Churchill knows the answer—life is a complicated business. To say, as they would, with Ruskin, that it is better to die than do an unjust thing is merely to evade the point. Justice is obscure. But death is simple; we can all of us die; even Aristides died and I have heard that he was not always just.

II

Where the Greeks failed it is not likely that we will succeed, with only emotion to guide us. Yet it is emotion alone that guides Mr. Churchill; and guides him quite often aright, for his heart is good. But he is not an artist. He has not that disciplined austerity which distinguishes the artist. Nor has he the artist's pity and understanding. He is too much the moralist. It is the moral aspect that interests him. He believes that those who touch pitch will be tarred. He is not Rodin. To Rodin every living thing had a beauty of its own; life was beautiful, and even ugliness. But to Mr. Churchill ugliness is ugliness; any fool knows that. He forgets that the knowledge of fools is no great matter, that the fool (in Blake's fine saying) cannot enter into Paradise be he ever so righteous. He believes, that we enter Paradise if only we can escape from life.   He gives this as his reason for writing romances.

III

There are those, he tells us in the the preface to *Richard Carvel,* who have found the world a bad place; somehow they have missed the joy of living, though they believe there must be joy in life; then suddenly they find it—or think they find it—between the covers of a book; the book is an escape; it pictures beauty and delight; it restores their faith in the world.

But does it?   Is that the world, filled with the chatter of beaux and belles who have no grocer to pay, the elegant postures of wits that never went to school?

And yet Mr. Churchill believes this to be the great service art can render—not to aid the confused that they may adjust themselves to the present, but to offer them an escape into the past, to drug their brains and silence their doubts, to blind their eyes to all the misery and tawdriness of our modern civilization.   They forget, he says.

Perhaps they do.   And since they are so anxious to forget they would probably not be of much use to us did they remember; we cannot look to them for help in clearing up the dirty mess from which they run away.

IV

But Mr. Churchill is all for escaping from life. He early discovered that life as he encountered it every day, at home, in the classroom, on the streets, was a vain and, seemingly, an empty business. It was not satisfying. Too often you had to go without. And it was drab. There was no fine raiment, no color, no cloaks flung carelessly across the shoulder; banners did not float from battlements above a lily-padded moat; gracious women did not smile down upon the head that bowed to kiss their fingers. He had been born out of his due time and into a commercial age.

And so he ran away. He re-created out of the crumbling ruins of the past a fairy world where he could play a more heroic part than that in which, by chance, he had been cast. There should be swords flashing in the moonlight, oaths by our Lady, and whispers in the garden where the sundial throws its shadow on the lawn.

It was a rare and joyous undertaking. And it was well enough while youth was still his and the future waiting with other possibilities. But now he is old. He is old and can make no other choice. He cannot go back. He has escaped from life. But when he came into this world life was all he had. Too late he realizes that he has sold his birthright for the figment of a dream. He is disillusioned.

It has been five years since he has indulged his fancy for make-believe, five years since he has written for publication; and he tells me that he will never write again. He wants peace, he says. He is tired.

v

As a matter of fact Mr. Churchill came into the world, if he was to prosper as a writer, at exactly the right moment. We were emerging from the aftermath of the Civil War. That reckless letting of blood had also let out the rebels who doubted our divinity. God had ordained that we should be one nation, a great nation, perhaps the greatest the world has ever known. A wave of patriotism swept across the country. It was no longer a disgrace, as once it had been, to be born an American. We were not the sons of younger sons, the children of misfits, descended from the men and women who had failed to measure up to the standards of the Old World. We were pioneers, discoverers, the adventurous who alone can take opportunity for what it is worth and make something of it.

Then suddenly we discovered that we had heroes and heroines of our own. Mr. Churchill helped us to this discovery. We were grateful to Mr. Churchill. He became immensely popular. His books sold by the thousands and have continued to sell. Only the other day *The Crisis* was voted one of the ten choice books of the past quarter century.

VI

Mr. Churchill had immense energy, some knowledge of history, a simple yet forceful style; his books made easy reading. And he had a feeling for costume. The old houses of Annapolis and Baltimore and Washington took hold of his imagination. He saw the men and women of colonial times walking the streets. He seemed to overhear their talk. And in recording that talk he hit upon the idiom that we, with less reading, had imagined for ourselves. This was the speech that we had invented and we recognized it as authentic. This was the past we liked to picture as our past; these were our founding fathers. If we had ever doubted that past, Mr. Churchill silenced our doubts. It was splendid and it was good.

Good! Ah, if it had been anything but good we would not have read Mr. Churchill's books. But he gave to everything that air of moral grandeur we demand and we were satisfied; we were happy, for we are Utopians; we want to believe that good triumphs. Listen to President Coolidge, in the latest of his contributions to political economy:—

"We have been successful beyond all others because we have been a people of vision. Our prosperity has resulted not by disregarding but by maintaining high ideals. Material resources do not, and cannot, stand alone; they are the product of spiritual resources. It is because America, as a nation, has held fast to the higher things of life, because it has had a faith in mankind which it has dared to put to the test of self-government, because it has believed greatly in honor and truth and righteousness, that a great material prosperity has been added to it."

Mr. Coolidge would like to make out that this is some recent discovery of his own, but Mr. Churchill knew it all long ago.

Richard Carvel towers above the young gallants of Mayfair because Carvel is virtuous; and he is virtuous because he is a Marylander. And in *The Crossing* David Ritchie is chosen to lead the frontiersmen because they will only follow one whom they can trust

and they believe implicitly in his goodness.   Even
old Jethro Bass, the crafty boss of a corrupt New
England political machine—to my notion the finest
and most interesting of Mr. Churchill's creations—
succumbs to the cleansing purity of a virgin's touch.
Indeed, it is precisely because we can be sure that
virtue will triumph before we reach the end of his
books that we like Mr. Churchill and his novels.   God
rewards the good.

VII

So it was that Mr. Churchill, dissatisfied with what
he knew to be the truth, made for himself and for
his family a glorious history.   It was our old friend,
the Inferiority Complex, at work performing miracles.   And it was successful because Mr. Churchill
was not the only one to look back with shame to
the crude beginnings of our wealth, the makeshifts
of the frontier, the loneliness and monotony of life
under the first half-dozen presidents.   No baths, no
literature,-no society, no sports, no theater, nothing.
It seemed too terrible to be true.   It just wasn't true,
that's all.   And when Mr. Churchill, out of his reading, showed us what might easily have been another
side, readers flocked to buy his books.

VIII

"In regard to my people," wrote Mr. Churchill,
answering a letter of mine, "I am chiefly English, with
a strain of Scotch-Irish, and a Dutch strain quite far
back, the De Witts and Van Horns of New York.
One of my ancestors was Jonathan Edwards.   An-

other was Margaret Van Horn Dwight, his granddaughter, who wrote the account of a journey across
Pennsylvania recently published by the Yale University Press, its date being about 1803. Through
her I descended from the Dwights, presidents of Yale.
My Churchill ancestor, John, landed in Plymouth,
Massachusetts, in 1643. On that side I am descended from the Creightons and Osbornes who
settled in Portsmouth. The Churchills, my immediate
forebears, lived in Portland, Maine, where my great-
grandfather, James Creighton Churchill, and his sons
were merchants in the West Indies trade, with their
own ships and plantations. I was brought up by
my mother's sister in St. Louis, where her father's
family was established, and educated at private
schools and afterwards went to Annapolis, where I
graduated in 1894. My interest in literature, however, and especially in American affairs, had grown
by that time to such an extent that I resigned from
the service at once and almost immediately began to
write *Richard Carvel,* which has to do with Annapolis, being my second book."

IX

Mr. Churchill was born in St. Louis, November 10,
1871, the son of Edwin Spaulding Churchill of Portland, Maine, and Emma Bell Blaine of St. Louis.
The first sixteen years of his life he spent in St. Louis
which was in fact, his home until he built Harlakenden
House at Cornish, N. H. In St. Louis, the opening
scenes of *The Crisis* are laid; and St. Louis recurs
as the scene of *The Crossing.*

At Annapolis, Mr. Churchill stood among the first five or six in his class. He helped reorganize the crew and was for a year crew captain. He played a good game of football. But his chief outdoor sports have always been fencing, tennis and horse-back riding.

On his graduation he worked for a time on the *Army and Navy Journal,* then joined the staff of the *Cosmopolitan Magazine,* living all the time at Irvington-on-the-Hudson and experimenting with fiction. In 1895 he married Miss Mabel H. Hall, resigned from the magazine, and moved to Cornish.

In 1898, while still gathering material for *Richard Carvel,* he published *The Celebrity,* an amusing if somewhat trivial hit at the then very much celebrated Mr. Richard Harding Davis.

In 1899, *Richard Carvel* appeared, becoming immediately the most popular book of the year in these United States. It was recently reprinted from new plates, the old plates having worn out.

And ever since, once about every two years, never taking advantage of his popularity, Mr. Churchill published some new novel or other, checking up history and making over the past so that it shall better suit our somewhat squeamish tastes.

He was at one time a member of the New Hampshire legislature, 1903–5; and at another, 1912, he ran for Governor on the Progressive ticket. He has, so Mr. Percy Mackaye tells me, done more for the free people of New Hampshire than any other resident of that State has ever done, giving freely of his time and money.

Mr. Churchill is the author of *The Celebrity,*

1898; *Richard Carvel,* 1899; *The Crisis,* 1901; *The Crossing,* 1904; *Coniston,* 1906; *Mr. Crewe's Career,* 1908; *A Modern Chronicle,* 1910; *The Inside of the Cup,* 1913; *A Far Country,* 1915; *The Dwelling Place of Light,* 1917; *A Traveler in War Time,* 1918.

OCTAVUS ROY COHEN

In that most bitter of all columns, *Prattle,* in the San Francisco *Chronicle,* Ambrose Bierce, twenty years ago, referred to Joel Chandler Harris as the man who had dragged a disreputable darky through the magazines so long and so far that he had worn all the black off him.

The question of blackness, of course, is one that applies to the darky. Just how black is he—for a man cannot be black in this country without being aware of it, and being aware of it, he must feel (again, in this country) inferior, an alien, more outlawed than ever Ishmael was? Life would be unendurable under such a burden, marked more plainly than Cain and scarred by the lash of inherited taskmasters, were there no possible, no imaginable compensations. Just how, then, does the darky compensate himself? What is his secret, the secret of his unfailing good humor, his patience and fine friendliness? How does he escape from persecution, and find forgetfulness?

Mr. Cohen has, though unaware of it, attempted to answer these various questions. He pictures for us the darky at play, Alabama darkies, crapshooters and chauffeurs, laundry wenches and colored maids—a glorious company, hilarious, on a frolic. One can easily understand that life is not without its beauty and its excitement if life can be as gay and adventurous as it would appear to be in Mr. Cohen's *Come*

Seven, Highly Colored, and *Sunclouds.* A shallow
life perhaps, a running-away and hiding, a refusal
to face the problems of being colored, being different
—but joyous and happy none the less.

Mr. Cohen is, of course, conscious of the fact
that in dealing with the darkies he is touching pitch
and may be tarred (and even feathered) for his
daring. This has made him fearful of coming too
near the truth. The truth about the darky is something that must be hushed up—in the South—and in
the North and West. But he loves his characters and
shows them as lovable, if rather futilely comic. Mr.
Cohen is just one of the many writers for the
Saturday Evening Post, and too much should not be
expected of him. He is not out to criticize but to
entertain.

II

He is a comic writer. To be a comic writer is a
profession in itself. It consists (apparently) of surprising the reader with apt quotations at inappropriate
moments, broadening the smile on the reader's
face into a grin of recognition when the not unexpected
is plumped out with all the astonishment of a con-
jurer taking cards from behind the callow youth who
has volunteered to act as assistant. You will get some
inkling of the technique to be used if I quote a few
of the titles to Mr. Cohen's stories—*Here Comes the
Bribe, The Ultima Fool, The Survival of the Fattest,
All's Swell that ends Swell, Alley Money, The Quicker
the Dead, His Bitter Half, His Wild Notes.* It consists in punning, but always on some familiar strain—

just as jazz is a ragging of accepted melodies. It is the stock in trade of Witwer. Only Ring Lardner and George Ade have, as yet, risen above it; and they are above it only at times when they are simple and unaffected.

III

But comedy is not Mr. Cohen's only claim to attention. He is the maker of several hair-raising detective stories—*The Crimson Alibi, Midnight* and *Jim Hanvey*—and the hero of the most amazing legend along Publisher's Row. . . .

It appears that Mr. Cohen had free-lanced and made a failure of it. The author of the first of the Florian Slappey yarns—the yarns that made him famous—could not sell them. No one wanted them —at any rate, that is what the editors told him. And things went from bad to worse. Worse still, and he was forced to hunt for a job. Twenty-nine rejection slips accumulated by just one inoffensive short story. Next Monday Cohen was to report at an office downtown. He was to become a clerk. But before he stooped so far in his conquests, having been refused by all the cheaper magazines, he decided to try Florian Slappey on the *Saturday Evening Post*. The week had not rolled away before the story, by return mail, had been accepted. Within the year Cohen had made $100,000. *The Crimson Alibi* was dramatized and played successfully—he sold forty-three short stories and published a novel. . . .

The moral is, of course, that you can never tell. Butter your bread and it may return, not upon waters,

but laden with honey and the sweets of Academe,
—which is the place good critics hail from.

IV

Mr. Cohen is a lean and hungry denizen of the
higher strata of Birmingham's literary set, a name at
which no Alabaman would think of swearing; and
with Hugh Wiley he tops the genial raconteurs who
have taken the darky for better or worse as stuff on
which to build a pleasant comedy. I do not agree
with the various newspaper reviewers who tell me that
his is the true darky, but there's no denying the fun
to be had in reading his books—providing, of course,
that a little goes a long way with you.

Mr. Cohen is the author of *Polished Ebony; The
Crimson Alibi; Six Seconds of Darkness; Gray Dusk;
Come Seven,* 1919; *Highly Colored,* 1919; *Assorted
Chocolates,* 1920; *Dark Days and Black Knights,*
1921; *Midnight,* 1921; *Jim Hanvey, Detective,* 1922;
Sunclouds,* 1924.

JOHN COURNOS

Voltaire was very angry when he wrote *Candide*. This was (to hear him tell it) a worthless world. You dreamed of El Dorado, of innocence and peace; you woke to—well, the France of 1750, the England of Wycherley and in America a wilderness of trees.

Not so bad, some of us might say—and certainly much better for Voltaire's book. . . .

Magnificent! That is a fitting description of *Candide*. Though angry, Voltaire was never more himself—and to be Voltaire was to be supreme, then . . . and even now.

II

Mr. John Cournos has, within the past few months, published a book—a tale, a romance, a satire—which he calls *The New Candide*.

Mr. Cournos is not a new Voltaire. Mr. Cournos is an American, born in Russia and living in London. Mr. Cournos lives at his ease, pleasantly, in a city where his heart has found rest and recreation and his mind delight.

But his book is none the less a very fine book. It might have been a bitter book—there is reason for bitterness when one views the world philosophically and notes the cruelty and folly of one's fellows. But Mr. Cournos knows—as Voltaire knew—that bitterness is useless. It is useless to rail against the inhumanity of man—one can but laugh, turn the page and laugh again, pricking a bubble here and there exposing what asses mortals be.

III

Dostoevski died in Russia in 1881—and three weeks later John Cournos was born, also in Russia.

Various conclusions have been drawn from this strange sequence of events. To Mr. Phillips Russell it seems fitting that Mr. Cournos should have come into the world just as Dostoevski left it. Mr. Russell insists that, in no small degree, Mr. Cournos has carried on the work relinquished by the great Russian at his death. But I am not so sure.

Dostoevski dead and Cournos living—yet I have not recently heard of any new *Idiots* or *Karamazovs*. How many thousands preceded Mr. Cournos into this world during that three weeks of full eventful mourning? How many in Russia? How many in America? And why should anyone bother to carry on the work of Dostoevski, having work of one's own to do? And Mr. Cournos has his own work.

IV

Mr. Russell quotes from *The Wall* a sentence that sums up the wisdom, and all the wisdom, Mr. Cournos has learned from life; "The good healer, Time, wears pain down to beauty."

This is a house of pain and life a tragedy, but time will give us ease. As we learn patience we will come to complain less. As we grow older we will find that our strength is enough for such burdens as have been laid upon us. We will come to joy a little even in our sorrow, to clap our hands and laugh.

So much for Dostoevski who could find no refuge anywhere. It is, I take it, the influence of Voltaire who thought of the world as a madhouse—or himself mad—he could never be sure which.

V

Before writing *The New Candidé*, Mr. Cournos wrote three books dealing with the life and adventures, at home and abroad, of a certain John Gombarov—*The Mask, The Wall*, and *Babel*.

When I read *The New Candide* I found it difficult to recognize the John Cournos I had already come to know (and to admire) through *The Wall, The Mask*, and *Babel*. Mr. Cournos has learned restraint. Mr. Cournos had been—not exactly verbose, but careful of detail, letting no instance and few saws escape him. His books were close-packed. His aim had been to write down life exactly as he saw and felt it— his own life, the life of a young man born in Russia, transferred to the new world of America, an unshaped and callous world, and, at last, escaping back to Europe, becoming mellowed and healed, in some degree, by the wisdom and quiet of an older civilization.

VI

Burton Rascoe has said that Cournos has succeeded in out-Wassermanning Wassermann. I am not good at comparisons; but I think that Cournos has succeeded (as I felt that Wassermann succeeded, in *The Goose*

Man, at any rate) in presenting a brilliant and at times a terrible picture of the complexities, the fervor and the romance of our modern ways of living.

VII

Mr. Cournos loathes machinery. He views with pitying contempt the mechanical perfections of a modern American city. Machinery, he would say, has its uses only in so far as it serves mankind. When it becomes the master—as eventually, if permitted to extend its power much further, it will become the master—it is remorseless, grinding men down until they become the slaves of the clock, feeble and passive, going a humdrum round—like the workmen in Ford's factories—without imagination and without resource.

Witness, says he, the narrow escape of the human race swept before the fury of the iron gods and demons of the late war.

VIII

But Mr. Cournos has no message. He has been a rover all his life. He is a gipsy, and his search has been, not, as Voltaire's was, for good sound sense, but for beauty—and beauty each man must find, as best he can, for himself.

IX

Mr. Cournos was brought to this country by his parents as a boy of ten—and as a boy he sold newspapers on the streets of Philadelphia in front of the offices of the newspaper of which he later became editor. But he was never happy in Philadelphia.

So soon as he discovered that he could earn his living by writing, he made off for London which had become, from his reading of Dickens, the city of his dreams. Of London he speaks with affection. He loves the crowded, twisted streets, the fog-drenched squares, the graying buildings—and the Cockneys. I am with him there. I should say that London is the finest city in the world.

Mr. Cournos has lived in London for ten years. At first he supported himself by doing newspaper work, hack-work, reviews and what not. About six years ago he turned to more serious writing and produced *The Mask*.

Let me advise you to read his books—they are excellent.

The Mask, 1919; *The Wall*, 1920; *Babel*, 1922; *The New Candide*, 1924.

JAMES OLIVER CURWOOD

Writing from Owosso, Michigan, on August 1, 1923, Mr. Curwood declared, on the fly-leaf of *The Alaskan,* that it was a rare privilege and honor to be allowed to dedicate the latest of his novels "to the big-hearted men and women of Alaska, the new empire rising in the North." Reading this declaration some months later I was moved to wonder that he should be so easily honored and to pity those to whom the privilege was denied. Why should the people of Alaska be chary of their favors? What have they ever done? Their hearts are large, of course; but when did their territory first become an empire?

I fell to pondering these questions, lost in a brown study. Supposing (I said to myself) that I too lived in Alaska, would my heart enlarge under the strain of keeping body and soul together in that world of ice and snow among the gutted hills? Would I feel called upon to thank Mr. Curwood? Or would it be enough to say, shyly: "Oh that's all right, old man"?

Which led to still other questions: Do the unfortunates recently visited by the kindly Mr. Harding actually read Curwood? And if they do what do they think of his so-called Romance? Do they ever say, "It's easy enough for you to talk; you live on a farm in Michigan and spend your week-ends in New York; we're exiled out here, cut off from civilization and after all civilization is what we're after, not the frontier—an occasional bath would come in handy?" Do they sometimes charge him with keeping back the best part of the evidence, ignoring the loneliness and the monotony as those who sing of war gloss over the horror and muck of the trenches, the maddening regularity of Mr. Kipling's boots marching up and down, marching up and down?

Who are Mr. Curwood's readers, anyway?

II

In one of those articles for which the *American Mercury* is justly famous, Mr. Lewis Galantiere reports that James Oliver Curwood is by all odds the most popular of American writers among the French. It used to be Jack London and Upton Sinclair; now it is Curwood. Edith Wharton has tried to establish herself as our literary ambassadress to France, but she has failed; her stories appear in the *Revue des Deux Mondes* and, so far as anyone knows, nowhere else, not even in books. But Curwood is encountered on all hands.

Galantiere explains Curwood's popularity by saying that "to the generality of Europeans, America is still the land of the cowboy and redskin, the prairie schooner and the bad man—the fellow in the autobus or in the metro sees the land of the free only through the eyes of Jack London and James Oliver Curwood. He is fascinated by stories of grizzlies and snow-shoes and gold-rushes; a two-gun man in a red shirt is his conception of a proper President of the United States."

In fine, those who voted for Roosevelt are apt to read Curwood.

III

Babbitt is another of his readers. Babbitt is forever planning a trip to the north woods; he reads the advertisements of the Canadian Pacific Railway—some of which, by the way, I write—and his heart is stirred by the glory of the towering trees, the everlasting mountains capped with snow, the fishing and canoe-trips along the Nippigon. He wants to get away from the confinement and tedium of his home and office in Cleveland, Toledo, Boston or Salt Lake. He finds it hard to get away. The wife is suspicious. "You men!" she says. There are children. There's the expense and his inexperience. Still he plans. He visits the sporting goods stores. He buys a blanket. He holds out as long as he can. The man across the hall in the Williamson Building is going. A client who came in yesterday visited Revelstoke last year. He hopes. But hope is vain. And so, too often, Babbitt is forced to compromise. He reads Curwood instead.

Curwood is the favorite author of the rotary clubs; he writes for he-men—and so, of course, the women read him. I have noticed that women of a certain suburban type are peculiarly drawn to the books intended, by their authors, for he-men.

IV

The Alaskan is the latest of Mr. Curwood's books. The Los Angeles *Saturday Night* tells me (in a review loaned by Mr. Curwood's publishers) that whatever I may happen to think of the book as literature, I must concede it real value because it is the only means left some of us whereby we too may visit the "wonderful, romantic open spaces of the west and north."

What, then, about the movies? And Burton Holmes? And the National Geographic Society's Magazine?

Besides, as the *Saturday Night* itself points out, Mr. Curwood is slipping. His hand is not as sure as once it was. In this, the latest of a long line of anomalies, he has mixed too large a spoonful of propaganda with his usual soufflé of topography and politics. Still, if you like your problems sugar-coated, the book may interest. There's the regulation gross villain, the beautiful girl and the never-failing hero, so manly and self-less.

v

A quotation will do no harm.—
Suddenly she faced him, her eyes flaming.

"You—and your suspicions and your brutality," she said, her voice trembling a little as she drew herself up straight and tense before him. "I came to you because I foolishly misjudged you. I thought you were different, like your mountains. I made a great gamble, and set you up on a pedestal as clean and unafraid and believing all things good until you found them bad—and I lost. I was terribly mistaken. Your first thoughts of me when I came to your cabin were suspicious. You were angry and afraid. You thought, almost, that I was unclean. And you believed I was a liar, and told me so. It wasn't fair, Mr. Holt. It wasn't fair! I believed you were big enough to think that I was not dishonoring you with my—friendship, even though I came to your cabin. Oh, I had that much faith in myself—I didn't think I would be mistaken for something unclean and lying!"

"Good God!" he cried, "Listen to me—Miss Standish——"

She was gone so suddenly that his movement to intercept her was futile. He dropped back, his blood cold, his hands clenched, his face as white as the girl's had been. He saw himself stripped naked.

VI

I call that writing. It has a familiar ring. You can't go wrong with stuff like that.

And where, toward the close he gasps, "Mary!" twice—twice because the first time she doesn't turn— and you know that happiness has come to them and their hearts are throbbing—there's even a little heart-like throb in her throat as she faces him—it's immense! As his publishers say, "You can't go wrong with a Cosmopolitan book." They're sure fine.

VII

Mr. Curwood is also the author of *The River's End*, a story of the Royal Mounted Police.

This was the first of Mr. Curwood's books to be published by the Cosmopolitan Book Corporation; and its history is almost as magical and preposterous as the story of any one of the seventeen novels he had put to press in the twelve years preceding, since first he quit newspaper work in 1907 to devote his entire time to literature.

Mr. Curwood had been in the habit of selling about ten thousand copies of a novel. Mr. Kinsey of Cosmopolitan took *The River's End* and from the dummy secured advance orders for one hundred thousand copies. This shows you what advertising and modern sales methods will do for an author—combined with Dean Cornwell's illustrations they are irresistible.

Indeed, to my notion, the illustrations are the best thing about the books. I like Cornwell and I like Lowderback; and they both illustrate Curwood—so I'm glad to have his somewhat exaggerated and often ridiculous stories.

VIII

Mr. Curwood, of course, when speaking of literature or art always uses quotes. Without quotes the words would be meaningless. With quotes they connote something anæmic or, as he would say, highbrow.

Yet he confesses that he once possessed temperament—at least, that's what he used to call it. Now he knows that it was nothing but magnificent egotism. He even went so far as to believe in inspiration once. But for the past fifteen years he has been living close to the heart of nature and (thank God, as he piously exclaims) he has learned different.

IX

There's royal blood in his veins too. His mother's great-great-grandmother was an Indian Princess. It's a long way back and Indian Princesses, even in their best days, were never much more than the daughters of petty chieftains—but it's there and that's something.

His father's uncle was Captain Marryatt, still remembered for his stories of the sea.

Curwood was born at Owosso, Michigan, June 12, 1878. Owosso is a small backwoods city, and Curwood's first exciting memory is of the circus which he saw when five years old. He did not see another circus until he was fourteen, because when he was six his father bought what was fondly supposed to be a forty-acre farm—it turned out to be a rock pile—and that was Curwood's only home for eight years. It was, however, an ideal home for the boy, with Lake Erie close by and behind it the mystery of wood and swamp. He got his first gun at eight and at nine he set to work writing his first adventure story. Some of these early stories ran to a hundred chapters and two hundred thousand words, with as many as half a dozen Indians or outlaws killed to the chapter.

He was expelled from high school, but by trapping he earned enough to put himself through the University of Michigan. Then he spent seven years on Detroit newspapers, from cub reporter to the editor of the *News-Tribune;* but he was never happy in journalism. He was always longing to get back to the woods again—to God's country, as he invariably terms the North.

Most of his stories are written out-of-doors. He has, I believe, a real affection for the forests and rivers of which he talks so much. To him they are romantic; and he strains after the fit phrase that he may convey to others the freedom and beauty he feels when over the border and away from the confining criticisms of those who speak of literature without quotes.

He has traveled thousands of miles on snowshoes, by canoe and packtrain, through the Hudson Bay Country.

Mr. Curwood is the author of *The Courage of Captain Plum*, 1908; *The Wolf Hunters*, 1908; *The Great Lakes*, 1909; *The Gold Hunters*, 1909; *The Danger Trail*, 1910; *The Honor of the Big Snows*, 1911; *The Valley of Silent Men*, 1911; *Flower of the North*, 1912; *Isobel*, 1913; *Kazan*, 1914; *God's Country and the Woman*, 1915; *The Hunted Woman*, 1916; *The Grizzly King*, 1917; *Baree, Son of Kazan*, 1917; *The Courage of Marge O'Doone*, 1918; *Nomads of the North*, 1919; *River End's* 1919; *The Country Beyond*, 1920; *The Flaming Forest*, 1921; *The Alaskan*, 1923; *A Gentleman of Courage*, 1924.

CONINGSBY DAWSON

An Interpolated Chapter, by Himself

I was born in a picturesque little town on the high-road between London and Oxford. The country for miles around is an almost primitive stretch of beech forest; hence again the inhabitants of this district are known as woodenheads and supposed to be proverbial for their density. Shortly before I was born a small-pox plague swept the little town of High Wycombe, killing the inhabitants in such quantity that, as in the Great Plague of London two centuries earlier, there was no one to nurse the sick and no one to bury the dead. It was found necessary to make the lowest characters in the town drunk before they could be persuaded to act as rough-and-ready undertakers. They were rough-and-ready enough; swinging lanterns and driving garbage-carts instead of hearses, they set out each night to collect the day's harvest of corpses. The house which my parents occupied at that time stood half way up a hill, the summit of which was crowned by the one and only cemetery. From midnight to dawn the grinding carts went by to the hoarse shouts of their ghoulish drivers, carrying the uncoffined dead to the pits which had been hurriedly dug. I have been told that the prenatal influence of these events accounted for the high-strung imaginativeness of my childhood. This imaginativeness was in no way abated by a lame nurse who had charge of me in Glasgow, to which city my parents moved when I was five.   Jack the Ripper was perpetrating his series of unchecked crimes.   My nurse, to make sure that her evenings would be undisturbed, informed me that the mysterious murderer inhabited the cupboard in my bedroom and would most certainly come out and have something to say to me if I made the slightest sound.   I am at loss even today to decide whether I am indebted or otherwise to this female purveyor of terror.   Short of driving me crazy, she stimulated my inventive ability to visualize mental images to the *nth* power.   Then she was found out and her morbidity limped away to work the same cruelty to other little boys.

My father was a preacher, lecturer and editor.   He had a passion for literature, paintings and everything that lent beauty to a humdrum world.   I used to accompany him on his treasure-quests and before I was ten was well acquainted with the leading categories of schools and periods.   My mother was also a keen reader.   It was a rule that for an hour every evening she should read aloud to me.   Through her I acquired an effortless knowledge of Tennyson, Browning, Shelley and all the leading poets of the nineteenth century together with the more colorful facts of their biographies.   At twelve I was forming my own library of standard works.   For every penny I saved towards the purchase of a book, my father made a practice of adding two more.   The belief that to create literature was the highest calling—a kind of self-appointed priesthood—was in my blood from my earliest recollections.

My first published attempt was a fantasy entitled *The Angel's Sin,* written at eleven, which brought down upon me the wholesale ridicule of my school-mates. They learned my composition off by heart and followed me home on foggy evenings shouting it at me. Till the age of seventeen my great ambition was to be a hymn-writer. I have a play-box stuffed to the brim with such pious concoctions.

At Oxford University my last two years I supported myself by journalism, writing a weekly column which was syndicated under the title of *The Quiet Hour*. Within two months of graduation I came to America, where with the visionariness of youth I essayed to earn my living by poetry writing. Macmillan published my first volume (six months' work) and the total receipts for me were twenty dollars. I then undertook a jour-ney into the Arctic in search of literary atmosphere. The result of which was a novel, which netted me $200, and a volume of short stories. As a comment on literary values, after seventeen years of rejection I sold the first of these stories—the first I ever wrote—only the other day for $2000. Then I settled down to four years of industrious scribing, making my home at Taunton, Mass. For four years' labor my total receipts were $600. This included seven volumes of literary criticism, three novels, and innumerable short-stories, all published both here and in England.

Deciding that something was lacking from my methods, I seized an opportunity that then offered to become literary adviser to the George H. Doran Com-pany. This experience was peculiarly educative, as the company was only just starting and I was able to watch the growth of a publishing business from its birth. At the end of three and a half years I had written *The Garden without Walls* and Sinclair Lewis succeeded me in the post of adviser.

I attribute the instant success of this, my first successful novel, to the discovery of one fact: that there is some one piece of knowledge on which each humblest individual is better informed than anybody else. Most young writers postpone their future by hunting through the world for an atmosphere which they borrow second-hand, whereas every one of us has an atmosphere of which he has absolute mastery within him. I puzzled my brains to discover what there was that I knew more about than anybody else and as a result decided that the thing I knew most about was knowing nothing. I chose that as my theme in *The Garden without Walls*. It was in every sense a novel of inexperience. My next was published almost on the day that the World War was declared. My third began to run serially when I was in a uniform.

I have heard men talk of the years they spent at the Front as time wasted from the point of view of career building. I can never understand them. War was the most fiery of all furnaces; if a man survived it, he had to come back to peace with a character which had been forged and pointed. If the war taught me nothing else, it taught me this: that courage is not a physical, but a spiritual quality and that, at its best, it embraces all the other virtues. While waiting for attacks, out on rest, in hospitals, I found time to write six war books which, while they afforded me companionship in the loneliest period of my life, served to distract public attention from my fiction writing when the war was ended. I had to convince the public all over again that I could write fiction, just as much as if I had never written a novel. Applying the old test as to the thing I knew more about than anyone else, I wrote *The Kingdom round the Corner* and again, a year later, after my tour in the starving countries of Europe on behalf of Mr. Hoover, *The Vanishing Point*. The last time I applied the test was during a two years' residence on the Riviera, in the creation of *The Coast of Folly*.

If I were asked to lay down rules for a literary career, I should say, "Don't write at all, if you can do anything else. Never attempt to write unless you have something that you can't help writing. When you've written your best, forget it; be convinced that your actual best still lies ahead."

FLOYD DELL

"I am prejudiced against booze and censorship, and in favor of Bolshevism and bobbed hair," says Floyd Dell—and by all that is fair, I should either hail him as brother or denounce him as a dangerous person; yet I hesitate, for he is neither one nor the other. When he says that he is prejudiced against booze, he means simply that he does not like it; and by favoring Bolshevism he is favoring the Russians against whom he will not hear a word; for Dell is the mildest of the radicals.

He is the mildest of the radicals and, perhaps for that very reason, the most persuasive. All his life, from high school days in Davenport when he contributed verses to *McClure's,* he has been known as a socialist—and yet only such timid tories as Burleson and Palmer have wanted to jail him.

II

"Mooncalf," he tells me, "particularly the early part, is more or less autobiographical. Maple, in the book, is a picture of Barry, Ill., where I was born in 1888; Vickley is Quincy, Ill., and Port Royal is Davenport, Iowa; and most of the people in the book, though not all, are real people. The book, in spite of an admixture of invention with literal fact, is a rather faithful account of my early life."

III

In those days Davenport was a ferment of art and the beginnings of art. Arthur Davison Ficke was busy on his first book of lyrics. Susan Glaspell was toiling, perplexed, over short stories for *The Black Cat*. George Cram Cooke, living on a farm to the south, enjoyed something of a local reputation as a wit. Octave Thanet, popular for years, was about to become a best seller with *The Man of the Hour*. George Randolph Chester had just left for more sophisticated worlds to conquer. Charles Edward Russell and his son, now the author of *Where the Pavement Ends,* graduating from local to Chicago newspapers, had left their influence as a guide to new reporters.

"I remember Dell, in those days," says Harry Hanson, "as a slight diffident lad who walked as if he were treading on eggs and smiled faintly and deferentially at whatever was said, especially when he did not believe it, and then would disturb a gathering of callow high-school youths by opening a serious debate on whether the egg or the chicken came first."

IV

Dell was a cub reporter on the Davenport *Daily Times,* gathering local items, recording train arrivals and departures, covering fires, shooting scrapes, the odds and ends that are used as filler by newspapers from day to day. It was a hard life and good training only in so far as it made Dell use his wits to find something better. It was not until he reached Chicago and,

on the resignation of Francis Hackett, succeeded to
the job of editing the literary section of the Chicago
Post that he really came upon congenial work. Almost at once he was recognized as the peer of the many
fine critics who have boomed out to the windy city the
worth of this book or that—they have been, almost
without exception, readable, interesting and provocative.

From Chicago he went to New York to *The Masses,*
to join Max Eastman, Art Young and Jack Reed—and
to be tried for treason.

V

"Rosemary and I," he says, in an essay in *Hearst's
International,* "lived in Greenwich Village. . . . Together we talked over everything. We were en-
chanted with each other's enlightened opinions. . . .
One evening there came a pause in our conversation. . . . The next minute we kissed. . . . We knew
that we were in love. Love makes people illogical.
. . . For a moment we almost forgot our intellectual
theories. We wanted to swear eternal fealty . . .
to belong to each other.

" 'Rosemary,' I said, 'I feel that I am on the verge
of promising—oh, all sorts of absurd and impossible
things.'

" 'Don't,' she said. 'It's dear of you to want to—
but you must not promise anything. . . . We have our
work. That's why we came here. . . . Chance has
thrown us together. But our destinies may carry us
apart, who knows when? . . . When the time comes,
and one of us falls in love with someone else, we won't

lie about it.   We will tell each other, and . . . and
part!' "

VI

So they set up house together; and Dell, trying desperately hard, found that the unconventionalities are
just as binding in their way as the conventions.   The
experiment was a failure.   At the first quarrel there
was nothing—no duty and no regard—to keep them
from flying apart.   They had their work, as Rosemary
had said; the work could not be interrupted by quarrels.
If they were going to quarrel then they must part.
And so they parted.

VII

Dell is now happily married, living at Croton-on-
the-Hudson, with a wife and child, and he looks back,
with a wise if somewhat lenient eye, on that earlier
trial at marriage as at the unreasonable tomfoolery
of two adolescents.   Happiness is worth quarreling
for, fighting for—it is worth everything.   To be free
is to be like a leaf blown from the tree, out of touch
with one's world—and homeless.

VIII

Dell published first a volume on education, *Were
You Ever a Child?*   He is especially apt and sympathetic when writing about children.   Indeed, it is
the boyhood of young Felix that makes *Mooncalf* so
fine and understanding a book.

Mooncalf is beautiful as it recounts the growing-up
of a young poet in various river towns in the Middle

West. I like *Mooncalf,* with its wise old men and all
the lovely girls Felix loved, the thrill of each new idea
as, with a boy's eyes, Felix discovered the world—
this desperate world, a world of wars and social op-
pression, of candy factories and libraries, of Lenin
and Harding and Dawes.

But *The Briary-Bush* I saw no reason for finishing.
It is a continuation of *The Mooncalf* with Felix married to Rose-Ann (a girl whom he had met at Hull
House) and both of them struggling to belong one to
the other and yet to remain at the same time free.
Why marry? Because if you're in love you must, or
so Dell seems to think. Yet in the end Felix and
Rose-Ann renounce their freedom, deciding the children are better, of more comfort and pleasure, than
theories no matter how modern.

IX

"Of dead writers," Dell says, "those whom I admire most are Defoe and Stendhal; among living
writers, Shiela Kaye-Smith—perhaps it is spelled
Sheila—I think it is."

It is.

"I have been," he says further, "influenced tremendously by H. G. Wells and Bernard Shaw. My
present plans are to go on writing novels and short
stories and books of criticism for the rest of my life.
My chief hobby is a determined avoidance of all forms
of exercise except dancing. I might add that I got
my education partly in a public library, and partly in
a socialist local, finishing it up by being psycho-
analyzed."

THOMAS DIXON

The son of a Baptist minister, of revolutionary stock, born on a farm in Cleveland County, North Carolina, January 11, 1864, Thomas Dixon was graduated from college at nineteen and elected to the state legislature before he was old enough to vote.

There you have the gist of his life. He has been elected to everything under the sun, and always before he was old enough to know what he was about. He went from Wake Forest College, with a scholarship in history, to Johns Hopkins. Next year he was back at Greensboro, studying law. At twenty-two he was admitted to the bar and to practice before the Supreme Court in Washington. Within a few months he had quit the law and entered the ministry as pastor of a Baptist church in Raleigh. From Raleigh he accepted a call to Boston; and from Boston to the People's Temple in New York City.

As a preacher, Mr. Dixon was a very fine writer. Taking Bob Ingersoll as his text, and giving Ingersoll what-for, he published four volumes of sermons. They had a grand reception. Immediately Mr. Dixon took to the lecture platform. He was going to stir his generation as it had never been stirred. But his success as a pulpiteer, bawling and shouting about sin, did not blind him to the further possibilities of still wider conquests. He would become a novelist. He knew what Mrs. Stowe had done. He would go do the same—or not the same. He'd simply turn her picture to the wall—for it was not in vain that he had been brought up in the South.

Mr. Dixon is a person of tremendous energy; and all the time that he was holding forth on the failure of the Protestant churches in New York, he was studying his audience. He knew what they would stand, what they needed, and what he would give them. At forty he was ready.

At forty he came out with *The Leopard's Spots*.

Now it is well-known—indeed, it is notorious—that a leopard cannot change his spots; and by the same token a nigger is always a nigger; he cannot doff his dirty hide or quit his hovel.

There's your theme.

And it's a corker. Countless pamphlets were written to prove that Mr. Dixon was right. Thousands, in doubt as to our rights to a monopoly of the good things of this world, rushed to enlist under the fiery cross. The day was Mr. Dixon's. Lincoln was forgotten and the gallant service of old John Brown. We were back in the halcyon days before the war, when white was white and black was black; and white was master, black a slave.

II

Yes, Mr. Dixon was right. Prejudice is the thing to play upon. And he has played upon it with a will. He has been an inciter to wrath, an appealer to fear and hatred—and he has had his reward. He has been carried on the shoulders of mobs; he has been acclaimed by backwoods editors as the chivalrous defender of an inviolable faith; but he has yet to stir a simple response in simple hearts; he has yet to bring aught but shame upon the Nazarene.

III

I have here on my desk a page torn from the Sunday edition of the *Daily Oklahoman* of Oklahoma City for February 26, 1911. This page is given over to advertising Mr. Dixon and his wares. Mr. Dixon is on tour. He is the distinguished author of *The Clansman* and he will positively appear in the leading rôle of his latest drama, his greatest drama, *The Sins of the Father*.

But there is a note of warning sounded before the page is through.

"On account of the enormous crowds surging to see this great attraction, many theatergoers may be disappointed in their efforts to secure seats or even standing room. The management therefore respectfully requests all and various, etc., etc."

You see, it is a great occasion and you don't want to miss it. The Old Dominion thrilled to Mr. Dixon's acting—so the Norfolk (Va.) *Ledger-Dispatch* reporter says, in his review. And in Raleigh Mr. Dixon's play won an ovation—if we can believe Joe Daniels' *News and Observer*. Noted clergymen have praised both play and actor. From Georgia and Tennessee tributes of one kind and another poured and pour in. There never was anyone like Mr. Dixon —it is not probable that we will ever see his like again.

IV

Yet I cannot weep. I have had more than my fill
of Mr. Dixon. He begins to nauseate me. I am
worn out with his lectures and novels and plays.
They are all too high-pitched for me. They are too
famous. They're away over my head. I want—
ah, here it is—Louis Hemon's *Maria Chapdelaine.*
Here is courage and here (if there be such a thing) is
a decent reason for believing in white supremacy—the
only decent reason we can ever have, a faith in our
own worth and the proof of our ability to stand the
gaff.

Mr. Dixon is the author of the *Leopard's Spots,*
1902; *The One Woman,* 1903; *The Clansman,* 1905;
The Life Worth Living, 1905; *The Traitor,* 1907;
Comrades, 1909; *The Root of Evil,* 1911; *The Sins
of the Father,* 1912; *The Southerner,* 1913; *The Victim,* 1914; *The Foolish Virgin,* 1915; *The Fall of a
Nation,* 1916; *The Way of a Man,* 1918.

JOHN DOS PASSOS

When in 1921 Dos Passos published *Three Soldiers* he was, for seven days, the horror and the wonder of his world. He had done a thing no full-blooded American would do—he had come out with the truth, the naked and unvarnished truth, concerning certain of our moral pretensions. It was outrageous, you may be sure; it was unheard-of.

But that was not the end of it. More remarkable still—or so it seemed to me, at the time, after Wilson and Burleson and Palmer—was the enthusiasm of those who backed him up in his stand, insisting that he had every right to speak his mind concerning our part in the war, or anything else that took his fancy. Their names, literally, ran up into the thousands.

It was inspiring. It was rare. Here was a sensitive chap in his twenties, his stomach revolted by the miseries and monotony of army life—and army officers were writing in to say that they quite understood; war had not changed since Sherman's time. Army officers and hard-boiled newspaper men and doctors, but (so far as I know) never a minister of the church of peace—the church, I say it with regret, had lost the war.

II

Three Soldiers was the second of Dos Passos' books. The first, *One Man's Initiation,* was the work of a gifted Harvard graduate with an urge toward realism. It was little more. But it showed the bent of Dos

Passos' mind. Dos Passos is effeminate; and as so
often happens with the effeminate, he has blood-
curdling notions—as Zola had blood-curdling notions,
and wrote about prostitutes from thinking on them and
sitting across the table from one, in a café one night.
The fevered dreams of adolescence were the dreams
of Dos Passos, and they came near to making a mis-
anthrope of him.

III

In *Streets of Night*, his latest novel, Dos Passos has
returned to the mood of *One Man's Initiation*. He
is older now and wiser, wearier maybe, and disillusioned; but he has not yet discovered that there are
things better worth his philosophizing than the petting
parties of students and the slow deterioration of the
same students after they have left college and gone
out into a larger world.

I declare I found *Streets of Night* tiresome, a repetition of every other novel of its kind—an attempt to
explain and excuse the nauseating satisfaction of the
younger generation, a hand book for inverts, a sort
of *Roger Bloomer* that (because not written in dialogue) knew no limits but carried its theme on and
on even to the suicide of minor characters. It was
poor stuff, coming, as it did, after *Three Soldiers*.

IV

Three Soldiers was great. It was especially great
because it was timely and because it needed doing.
Re-reading it a while back the wholesale stupidity and
waste of war overwhelmed me. It does not sidestep

and gloss as the more likable Sir Philip Gibbs will always continue to do—because Sir Philip has finicky tastes and a certain reticence. The book calls a spade a spade and makes free with bastards. You are back in the army camps with all their repressions, buck privates and sergeants around you, and nothing but drill and menial tasks to relieve the monotony and degradation of their talk. It is a better book for us than Barbusse's *Under Fire*. It tells of our army and was not written by a man worn out with four years in the trenches.

v

However, to date it is not as a novelist at all but as the author of *Rosinante to the Road Again,* a book of essays, that Dos Passos has done his best work. *Rosinante* comes near to being one of my favorite books. Perhaps because I have an unguarded affection for Spain and things Spanish—probably because it is so well written, so lilting, so perfect an expression of the lazy man's philosophy and the lazy man's charm.

Be that as it may, I recommend *Rosinante to the Road Again* without reservations.

Mr. Dos Passos is the author of *One Man's Initiation,* 1918; *Three Soldiers,* 1921; *Rosinante to the Road Again,* essays, 1922; *A Pushcart at the Curb,* a book of poems, 1922; *Streets of Night,* 1923.

THEODORE DREISER

Whenever I am asked to name the greatest novelist in America, though I may think the order a large one —and yet withal trivial and silly; in my more rigid moments such orders always seem silly to me—I invariably answer, Dreiser. And I think I have good reasons for such an answer. More than any other Dreiser moves me. This is a wonderful and terrible world to him; and his are wonderful and terrible books, filled with pity and understanding. They are more humane than the novels of Hardy, larger than the novels of Galsworthy. They are not marred as, at their worst, are the novels of Wells and Bennett by cheapness, the scarcely laudable showing-off of the Cockney. So far as I am aware, only Conrad, among the men, can be compared in reverence to Dreiser. . . . And as you can see, none of my comparisons are made with Americans. In America Dreiser is unique. "The one man," Harris Merton Lyon said, a dozen years ago, "worth the lot of them."

II

"The one man, my masters," said Lyon, "worth the lot of them . . . a fellow whose work reveals at once that lucidity and that inscrutability which we accord to the seer . . . mysterious . . . interesting.

"Imagine," said he, "a man, long, loosely put together, with design obtuse, blunted or slack where in most individuals nature makes for acuteness and taut-

ness.   A lolling gait; a lolling head; unbeautiful, un-
arresting, prematurely grizzled.   Somewhere between
forty and fifty. . . . . A loose mouth, chin blunted and
rather small; bluish gray eyes, large, lolling eyes; perhaps neurotic, and meaning nothing, save perhaps in
anger.   Simply a tall, ungainly, unlovely man with
something of the cast of Oliver Goldsmith's features.
Something lumpish, something rankly vegetable is
evoked.   What?   A huge rutabaga; a colossal, pith-
stricken radish.   In this body dwells this interesting,
this amazingly fascinating mind.   He sits, lolling his
head, articulating with a drone. . . . 'Well-ah . . .
Well-ah . . .' folding a pocket handkerchief eternally
into a strip, folding the strip itself together accordion-
wise.   Theodore Dreiser, mysterious and powerful.''

III

Or there is Sherwood Anderson's picture of him, as
part of the foreword to *Horses and Men:*

"Theodore Dreiser is old—he is very, very old.   I
do not know how many years he has lived, perhaps
forty, perhaps fifty, but he is very old.   Something
gray and bleak and hurtful, that has been in the world
perhaps forever, is personified in him. . . .

"Long ago, when he was the editor of the *Delineator,* Dreiser went one day, with a woman friend, to
visit an orphan asylum.   The woman once told me the
story of that afternoon in the big, ugly gray building,
with Dreiser, looking heavy and lumpy and old, sitting
on a platform, folding and refolding his pocket handkerchief and watching the children—all in their uni-
forms, trooping in.

" 'The tears ran down his cheeks and he shook his head,' the woman said, and that is a real picture of Theodore Dreiser. He is old in spirit and he does not know what to do with life, so he tells about it as he sees it, simply and honestly. The tears run down his cheeks and he folds and refolds his pocket handkerchief and shakes his head."

IV

Burton Rascoe, in his "Bookman's Day Book" in the New York *Tribune*, told a while ago of an evening spent with Dreiser, Mencken, W. C. Fields and others:

"Dreiser kept rolling up his handkerchief and letting it unfurl again, trying very hard now and then with some gibe to get Mencken's goat, and altogether having much more fun than I have ever seen him have before. . . . Mencken allowed that 'Say what you will, fellows, the greatest living poet is Kipling,' and Dreiser chimed in, 'And he wasn't such a slob as a short-story writer. What about his Indian stories, and what about *Kim?* Where do you find fiction any *better?*' . . . Fields entertained us with anecdotes until tears of laughter streamed down Dreiser's cheeks."

V

Once while riding in the subway with Harris Merton Lyon, Dreiser showed Lyon a paragraph in the *Evening World* beginning, "Let us introduce you to the work of Rudyard Kipling." Lyon scoffed, saying that such work was already known to everyone. But Dreiser said, "No, people have to be introduced to everything."

VI

This is, as I have said, a wonderful and terrible world to Dreiser—but to how many others? Watch your neighbor. Does he know anything about the beauty, the joy, the thrill of living? And not alone your neighbor, but your Mayor, your Senator, your President—would you say that they are living as in old barbaric times Mithradates King of Pontus lived or Plato or that dear serpent of the Nile whose slave was love? Are they not rather shirt-fronts stuffed out with inherited misconceptions and question-begging compromise? Imagine your Mayor, your Senator, your President under a gallus moon—imagine them before the grave and daring canvases of Goya or listening to the seductive music of the Russians—put them beside even so harassed a young man as the Prince of Wales and see how dead they are. Such people must, in Dreiser's words, be introduced to everything. They have not looked upon the stars within their memory or yours. They do not know the mountains move, shifting under their weight of clouds. To them the sea is something to be crossed that they may the sooner come to London or to Paris.

VII

And Dreiser is the one to tell them all they ought to know. Everything is wonderful and new and strange, mysterious to Dreiser—so everything, the cricket on the hearth, green gables, myself, the color of the city, is recorded in Dreiser's books. . . .

"Turn," says Mencken, "to page 703 of *The Genius*.

By the time one gets there, one has hewn and hacked one's way through 702 large pages of fine print—97 long chapters, more than 250,000 words. And yet, at this hurried and impatient point, with the *coda* already begun, Dreiser halts the whole narrative to explain the origin, nature and inner meaning of Christian Science, and to make us privy to a lot of chatty stuff about Mrs. Althea Jones, a professional healer, and to supply us with detailed plans and specifications of the apartment house in which she lives, works her tawdry miracles, and has her being. . . . A Dreiser novel, at least of the later canon, cannot be read as other novels are read—on a winter evening or summer afternoon, between meal and meal, traveling from New York to Boston. It demands the attention for almost a week, and uses up the faculties for a month."

VIII

But who cares? The faculties have been well used, and the time was not wasted—as Mr. Mencken knows. . . .

"The notion," says Mr. Mencken, "that Dreiser is a mere representational realist, which is to say, a mere photographer, is utterly absurd. It is held, to be sure, by his chief academic opponents, and it seems to be held, too, by some of his imitators, but it is absurd nevertheless. The virtue of such a book as *Jennie Gerhardt* does not lie in the fact that it is accurate and life-like as representation; it lies in the fact that, in some way that is hard to analyze, Dreiser manages to make us see the world through Jennie's eyes, and so gives us an understanding of her pitiful tragedy.

Superficially, she is simply a girl of loose morals, living in contempt of the Mann Act. But actually, in Dreiser's highly skillful hands, she becomes a representative of the agony of all womankind. The last scene of the book, with Jennie looking through the train-gate as Lester's carcass is loaded into the baggage coach, is surely not mere photography; it is poignant and unforgettable tragedy. To argue that it cannot be tragedy because Jennie is a poor simpleton—in other words, that simple folk cannot know disaster and despair—is to argue plain nonsense."

IX

As good a portrait of Dreiser as any can be found in Dreiser's *The Genius* where he tells on page 65 of Eugene Witla—since, rightly taken, as Anatole France has said, all romance and all criticism is autobiography.

"With Eugene convention meant nothing at all, and his sense of evil and good was something which the ordinary person would not have comprehended. He was prone to like all sorts and conditions of human beings—the intellectual, the ignorant, the clean, the dirty, the gay, the sorrowful, white, yellow, black. . . . To him a human being was a human being. The ruck of misfits or ne'er-do-wells he could laugh joyously with or at. It was all wonderful, beautiful, amusing. Even its grimness and tragedy were worth while, although they hurt him terribly at times. . . . He was truly your flamboyant youth of talent when he got to talking—when he had a truly sympathetic ear. He loved to boast to someone who really admired him."

X

"People in general attach too much importance to words," Dreiser says, in *Sister Carrie*. "They are under the illusion that talking effects great results. As a matter of fact, words are, as a rule, the shallowest portion of all the argument. They but dimly represent the great surging feeling and desires which lie behind. When the distraction of the tongue is removed, the heart listens."

XI

Mr. Mencken has said that there seldom comes a time when Dreiser will not digress to expound his various philosophies. But I like the digressions of Dreiser. I want to be told of the habits of Sister Carrie—or of any other habits concerning which Dreiser is informed. . . .

"Habits are peculiar things. They will drive the really non-religious mind out of bed to say prayers that are only a custom and not a devotion. The victim of habit, when he has neglected the thing which it was his custom to do, feels a little scratching in the brain, a little irritating something which comes of being out of the rut, and imagines it to be the prick of conscience, the still small voice that is urging him ever to righteousness. If the digression is unusual enough, the drag of habit will be heavy enough to cause the unreasoning victim to return and perform the perfunctory thing. 'Now, bless me,' says such a mind, 'I have done my duty,' when, as a matter of fact, it has merely done its old, unbreakable trick once again."

There is something endearing, to me, in the man who can be so simple in his comments on habit—so direct, so naïve. He is good. Let his persecutors denounce him as obscene—they are mad, driven mad by the desire to see something evil in the natural evolution of God's handiwork.

XII

Dreiser is sane because he is not easily shocked, because he is not horrified when in the presence of folk less fettered than himself. . . .

"That's her—the Butler girl," one railroad clerk says to another in *The Titan*. "Gee! a man wouldn't want anything better than that, would he?"

It was, as Dreiser says, the spontaneous tribute that passion and envy invariably pay to health and beauty. On that pivot swings the world.

XIII

When he speaks of home he is equally direct and honest.

"A lovely home atmosphere is one of the flowers of the world, than which there is nothing more tender, nothing more delicate, nothing more calculated to make strong and just the natures cradled and nourished within it. Those who have never experienced such a beneficient influence will not understand wherefore the tear springs glistening to the eyelids at some strange breath in lovely music. The mystic chords which bind and thrill the heart of the nation, they will never know."

XIV

He is sometimes apt and unerring in his metaphors —"the heat of his passion was already melting the wax of his companion's scruples."

He has a sense of the forlorn loneliness of a first unrequited love—"He worshiped her from afar but she never knew; she never knew what solemn black eyes burned at her when she was not looking; she left Alexandria, her family moving to another town, and in time he recovered, for their is much of beauty; but the color of her hair and the wonder of her neck stayed with him always."

XV

"I have just turned forty," Dreiser said in *A Traveler at Forty*—he was born at Terre Haute, Indiana, on August 27, 1871. "I have seen a little something of life. I have been a newspaper man,"—he entered newspaper work, on the Chicago *Daily Globe*, June 15, 1892—"editor,"—he was editor of *Every Month*, a literary and musical magazine, 1895–8; of *Smith's Magazine*, 1905–6; managing editor of *Broadway Magazine*, 1906–7; and editor-in-chief of the Butterick publications, *Delineator, Designer, New Idea, English Delineator*, 1907–10, about the time Arnold Bennett, in London, was editor of *Woman*—"magazine contributor, author, and, before these things, several kinds of clerk before I found out what I could do.

"Eleven years ago I wrote my first novel, which was issued by a New York publisher in 1900 and sup-

pressed by him, Heaven knows why. For the same
year they suppressed my book because of its alleged
immoral tendencies, they published Zola's *Fecundity*
and *An English Woman's Love Letters*. I fancy now,
after eleven years of wonder, that it was not so much
the supposed immorality as the book's straightforward,
plain-spoken discussion of American life in general. We were not used then in America to calling a
spade a spade, especially in books. We had great admiration for Tolstoi and Flaubert and Balzac and de
Maupassant at a distance—some of us—and it was
quite an honor to have handsome sets of these men on
our shelves, but mostly we had been schooled in the
literature of Dickens, Thackeray, George Eliot,
Charles Lamb and that refined company of English
sentimental realists who told us something about life
but not everything. No doubt all these great men
knew how shabby a thing this world is—how full of
lies, make-believe, seeming and false pretenses it all is,
but they had agreed among themselvs, or with the public, or with sentiment generally, not to talk about that
too much. Books were always built out of facts concerning 'our better natures.' We were always to be
seen as we wish to be. There were villains to be sure
—liars, dogs, thieves, scoundrels—but they were
strange creatures, hiding away in the dark, unconven-
tional places and scarcely seen save at night and per-
adventure; whereas we, all clean, bright, honest, well-
meaning people, were living in nice homes, going our
way honestly and truthfully, attending church, raising
our children, believing in a Father, a Son and a Holy
Ghost, and never doing anything wrong at any time

save as these miserable liars, dogs, thieves, et cetera, might suddenly appear and make us. Our books largely showed us as heroes. If anything happened to our daughters it was not their fault but the fault of these miserable villains. Most of us were without original sin. The business of our books, our churches, our laws, our jails, was to keep us so.

"I am quite sure that it never occurred to many of us that there was something really improving in a plain, straightforward understanding of life. For myself I accept now no creeds. I do not know what truth is, what beauty is, what love is, what hope is. I do not believe anyone absolutely and I do not doubt anyone absolutely. I think people are both evil and well-intentioned."

XVI

Of course, Dreiser cannot claim to have originated this non-committal philosophy of his. It is as old as man himself. It is the tolerant fatalism of the East. When Pilate in Judea asked, What is truth?—he was making the confession that Dreiser makes. There may have been many who were cocksure but since time began there have been many more who did not know. Life, said Euripides, is a song sung by an idiot, dancing down the wind—or, to quote Macbeth, a poor player who struts and frets his hour upon the stage. We are bemused. There is so much to learn—time is so short.

Nor is there anything new in Dreiser's assertion— it was King Richard's—that there is a soul of goodness in things evil. There is much good in Falstaff

and more than a little of the bad boy in Prince Hal.
There was good and evil in Cæsar—and Plutarch
knew it. The soldiers of King David who followed
him to battle recognized the evil that he did in taking
Bathsheba to wife—but they knew him too for the
Lord's annointed.

But Dreiser is right in saying that in America we
have a horror of criticism. To tell me that Babbitt is
a fool is like calling my brother a fool—for the aspirations and terrors of Babbitt are my brother's terrors
and aspirations—they might very well be my own.
Nor do we read here that we may have our horizons
broadened, but only to pass the time; and since we are
all of us the victims of inferiority, it is no pastime to
be told unpleasant truths—it only makes us mad; and
so long as it was possible we suppressed the authors
who dared such tactics. Now that their name is
legion, thanks to Dreiser, we can no longer suppress
them.

XVII

"Of all the personages in the Dreiser books," says
Mr. Mencken, "the Copperwood of *The Titan* is perhaps the most radiantly real; he is accounted for in
every detail, and yet in the end, he is not accounted for
at all; there hangs about him to the last that baffling
mysteriousness which hangs about those we know most
intimately."

XVIII

"Novels are a mere expression of temperament anyhow," Dreiser says.

XIX

"I am not really a princely soul looking for obsequious service," he tells us. "I am, I fancy, a very humble minded person, anxious to go briskly forward, not to be disturbed too much and allowed to live in quiet and seclusion. . . . There is in me the spirit of a lonely child somewhere and it clings pitifully to the hand of its big mamma, Life, and cries when it is frightened; and then there is a coarse, vulgar exterior which fronts the world defiantly and bids all and sundry to go to the devil. It sneers and smirks and jeers bitterly at times, and guffaws and grins and has a good time laughing at the follies of others."

Mr. Dreiser is the author of *Sister Carrie*, 1900; *Jennie Gerhardt*, 1911; *The Financier*, 1912; *A Traveler at Forty*, 1914; *The Titan*, 1914; *The Genius*, 1915; *Plays of the Natural and Supernatural*, 1916; *A Hoosier Holiday*, 1916; *The Hand of the Potter*, 1917; *Free and Other Stories*, 1918; *Twelve Men*, 1919; *Hey Rub-a-Dub-Dub*, 1920; *A Book about Myself*, 1922; *The Color of a Great City*, 1923.

HARVEY FERGUSSON

When I asked Mr. Mencken to nominate someone or other for inclusion in my book, he named Harvey Fergusson as the best of the new men; and having read Mr. Fergusson's three novels I am of a mind to say that Mencken, though dogmatic, was right. There is passion and color to *The Blood of the Conquerors,* that tale of a dying race; there is truth and accuracy to *Capital Hill,* which pictures the success of an astute jobholder in Washington; there is a new note, monotonous and faithful, to *Women and Wives* where Mr. Fergusson recounts the failures of a young man with a splendid past and the various adventures of the women who put their faith in him. Mr. Fergusson is versatile and Mr. Fergusson is observant, and—best of all—he has gone to some pains to learn the rather difficult art of writing. He can describe the desert of New Mexico as I, for one, have never seen it described—the towns, the buttes, the miles on miles of sage-brush and sand. He can turn, in the next chapter, to New York and setting his hero down to supper give you the very tone of hotel life and the rather shabby treatment one in earnest may expect from a married woman who is merely playing with intrigue. He has plumbed the pretense and chicanery of that unscrupulous humbug, our professional politician. And through it all he has remained critical, though taking neither one side nor the other—he has retained his faith in the vigor and hearty mirth and good clean earth that is America.

II

The Blood of the Conquerors is a novel of the American Southwest where Mr. Fergusson was born and where he grew up. It deals with the people Mr. Fergusson knows best. To know any one well is to love that any one, though he be sinful and vain; and Mr. Fergusson loves his characters. In especial he loves Ramon Delcasor, the son of countless generations of *hidalgos,* a born lord of the soil—the painted buttes and sun-baked plains are his natural heritage. Ramon struggles—helplessly, to be sure—against the encroachments of the puritan and schemer, hoping to save the spacious hospitality and courage of his ancient civilization from complete effacement at the hands of penny-wise boosters. But the Yank degrades the Spaniard; the Yank has all the advantage. It is the material things the Yank seeks while the Spaniard is tormented with a sickness of the soul. For an hour of ease the Spaniard will barter his birthright to the Yank.

Mr. Fergusson watches this strange unequal struggle with interest; and as, step by step, he makes known to us the changing fortunes of Ramon, the book assumes epic proportions, the drama becomes enthralling. These people live. They have their vagaries. They drink, they gamble, kiss and grow indifferent. They make history—and their history makes fine reading.

III

Capitol Hill is quite another story, the story of Washington, of government clerks and their girls, of débutantes in search of a thrill and kept women with their paramours. This, as Mr. Mencken has said, is the Washington that really runs the country, the Washington of the Press Club, of the professional jobholder—the lobbyist and congressman. These second and third rate people are infinitely more powerful than the so-called diplomatic set, because their name is legion, because it is numbers that count in a democracy, because they are the commonplace of America. They are the people who came from Ohio with Harding and from Massachusetts with Coolidge. Theirs are the little parties at houses on K Street, theirs the wires to Slemp, and theirs the pride and glory of corruption.

Ralph Dolan, the central character, is just such a one as could succeed in a government that goes by favor. He is our present Casanova, living by his wits, by cards, with women for his hours of ease and brave talk his best contribution to civilization. He is—again to quote Mr. Mencken—as authentic as Babbitt or Carol Kennicott.

IV

Women and Wives, though the scene remains in Washington, deals with yet another world, the world of failure, the world of the boy who graduates from college with honors, marries early and, on the salary of a government clerk, proceeds to make a drudge of the lovely and intelligent girl whom he has married. It is the tale of the *Doll's House* in terms of a three room flat, a relentless study of the uses to which we put our dreamers. Jim is not really a bad sort—he is just futile—vain and preposterous. As Mr. Fergus-

son says, the strong and free sin blithely and forget,
but Jim sins miserably and stews in the juices of regret.
And such sins! Bootlegger whiskey drunk by himself
as he sits alone in his room reading Conrad and Kipling—a flirtation with his stenographer.

V

In *Women and Wives*, Mr. Fergusson gives us a
glimpse of the bathing beach, at the Basin, in Washington—the beach which is so often pictured in the
Sunday Supplements—

"Jim, after donning a bathing-suit in a dim cell,
dank from the feet of former occupants, emerged and
surveyed the scene in disgust. It was an impressive
demonstration of the ugliness of the human race.
These people, he thought, would have been bad enough
in their street clothes, but in bathing-suits they were
terrible to look upon. That is, most of them were.
A few, slim sweet girl figures led the eye captive, and
a few muscular, sunburned young men sported like
otters, swimming swiftly hand over hand with their
faces buried deep in the water. But most of the crowd
was made up of beings preposterously, bulbously fat
and of others painfully thin. Their wet suits spared
the beholder no detail of their unloveliness. Why
was it, Jim wondered, that only man of all the animals
could not keep his natural proportions, but either
bulged or shrivelled?"

VI

Mr. Fergusson tells of Marion and how she had
reduced her ankles with rubber bandages and with

rubber bandages warded off a double chin.   Her eating was controlled by science; her complexion was under the care of experts; her blonde hair was waved to perfection; and she exercised.   Neither travail, passion, weariness, worry nor toil touched her at all. She was a thing of unspoiled beauty, dwelling alone in the glass tower of her egotism.   But she had the rare grace of being interesting; and she interested Jim's wife, Catherine.

"Catherine had been forced to realize that persons who devote their lives unselfishly to great causes are often tiresome.   And still more tiresome were often those who led lives of self-sacrifice and devotion to others.   They were wont to talk about their sacrifices and devotion too much.   They had the impenetrable complacency which so often goes with self-conscious virtue.   They were admirable, but they were bores."

VII

Jim has an affair that finally wrecks his marriage; and the woman in the case wins him because she appeals to his vanity.   Catherine makes him feel his inferiority, the futility of his gorgeous dreams, the worthlessness of his promise: but Fanny——

"A woman's love," says Mr. Fergusson, "be it ever so sensuous, is also always either a succor to helplessness or a tribute to superiority.   But a man loves, above all, a reflected and glorified image of himself in a woman's mind.   He will endure vast stupidity in his mate if only it is not blind to his merits, and great weakness if only it clings trustfully to his strength.

A woman's vanity is mostly pride in the body she has to give, but a man's vanity is the very essence of his being."

VIII

Jim has one last futile vision. He had gone camping up the river—

"It was such a forest that he had loved—a forest where his imagination could play with strange and lovely things of his own creation.

"As he peered into its draped and shadowed arches and listened to its soft sibilant voices, he was unaccountably filled with a quiet ecstasy. Life now seemed to him as simple and beautiful as a tree. He perceived that he had been all his life toiling and fretting at useless tasks, and he felt certain that he could simply turn away from them and do delightful things. Life gives what you ask and is what you think it—that was the mystical wisdom of his mood.

"He and Catherine had quarreled, they had grown cold to each other. And it seemed to him that he could bring their love to life again with a kiss. They had quarreled; well, they would make up! How sweetly they would make up. He had been untrue to her. What of it? How clearly he saw now that he had but loved some image of her in another woman, that he had been chasing the ghost of an emotion that she had aroused. Love and life were there, waiting, but he had grown blind to them. He had been putting buffers between him and his desire.

"He turned and went quietly out of the forest as a penitent goes from church, with his soul purged and at peace."

IX

Mr. Fergusson has very kindly jotted down a few autobiographic notes to make my account of him and his doings more complete. . . .

"My father, Harvey Butler Fergusson, came to Albuquerque about 1882. He was the son of Sampson Nolan Fergusson, of Dickens County, Alabama, a physician, planter and large slave owner, head of the Masonic order in Alabama, a captain in the Confederate Army and a member of the original Ku Klux Klan. My father's mother was named Poyos and was Huguenot French from Charleston, S. C. My mother's parents were both German immigrants. Her father, Franz Huning, was a pioneer who came over the Santa Fè trail in the forties, and once owned most of the land on which Albuquerque now stands.

"I was born in Albuquerque in 1890, about eight years after the railroad reached it, and so spent my boyhood in a western town of a few thousand people, which was just passing out of the frontier stage. I was the typical sensitive member of my generation, somewhat at odds with my environment, awkward and shy. Such a child usually finds his escape in books. I think the most distinctive thing about my childhood was that I found my escape in going outdoors. I used to make all-day expeditions afield at the age of six. I owned a shot gun and was a hunter at the age of nine. I had a horse at eleven. I went always alone, not being allowed to hunt with anyone else for fear of accident. I was a good shot and rider, but played no games with other boys. I was a naturalist and made collections and kept notes. My only reading was popular natural histories. I was a graphic artist from an early age and drew pictures incessantly, mostly of birds and animals, though I also sketched landscapes. My parents repeatedly offered me instructions in drawing, but I always quit after one lesson, being profoundly averse to any kind of routine or discipline or anything that interfered with my freedom. I was self-reliant and self-sufficient to an unusual degree, with a great capacity for solitude, but very little capacity for getting along with others. I had the outcast, guilty feeling characteristic of such boys, and always thought of myself as one who had no place in life as he saw it about him.

"At the age of sixteen I had written a journal about twenty thousand words in length, some poems and prose poems and many short notes on birds and animals.

"My education was in the local schools, with one year at the New Mexico military institute, one at the University of New Mexico, and then three years at Washington and Lee University, Lexington, Va., where I took a B. A. degree at the age of twenty-one.

"My real education was undoubtedly afield and in my own efforts as a writer and graphic artist. I developed necessarily a good habit of observation. It seems to me much of my viewpoint was formed in those years. I look at the human spectacle with the same detached, scientific curiosity that I developed as a boy out-of-doors, and it has always seemed to me that this detached, impartial view of things is the most distinctive thing I have. I always regard a character, too, as an organism in a certain environment, rather than as a social unit. Man is to me primarily the strangest and most interesting of the mammals.

"During my college life I was a solitary, a sarcastic and unpopular fellow, nearly always gloomily in love.

I used to go off hunting in the Virginia hills. Had a profound contempt and aversion for so-called college life. During my last year in college I began reading a good deal for the first time. I remember reading Tolstoy's *Anna Karenina,* and being tremendously inspired by it.

"I had an artistic instinct of some kind from an early age. I believe that what turned me toward fiction was the need for studying people. When I got out in the world I found that I had an appalling ignorance of people. I had a profound social maladjustment. I therefore began studying people. I made notes, read psychology, tried to understand my own kind as I had tried to understand wild animals.

"When I left college I went into the U. S. Forest Service in New Mexico and after two seasons as a timber cruiser, took the examination to become a forest ranger. I thought of this as a life work, greatly prefering the mountains to any civilization I had seen. My father, who was then a member of congress from New Mexico, objected to this course and sent for me to come to Washington. He got me a government job and sent me to night law school. I passed up both in less than a month and went to work as a cub reporter on the Washington *Herald.* After a few months I got a job in Savannah, Georgia, on the *Morning News.* Stayed there about six months and went to the Richmond *Times-Dispatch.* I was full of nomadic urge. I was soon back in Washington on the bureau of the old Chicago *Record-Herald.* In less than a year I passed that up and went back to New Mexico, where I spent four months and all my money wandering around the country with a friend. We had two pack horses and camped out, spending our time hunting and fishing. I wrote stories that were no good and a journal of the trip which I can still read with interest. I also composed poetry.

"Returning to Washington broke, I took a job with Frederic J. Haskin, who syndicated a newspaper feature called the Haskin letter. This job suited me peculiarly well and I held it down seven years. About twice a year Haskin would let me go on long trips in search of material; and this made the thing tolerable to me. I have never spent a year in one place in my adult life. I went all over the Eastern United States, into maritime Canada, South to Cuba, Porto Rico, Santo Domingo, and Panama. Between trips I read extensively, having a card to the Library of Congress. I soon obtained complete editorial control of the Haskin letter. My employer did not even read it after it was printed. I wrote into it all my impressions, theories, everything. The only check on me was the number of kicks I got from astonished editors and readers. During this period I achieved some intellectual sophistication entirely by my own reading and thinking. I knew hardly anyone who could share my ideas.

"I wrote my first short story while in Richmond at the age of twenty-three and sold it to the *Black Cat*. I continued writing short stories all through my newspaper experience and sold a few to cheap magazines. But I did no good work. I did not dare to write my most original ideas because I saw that they were unfit for magazines, and I did not see any other medium of publication. My efforts to be a magazine writer ended at the age of twenty-seven, when I wrote an adventure story about thirty thousand words in length. It was commonplace and I knew it. The next year I began a realistic novel of New Mexico as I knew it. I imagined I was writing something very radical and

startling and something that would probably never
be published.   I finished the thing in about a year and
a half by working Sundays and vacations.   This was
The Blood of the Conquerors.   I took it to Henry
Mencken, who pronounced it good and gave it to
Knopf to publish.   Following this I gave up my job
and went to New Mexico and wrote *Capitol Hill,* into
which I poured all my disgust with Washington.   I returned to Washington, made a stake by doing newspaper work, and again retired to my native heath to
write *Women and Wives.*   Last fall I went to New
York, where I wrote short stories and articles and did
publicity work.   I am now back in New Mexico again
and about to start my fourth book.

"During my period of heavy reading in Washington
I passed under many influences.   I had a period of
Bernard Shaw and Ibsen, and another when decadents
like Wilde, Hearn and Gautier were my models.   But
the novelists that influenced me most, in about the
order named, were Maupassant, Turgenieff, Tolstoy,
Flaubert, George Moore and Thomas Hardy.   I
never found anything I liked in American fiction except
Huckleberry Finn and a few of my contemporaries,
who came too late to influence me much.   Wells, Bennett, Galsworthy and W. L. George all mean little
to me.

"Undoubtedly my three novels were built on the pattern of the Gallic novel form as used by the writers
who influenced me most, with some added insight
gained from psychoanalysis, of which I have read
everything I have been able to get.   I cannot, however, lay claim to a finished method or theory of the
novel.   I hope and believe that my technique is still
developing and that my future work will be different
from what I have done.   I am much interested in the

work of experimentalists, such as James Joyce and Waldo Frank. I believe the long-winded novel is going. I look upon my own work to date as too long-winded and detailed. I believe fiction has got to break through the surface of the social spectacle and get at the essential personality of man more than it has done heretofore. At the same time, I am a partisan of no special method for doing this. Most æsthetic theory seems to me ridiculous. An artist can proceed only by following his instinct with what skill and courage he has. I think he should seize upon whatever method, new or old, seems best to fit the creative purpose of the moment. What he wants is the form that will give the most complete release to his creative energy. His success is measured by the amount of vitality he gets into his creations—by the extent to which his material is fused and moulded in creative heat. This is felt by the sensitive reader as clearly as he might feel the impact of a blow.

"If the novel be defined as an imaginative record of human experience, I believe that it is almost as fundamental a part of life as bread or love. I would put upon it no limitations or dogmatic imperatives, but let it try to be as free and various as the thing it seeks to represent."

F. SCOTT FITZGERALD

If I were given to prophecying I should certainly predict, once his mania for writing ephemeral short stories is done with, a great and glorious future for F. Scott Fitzgerald; and I should base that prediction upon the irony, the beauty, the wit of *This Side of Paradise* and *The Beautiful and Damned*. There are two books unique in American literature, though imitated a thousand times. They are the young man sowing his oats, reaping his whirlwind, muddled, worried, triumphant and moody, with his gay colors and gray castles tumbled in a heap. They have form, ease and variety. They are utterly fearless, shirking no conclusions, true to their characters.

If a chap is a bounder, selfish and conceited, soon or late his friends will find it out. Fitzgerald knows this. But that does not blind him to the fact that the chap may be immensely interesting and, in his way, tragic and likable. The chap may be generous; the cad may be a pose—as it was with Byron. Or the loss may be a woman's, some woman who has put her trust in him. But not always. Sometimes the loss is ours. If I remember right, Sidney Carton was a sot, but his is the only name one regrets and recalls when *A Tale of Two Cities* is done with—as, in the course of the years, most books are done with, becoming only memories, half and more than half forgotten.

II

But it is not so much his characters that matter, to Fitzgerald and in his books, as what is done with them. In *This Side of Paradise* they are given their heads, in *The Beautiful and Damned* rope. Yet when they threaten to run away or hang themselves, Fitzgerald does not wring his hands and say, "I told you so." Nor does he stand idly by and shrug his shoulders, murmuring, "The funeral is theirs." He lets them play their piece out to the end; and they become, even for the dullest, tragic comedians, dangling helplessly on the threads of destiny and time. Rightly understood, they are heroic—and Fitzgerald understands them absolutely.

III

"My third novel," he says, "is just finished and quite different from the other two in that it is an attempt at form and refrains carefully from trying to 'hit anything off.' Five years ago the new American novels needed comment by the author because they were facing a public that had had very little but trash for a hundred years—that is to say, the exceptions were few and far between and most of them were commercial failures. But now that there is an intelligent body of opinion guided by such men as Mencken, Edmund Wilson and Van Wyck Brooks, comment should be unnecessary; and the writer, if he has any aspirations toward art, should try to convey the feel of his scenes, places and people directly—as Conrad does, as a few Americans (notably Willa Cather) are already trying to do."

IV

Mr. Fitzgerald was born in St. Paul, Minn., Sept.
24, 1896.   He spent his early years traveling with his
family here and there through America, living for a
while in Syracuse and for a while in Buffalo.   His first
reading was entirely confined to Henty, Alger and
Ralph Henry Barbour.   At college he was influenced,
almost exclusively, by Wells and Compton McKenzie
—as he says, "see *This Side of Paradise* which treats
all this very fully, being to a large extent autobiographical."

V

That incorrigible gossip, Burton Rascoe, in the New
York *Tribune,* tells of a luncheon with Edmund Wilson during which Wilson remarked that Fitzgerald
mispronounces more words than any other educated
person he (Wilson) has ever known; going on to say
that when Fitzgerald is with Ring Lardner, Lardner
is forever correcting Fitzgerald's pronunciation.
However, no harm is done as Fitzgerald never remembers the correction from one moment to the next.

VI

Among other wise sayings Ed Howe has said that
somehow we always hate to tell a man that he can't
spell.   Spelling, nevertheless, is a part of writing.
The history of a word is in its spelling—whence it
hails and who has used it, Latin or Greek or Teuton,
and where, under what moon, across what council table, for whose ears.   This is my only excuse for re-

ferring to the spelling of Fitzgerald in a recent letter to me. . . .

Fitzgerald is free from all feeling for words. He uses them or abuses them as suits his fancy. He coins them anew. They are divorced from their past, made over, becoming utterly modern tramps as are so many of Fitzgerald's best liked characters, and somehow individual—awhile, Ralph Henry Barber, Sarycuse, Compton MacKenzie, Van Wyke Brooks, Nietchean Gertrude Stein, traveling. . . .

But don't let that worry you: the man's an artist just the same.

VII

"When, in St. Paul and about twelve," says Fitzgerald, "I wrote all through class in school in the back of my geography and first year Latin and on the margin of themes, declensions and mathematic problems. Two years later the family decided the only way to force me to study was to send me to a boarding school. This was a mistake. It took my mind off my writing. I decided to play football, to smoke, to go to college, to do all sorts of irrelevant things that had nothing to do with the proper mixture of description and dialogue in the short story.

"But in school I went off on a new tack. I saw a musical comedy called *The Quaker Girl* and from that day forth my desk bulged with Gilbert and Sullivan librettos and dozens of notebooks containing the germs of dozens of musical comedies.

"Near the end of my last school year I came across a musical comedy score lying on top of the piano. It was a show called *His Honor the Sultan* presented by the Triangle Club of Princeton University. That was enough for me. The University question was settled. I was bound for Princeton.

"I spent my entire freshman year writing an operetta for the Triangle Club. I failed in algebra, trigonometry, coördinate geometry and hygiene, but the Triangle Club accepted my show, and by tutoring all through a stuffy August I managed to come back a sophomore and act in it as a chorus girl. A little later I left college to spend the rest of the year recuperating in the West.

"The next year, 1916–17, found me back in college, but by this time I had decided that poetry was the only thing, so with my head ringing with the meters of Swinburne and the matters of Rupert Brooke, I spent the spring doing sonnets, ballads and rondels. I had read somewhere that every great poet had written great poetry before he was twenty-one. I had only a year and, besides, war was impending. I must publish a book of startling verse before I was engulfed.

"By autumn I was in an infantry officer's training camp with poetry in the discard and a brand new ambition—I was writing an immoral novel. Every evening, concealing my pad behind Small Problems for Infantry, I wrote on a somewhat edited history of me and my imagination. And then I was detected and the game was up. I could write no more during study period.

"This was a distinct complication. I had only three months to live—in those days all infantry officers

thought they had only three months to live—and I had
left no mark in the world. But such consuming ambition was not to be thwarted. Every Saturday at
one o'clock I hurried up to the Officer's Club, and there,
in a corner of a room full of smoke, conversation and
rattling newspapers, I wrote a one-hundred-and-
twenty-thousand word novel on the consecutive week-
ends of three months. There was no revising; there
was no time for it. As I finished each chapter I sent
it to a typist in Princeton.

"I went to my regiment happy. I had written a
novel. The war could now go on. I forgot paragraphs and pentameters, similes and syllogisms. I
got to be a first lieutenant, got my orders over seas—
then the publishers wrote that though *The Romantic
Egotist* was original they could not publish it. Six
months after this I arrived in New York and presented
my card to the office boys of seven city editors asking
to be taken on as a reporter. I had just turned twenty-
two, the war was over, and I was going to trail mur-
derers by day and do short stories by night. But the
newspapers sent their office boys out to tell me they
didn't need me. They decided definitely and irrev-
ocably by the sound of my name on a calling card that
I was absolutely unfitted for a reporter. Instead I
became an advertising man at ninety dollars a month,
writing the slogans that while away the weary hours
in rural trolley cars. After hours I wrote stories—
from March to June. There were nineteen all together; the quickest written in an hour and a half, the
slowest in three days. No one bought them, no one

sent personal letters. I had one hundred and twenty two rejection slips pinned in a frieze about my room. I wrote movies. I wrote song lyrics. I wrote complicated advertisement schemes, I wrote poems, I wrote sketches. I wrote jokes. Near the end of June I sold one story for thirty dollars.

"On the Fourth of July, utterly disgusted with myself and all the editors, I went to St. Paul and informed family and friends that I had given up my position and had come home to write a novel. They nodded politely, changed the subject and spoke of me very gently. By this time I knew that I had a novel to write, and all through two hot months I wrote and revised and compiled and boiled down. On September 15 *This Side of Paradise* was accepted by special delivery.

"In the next two months I wrote eight stories and sold nine. The ninth story was accepted by the same magazine that had rejected it four months before. In November, I sold my first story to the *Saturday Evening Post*. By February I had sold them half a dozen. Then my novel came out. Then I got married. Then I wrote *The Beautiful and Damned*. Now I spend my time wondering how it all happened."

VIII

"I am a pessimist, a communist (with Nietschean overtones), have no hobbies except conversation—and I am trying to repress that. My enthusiasms at present include Stravinski, Otto Braun, Mencken, Conrad, Joyce, the early Gertrude Stein, Chaplin and all books about that period which lies between the V and XV centuries."

Mr. Fitzgerald is the author of *This Side of Paradise,* 1920; *Flappers and Philosophers,* 1920; *The Beautiful and Damned,* 1922; *Tales of the Jazz Age,* 1922; and *The Vegetable,* 1923.

WALDO FRANK

I have forgotten the exact words used by the always fastidious Professor Sherman, in an essay on Sinclair Lewis, but the effect (upon me, at any rate) is something about a perverted slayer of all that is clean and beautiful in life, as though Frank were akin to Leopold and Loeb. And that's the sort of criticism Frank gets. Helpful, isn't it? He has fallen, we are told, among thieves; but the conscript fathers hurry by on the other side, leaving him to my tender mercies and the benedictions of Gorham Munson.

II

Quite frankly I confess myself of those who can make only head or tale of Frank's books—I know when I am holding them right end up, and little more. Yet I am not blind to the great service he is rendering American letters, broadening our horizons, revivifying the language, refusing to be comforted lest still other innocents be slaughtered in our fear of usurpers, in our terror of any change, our worship of the rights of property. . . .

I remember loaning *Rahab* to Reed Rowley in Cleveland and hearing his laughter as he began to read; "Spring . . . a southern city in song. A city drifting fading into the wide arms of earth, into trees, fields running under grass . . . trees . . . fields running under grass. . . ." It struck Rowley as ridiculous; and for us, perhaps, it is. But the loss is ours.

If you can see the earth moving, laboring, under the grass, you have fine eyes, you have vision, your wits have not been dulled by long use in trivial affairs as ours have been.

III

Or take yet other words and other occasions—the word "great," for instance. You know what it means —or should mean. It is a fine word, a word to use sparingly—not all things can be great. Michelangelo perhaps or Goethe or the Taj Mahal or Milburn's polo and Vance's pitching. There are some, no doubt, to call Charles Lamb great or Alexander Hamilton; but scarcely Taft and Fairbanks. Yet there's no plumbing the folly of one's fellows. Language may have no limitations for some. Even a fine word will be bandied. There's no telling. Major Hughes— I've mentioned him before—just the other day, in the *American Magazine,* gave his reasons for insisting that his father be called great. . . .

I wonder if Major Hughes knows how words are made. Could he, pressed by the desire to evoke some new monster, some new miracle of the sky or the waters under the sky, coin us a word? Or can he, now that he has made "great" a term for circuit judges, give us five letters to take its place, a connotation for God or the verses of Keats?

IV

Well, if he can't, no matter—Frank will—for that is what Frank is doing, lifting again the fingered and inky language that we have so misused and in the anguish of his love giving it new life.

V

Words are made—they don't just happen. And they are precious and very dear, for in them, careless though they seem, they hold all that men have ever dreamed or seen of beauty, terror and romance, since first a woman waited for her lover or men went out to wrest a living from the earth.

VI

There is, to digress, the story of the Carthaginian traveler, Hanno, who, before Rome humbled his ancient city in the dust, went to explore the jungles of North Africa. He traveled far, for he was even more curious and gifted than Messer Marco Polo. One day he came upon a family of apes, huge apes, larger, far larger, than the tallest and strongest soldier in his guard, with long hairy arms and tremendous shoulders, huge bellies and fists that would crunch a stone. In his journal he named them "Gorillas." Hanno is dead, Carthage razed, Rome fallen; Latin and Greek done with; the world has witnessed the crucifixion of Christ and the birth of Mohammed, the torture of Galileo and the healing faith of Lincoln —centuries have gone and come—nothing remains out of the past but that one word. Conceive, if you can, the matchless imagery of that word—define (now that Major Hughes' father has attained greatness—or, rather, had it thrust upon him) define me that far-flung traveler who named, once and forever, the gorilla.

VII

Dante, when all about him wrote in Latin, chose the common speech of common folk as the medium of the *Divine Comedy*. In much the same way, Frank (and, of course, Lardner) employs the talk of the press room and the tenements. And what Frank writes is, really, poetry. I quote at random, for I am no authority upon his works; "The air moved toward the mountain; the waves and the trees and the earth moved toward the mountain. All the world moved gently upward toward the mountain like a tide. The mountain moved toward earth, spilled water and spread trees in it."

It is an echo from the *Psalms* wherein the hills stand up and clap their hands.

VIII

Something of his philosophy is in a paragraph from *The Unwelcome Man,* his first novel: "Scan the book of life and the nature of the heroic becomes plain. It is the deliberate negation of what is sense and rote, of that which the interminable average makes life; it is the disavowal of all laws, the compliance with what is but a shadow, a shred, a suggestion. It is the leaning on an instant and the despising of all time. It is the paradoxical resolve to prove a spot of star greater and wider and more important than the mass of earth. It is the truth. And it is even more, for it is the acting on it."

IX

I quote from Gorham Munson's biography of Waldo
Frank—

"Frank was born August 25, 1889, at Long Branch,
New Jersey.   His mother came from Alabama . . .
his father is a lawyer, for long active in political reform movements in New York.   There were three
other children.

"Frank received his first formal education in the public schools of New York City.   At four he had written
a brief play; at sixteen a novel which a New York
publisher accepted, but which his father wisely with-
drew.   In 1906 he went abroad for a year.   Then
came Yale.   Frank was quite definitely a rebel.   In
his senior year he conducted a signed column of dramatic criticism for the New Haven Journal-Courier.
After graduation in 1911 he ranched in Wyoming, did
newspaper work for the New York *Evening Post* and
the New York *Times,* and wrote plays.   In 1913 he
went again to Europe for a year, living in Paris and
Germany.   He came back to New York in 1914, lived
on the East Side and free-lanced as a writer.   In 1916
he joined with James Oppenheim to found *The Seven
Arts;* and the same year married Miss Margaret
Nawnburg, the pioneer in applying psychoanalysis to
education, founder of the Walden School.   In 1917
when war was declared, he registered as a conscientious objector and, though sick and discouraged a little,
wrote *The Dark Mother* while waiting to be carted
off to jail.   However, no summons came.

"Some mention must be made of his friendship for
Sherwood Anderson, Romain Rolland, Jules Romain,
Jacques Copeau and Leo Ornstein.

"With the birth of his son in May 1922, he moved to Darien, Conn.

"He has now in preparation a book on Spain, a play and a three volume series to continue histories of David and Tom started in *The Dark Mother.*"

Mr. Frank is the author of *The Unwelcome Man,* 1917; *Three Psalms,* with music by Ernest Block, 1911; *Our America,* 1919; *The Dark Mother,* 1920; *Rahab,* 1922; *City Block,* 1922; *Holiday,* 1923; *Salvos,* 1924.

NEWTON FUESSLE

Betwixt two worlds life hovers like a star—

We are such stuff as potters use, moulded by time and circumstance—and easily broken. The end, for all, is death—and the beginning, for some of us live, as Conrad lived, in the shadow of death, oppressed, and saddened because life must end—because, even before the end, with the passing of youth, the best of life is gone. It is an old story—and a new one—as new as youth.

Conrad was the poet and romancer of youth. All his writing life he dredged among the memories of his twenties, bringing to the surface pearls and gold, the precious freight of long-sunk argosies—ships that had set out with what brave hopes and what schemes for fortune and adventure among far blessed islands in uncharted seas.

"And this is all that is left of it! Only a moment! a moment of strength, of romance, of glamour—of youth! . . . A flick of sunshine upon a strange shore, the time to remember, the time for a sigh, and—good-by!—Night—Good-by——"

II

Conrad is dead and Fuessle is dead—both because the lungs are weak. Both because, shouting in the face of an indifferent fate, they wore themselves out. One was an inland Pole and the other a lubber from the greatest Polish city in the world—Chicago. They were both of them romancers, writing realistically of their preposterous heroes.

III

But you tell me Conrad was unique—and so he was. That combination of genius and pity, of brooding and a furious temper, of old days spent under the tropic sky among the jungles of a savage people and recalled with something of regret to break the quiet of an English countryside, was single—not to be found again, forever precious and alone.

Yet there was about Fuessle, for all that he was a German, something of the yearning of the Pole, something of the Pole's dissatisfaction with things as they are, and the Pole's heady dreams of beauty—

"Rudolph adored her. But his romantic yearnings sought no more definite expression than mute worship from afar. He contented himself with feasting his sad, hungry eyes upon her face, with waiting for the deluge of an occasional smile——

"They were playing a Viennese Waltz. The strains were wholly strange to Rudolph, but their luminous coloring, their fleet measure and whimsical phrasing attracted him mightily—stole through his being like rich, narcotic vapors——"

IV

And yet, of course, the chief influence in Fuessle's life, as a writer, was Dreiser. It is impossible to know Dreiser and not be affected by him—and Fuessle knew Dreiser very well. Fuessle's themes were Dreiser's.

His mind dwelt upon the futility of existence and contrasted that futility with 'the splendid and ambitious hopes that buoy us up in spite of a thousand disappointments. We do not quit and resign ourselves to the void because we cannot believe this is all there is to life—this going down to the office and this coming back, hiding forever our true faces from the world, facing the world in a mask.

v

In *Main Street* Sinclair Lewis wrote the story that Fuessle should have written. In *Main Street* Sinclair Lewis wrote the story that is the story of every artist and every poet, every lover throughout this broad and posturing land. He did not write as we others would have written. He overloaded his fable with details; he was at times superficial and at times tiresome, talking (for the most part) in the idiom of Babbitt—but talking at Babbitt; and that is what Fuessle should have done. Babbitt with his lazy optimism and foolish smile plumped himself down in Fuessle's chair, the good things of this earth at his elbow—and Fuessle should have dumped him unceremoniously to the ground. But Fuessle never did. There was a diffidence about Fuessle that was my constant despair. I felt that if he were not so everlastingly tactful, so self-effacing, so good he might have stirred us, till, with a shout, we accepted his doctrine and—bought his books.

We did not buy his books. We did not buy them because we felt sure that they contained nothing for us—they were too well modulated. Mencken has the right accent and the right vocabulary for rousing that sleeping beauty that is our best self. You must bump the boobs and show them that even the obvious may be shocking, that botany (in our little code of morals) can be obscene and beer a drink fit only for loafers and thieves.

VI

With Fuessle's death we lose one of our most lovable and one of our most promising novelists. And by "lovable" I do not mean that he was not as well hated as loved—by "promising" I do not say that he left no good work done. In the offices of the National City Company where Fuessle was connected with the advertising and publicity staff (1919–20) there are officials who will tear their hair if you mention his name—there are officials elsewhere who denounce him with scorn—and officials who (*mirabile dictu*) knew his worth. And in *The Flail, Gold Shod* and *Jessup* he wrote three fine novels—I am of a mind to agree with his brother (that astonishing brother who has convinced a nation of inadvertents that halitosis is an insidious thing) that ten years from now Fuessle's books will be better regarded than they are to-day.

VII

Just one instance of that critical befuddlement which he encountered—and from Mencken who is the archevangel of what is, if not the best in execution, at any rate the best in spirit and purpose in American literature. Mencken is, of course, a busy man and makes no pose of being infallible. He is further extremely valuable—invaluable, almost—a host, in himself, of good things. Mencken accepted certain of Fuessle's stories, later to be incorporated in *Flesh and Fantasy,* for publication in the *Smart Set,* of which Mencken was then editor. But when the book came out Mencken slated it in his usual quick-witted and slashing style. Fuessle could make neither head nor tail of such doings. If his stories were good enough for the readers of the magazine when edited by Mencken, why not good enough in book form? Why—?

But this is only to show how little real help the novelist receives from American criticism. Criticism is not detailed. It is a business of broad strokes— this is excellent or this will never do—but seldom why one or the other.

VIII

Fuessle was born in Chicago, October 16, 1883, the son of a Methodist minister who, even now, in his eighties, is still preaching every Sunday in a parish on the outskirts of that metropolis of the West. Fuessle was christened Newton Augustus Fuessle, educated in the public schools and at the University of Chicago. Immediately upon graduation he went into the newspaper business. He was a reporter in Omaha, in Seattle, and Chicago. Then he got a job in Detroit with Packard and later with Chalmers, in the advertising departments. He married, and the year before he died became the father of a daughter. He was very successfully married. Indeed, Mrs. Fuessle was probably the strongest and best influence in his life. The

books he wrote were in reality written in collaboration
with her.

IX

In 1919 he wrote down for me the salient points in
his philosophy as a novelist—

"A few cogent literary saints have spread Newton
A. Fuessle out into a dual personality. He can't
write fiction when he's hungry. He can't write fiction
when he's cold. He can't write fiction in the day-
time. He can't write fiction when he's worried about
bills. He can't write fiction unless he is surrounded
by creature comforts. He can't write fiction without
good cigars and plenty of them.

"He therefore spends most of his time making it
possible to spend part of his time in sincere, unhamp-
ered literary production. His office is on Wall Street.
But instead of finding that a cold, calculating business
career is smothering the artist in him, it has on the
contrary helped cultivate two artists in him. At dusk,
his creative faculties swing automatically into action.

"He believes that the present enormous quantity
production of fiction is a curse; and is satisfied if he
can spend several hours a day on a novel under working conditions that suit him. He believes that extravagant tastes are inherent in every imaginative
writer, and that tossing off rapid-fire tales under high
pressure to get the money is all too likely to follow if
a fiction writer's income depends entirely upon his roy-
alties. He has seen too many writers of promise cave
in under the strain and descend from their best to their
worst, to be willing to step lively on the same tread-
mill.

"Mr. Fuessle declares that the markets are overwhelmed with jaded, strained, unimportant new books by established novelists who dash them off because they need a new car, a new house, or a new wife. He hates writing that has become a habit, and which rushes into print whether or not the novelist has something new to say, something important to set forth, something to picture sincerely. He blames modern merchandising and advertising for the enormous markets they have created for shallow and mediocre fiction by flooding the country with magazines that have largely become primarily portfolios of advertising.

"Mr. Fuessle's own apprenticeship in letters was served at what he calls the altar of the false gods of fast and furious writing for the notion-counters of magazine fiction, where the whole cry is for novelty instead of truth. He must have written and sold nearly a million words of short stories before it began to dawn upon him that nearly every master he had studied had to tear himself loose from the short story before he found the way to something more than fragmentary expression of what he knew about life.

"The short story has gained its popularity in America, (he declares), because of the ease with which the lazy, the superficial, the dilettante-minded can dabble with it and market their manuscripts. The short story is the china-painting of fiction. Even in its more finished development, it usually remains the mere trapeze-work, the acrobatics of fiction, neurotic instead of natural, smart instead of true. Even Guy de Maupassant attained greatness in but a few short stories in all his voluminous production in this form. We can search almost in vain for the real de Maupassant, the real Tolstoy, the real Balzac in their short stories. One must go to their novels to get at their understanding of life. The short story puts the premium on the arrangement, the distortion, the playing with the facts of life. The novel, on the contrary, puts the premium where it belongs—upon a revelation of the deeper currents of motive and experience. By the novel, I mean of course, the record of the evolution of character."

X

"It is far from my intention," Fuessle said, "to condemn the short story in its entirety, or to argue that it does not have its legitimate field. As an apprenticeship to more comprehensive endeavor in writing, as an interlude between more sustained efforts, the short story has an important place. But it seems too bad that so abrupt, breathless, fragmentary, and restricted a form should attain such popularity in America that its whole tendency is to withhold a writer's efforts from the longer-lived and more satisfying novel.

"Surely it is one of the tragedies of American literature that writer's such as Poe and O. Henry and Harris Merton Lyon died without leaving us a novel. One hopes that gifted contemporaries like Edna Ferber and Fannie Hurst will not lay down their pens before they have bequeathed to the world their share of novels and revealed to us more fully than they can in short stories, their singular comprehension of life.

"When I speak of the responsibility of the novelist, I mean it in an artistic rather than a moral sense. The reader can get no more out of a novel than the author puts into it. So much sham and pose and pre-

tense have taken possession of the people who write
and publish books that one sometimes feels like running
screaming out of a bookshop.

"My conception of what should go into a novel in
order to make it worthy of being sold and read, is
stated from the point of view of one who has bought
and examined, and thrown away large quantities of
books for the sake of finding the few that I wanted to
keep. I believe that a novelist who is unwilling to express as truly as possible his own reactions to his contact with life, has no business wasting your time and
my time with his fiction. Unless he possesses the candor and the willingness to do that, he is adding nothing
new to the net recorded sum of human experience. I
do not say that a novelist should write his autobiography into his novel. Lord forbid! But I do imply
that unless I can see an important phase of myself in
each of the characters I undertake to present, and interpret my characters in terms of my own reactions of
life, I cannot imbue a character with anything ap-
proaching truth."

XI

And that is exactly what he did—he understood and
sympathized and suffered with the thwarted and un-
satisfied creatures of his fancy. He knew that the
world was beautiful and that life was good, but somehow (it seemed to him) man had made a botch of
living.

XII

Fuessle died in Middleton, Mass., March 18, 1924,
after a brief illness of six weeks.

XIII

Fuessle was the author of *Flesh and Fantasy,* a book of short stories, 1919; *The Flail,* 1919; *Gold Shod,* 1921; *Jessup,* 1923.

Hugh Walpole pronounced *Gold Shod* one of the best of America's novels; and Burton Rascoe never tires of numbering Fuessle with the twelve best writers in America.

HENRY BLAKE FULLER

Were I the editor of a weekly review looking for the perfect reviewer to take charge of my literary department I should know that my quest was ended once Mr. Fuller had consented to act for me, for he is, in my opinion, as a man of letters, easily among the first of living Americans. He has scholarship and the best of good taste, charm and grace of style, wide reading and instant sympathy. He is at home with Mary Stuart and the Maid of Orleans, with the sages of Concord and Camden and the Lake Country. He realizes that Carlyle does not need to be right to be moving and profound. He would not improve upon Jane Welch or Mrs. Wharton. He is familiar with Marlowe's mighty lines and the terrific tragedies of Kyd. He knows the farces in which Garrick played and the comedies of Molière. He has read Vanburgh and Hebbel, Corneille, Goldoni, Eugene Field, D'Annunzio and Mathilde Serao. He can quote from Lessing, Diderot, Strachey, Menander, Firdusi and Franklin. I read him recently on the loves of Sarah Bernhardt and he was all attention. He would be as considerate of the platonism of Dante or the grave passion of Abelard, the lechery of Villon and the hopeless adoration of Keats. And, to top it all, he is a gentleman.

He is a gentleman! Those words proclaim at once his weakness and his strength. Yet they mean more than any casual reading done while running would lead the unobservant to believe; for your writer is by ordinary a bounder. Your writer takes, he says, all life for his province—or, at any rate, so much of it as he can see and understand; and it still remains true, as it was when Wilde wrote his *De Profundis,* that of two men in prison one will look out upon the stars and the other on the filthy pavements of the prison yard.

II

A generation ago Mr. Fuller wrote his *Chevalier of Pensieri-Vani* and in his first sentence he told us how the Chevalier halted his traveling-coach on the brow of the Ciminian Forest to look down upon the wide-spread Campagna di Roma. The Chevalier was a dilettante cut to the measure of Mr. Fuller's mild æstheticism and he dabbled in archæology and the lesser improprieties of minor poets. He would naturally make a sentimental journey through Italy. But his journey was bound to end, in a lodging above the Arno, in a fit of despondency. It had meant nothing, with his doubtful Madonna and his all too genuine Contessa. He was forced, as Mr. Fuller has at times been forced, to write himself down a failure.

Twenty-seven years went by and Mr. Fuller published *On The Stairs;* and there, in a sentence, he explained that failure. It is impossible, you see, to be an artist and give yourself out; to be a gentleman and hold yourself in; you end by being nothing.

III

Mr. Fuller is, in Rossetti's use of the word, an amateur, a lover and appreciator of the beautiful rather than a craftsman with rolling eye and a passion for creation.   There have been long periods when he has written nothing and published nothing, 1901–1908, 1908–1917; and in those periods, so short is memory, he seems to have completely disappeared and to have been more or less forgotten, his name misspelled—as in William Archer's *The American Language,* 1899, where he is referred to as Henry Y. Puller.   Only Mencken and Huneker were loyal—or Mr. Hamlin Garland in whose *Son of the Middle Border* he appears again and again, and always vividly, suggestive and stimulating.

IV

He was born in Chicago, January 9th, 1857.   His family had been well established in the city for two generations—his grandfather, Henry Fuller, being one of the first to settle around Fort Dearborn.   On both sides of the house he is English; his father's people landing in New England soon after the Mayflower; and his mother's immediately after the War of 1812.

He started life intending to become a composer; and since he had some notion about the freedom of the arts and both his father and his grandfather were merchants, wealthy and well-respected, he decided that first he must make himself independent.   So he took a job as bookkeeper, saving his money and finally leaving home for a two years' sojourn in Italy.   There the idea of the *Chevalier of Pensieri-Vani* was born; there the book was written at odd moments, stuffed away in a trunk, a jumble of notes, to be rescued and copied and started on a dreary round of the publishers' offices, to be invariably returned unwanted, and finally to be brought out at the author's expense, to win some praise, enjoy a short success, and go the way of forgetfulness.

Then followed *The Chatelaine of La Trinité* wherein Mr. Fuller joins his realist-romancer Fin de Siècle, in a search for the soul enshrined in woman's body.

A little later he came under the influence of William Dean Howells and began to discover Chicago and to write about Chicago and, for the first time, to produce real flesh and blood women in Camelia McDodd and Cecelia Ingalls of *The Cliff-Dwellers*.

Followed stories of Chicago art-life, *Under the Skylights,* and of Americans traveling in Europe, *From the Other Side*.

V

"As may be gathered," he says, "I am as much concerned with form and technique as with any of the other elements involved in fiction; all because these two features seem to be increasingly disregarded by the ordinary reader. I have been helping my friend, Miss Harriet Monroe, of *Poetry,* as one of her advisory committee; and during the earlier days I helped her on proofs and looked after some of the routine of her printing. The atmosphere of free verse prompted me to try some free verse myself, as applied to the short story; hence *Lines Long and Short,* 1917. Then the vogue of the long and amorphous novel led me to revive my novel-writing (after a lapse of some years) in a briefer, compacter form; hence *On the Stairs,* 1918, together with my discussions of the matter in *The Dial*.

"I was in Europe in 1879–80, in '83, '92, '94 and '97. These trips supplemented some schooling in Chicago and in a Wisconsin Academy. During these later years I have had to keep in America and almost altogether in Chicago, where practical concerns have often been unfavorable to literary production. This circumscribed locus—together with changes naturally brought by time itself—will account, I suppose, for certain alterations in field and in themes."

GARET GARRETT

(AS SEEN BY MYSELF AND THE MESSRS.
DUTTON, HIS PUBLISHERS.)

An author once sent a short story to a magazine editor who promptly returned it saying that though he liked it very much, one of the principal incidents was altogether too improbable. Whereupon the author replied: "Sir, the incident to which you take exception is the only true thing in the story. All the rest is imaginary."

Much the same sort of thing has happened again and again to Garet Garrett, author of *The Driver* and *The Cinder Buggy*. Bernard M. Baruch tells one story: "One day I heard a man commenting on one of Garrett's stories in the *Saturday Evening Post* regarding an old Wall Street incident, say that such a story was virtually impossible. I turned to him and told him that as a matter of fact all the details in the story, excepting the names of securities and individuals, were absolutely correct. I know because it was a story regarding myself."

II

All his life, Garet Garrett has been a newspaper man, with the Cleveland *Press,* Washington *Times,* New York *Times,* New York *Evening Post,* New York *Sun,* and New York *Tribune.* At one time he was one of the best known financial reporters on Wall Street. He was one of the founders of the *Annalist,* the financial appendix to the New York *Times.* He has written many stories about Wall Street for the magazines. During the war he went to Europe as a special writer of financial articles for the daily press.

III

With his knowledge of Wall Street, its financial powers, their giant operations, their deeds of daring, helping to build America, it is not strange that Mr. Garrett should use his hard-won material in his stories. The achievements of a Harriman, the coups of a Morgan, the heroism of a Hill—the intrepid spirit of the American pioneer in business—are portrayed in his books with fidelity and detail. Sometimes they seem too dramatic to be real. Yet Wall Street men, in speaking of *The Driver,* say, "The thing that impresses us is his fidelity to the truths of life."

IV

In *The Cinder Buggy,* Mr. Garrett has given us another superhuman novel of American life, with the development of one of America's great industries as the background.

With the two-wheeled, bow-legged "cinder buggy" (which carries the slag of the iron furnace away to the dump) as his symbol, he has written a romance of iron and steel and something of the romance and horror of the lives of the men and women who live in

Pittsburg, Cleveland, Gary and other steel towns.
One thing is notable: Mr. Garrett cannot write love
stories. The gentle passion always makes a financier
of him.

GEORGE GIBBS

George Gibbs, the author of many popular novels, was born March 8th, 1870, at New Orleans, La. His father, an officer in the United States navy, died at Trieste, Austria, while serving as fleet surgeon with the European squadron.

When a midshipman at Annapolis, Mr. Gibbs began his career by making sketches of the officers and writing verses—afterwards published (as he says, fitly) in a volume called *Junk*. This book the author considers his second distinguished failure, the first being his resignation from the naval academy, as one result of having given rather more time to caricature than to trigonometry.

Mr. Gibbs' art studies began immediately. He worked at night in the classes of the Corcoran Art School and the Art Students' League at Washington, where he was then living. "My days," he says, speaking of this time "were devoted to writing very poor short stories which steadily went the rounds of all the magazines of the country, only to be returned in the course of time, making me richer in experience and poorer in the cost of postage. After a while it became necessary for me to make money, for I had gone into debt and had no way of getting out. So I started writing specials from Washington to the New York *Sun*, *Times* and *Herald*, to such good purpose that I was enabled to finish my studies in Washington.

"My first drawing for publication was sold to myself and printed in the ill-fated *Junk* book aforementioned. My second went to a weekly newspaper, and my third to *Vogue*, then in the first years of its existence. These early drawings were done without models, and were rambling imitations of the work of better men than I. The princely ten dollars from *Vogue* raised my hopes into the realms of bliss and I figured that I could make a very decent living by illustrating. (This was before I began writing newspaper specials.) But the checks came at long intervals, and that was the hardest part of my life."

II

Mr. Gibbs was educated in public schools, at a boarding school near Geneva, Switzerland, and at the United States Naval Academy. He began writing novels years ago; and for a number of years he has not only found time to illustrate the successful books of other writers, but has also contributed one or another of the season's best sellers.

The Bolted Door, written about ten years ago, quickly ran through a dozen editions. Since then he has written *The Forbidden Way, The Silent Battle, Madcap, The Flaming Sword,* and *Paradise Garden,* all of them, quantitatively speaking, great successes. Three or four years ago Mr. Gibbs' novel of the season was *The Yellow Dove,* a story of the secret service, a war story. This book ran through seventeen large editions and is still selling—thanks to Appleton's efficient publicity department.

Mr. Gibbs' next novel was another story of the war, *The Secret Witness.* It is a story of the German

and Austrian secret service bent upon the destruction
of a British diplomat who accidentally overhears a plot
made by the Kaiser and the Archduke Franz Ferdinand. The book is extraordinary (to my way of
thinking) for the liberties Mr. Gibbs never fails to
take with alien enemies or any such as may be the
bugbears of the thoughtless and shallow.

The Secret Witness was followed by *The Golden
Bough,* the story of an American soldier's adventures
in Germany. Then came *The Black Stone,* a tale of
adventure amid the burning sands of Arabia. . . .

As you can see, Mr. Gibbs' career as a novelist has
been a hectic one—one passionate romance after another.

III

The Splendid Outcast, Mr. Gibbs' next book, found
an even wider public than any of his earlier volumes.
Its scenes are laid in Paris; and it pictures the Apaches
of the underworld there. Naturally the one hundred
per cent American hero and the glorious heroine, who
is his hoped-for lady, made instantaneous appeal to the
one hundred per centers. They bought the book—
they told others to buy.

The Vagrant Duke is the next title in what his publishers call the "Gibbs galaxy of successes." It is the
story of a duke exiled from his duchy, a duke who
makes good in a new world, in spite of many handicaps,
a duke drawn into strange plans of high adventure, deceit, treachery and excitement—it reads (to me) like
the precocious musings of an incipient Dumas.

IV

Youth Triumphant shows a further step in Mr. Gibbs' progress as a writer. In this story the author again exhibits that penchant for mystery and adventure that made his earlier novels so popular with some of the (emotionally speaking) younger set. It is the story of Patsy, a Bowery waif, and her transformation into a charming and dashing young society leader. It comes after Shaw's *Pygmalion* and is not (as perhaps you will not be surprised to hear) so well done.

In *The House of Mohun,* Mr. Gibbs gives us—as he was sure to—his notions of the flapper and his answer to the flapper's various problems.

Fires of Ambition, Mr. Gibbs' latest book, is a consideration of that now hackneyed theme, a woman's choice between marriage and a career. Mary Ryan, titian-haired, freckle-faced and Irish, is confident that she can rise to whatever heights she chooses. She starts on her career with a $25 a week job, climbs by leaps and bounds, not only in a business way, but in a social way as well—trust Mr. Gibbs to do right by Mary. Then she surveys the life she has made for herself (with Mr. Gibbs' help) and asks herself, "What are these things I have fought for? What are they in comparison with the love I might have had?"

What indeed? For I can tell you that love is not doled out by Mr. Gibbs. He showers it upon his characters with both hands. They are thrice blessed.

And they could have money too, without all the bother of making a career, if they would only ask for it. Nothing is impossible to Mr. Gibbs—when he sits down to write.

ZANE GREY

His novels appear simultaneously as movies, serials and in book form. His readers are legion—all those who ache for the wide open spaces and those who like their romance served with a little moral doctrine. In fact, morality and space are the chief points of his interest. His lovers are chaste and they have all out-of-doors in which to roam; but they always end up happily. And this is as it should be for they are good and virtuous. Not for them the rough and tumble of life, the lures of the flesh. They are home-keeping folk. As most of us are. And so, when war was declared, Mr. Grey became the favorite author of the A. E. F. He is the favorite still with those whose chief delight is in the performance of duties.

II

As hunter, fisherman and explorer he first began to attract attention in *Field and Stream,* with articles on black bass. Then followed *Roping Lions in the Grand Canyon* and *Down An Unknown Jungle River,* which was the account of a trip Grey made exploring in Mexico. Jaguar, puma, deer, poisonous snakes, wild fowl—all these have felt his descriptive powers. Much writing and traveling have made him an authority on big game. He has won prizes in fishing contests. He was once a professional ball player. He is always a hero to his readers.

Riders of the Purple Sage was his first serial.

III

Zane Grey was born in Zanesville, Ohio. His father had been a backwoodsman, a farmer and hunter, but later became a doctor. His mother, with Indian blood in her veins, was a descendant of the frontier Zanes who founded the town of Zanesville. Young Grey was educated at the Zanesville High School and the University of Pennsylvania. The favorite authors of his youth were Scott and Fenimore Cooper; and they are the authors who have most influenced his writing. But he has always preferred swimming and hunting and fishing to books. He played baseball at college, was a member of the Orange Athletic Club of East Orange, New Jersey, and finally became a professional ball player with the Newark Eastern League Team, transferring to the Tri-State League and to Jackson in the Michigan League. But his parents persuaded him not to enter the major leagues, so he gave up ball and took to hunting. Hunting has been his hobby and his avocation ever since. His writing is really incidental. Yet it is as a writer that he is best known.

He is the author of *The Desert of Wheat, The U. P. Trail, The Border Legion, The Heritage of the Desert, Ken Ward in the Jungle, The Light of Western Stars, The Lone Star Ranger, The Rainbow Trail, Riders of the Purple Sage, Wildfire, The Young Lion Hunter, The Young Forester, The Young Pitcher, Desert Gold, Riders of the Wasteland.*

HERMAN HAGEDORN, JR.

Jones and I were coming from a dance, dressed in our neatest attire. We had to change cars, and stood for a while waiting on the curb. A congenial souse came over to stare at us. He stared long through his blurred eyes. Finally he made up his mind. "Harvard," he murmured; and again "Harvard." He was far from right—Jones did the billing for a foundry; and I was shipping clerk for a glass house— but, at any rate, he knew that there is such a thing as Harvard, and that as Harvard it has distinct characteristics.

I am not sure that I know what those characteristics are. They seem rather negative than positive. You hold yourself aloof a little and give the tone to an otherwise crude civilization; you are leaven in a mass of unseasoned humanity.

II

Harvard will always give us tone. Harvard is nice. All the philosophers are at Harvard and most of the Jews from South Boston and as many Lowells as they can crowd in. Bliss Perry is at Harvard—and Copeland—and Professor Baker who contrives a workshop out of that theater which Shaw refers to as the elder sister of the church. A strange and motley crew. Perry boasts that he hasn't read a novel written since 1910—the younger realists shock and upset him; Copeland is busy getting the restless immature

into the right grooves; Baker has produced a harvest of
Romances and *Yous and Mes, Mamma's Affairs* and
—to prove his versatility—Eugene O'Neill.

Yet there are those who make a religion of Harvard
—the legal minds who keep us out of jail, and the
men and women who understand mob psychology.

It is to these latter that Herman Hagedorn belongs.
He has swallowed Harvard without a glance at Princeton or Notre Dame; he never considered the Army.
All the various things that Harvard stands for he
stands for.   It's a religion; and naturally his chief
saint is T. R., the first of Harvard's major prophets;
Mr. Hagedorn has devoted years to the study of T. R.

III

Born July 18, 1882, Mr. Hagedorn is the author of
two novels, *Faces in the Dawn* and *Barbara Picks a
Husband,* and of two lives of Theodore Roosevelt, one
for boys and one for adults.   The novels are out of
print and (so I hear) forgotten; but the lives of
Roosevelt go on, edition after edition.   This is as it
should be.   The novels were light and supercilious;
the Roosevelt books are a distinct contribution to the
legend that makes a false and faultless hero out of
T. R.—they are the sort of books we, in need of heroes,
like and insist upon—the conventional biography of
the conventional statesman, a straw man fighting for
the right against other men of straw.

IV

Hagedorn was born on Staten Island.   He doesn't
know where, but he remembers being told that there

were a lot of mosquitoes round about and he has seen a picture of the house, taken in the manner of the eighties, with men and women crowding the windows or leaning against piazza posts, sitting in rockers and on the porch steps. That house is always joined in his memory with memories of the pleasant people gathered there, graciously attentive, incredibly young as he looks back now and thinks how old he once considered them.

At the age of three weeks or thereabouts he moved to Brooklyn; and it was in Brooklyn that he first discovered the terrors of school.

"I did not like school very much," he says. "My first school was a girls' affair where boys were merely suffered, and my second was a pseudo-military academy, presided over by a Prussian martinet with a scarred face, who wore a flat-topped derby and used to call on my father Sunday nights and keep him up until after midnight, to my father's intense indignation. There were other reasons too why I did not like school. My way to it lay through a region where what are known as 'micks' abounded; and they kept me in a continual state of terror.

"School began to be a delight when I became sixteen and was sent to the Hill School in Pottstown, Pennsylvania. The Hill opened the world of boys to me, and one or two other worlds, in time. The principal, John Meigs, was, next to Theodore Roosevelt, the most positive personality I have ever known, a man of deep tenderness and extraordinary power, warm-hearted, hot-tempered, indomitable. His wife was known as 'Mrs. John'—a torch of a woman with the ability to take a boy's character apart before his eyes to show him how it worked, and to put it together again and hand it back to him as one would a watch. 'Now see that you don't let it run down.'

"It was at the Hill that I felt the first faint impulse to write. There was a school monthly, the *Record,* which seemed very important to those of us who wanted to become editors of it, and we all wrote a great many unspeakably bad things for it. I left the Hill in 1901. The first thing that I ever published in what I called a 'real' magazine—though it wasn't—was a sentimental allegory in an ephemeral four-by-six pamphlet called *Heart's Yarns.* I remember the hearts all over the white cover. I was office-boy in a wholesale dry goods house after that, an occupation I loathed; then for a few months I attended a business college (my father objected to my handwriting) spent my time editing the school magazine. My father agreed with a sigh that I did not seem fit for business and allowed me to take a position with the *Reader,* a literary monthly which attempted unsuccessfully to compete with the *Bookman.*

"My salary—ten dollars a week—seemed to me at the time quite tremendous. In dry goods I had been getting four, with the promise, after a year, of a dollar raise.

"The *Reader* did not amount to much, but on its staff were a number of men who had come under the influence of Barrett Wendell, George P. Baker and the others of the Harvard group. They pointed out to me that I did not know very much and that what I needed was a year or two at college under these men. The idea seemed sound. I went to Harvard for a

year and stayed four. They were quite wonderful
years—years of reading and endless writing and fellowship and discovery. I discovered standards, I discovered people, I discovered the beauty and fascination and terror and ruthlessness of life. I wrote a
good many verses and stories, which were published
in the *Harvard Monthly* and which won some favor;
and ended my college career in a totally unexpected
blaze of limelight owing to a class poem called *A
Troop of the Guard,* which happened to catch the
public.

"I went abroad and studied or pretended to study,
one semester at Berlin University; returned to America, married and settled down as an instructor of English and Comparative Literature at Harvard. I stayed
there for two years, but I was not much of a success
as a teacher. I was trying to serve two masters, the
college and the Muse, with the result that my teaching
was half-hearted and my writing academic. I broke
away and took my family West. We went to Santa
Barbara and settled in a gorgeous spot overlooking the
sea, intending to stay a year, or forever. We stayed
six months. The place was lotus-land. It was no
place for work, not for work that meant something.
We returned East and bought a farm in Connecticut.
There was nothing lotus-landy about life after that.
We found that living on a farm nowadays is an exacting and difficult business. We all learned what it
meant to work; we learned a great many other things;
we saw light on many 'literary' misconceptions.

"The Great War hit me hard from the start, for
brothers of mine were fighting in the armies of Ger-

many.   My own neutrality was never such as the
President would have approved; but what there was of
it died when the *Lusitania* went down.   I hoped the
United States would go to war with Germany in 1915.
When we did not, and still remained neutral in 1916,
I joined with three other men, Julian Street, Porter
Emerson Brown and Charles Hanson Towne, in start-
ing the Vigilantes with the idea of making it a sort of
megaphone through which to preach national duty.
The war came at last.   The Vigilantes did a little
something in the waging of the war at home."

V

The War!   How long ago that seems; and what a
pest the Vigilantes and the rest of them were, preaching duty to a lot of poor miserable devils who must
go out and die.

The Vigilantes are all living.   They are a little out-
moded, but they are remarkably fat and well-fed.
Sam Adams tells me that he honestly believes that if
Julian Street should suddenly and inadvisedly take to
exercise he (Street) would drop dead.   And I know
that Towne is happy.

VI

Through the years Hagedorn wrote and published
a number of books, volumes of verse, plays, novels,
propaganda, and that *Boy's Life of Theodore Roosevelt* to which I have referred.

The best of them, a narrative in blank verse called
The Great Maze, no one seems to care for.   It is a
modern story, in modern settings, but the names are

the names of heroes known to the Greeks—Aga-
memnon and Clytaemnestra, Ægisthus and Iphigenia.
These names it is, perhaps, that frightens away the
possible reader.

(Mr. Hagedorn tells me it is the names. "They
read the names," he says, "and think it old stuff. Too
bad.")

VII

I asked Mr. Hagedorn to make himself "vivid and
real" to my readers.

"Perhaps I will some day," he answered, "but it
won't be in a letter. It will be in a novel and your
readers will never know it."

Now I don't like that. I haven't the faintest notion who my readers are, but I'm not going to have
them insulted off-hand and their knowledge—even such
knowledge as they may acquire in the future—limited
to the prophecies of a Connecticut farmer. No.

I've a good mind to tell him he doesn't know what
he's talking about.

VIII

"I am not a very important person," he says, "and
my preference in salads, concerning which you inquire,
will make no dish famous. I have ambitions, of
course, but they are not the sort of ambitions which
would be of interest to the general run of folk; there's
nothing very splendiferous about them. At present
I am very much more interested in public affairs than I
am in books, ancient or more, my own or anyone's
else; I may never write another book; to be a part,

even a small part of the drama which is unfolding itself from day to day seems at the moment of far
more consequence than any book which I am ever likely
to write.

"Really I am out of place among 'novelists.'   I am
just a man at a flat-top desk three hundred feet above
the ground, staring day after day at a huge map of
the United States and wondering how Charlie Jones
of Sipes Springs can be persuaded to mould himself
and his government a little nearer to the heart's desire
of Washington and Lincoln and Roosevelt.   Some of
my friends intimate that I am a lost soul.   I let it go
at that."

Mr. Hagedorn is the author of *The Silver Blade,*
1907; *The Woman of Corinth,* 1908; *A Troop of the
Guard* and other poems, 1909; *The Horse Thieves,*
1909; *Poems and Ballads,* 1912; *Faces in the Dawn,*
1912; *Makers of Madness,* 1914; *The Great Maze—
The Heart of Youth,* 1916; *You are the Hope of the
World,* 1917; *Where Do You Stand?* 1918; *Barbara
Picks A Husband,* 1918; *The Boys' Life of Theodore
Roosevelt,* 1918; *Life of Roosevelt,* 1919.

He is a member of the executive committee of the
Roosevelt Memorial Association and the Loyal Order
of Moose.

HENRY SYDNOR HARRISON

Mr. Harrison is the author of *Queed*.

I am not old as youth is counted in this city of gray-beards, yet my mind runs back with something of a senile trot to that glorious and crowded autumn, in 1911, when not to have read *Queed* was to have left unread the one book every one was reading.

Eheu fugaces—how time flies! To read *Queed* to-morrow would be a labor, a task, everyone—the same everyone who was all agog with its interest a generation gone—would scorn. There is for us, of the Fitzgerald and flapper era, no stuff of dreams in *Queed*. *Queed* is outmoded: and even on my dusted shelves *Queed* gathers dust. Thieves might break in and make off with *Queed* and I be none the poorer.

So creeps in, with petty pace, from day to day, this life of literature; and those who yesterday were strutting where Poe drank deep, to-day are one with Jamsshyd, stamping like wild asses about the groves of Arcady. Milton could not be more mute than they. Indeed I think that Milton, from the grave, across the centuries, speaks with greater persuasion than they (whose books were made to sell) from their chairs, in the Century Club. For if a book be made to sell and ceases selling, it ceases to exist. But books made for the heart endure so long as hearts, like to the author's, beat. That is the value of sincerity. Speak true and through the ages those who seek truth will list to you. Speak vanity and only the vain will be your audience—

and the vain are fickle, following ephemeral mode upon mode as ephemeral.

II

In *The Advance of the English Novel,* Professor William Lyon Phelps, that lion of the unicorns, hailed Sydnor Harrison as not only a clever novelist, but more—as a valuable ally of the angels!

Alas for hailing—it melts with Villon's snows. Big-breasted Bertha and slow-footed Joan are not more allied with the angels now, in death, than the Professor and his advances. Nor need you stop but one in three to find this out. Stop all! Aye, stop the wedding-feast itself and offer pennies to those who name the angels' choice among our novelists—it will not cost you twopence for those who single Harrison out of last year's books.

He has come down from his high place and fools rush by where he was wont to tread.

III

Queed was quizzical. *Queed* was intended as a gentle man, good and o'er-flowing with the milk of kindness. But in his latest, *Sister Theresa,* Mr. Harrison has turned his heroine into a harridan, letting her kick, bite, scratch and wrestle in the clinches. Of all vile-tempered creatures she's nearest to a vixen. This, too, after *Angela's Business* which, according to Marshall Field & Company, was the best selling book in their book section in 1915, in Chicago, solely because it appealed so to the women.

Mr. Harrison is not gallant. The women buy his

books and then he pictures woman—or, at any rate,
one fit to be the central character in his romance—as
but little removed from the savage. Scratch her—
and she's a tartar.

IV

When I first wrote of Mr. Harrison, in 1919, I
quoted from a letter of his written at Dunkirk in France,
sometime in March, 1915—"I expect to have my own
ambulance to run after a while"—and said that running after one's own ambulance was not exactly what
I should expect, even in France: adding, "but then, of
course, I'm not a clever novelist."

The joke was feeble; but for it I received a half page
editorial in the Richmond *Times-Despatch,* where Mr.
Harrison had at one time been a book-reviewer and
editorial writer.   I was hailed as though I had been
Columbia and roundly put to task—the task being that
I should read Mr. Harrison's books again and learn
from them, as from an aunt, to be wise.

I have tried.

It was a trial of error—Mr. Harrison is not for me.
I cannot picture him, (as he pictures himself in the
letter I quoted), sitting on a hard bench, at a table of
dirty bare boards, when not engaged in transporting
the *malades* and *blessés* during the late Great War, and
say: Here is my man!

But I can let you choose him if you will; and I can
make some mention of the fact—which he singles out
for special mention in *Who's Who*—that he was with
an American Ambulance in France from March to June
in 1915.

In the same letter—I forgot to add—he says that he had forgotten to say that he wore a khaki uniform and might be (from a distance) mistaken for a soldier —however, we all make mistakes.

V

Shortly after his birth at Sewanee, Tennessee, February 12, 1880, his father resigned as professor of Latin and Greek at the University of the South, and moved to Brooklyn, N. Y., where he founded the Brooklyn Latin School.

In Brooklyn Mr. Harrison grew up, a student at his father's school, and later an undergraduate at Columbia, receiving his A. B. in 1900 and an M. A. in 1911.

On graduation he taught in his father's school for three years. Then the father died; and the family moved to Richmond.

VI

"As a kind of natural recoil from the cloisterliness of the schoolmaster's life," Mr. Harrison says, "I had an earnest ambition to whirl in the business world, and the result of this desire was a partnership with a man to manufacture bamboo furniture. The enterprise lasted about a year, cost me a pretty penny and cured me of addiction to commerce.

"About the time I was winding up with the bamboo works, my friend, Mr. John Stewart Bryan, whose family own the Richmond *Times-Despatch,* invited me to join the *Times-Despatch* staff as a book-reviewer. I was soon set to paragraphing; next to rhyming; before a great while to writing editorials, and as the

years ran on, I turned over the reviewing to another
hand, and gave all my time to the editorial page.
Finally, in November, 1908, circumstances made a reorganization of the staff necessary, and I was appointed
chief editorial writer. The post was in every way a
desirable one; but newspaper work was never my goal;
my heart was never in it; I always wanted to write
books, and when I had put by enough to stand off the
wolf for a few months, I burned my bridges by re-
signing my position and claiming all my time for my
own.   I could give myself a year's chance and I
thought that if I ever could do anything I could do
it in a year.

"In the meantime, my brother had removed to
Charleston, W. Va., to practice law, my mother and
sister had followed him, and finding myself no longer
bound to any particular chair, I joined them within a
few days after my resignation went into effect. . . .

"I wrote *Queed* entire, from the first vague gropings
for ideas to the consignment of the manuscript to the
express office, in a little over four months. . . .

"The point of origin of my desire to write is
shrouded in obscurity, but I think it must date back to
an early period.   When I was nineteen I sold a short
story to the New York *Sunday Herald*—I got $11 for
it, I think—and that was the first money I ever got out
of fiction.   By the way, that was hardly fiction at all,
for though I gave it a fictional form, the incident I recounted had really happened to an acquaintance of
mine.   A year or two later I had two little stories in
the Editor's Drawer Department in *Harper's*.   In the
years that have since elapsed I have published a num-

ber of short stories—perhaps ten or twelve in all—
scattered around in various magazines."

VII

Mr. Harrison is unmarried, a Democrat and Episco-
palian, and a member of the National Institute of Arts
and Letters.   He is the author of *Captivating Mary
Carstairs; Queed*, 1911; *V. V's Eyes*, 1913; *Angela's
Business*, 1915; *When I Came Back*, 1919; *Sister
Theresa*, 1922.

BEN HECHT

A. E. Orage, the English editor and critic, divides the history of American literature into three ages— the age of Emerson, of Whitman and the present age, the age of experiment.

This is, I presume, as good a division as any, though it leaves out of consideration what are (for me) the most interesting influences in the development of the modern American novels; the influence of the frontier and the influence of the sickly sweet sentimentalists who were making a second Hellas out of their little localities. It leaves out Bret Harte, Fenimore Cooper, Mark Twain, Hamlin Garland and the historians of the trek westward—and Washington Irving, the daddy of George Cable, James Lane Allen, Thomas Nelson Page, Mary Johnston, Mrs. Freeman, *et al.* . . .

However, I am not writing a history of American literature but of Ben Hecht who belongs, if anybody does, to this age, the age of experiment.

II

Now the age of experiment owes its inspiration entirely to one man. It is an age that seeks for truth, without affectation and without simpering. The first and the lustiest of such truth-seekers is old Ed Howe of Atchison, Kansas. With the publication of his *Story of a Country Town,* the bombast of Whitman was merged with the pity and realism of Dreiser and the preoccupations of Masters and Sherwood Anderson.

Ben Hecht stems from Anderson through Masters to the Missouri of William Marion Reedy and the Kansas of Howe.

III

Hecht will, of course, deny all this. He thinks himself an original fellow, taking no ideas as his own that have not been imported from Remy de Gourmont and Huysmanns or from the Russia of Dostoievski and Tchekov. Nevertheless I will stick to my say-so. In America Hecht is unthinkable without first thinking of the (literally) amazing Howe.

IV

Hecht is the bad boy of our newer pandemonium. He has been threatened with jail and (I doubt not) with tar and feathers. He is going to show us up, expose the meanness and filth that is in the heart of every man and so by shouting *Tu Quoque* prevent us from judging our neighbors too harshly. He goes about it all without ferocity, in a very businesslike way, but he is apt to be such a scourge to our next ten years as for twenty years past Shaw has been to the complacency of the English. He has a fine detached air that keeps him from becoming himself too deeply involved and so he can instantly dramatize our major transgressions as he dramatized the comic opera *putsch* of Ludendorff in Munich, setting everything off in just the right light, in *Eric Dorn* before the shouting had finally died down or the captains and the kings departed to their

Ben Hecht

accustomed obscurity. So he will satirize our future
Napoleons, the Falls and Sawyers, McGees and Fal-
lons, who will be with us next year and the next. Their
brief candles, lighting up a moment's strutting on the
stage, will be for him a rushlight whereby he can com-
pose at once a fitting climax and an epitaph for their
exertions and their failures. He will need no more
than a hint, for he is ingenious and, after a dozen years
on the Chicago *News* and *Post* and whatnot, extremely
wise in the ways and tricks whereby we bamboozle
the stranger within our gates and, sometimes, ourselves.

V

Then, too, he is quite without shame, having in its
stead a sort of fierce pride in his own integrity. He
will do anything and say anything that he himself believes to be right; and you cannot silence him by insisting that no one else has ever talked or acted that
way before. He cares not a damn how anyone else
talks or acts. He is being faithful to his own self—
and that is his only concern.

VI

Ben Hecht was born in New York City, attended
high school in Racine, Wisconsin, then went to Chicago
to work as a newspaper reporter. He never wanted
to go to college, never asked to go, and he has not
now any sympathy with colleges or the conceptions of
college men. His college was a turn, at eighteen or
thereabouts, as an acrobat in Costello's road show touring the country towns of Wisconsin.

VII

Let me give you his portrait as it is given by Harry Hansen in that excellent volume of his, *Midwest Portraits:*

". . . a lad just passing the twilight zone of youth, with the face of a man who dreams at times, and at other times plans; a round face, which will be chubby, or florid at fifty; the face of a Balzac, or an Alexander Dumas. A man with a certain careless air about wearing clothes that hang loosely upon him, and a certain recklessness in knotting his tie, and yet making occasional overtures to fashion in the manipulation of ˑ heavy cane; a man with soft, dark hair often dis-ˏeveled, falling loosely over his forehead; brown eyes soft, kindly; the mouth, most expressive of all, sensitive with a touch of the sensuous, and on either side two deep furrows that come out sharp and clear when the lips part in disdain, or mockery, or sarcasm, or mild, quiet invective. . . ."

A provocative person, as you can well see. And he has provoked no end of comment, this one trying to damn him as the greatest rascal unhung and that one exalting him as a smasher of idols, street urchin and intellectual. . . .

As a matter of fact, just at present, Ben Hecht is a young writer in search of a vocabulary. His interest in people is only a passing interest. But his interest in words is devouring. He wants to express himself, to spatter the world with ink of his own choosing. He is vain. And people only attract his attention in so far as they are useful to the making of his books.

They are neither the villains nor the heroes. He is
the hero. And in clearing the stage for a place where
he may rant he has naturally rudely brushed aside certain touchy individuals—and they have roared.
Therefore his reputation for discourtesy and *schwei-
nerei*.

VIII

But he is not especially swinish—for all of *Fantasius
Mallaire* which was confiscated and banned as filthy.

I have had but a passing glance at *Fantasius Mallaire*, but to me it seemed no worse (though more
elaborate) than the usual dirty story that is, at one
time or another, the highest form of humour and romance for so many men.

IX

No, I am convinced that Ben Hecht is just being himself and, except for his energy and wit and shameless-
ness, I do not find him at all unusual.

Take his reading. It began with the effeminate and
cruel romancing of Theophile Gautier, passed to the
pyrotechnics of Huysmanns, and halted a moment,
thrilled by the passions of Anatole France's *Red Lily*.
Then came Arthur Symons and George Moore,
Mallarmè, Verlaine and Baudelaire.

It is the reading of Van Vechten's Gareth Johns, of
young Hart Crane, of Sam Loveman and a thousand
others who some day will want to write in this country.

X

"I could not stomach Victor Hugo and Balzac,"
says Ben. "I was bored to tears by Balzac. Rous-

seau I considered a great big thumping fool, especially in his confessions. But for action and romance give me Dumas—I have just bought a fine leather set of his books. At that I think I got more out of Huysmann than anybody else."

XI

What is it then, that sets Hecht apart—for certainly an inability to stomach Hugo and Balzac, a consideration of Rousseau as a fool, a liking for Dumas and Huysmann, will not do it?

It is not simply that Ben has taken his good where he has found it, but in giving it forth again as his own he has obeyed that timely injunction; Be your age (or yourself), kid.

XII

Of the early American writers Hecht approves only of Hawthorne and Poe. He likes the rhythm, the excitement and movement of Poe, and the activity of Hawthorne and Hawthorne's absence of prudery. Longfellow, Lowell, Holmes and Whittier bored and bore him. Whitman was the god of a literary clique that did not interest Hecht; and so, for the sins of his idolaters, Whitman was banished. Stephen Crane is the only writer of that earlier generation to whom Hecht can be at all fair. To-day, of course, it is Mencken. It is Mencken with such a vengeance that sometimes Hecht reads like a paraphrase of the, though by no means immaculate, immense and robust Baltimorean.

XIII

I must interrupt for a moment to ask why no one to-day reads Thoreau. To me, to-night, he is the greatest writer America has as yet produced. "I have traveled much in Concord," is in itself a priceless observation. But observation is not the only gift Thoreau has brought us. He has brevity and simplicity and the courage of a seer. I would like to see the tree of his knowledge bearing fruit.

XIV

"The culture which loves the cadence of line, the sparkle of words, the piquant acrobatics of phrase, is still unborn in America," says Hecht.

Hecht is a provincial or he would know that that sort of culture was unborn in the England of the Restoration, the France of Molière, the Italy of the Renaissance. It is only the few who care for words for their own frail sakes. It was piquancy of line and phrase that condemned Whistler and Wilde to a limited audience. It was sparkle and cadence that left Saltus and Huneker talking to themselves, that made Synge's plays financially a failure.

Because Huysmanns' books are there, Hecht thinks that France bubbled with just such gorgeous metaphors, that in the drawing-rooms of St. Germaine there was repartee rather than monotones; and comparing that Paris of his imagination to Chicago he condemns America. But Huysmanns' best admirers have not been Frenchmen at all, but Englishmen and Irishmen and Yanks.

However, Hecht has done his best to prepare for just such a culture as he wishes to see born. In *Eric Dorn, Gargoyles* and *The Florentine Dagger* he has given that culture something to feed on.

XVI

The appearance of *Eric Dorn* really was an occasion. It is one of the most written books in America. It does with enthusiasm and facility what Van Vechten strives to do with study and perseverance. It flings exotic words about, strange words, daring and harsh and arresting, gaily and with abandon. The story is no never mind. It is merely the story of a man divided between his wife and a mistress and leaving them both for the honor of loving adventure more. It is the telling that counts, and the telling is reckless and witty, apposite and novel.

XVI

I believe that Hecht will finally desert the novel for the stage, as Shaw did; and when he does I believe we will have, for the first time in our theater, a writer of comedy to equal Donnay and Ludwig Thoma and Georges de Portoriche. He will not challenge George Kelly, though he has more style than Kelly, or Kaufmann and Connely, because he is of the tribe of Molière while they are, one and all, Ibsenites.

JOSEPH HERGESHEIMER

I have been in my time a rooter for Mr. Hergesheimer. With what I took to be great sarcasm, in 1919, I quoted the judgment of Mr. Arthur B. Maurice upon him.

Mr. Maurice was for years the editor of the *Bookman,* a critic referred to and deferred to by some.

In September 1918, in the *Mentor,* Mr. Maurice reviewed our modern American novelists, devoting a page to Rex Beach, another to Robert W. Chambers and a third to Stewart Edward White. At that time Mr. Hergesheimer had published only four volumes, three novels and a book of short stories—*The Lay Anthony, Mountain Blood, The Three Black Pennys* and *Gold and Iron.* Mr. Hergesheimer was not, according to Mr. Maurice, as worthy of notice as was Beach or Chambers or White. Mr. Hergesheimer's books did not sell very well—few books published by Mitchell Kennerley ever do. Therefore Mr. Hergesheimer was given only one sentence in Mr. Maurice's elaborate resumè. "Mr. Hergesheimer," said Mr. Maurice, "has won a place among writers by reason of his picturesque style and original invention."

Indeed, said I, and is that all?

I then went on to show that Mr. Hergesheimer, by reason of his picturesque invention and original style, with Cabell and Dreiser and one or two others, topped the lists of American novelists.

227

II

But I am not now so enthusiastic about Mr. Hergesheimer—the necessity for being well-met is too heavy upon him.   He is self-indulgent; his airs are a trifle superior, his English (at times) appalling. Again and again his sentences have neither rhythm, reason nor construction.   It seems as though he put in commas just to prove that commas are not yet out of fashion for all that Mr. Shaw has discarded them.

III

I have no liking for the professional novelist.   A novelist is either an artist or, to me, he is nothing. Mr. Hergesheimer (an artist) has deliberately chosen to make a profession of novel-writing.   He believes that certain benefits, applause and fawning, accrue naturally to the novelist.   He thinks that the novelist should be gaped at—just as the Prince of Wales is gaped at, or Thomas Meighan.   And so he pretends at one time to be the Prince of Wales, and at another Thomas Meighan.   He poses in hotel lobbies and is delighted when waiters recognize him as the author of that serial running in the *Saturday Evening Post*.   In short, he is or hopes to be something of a matinée idol. Even as a boy I could not stomach matinée idols.   To me the attitudes of Joseph Hergesheimer are often farcical and ridiculous.

IV

Mind you, Mr. Hergesheimer has every reason for being proud of himself—more reason, surely than any

matinée idol you or I can think of.   But if you stand
off and kneel before a graven image of yourself—if
you know that you are great—you must kneel before
your characters for it follows naturally that they are
great since they are yours.   And that is exactly what
Mr. Hergesheimer does.   He exclaims over the
children of his fancy as though they were no less astounding than he knows himself to be.   And they are
astounding even when they are, as Meta Beggs was,
no more than country school-teachers.

Listen to Mr. Hergesheimer on Meta Beggs:

"Meta Beggs was the mask, smooth and sterile, of
the hunger for adornment, for gold bands and jewels
and perfume, for gophered linen, and draperies of silk
and scarlet.   She was the naked idler stained with an-
timony in the clay courts of Sumeria; the Paphian with
painted feet loitering on the roofs of Memphis while
the blocks of red sandstone floated sluggishly down the
Nile for the pyramid of Khufu the King; she was the
flushed voluptuousness relaxed in the scented spray of
pagan baths; the woman with white-piled and powd-
ered hair in a gold shift of Louis XIV; the prostitute
with a pinched waist and great flowing sleeves of the
Maison Dorée.   She was as old as the first vice, as
the first lust budding like a black blossom in the morbidity of men successful, satiated."

She was, as you can see, a skit.   But silly and vain
as she may have been she was not one half so vain or
silly as Mr. Hergesheimer.   For Mr. Hergesheimer
is deliberately deceiving himself and us about Meta
Beggs.   Meta Beggs is a country school-teacher in the
Virginia Mountains, in *Mountain Blood;* and for her

Gordon Makimmon destroys his marriage with Lettice
Hollidew. That is all. To Gordon, of course, Meta
is desirable as in Sumeria, to some, Mr. Hergesheimer's naked idler was desirable; she is unashamed in
her passions as was the Paphian; she is provocative
(for Gordon) as, to King Louis, were certain of the
women of the French courts. But all this does not
make of Meta a Paphian, a naked idler, or a noble-
woman of France. She remains, despite Mr. Hergesheimer's extravagant comparisons, always a country
school-teacher, the third party in an ill-starred marriage, a marriage made, in the first place, for money.

V

It is the same with *Linda Condon.* Cold and immaculate, empty and childish, she fires such a conflagra-
tion of love as only the loving—Manon or Ninon de
l'Enclos, Lucy Feveral or Nell Gwynn—could have
fired. . . .

I say this dogmatically because Mr. Hergesheimer
is dogmatic. He tells me that Linda was another
Helen and that for her dear sake the world went up
in flames. Frankly, I don't believe it. Not all of
Mr. Hergesheimer's geese can be, by a simple stretching of the imagination, swans as lovely as Pavlowa.

VI

Mr. Hergesheimer is a platonist. He was a platonist in *The Lay Anthony,* a platonist in *Linda Condon.*
"It was not," he says, "what the woman had in common with the rabbit that was important, but her difference." The difference is at once moral and

æsthetic. It is the difference between organic and in-organic matter, between a woman and her portrait on the wall. Yet as a matter of fact—and Mr. Herges-heimer understands this in *Balisand*—it is only in so far as she is woman, at one with creation, the female of the species as Kipling has called her, that woman can exercise such power as Mr. Hergesheimer tells us his women have over men.

VII

But if I quarrel with his slurring over of the simpler biological aspects of sex, it is not because Mr. Herges-heimer's women are not wonderfully successful as decoration. They lend beauty and grace to his scenes. They are a fitting background for the gorgeous and intricate designs he fashions with the words that now (almost) he has made his own—colorful words, per-fumed and decadent, the words of a painter, of some old catholic cardinal, Latin words, heavy with all the brocade and silver and jewels of the Renaissance. Mr. Hergesheimer is a stylist, an artist—for all that I believe the world holds more than can be dreamed of in his philosophies.

VIII

"But personally," he says, "I am without interest, I live in a very old long low gray stone house beyond a little town, a pleasant place and a pleasant interior with wide fireplaces and walnut furniture and bright archaic rugs. I have been married for eleven years" —I quote from a letter he wrote to me in 1918—"and have no children. My pleasures are very common-

place—rock bass fishing, golf and the reprehensible
game of poker; in these I am successful (or it may be
luck) only in the fishing."

IX

I shall quote further from that letter:

"The grandfather with whom I lived as a child and
boy, my mother's father, was Thomas MacKellar, a
Scotch-American typefounder and hymn-writer. My
father's family had lived for a respectable number of
generations in Philadelphia. He (my father) was an
officer in the United States Coast and Geodetic Sur-
vey; a stout and, to me, largely strange individual
with bright blue eyes and temper and cheeks bronzed
with exposure. As much as anything I remember him,
in the rare hours when he was home, playing fright-
fully on the fiddle—yet there is another memory, perhaps more significant than the melancholy strains of
The Arkansas Traveler . . . my father bending over
a large table of trestles, drawing with beautiful patience huge intricate maps.

"My grandfather's house was rather large and of
stone, with a tower on the façade and supporting
porches; it was in a suburb of Philadelphia, a place of
smooth lawns and solid houses and shaded streets; our
grounds swept back and down to the stables and the
coachman's house hung with wistaria; there were a
great many fruit trees with their succession of blos-
soms and a fountain with stone cupids, a basin and
gold fish in the front. All the memories which have
power to stir me are of the various aspects of nature
and places—I remember perfectly the character of
trees at Woodnest, though I haven't seen them for
thirty years; I remember them hung with Chinese lant-

erns on the Fourth of July and cased in clear ice in January.

"The dwellers were its owner, always old with a short beard and steel-bowed spectacles, vigorously Presbyterian; two still more ancient great-aunts, like shriveled and blasted apples; another excessively genteel, unnatural black hair and a proud face with crisp surah silks and black enameled gold chains; my mother and myself. It was not a haunt of noise and I was sick more than a little. At four of summer afternoons we'd drive out, two sleek fat horses in a barouche—grandfather in a coffee-colored duster, Aunt Henrietta erect and elegant with a carriage parasol like a mauve carnation, the coachman permeated with an odor which I have since come to recognize as whisky . . . down by the Park we drove, a way by a jade shadowed stream with perhaps a rowboat on it from one of the small landings, a way cool and green—Hooker's green number two, painters would call it.

"The house had long heavy window draperies, white marble mantles and tall glimmering mirrors in gold frames, onyx-topped tables and a formal parlor with lovely Chinese cabinets and smooth incurably domestic paintings of the Dutch school. I recall it best late on Sunday afternoons filled with the wailing organ music of my grandfather's playing. . . . Nothing, I am certain, has since had any such powers to impress itself ·upon me as that period. At perhaps my nineteenth year every one, it seemed, died at once."

X

"Looking back," he says, "over the whole field of my work a very few things are evident, and principally that I always write about people, men usually near

forty, who are not happy.   The story at bottom is
nearly always the same—a struggle between what is
called the spirit and what is called the flesh—the
spirit is victorious—that is why it seems to me my
books are happy books. . . .

"And I am, of course, conceited—though the cheap-
est mind in the world, the most venal editor, by
merely talking long or loud enough, can send me home
full of confusion and apologies.   Part of my conceit
lies in the opinion that I do women extremely well,
particularly girls, the lovely girls Turgenieff understood so completely.   I'd like to write a novel about
a girl of fourteen, slender with a black bang and blue-
black eyes, in a modern hotel with porphyry columns
and turkey red carpet, against a background of cold
gorged women in dinner gowns; most probably I never
shall, but I'd like to; the necessary sex, gossamer-
like, an affair of sprigged cambric, might seem in-
decent to the American public gesture—yet anything
that is beautiful will do; what I mean by beauty is the
quality of a courageous purpose maintained against the
hopeless and transitory aspects of life and death.   The
transitory in especial—everlasting flowers are the stu-
pidest imaginable; this is clear enough: that things are
fine and pinch the heart only if they are addressed to
fatality.   How long would you keep a muslin rose out
of the waste basket?   It is the same with youth and
love—love matched against death and the loser in the
degree of its perfection.

"Yet this doesn't account for the setting of most of
my stories back in the Victorian period, nor for the
fact that in Italy I paid no attention to the heroic
quattrocento and read nothing but in the last part of
the eighteenth.   I made no effort toward 1840—that
involves an enormous, distasteful amount of work for

which I have the worst preparation in the world, except in the way of persistence. I am always being urged to write about to-day, but my imagination goes perpetually back to crinoline and ormolu and sparkling hock. These things have for me the envelopment necessary to the calling out of an emotional effect; they are all of a tone, wistful and gay and lost; and the story, the elements involved, must be as simple as possible, the qualities that have always been potent. . . . Yet nothing is asserted for the future."

XI

"What remains?" he asks. "I practically never went to school, and when I did it was days wasted; I read trash, or (at least) that is what it is everywhere called, until I was eighteen; I then progressed (or retrogressed?) to Joseph Conrad, from Conrad to Turgenieff, from Turgenieff to Jeremy Taylor, from Taylor to George Moore, from Moore to almost nothing. . . .

"After fifteen years of labor—that for any result might as well have been spent in invisible ink—and now a number more, I write quite easily, about twenty-five hundred words long hand a day; this my secretary types; it is then polished and polished and typed again; that, in the books, with three or four proofs shifted in a manner which must make any typesetter's mind seeth with anger—scarlet to crimson, crimson to vermillion, and back to scarlet—no, geranium. I write all the time; it is a disease really, and anything else irritates me out of all reasonable proportion. I'm naturally lazy and inaccurate and procrastinate without end . . . a more unsuitable person to be the victim of a hopeless and ideal pursuit you can't imagine. I have no dogmatic religion; I like the music of Christopher Gluck better than any other; I keep airdale terriers and no cats; I think James Branch Cabell writes beautifully."

XII

All this, as I have said, is quoted from a letter written in 1918. Under date of May 13, 1924, he wrote me further:

"I am practically at the first page of an autobiographical fragment covering almost precisely the period that has gone since I met you. It will be perhaps sixty thousand words and entirely confined to the setting of my house. . . .

"How I have changed it would be difficult for me to say. Certainly I read less, I care for fewer books, and I return almost not at all to those I used frequently to read. In *Balisand,* which I have just finished, for me a long novel laid in Tidewater Virginia at the end of the eighteenth century, I have deliberately omitted every particle of the description of surfaces. That, after so much that was different, God knows is drastic enough. I still have, personally, a great love for an old walnut table, for flowered muslin on the right kind of young thing; I like to regard them in reality; but they no longer engage me in books. This without committing myself for all the future. Curiously enough, for the past two years I have been more than ever absorbed in early and fine American furniture, in beautiful early glass; since I have largely rebuilt The Dower House, and tried to put in it the rightest furnishings I could find. In my house but not in my book.

"I am beginning to find a wide difference between man as an immemorial animal and what has happened to him in the present civilization or lack of civilization. It seems to me that I am growing less interested in intellectual and æsthetic values and more concerned with qualities which appear to me quite timeless. Perhaps I am merely growing old-fashioned . . . or old. *The Lay Anthony,* was published in 1914, this is no more than 1924, and in the ten years I have written how many—maybe seventeen books. I don't know without looking. Yes, and endless stories and papers."

XIII

The Lay Anthony was published in 1914, and I feel again as I write the thrill I felt then on the first reading. . . .

Mr. Llewellyn Jones, the literary editor of the Chicago *Evening Post,* has said that he was the first, if not the only commentator on that early novel to prophecy from it the future of Mr. Hergesheimer. But that is not true. Mr. Mencken (a busier man than Jones will ever be) laid aside his other concerns to shout vociferously for Hergesheimer and his book. In all of Mr. Knopf's advertisements (after he had taken over *The Lay Anthony*) my name was quoted in hearty approval. Indeed, it was impossible to escape the promise of that retelling, in modern terms, of the platonic romance of Dante and Beatrice. I said then and I believe now that it was as surprising a first novel as any in a decade. . . .

Mr. Hergesheimer has since confessed that, his being a 'prentice hand, he was not altogether successful

in *The Lay Anthony*.   But the failure is apparent only
to the captious.   Perhaps the book was overwritten—
it is a fault Mr. Hergesheimer is not yet completely
done with—but it was worth writing; and it brought
to American letters an unexampled use of color, of reds
and purple and gold, the heady fragrance of lilacs
blown by an April shower across cool shaded lawns,
the sudden burgeoning of spring, and the reverence
and chivalry of the Authorian legends. . . .

Secretly but in an entirely natural manner, says
Mr. Hergesheimer, Anthony Ball was ashamed of
being, in the exact physical sense, pure.   He carefully
concealed his purity in a great show of worldly wisdom,
in an attitude of cynical indifference towards girls.
He played baseball, drove an automobile, talked till
all hours in back rooms; but every once in a while he
cleansed himself by spending long hours alone in the
open country, on the river, under the trees.   Then he
meets Elizabeth Dreen; and for her he goes out to
seek his fortune in the world—for her he guards, as
did the anchorites of old, against incredible temptations, the chastity that is his chief claim to respect.
But Mr. Hergesheimer is something of an ironist; and
in the end, at news of the death of Elizabeth, drunk,
on a bed in a bawdy house—but still, in the exact physical sense, pure—Anthony dies to establish an alibi for
a besotted police officer. . . .

The book is melodramatic, and it may be impossible,
but there is no denying the interest it arouses and no
escape from the atmosphere, as of a waking dream,
that Mr. Hergesheimer evokes with his use of strange
and heavily-freighted words.

XIV

Mountain Blood is the story, as I have said, of Gordon Makimmon, Lettice Hollidew and Meta Beggs— a sombre and, at times, a moving tale.

XV

The Three Black Pennys, which came next, gave Mr. Hergesheimer a reputation in England so that you often hear it said of him that he is the only American novelist seriously considered by the English.

Through three generations he follows the fortunes of the Penny family while their steel mills prosper and decline. We begin with Howat Penny in 1750.

"Something deep and instinctive in him resisted every effort to make him a part of any social organization, however admirable; he never formed any personal bonds with humanity in particular. He had grown into a solitary being within whom were immovably locked all the confidences, the spontaneous expression of self, that bind men into a solidarity of common failings and hopes."

The affair of Howat Penny with Ludowicka Winscombe, Polish wife of a gentleman from the Court of King George, makes up the first part of the book.

In the second part the aging Jasper Penny, Howat's great grandson, plays out a belated love-affair to a melancholy climax.

The third part is concerned with Jasper's grandson, a dilettante in whom the fierce Welsh blood of the Pennys has run thin. From his window, "below on the right he could vaguely see the broken bulk of what had been Shadrach Furnace, the ruined shape of the past. The Pennys no longer made iron. His father had marked the last casting. They no longer listened to the beat of the trip-hammer, but to the light rhythm of a conductor's baton; they heard, in place of ringing metal, a tenor's grace notes. It was fitting that the last, true to their peculiar inheritance, should be a black Penny."

Jasper tries vainly to prevent his cousin Mariana from keeping the man she loves.

XVI

Then came *Java Head,* the first of Mr. Hergesheimer's popular successes, a serial in the *Saturday Evening Post,* a movie and an amazing recreation of the old seaport town of Salem, with, for contrast, the most detailed and decorative of Mr. Hergesheimer's many gorgeous women, Tao Yuen, a Manchu, as the central character around whom revolves the intrigue that brings down in ruins the whole world of laughing girls, sea-roving ships and sailors, an opium eating clerk, Captain Ammidon and his first love, Nettie Voller.

XVII

With *Linda Condon* the platonism of Mr. Hergesheimer reached its peak. Here is the story of the black-banged girl, against a background of gorged women in dinner gowns, to which Mr. Hergesheimer refers in the first letter I have quoted—an intricate, unemotional and very lovely book—a little masterpiece, as Van Doren has called it.

XVIII

In *Cytherea,* for the moment Mr. Hergesheimer got down to brass tacks and up to date, poring over the problem of a middle-aged married man who wants just one more fling at the pleasures and excitements of loving before he settles down. *Cytherea* caused something of a scandal among the more delicate minded, but it delighted Ludwig Lewisohn who believes that life is best when it is labored and that a kiss taken after much thought is worth a dozen stolen or used at random for nothing but a kiss—a kiss, says Lewisohn, should be the symbol of a passionate and reckless destiny. And that is what *Cytherea* tends to prove; at any rate, that is the conclusion reached by Lee Randon. He cannot go quietly to a rendezvous with his doll-lady but must abandon everything, as boys are abandoned in the throes of first love.

XIX

The Bright Shawl, like so many of Mr. Hergesheimer's books, is a *tour de force,* proof that Mr. Hergesheimer is at home in Cuba as he was at home in Philadelphia, in the New York of *Linda Condon,* the Salem of *Java Head,* the Virginia of *Tol'able David* and *Mountain Blood,* the steel towns of *The Three Black Pennys*—yet I could not finish *The Bright Shawl.* Long before the end I had lost all interest in Charles Abbott and the idealism which drew him into Cuba's rebellion against the tyranny of the Spaniards. But Hugh Walpole has said that America should be proud, quietly but surely, of *The Bright Shawl.*

XX

Llewellyn Jones insists that Mr. Hergesheimer is the foremost American novelist—just as Professor Sherman insists that Sinclair Lewis is, while others claim as much for Cabell or Dreiser.   I see no reason why we should not have a dozen first-rate novelists—I think we have a dozen as interesting as Mr. Hergesheimer or Cabell or Lewis—but I see no reason why Mr. Hergesheimer cannot always be numbered among the best.

ROBERT HERRICK

You can name Mr. Herrick in the same breath with
Galsworthy, and then forget Galsworthy—Mr. Herrick towers above him like a giant. Hr. Herrick has
none of that amiable piety and wit which is Mr. Galsworthy's contribution to literature. Mr. Herrick does
not pity the poor. Himself a fine upstanding man, he
knows that the poor are fine and upstanding. He offers them no dole for which they would no more think
of begging than you or I. Nor does he interfere with
his characters, making them one thing in themselves
and another in his books. He does not tell us that
Clara, Galsworthy's *Fugitive,* because of a loathing for
the marital bed, leaves her husband to become, in a
half hearted fashion, the mistress of a hack in Grub
Street. Mr. Herrick is no medieval romancer. He
knows that, even in a money-mad age, woman is not
entirely dependent, for her support, upon men—half
paragon and half fool. The breath of life is in Mr.
Herrick's women and the grace of an unfailing honesty.
He takes no straw to stuff their hearts, making dolls
of those who, if they are to move us, must have good
clean earth as their substance—and the wide heavens
for a roof.

Not that he has exalted woman. Far from it. He
has been only reasonable and realistic about her. She
does not have to pretend to any virtues not her own
to win his interest and consideration. He has, as

243

Clark's Field proves, ample faith in her if only she be womanly.

II

"I am afraid I have been very little tolerant of the merely entertainment aspect of fiction," says Mr. Robert Herrick. "The magazine story and the boy-and girl novel have no significance to me whatever. Little more has the adventure tale of cowboys and Alaska. All that seems to me meretricious and ephemeral. Since Howells' strong earlier work, I consider that there has been little American fiction of good quality—Frank Norris, London, some of Phillips' books, two or three volumes by Mrs. Wharton, are among these. I feel that American novelists are afraid of being dull, and have the irritating American defect of not taking themselves seriously enough."

III

Mr. Herrick was born in Cambridge Mass., April 28, 1868, and educated at the Cambridge Latin School and at Harvard, where he graduated with the class of 1890. His father, Dartmouth '35, a lawyer practicing in Boston, was the author of several legal books, notably *The Town Officer,* which is, so I am told, still in use. With him the academic tradition begins. All the earlier Herricks, in this country, were farmers. The original ancestor, a nephew of the poet's—the name Robert appears in every generation—settled in Salem in 1638.

"My father's branch of the family," says Mr. Herrick, "moved, in two hundred years, about thirteen

miles, to Boxford, Mass., (near Andover), where my
uncle still cultivated the ancestral farm quite profitably,
ran a saw-mill and a cider-mill, as well as a herd of
cattle, all of which were familiar memories of my
youth, for we spent about five months of the year in
an old French-and-Indian-War house with a double
cellar, about a mile from the Herrick place.   Until I
went to college, Boxford had more significance to me
than Cambridge.   My mother's family came from
Boxford.   Her father (an Emery) was, for fifty
years, pastor of the First Congregational Church at
Weymouth, near Boston.   (The immediate families
related to us—Hale, Welsh, Manning and Peabody—
were preserved in the middle names of my brothers
and sisters; I doubt if a single one of my ancestors
came to this country later than the middle of the
seventeenth century; this shows the thorough New
Englandism of my descent—and, by the way, the Man-
nings, my grandmother's family, were related to Hawthorne.)   My grandfather Emery was said to have
been something of a revivalist in his early years; also
to have loved a good horse; and, for a fact, he raised
a family of three children, sent them all to good
schools, and saved quite a small competency, all on a
salary that was not over one thousand dollars a year.
He was a charming old gentleman—and very much the
gentleman, as I have heard Mrs. William James, who,
in her youth, was one of his parishioners, often declare.

"My course of study at college was largely literary.
At that time the English department, under Child,
Adams Sherman Hill and Barrett Wendell, was es-
pecially strong.   Hill and Wendell had created the

new method of teaching composition. I had always wished to write, and it was but natural that I should gravitate toward courses in English composition; also into the editorship of the *Harvard Advocate;* and, later, of the *Harvard Monthly.* There was, at that time, a brilliant set of young men of literary tastes, among whom were George Santayana and Norman Hapgood; also the poet Moody and Mr. R. M. Lovett, now editing *The Dial* in New York. All these men and many others, were editors of the *Harvard Monthly,* which had been founded in 1886 under the influence of Mr. Wendell—and it did more for me than anything else Harvard offered me, both the exercise of writing for it and the association with the editors.

"The year '87, however, I spent, not at college, but in travel. A friend and classmate who had broken down in health, asked me to become his traveling companion, and, together, we made a long journey from New York to the Bahamas, Cuba, Mexico, California, Alaska, returning by the Yellowstone Park to Colorado and the East. For a boy of eighteen, who had never been out of the state of Massachusetts except for a brief visit to Broadway, once, such a journey covering nine months was a revelation of romantic scenery, strange peoples, as well as the vast extent of our own nation. I remember with special vividness the weeks spent in Mexico, also the months spent in the Yosemite Valley, which was then a wild and remote paradise. On the way to Alaska we were joined by my friend's father, together with President Gilman of Johns Hopkins, and Professor Lewis Dyer of Oxford.

There were also on the boat Mr. Butler, then an instructor at Columbia, and various notables of the United States Senate, who amused themselves with poker in an inside cabin while we journeyed through the marvelous glacier scenery of the far north. That year of travel was undoubtedly worth a great deal more to me than several years of college. At any rate, it awakened my appetite for travel of which I have done a good deal in later years.

"As the spring of 1890 drew close, it became imperative that I should find some job. I had written a good many stories for the college magazines—I had, as editor in chief, nearly wrecked the *Harvard Monthly* financially by publishing the first English translation of Ibsen's *Lady from the Sea*. But my ideals in literature had been formed largely on the contemporary French school, which would not assist me in placing my fiction with the American magazine of that time. One of my college friends, Professor George Carpenter, was undertaking to organize an English department in the Massachusetts Institute of Technology and asked me to join him. I taught there for three years under Professor Carpenter, and learned my profession from him. When he was called to Columbia, in 1893, I accepted a call to the new University of Chicago, to organize the teaching of rhetoric and English composition on the Harvard method. I can very well remember the forbidding aspect of the unfinished buildings, the muddy and unfinished campus and the variegated stretch of the Midway, on which the University fronted, which was then in full blast during the closing weeks of the great World's Fair.

To plunge from orderly Boston and more orderly Cambridge into the unfinished bustle of Chicago and the World's Fair was a large experience for a young man of twenty-six.

"I have retained my connection with the University of Chicago ever since 1893 although, of late years, I have not been in residence except for three or six months of the year, and have been relieved of departmental and faculty routine. I may say, here, that I have not found any inherent antagonism between teaching and writing, both of which I have practiced constantly; and I have never, in the twenty-five years of my connection with the University, felt in the slightest degree hampered in anything I have written or said. I had begun to publish stories before I left Boston, the first one in *Scribner's Magazine*, to be followed shortly by several in the *Atlantic Monthly*; and, in 1896, while I was in Europe on a year's absence, began my first novel. From that time, my books came on about every other year for the next fifteen years or so. While I was writing novels, I also edited manuscripts, collaborated in a text book for secondary schools, which has had a long and lucrative career; wrote stories and articles for the magazines; in short, did all the many necessary journeyman jobs. But the main thing was the novel! I wrote my novels, usually, in the long vacations which I took from university work somewhere in the East, in the New England country. *Together* was written partly during the year spent in Cornish, N. H., partly in a cold winter at Bethel, Me. Other books written in the solitude and beauty of that little Maine town, near the White

Mountains, were *The Healer* and *The Master of the Inn*.

"Of late years I have lived, during half the year, on the Maine seacoast, near Portsmouth, in York Village, where I have a small house and a few acres. There I have written *His Great Adventure, Clark's Field, The Conscript Mother* and *The World Decision.* I lead a very simple life, writing three or four hours in the morning and spending the rest of the day in my garden or walking in the country. I find that city life fatigues me and distracts my attention from my work. My stories come to me in solitude and in the country.

"To return, for a last few words, to my contribution to the American novel: you will find my critical opinions on the subject in a two-part article published in the *Yale Review* during 1915. I think the one subject, consciously or unconsciously, always to be found in my books is the competitive system—its influence upon men and women. Whenever I look back into these books, I find the one insistent question implied in almost every chapter, What is success? Various forms of success and the interpretation of success are there portrayed. Of course, the novels differ widely in point of view, and in background. Many of the early ones were concerned with business because, although I had no business experience directly, I have lived many years of my life in a great business center, where commercial life was the one dominant interest and commercial standards were the standards of the community. Looking at the books from another angle, you will find they fall into two classes—those strictly of realistic technique, such as *The Memoirs of* an *American Citizen* and *The Common Lot;* and those of a freer, more poetic technique, such as *The Real World, A Life for a Life* and *Clark's Field.* I need scarcely say that these latter are the books nearer my heart, but they are not the ones which appeal most widely to the public."

EMERSON HOUGH

Mr. Hough is dead; but he hadn't been dead very long before there was a great commotion in the *International Book Review*. Stuart Henry, reviewing *North of 36*, the last of Mr. Hough's novels, a tale of the great southwest, said that he didn't believe the half of it—and all the cowboys wrote in, from Texas and Oklahoma, to say that this same Henry didn't know history, for if he knew history he'd know that thousands upon thousands of cattle were driven north over the trail to Kansas City every year until as late as 1889; and that the towns Henry called villages were really towns, cow towns; and some of their oldest inhabitants were still living and could testify that there had always been more than one residence to each saloon as far back as anyone could remember—which was pretty far, what with the droughts and humidity.

It was a debate such as Hough would have enjoyed, for Hough was meticulous and a stickler for having facts just so. When he described a hitch he got it right so that every sheep-camp-tender could recognize it at once as the Diamond Hitch or whatever hitch it might be. (It has been long since I have gone down the trail with pack-ponies, and my vocabulary is not what is used to be.) But Hough lived in the out-of-doors and his mind ran to surcingles and saddles and riatas; he knew a *vaquero* from a cow-puncher; and he could swap yarns with the best of them. A campfire was the hearth at home to him.

II

Stuart Henry said that Hough, (born in Newton, Iowa, June 28, 1857), did not go west until the frontier days were done; that he was and always had been a tenderfoot; and that the tales he told were the tales he had listened to as a greenhorn, tales designed particularly to flabbergast the gentle and credulous East.

"This is amusing," said William MacLeod Raine, in rebuttal. "The guns of the Lincoln County cattle war were still echoing in New Mexico when Emerson Hough located in the little town of White Oaks. Billy the Kid, most notorious outlaw ever known in the West, was still dodging in the chapparal close to the village where Hough was a reporter on the White Oaks *Golden Era.*"

And so on and so on.

Hough has his defenders and those who take him lightly, with a grain of salt.

I must confess myself of the latter. He was on the ground—but what of it? Is every old timer a fit historian of the times through which he has lived? I care no whit whether Hough was a tenderfoot or whether his feet, in forty years, grew as tough as whip-leather—he was a poor judge of circumstance. It is all a matter of accent; and he threw into bold relief the utterly trivial and irrelevant. He made heroes of very ordinary men; and to the end of his days his burden was the burden of the white man. He was a Nordic—we were superior to the Mexicans, to the Spaniards, to the breed; the earth and its fulness was ours by right of conquest and inheritance.

III

Hough thought of himself as a great romancer, but all his romance is strength and awkwardness. There is no single lovely gesture in any one of his books, nothing to touch the heart, no grace of form or phrase. His prose is ordinary, the prose of a reporter. Over and over he repeated his trite situations—hard riding, unselfishness, an unresisting endurance of want and makeshifts; no hopes of anything better, no recognition of the good that has gone before. And the world his people inhabit is equally trite, without beauty. The people themselves are abrupt and ungracious.

IV

Mr. Raine says that Hough has told the truth about New Mexico. Has he? I know better. He told the truth as he saw it, but the real truth is in Harvey Fergusson's *The Blood of the Conquerors.* The real truth is that these people whom Hough exalts were bounders, coarse-grained and common, usurpers and destroyers. The Indian had a finer civilization than they; and the drama of that world of ambush and scheming, the pathos of it and the charm, was all in the passing of the *hidalgos*—is told, with understanding and insight, in *The Blood of the Conquerors.* As history and as romance, *The Blood of the Conquerors* is worth Mr. Hough's entire output of twenty-eight volumes and the land knows how many magazine articles.

V

"For fifteen years," Mr. Hough once said, "I was engaged in professional out-of-doors journalism. I have been a sportsman all my life, and my father before me. In this capacity I have traveled in almost every state in the Union, in New Brunswick, Quebec, British Columbia, Alberta, Manitoba, Saskatchewan, the Northwest Territory, many parts of the Sierras and American Rockies. I confess to rather a vagabond life. Sometimes I wonder if I ever slept under one roof thirty nights consecutively. At least my frequent trips into the open have done me a great deal of good physically, and have afforded me pretty much all the happier moments of my life—it is impossible to fret over things when wading in a trout stream, following a good dog, or riding a good horse.

"I still have my old cow saddle, I suppose a dozen rifles or so, half a dozen shotguns, as many fly rods, salmon rods, etc. I do not know whether I would rather fish for salmon, bass or trout, but have pretty much gone out of all bait fishing for the fly.

"I have killed, if I make the count fairly, or helped to kill, either fourteen or fifteen bears, nine of them grizzlies. I may have the count wrong by one. I am rather fond of grizzly hunting, but must confess I never had any kind of an adventure with a bear. I would rather shoot Bob White quail than grizzlies, and believe them about as dangerous.

"I have killed examples of most of the big game in the country—including my buffalo, which I killed as late as 1886. I think I have between a dozen and a dozen and a half of mounted heads—the taxidermist has most of them now, for the Missus kicks on them littering the house. . . .

"I presume that, after all, though I am best known as a writer of fiction and magazine articles, my real life's work has been in the open and has to do with the literature of out-of-doors.

"My first book, *The Singing Mouse* stories, had to do with out-of-doors. My next book—and the one which gave me my first real chance as a writer—was *The Story of the Cowboy.* My first novel, *Girl at the Halfway House,* dealt somewhat with the out-of-doors and with the West.

"I have liked the early life of Americans as a field for study more than anything else I have ever handled. Often as a boy I regretted that I was not born in the time of Carson and Frémont. I still regret that. I believe I would have fitted into the life of that time better than I do into that of to-day."

VI

You can get from all this some impression of the man as a stylist, and some impression of the man himself. He ran away from life, from his fellows, from the America of Gary and Dawes and Bryan; he hid in the forests; he played at being back in the days of the great explorers. I do not blame him—indeed I sympathize with him—he was too unsettled and too unaquisitive to make a go of things in our metallic marts of trade. He was not a schemer, but a boy with a boy's love for beckoning roads and the hunter's trail.

VII

"I started in life," he says, in an article in the *American Magazine*, "with a very small equipment. I had a university education, perfectly good and perfectly worthless. In line with the traditions of my family I was intended for the practice of law, and was admitted to the bar. Perhaps the ambition to write was mine from early youth—I don't know. I remember that in the course of my law studies I used to snatch time to write 'pieces,' as we called them in those days. Some of those early sketches found print in the magazines of the East before I was admitted to the bar.

"After I was admitted to the bar my first location was in a small town in New Mexico, half mining camp and half cow camp, the capital of an inland empire of wild life such as cannot be found anywhere on the surface of the earth to-day. In this rugged field, among those splendid and sterling men, in an atmosphere not too law-abiding, but always just and broad, I got my first actual impression of life on my own. I learned there to respect a man for what he really is, not for what he has or for what he pretends to be."

VIII

Hough always stressed the importance of keeping one's independence, in thought and action. Take less money, if necessary, (he would say), but be free.

He offered William 'Ernest Henley's *Invictis* to "every young man, every beginner and every striver, of whatever age," insisting that it ought to be included in every business college course, that it showed the only road to success and—what is better—what success should be at the end of the road. On all occasions he quoted the boastful and empty words:—

> "Out of the night that covers me,
> Black as the pit from pole to pole;
> I thank whatever gods may be
> For my unconquerable soul."

No soul is unconquerable. As Shaw said of Carpentier, even genius can be defeated. But the lines had sound; and their rhythm persuaded Hough that they must have sense, too:—

> "It matters not how straight the gate,
> How charged with punishment the scroll;
> I am the master of my fate;
> I am the captain of my soul!"

It is like a drunken mouse saying, Bring on your cats! It was the beaten Henley proclaiming, in the face of his conquerors, that he was tough and you couldn't hurt him. If he was tough he made a tough of himself, for Henley had genius and power of a sort, as his essays on Burns and Fielding show. I have an affection for Henley, but his poem is drivel.

IX

When Hough died in 1923, the *Saturday Evening Post* said, editorially, of him:—

"Death brought to a sudden close on April thirtieth the labors of a great patriotic American. Millions knew that Emerson Hough stood in the forefront of American novelists, yet only hundreds were aware of the devotion that actuated a long life spent in the single-hearted service of his country. It is well within the truth to declare that Mr. Hough's dominant passion was love of his native land, her history, her institutions and all that goes to make up what we call America. Those who knew him best say that his vision and his capacity for feeling were such that to him America was a great, all embracing personage, as it were, a benign goddess or a kind of glorious mother."

And this, too—*pace* the *Saturday Evening Post*—in an age when we are trying to transcend the narrow bounds of nationality and create a league of nations under which we shall be, not Americans or Swedes, Yanks, Micks, Wops and Frogs, but men in a world of men. In so far as Emerson Hough was American, wholly and only American, in so far he fell short of being worth-while. Pride of race, as Doctor Johnson said, is the last refuge of the blackguard.

X

Mr. Hough was the author of *The Singing Mouse Stories*, 1895; *The Story of the Cowboy*, 1897; *The Girl at the Halfway House*, 1900; *The Mississippi Bubble*, 1902; *The Way of the West*, 1903; *The Law of the Land*, 1905; *The King of Gee Whiz*, 1906; *The Story of the Outlaw*, 1906; *The Way of a Man*, 1907; *Fifty-Four Forty or Fight*, 1909; *The Sowing*, 1909; *The Young Alaskans*, 1910; *The Purchase*

Price, 1911; *John Rawn—Prominent Citizen*, 1912; *Lady and the Pirate*, 1913; *Young Alaskans on the Trail*, 1914; *Out of Doors*, 1915; *Let us Go Afield*, 1916; *The Magnificent Adventure*, 1916; *The Man Next Door*, 1917; *The Broken Gate*, 1917; *Young Alaskans in the Far North*, 1918; *The Way Out*, 1918; *The Sagebrusher*, 1919; *The Web*, 1919; *The Covered Wagon*, 1922; *North of 36*, 1923; *Mother of Gold*, 1924.

E. W. HOWE

Here is the finest figure of the lot, the man who has
made all our later realists possible, a contemporary (as
William Allen White has said) of the great Russians.
And yet withal a kindly man, one who watches with a
sort of pained wonder the obscene contortions of
Anderson and Bodenheim; one who is shocked (and
confesses to finding some fun in being shocked) by the
frenzied antics of the younger generation; one who
(because he delights in blunt honesty and forthright
speech) cannot understand the witty innuendoes of
Cabell and Van Vechten. . . .

I admire Van Vechten and Cabell, Bodenheim and
Anderson, bobbed hair and frenzied antics—but I repeat; Here is the finest figure of the lot, the most
admirable, the most lovable, the most sane.

II

"What do you think of Shaw?" I asked him.

"I think he is the smartest man now writing," he
said "—or was until he became old. He is lately a
little maudlin, as all old men are."

"And Ibsen?"

"I don't care for Ibsen or his plays. I have a book
of his sayings and have found only three that I thought
very good. In a similar book by Shaw every one
would have been good and some of them brilliant.
But then I never have been greatly impressed with

what we call literature.   American literature is largely
a disturbance."

III

It is certainly disturbing.   When I think of what is
happening to me, how one day I pity the great inert
masses with Struthers Burt and the next day abuse
them roundly with Red Lewis; how one hour I am
in the seventh heaven because two lovers have met and
the next cast down because some paltry misunder-
standing has separated them; how I have wept beside
the waters of Babylon and thirsted for the blood of
Herod; when I think of how my soul has been corrupted by books and my heart disturbed and my liver
made to complain, I know that, with little reading and
much toil, Ed Howe and I have at last come to an
agreement with Anatole France. . . .

"Those who read many books," Monsieur France
has said, "are as opium eaters, living in a dream.   A
subtle poison penetrates their brains, making them in-
sensible to the real world.   Books are killing us—we
have too many of them.   Men lived for ages without
books—and those were the years in which they passed
from barbarism to civilization.   For they were not
without poetry—they knew their songs and catechism
by heart."

IV

"I admire Mencken," says Mr. Howe, "but he is
mean.   A useful writer should be candid and truthful
without being mean."

Mr. Howe is never mean.   He tells of a man in

Atchison who is so worthless that instead of putting off until to-morrow he puts off until Monday the things that he should do to-day; but Mr. Howe makes no comment.   He does .not fly into a rage and condemn the man as a boob, a Chatauquafan or an imbecile professor.

So, too, when he says that a woman ought to be pretty to console her for being a woman at all— there is no malice.   It is the male viewing out of a full life what he takes to be the slavish round of his women-folks.

V

On page one of *Country Town Sayings* he advises us to be better than the average because average wages are pretty low.

There, in essence, you have his practical philosophy. We are to take the world as we find it and adapt ourselves, accept the world's standards, because the world is the market to which we must carry our wares if we are to sell them.   Do not waste your time in useless rebellion.   Do not dissipate your energies in futile whining.   You can get better than average wages if you will do better than average work.

VI

Mr. Howe lives in Atchison, Kansas, and, oh, seen through his eyes, Atchison is a rarely interesting and a rarely human place.

There is, for instance, in Atchison a man who claims that the minute he hears a woman's voice he can tell whether she wants to vote or not.   And there, as elsewhere, cheap people are noisy—like cheap automobiles. Nearly all the trouble in Atchison—or in the world, for that matter—is due to the fact that half the people are men and the other half women. Some of the men are too active, stirring up unnecessary trouble; most of the women insist that men can never understand how much work there is around a house.

Unsupported gossip will be believed in Atchison where sworn testimony will not. And about all you'll find at a big celebration in Atchison is a big crowd.

The girls in Atchison say of a certain rich bachelor: "He has money, but he wants it all himself."

A while back an Atchison man was moody and silent for several days. His women were sure he was meditating some devilment. Then he came down with typhoid fever.

VII

In Atchison, it seems, every time you look at a twelve year old boy he needs a new pair of shoes.

VIII

Mr. Howe always gives a woman what she wants without any useless arguing. Argument is disagreeable. Besides she'll have her own way in the end anyhow.

IX

Mr. Howe has a great respect for women. As his secretary, Miss Nellie Webb, says in a letter to me— he likes a womanly woman.

Still he is philosophical about them. Their eternal

question (he says) seems to be, How much a yard? And when they get invited to a party they are never satisfied—they want to be asked to help receive.

X

He believes that having two love affairs at the same time is more trouble than twins.

XI

He says that he is rough and that his heart is hard, yet he is curious as to just how far a young man can go in his attentions to a young girl and still withdraw with honor. Is he bound (Mr. Howe asks) after he has squeezed her hand?

He says that he has never known anyone who could play the guitar, though he has yet to meet the man, woman or child unwilling to try.

XIII

He says . . .

But, there, I could keep on forever. He has said so much, and all of it timely, most of it witty, the wisdom of an exceedingly able and tolerant observer. Get *Country Town Sayings* or get that book Mencken edited, *The Anthology of Another Town.* You will never regret a thorough acquaintance with Howe.

XIV

There is no more courageous figure in the somewhat crowded lists of those who make our novels—"the only man I know," William Allen White has said, "who is not afraid of the truth."

Nor is the truth the only thing of which Howe is not afraid. He is unafraid of lies. He is not to be silenced by intolerance or quieted by prejudice, by loud mouthings and the threats of our professional Luskers.

XV

Away back in 1881 he wrote the most sensible essay on prohibition that, to my finding, has ever been written in this or any other country. A "temperance lecture" that dismisses such anarchy as we are now faced with as pernicious pettifogging. You will find it all, in black and white, on pages 177 to 182 of the first and last editions of *The Story of a Country Town*. Why make a hero of the drunkard? Howe asks. Or exalt a bad habit by speaking of it as though it were some Lucullan vice?

XVI

You will find the history of *The Story of A Country Town* in the preface to that faithful and enthralling study of life in a small midwest American community of fifty years ago.

Night after night Howe sat at a kitchen table, alone, laboriously penning his careful and sympathetic record of the people and the world he knew so well, so wonderfully well—every word written after a hard day's work as editor and publisher of a small town evening newspaper, not a line while the sun was shining. "In almost every chapter," he says, "there is some recollection of the midnight bell."

I am told, that, among writers, two or three thousand words is considered a good day's work. But not

by Howe. *The Story of A Country Town* was written after Howe had already finished five thousand
words or more as his day's stint on the Atchison *Globe.*

XVII

But the hardest and most discouraging moments in
the life of a beginning novelist come, as often as not,
after the book is written. It was so with Howe. A
dozen times *The Story of a Country Town* was refused. Every reputable publisher of whom Howe had
ever heard was given his chance at the book; and they
all returned it as unavailable. The outlook seemed
hopeless. But Howe was not only an editor, he was a
printer, and in his day he had been a champion printer.
He set to work on *The Story of a Country Town.*
The *Globe* print shop, a newspaper office by day, was
turned into a book publishing house at night.

The book was set up by hand, and printed on a job
press, four pages at a time. Then the type was dis-
tributed the same night, to be ready for use on the
Globe next morning. Night after night the work progressed, until at last it was finished, and the pages
bound into a thin green-covered volume, to be cherished
in the libraries of Atchison, a first edition of two thousand copies, worth, the proud author will tell you, $4 or
$5 a copy to-day.

XVIII

Mr. Howe's literary education at that time, 1882–3,
was limited. He had read a few of the classics and
not much else. But he had certain violent enthusiasms.
One was for Dickens, another for Howells and a

third for Mark Twain. When his book came out he
sent copies to Twain and Howells—I am assured that
he would have sent copies to Dickens had Dickens still
been living. . . .

About that time Barney McCauley hit town with his
troupe, playing *The Messenger From Jarvis Section.*
McCauley and Howe struck up a friendship, and in
due course McCauley received a copy of *The Country
Town.* McCauley read it, with enthusiasm. He sent
it on to a friend of his writing about books and race
horses for the New York *World.* In less than two
weeks a flattering two column review of *The Story of
a Country Town* appeared in the *World.* And about
the same time, almost the same day, the *Century Magazine* came out with Howells' now famous review.

The publishers went crazy. Every day telegrams
poured in on Howe, from Boston and Chicago and New
York—"make no contract until you receive ours, which
we are mailing to-day."

Howe, characteristically, closed with the company
whose contract arrived first—Houghton-Mifflin.

XIX

The Story of a Country Town went through twenty-
five editions in two years and has recently been reprinted by Harper's in response to a popular demand
for more of Howe.

XX

Of the three books of travel letters written by
Howe, only one is now in print, the letters from Australia and Africa.

XXI

Mr. Howe was born at Treaty, Indiana, May 3, 1854, the son of Henry and Elizabeth (Irwin) Howe.

Let me quote from a letter I have received from Miss Nellie Webb, for twenty six years a reporter on the *Globe* and, since 1910, Mr. Howe's secretary:—

"Mr. Howe's father was a Methodist preacher. When Mr. Howe was a little boy he used to ride around behind his father, on a roan pony, and they used to hold meetings. Mr. Howe's father preached and the little boy used to stand on the pulpit and sing old camp meeting hymns. He had a musical voice, which he retains, although he is now seventy years of age.

"His father was very severe, and believed in whipping. When he was so little he had to stand on a stool to do the work Mr. Howe was obliged to set so much type a day, or get a whipping. Because his father, the Methodist preacher, was also a newspaper man. When Mr. Howe was thirteen or fourteen he was wandering around making his own living setting type. He was fast at setting type, and in Salt Lake City used to race with the fastest typesetter and win. That was when he was sixteen, maybe, or thereabouts. His father being a hard taskmaster had taught him how to work effectively, and for that I have often heard him express gratitude. In after years Mr. Howe's father lived at his home, and it was Mr. Howe who took care of him, sending him to Hot Springs and elsewhere, and there was a tender feeling between the two men. Mr. Howe's father was a strong rugged type, and Mr. Howe is that type, I believe.

"Mr. Howe's unhappy wretched childhood made

him the best of fathers. He has two sons and a
daughter. All successful and not a one of them ever
gave him a moment's anxiety. Mr. Howe never spoke
harshly to them. He is now and always has been a
gentle man.

"But when it comes to thinking he sees things clearly.
I believe it is only the terrific oceans of sentimentalism
which has submerged humanity so often and from
which, every so often, we have to be rescued that
makes Mr. Howe so completely and utterly materialis-
tic. He does not believe material things are hideous.
He believes that it is the material things of this world
that plant us firmly on our feet and help us over the
rough places. He has plenty of sentiment, although
he loathes sentimentalism.

"When Mr. Howe was editor of the *Globe* he was
first of all a reporter. News seemed to stick to him.
He used to bring in the hidden items—by that I do
not mean scandal, but honest-to-goodness news. He
used to seem to get hold of everything that happened,
just before it broke. And when he knew an item he
printed it. No item was too small for him to write.
In fact, the other reporters wrote the big items that
every one knew. Mr. Howe often brought in two
hundred items a day. He wrote paid locals. In
those days of horses and buggies he had a little old
horse and a buggy, and evenings and Sundays used
to ride around. Atchison is just across the river from
Missouri. Mr. Howe used to drive over in the Missouri hills and out over Kansas farms. Everywhere
he was known; and farmers, their wives and children
used to give him news. They used to come out to the
fence and call to him to give him news. He used to
send us reporters around the byways to pick up news.
'If it is not in the *Globe* it did not happen,' people

used to say in those days. The paragraphs which
have made Mr. Howe famous were none of them
forced. He used to have flashes as he talked to people, or observed people. So his paragraphs fairly
reek with human nature. . . .

"In the old days of his editorship Mr. Howe rather
rúled the town. He was the good wife who makes
her husband believe he's the boss when really she is.
He had a clever way of handling situations. He was
and is appreciated in Atchison. Once the town gave
him a silver water set, once a gold repeating watch,
once a loving cup—which shows, I think, that Mr.
Howe is what every man should be: respected and
liked in his home town."

XXII

Respected and liked! He should be loved—for I
could go on and prove, by a thousand instances, that he
is the most lovable and admirable person now writing
in America and the most influential—for I am certain
that a comparison would bear me out when I say that
Ed Howe's Monthly has the most intelligent subscription list of any periodical in these United States, editors, statesmen and bankers, poets and dramatists and
scholars, historians and mere men and women. And,
for me, at any rate, considering the benighted and
lachrymose and craven age in which it was written, for
truth and understanding, for pity, irony and grace of
thought, *The Story of a Country Town* is by all odds
the best novel made much of in this exciting and timely
historillamoris of mine.

Mr. Howe is the author of *The Story of a Country
Town*, 1883; *A Moonlight Boy; The Mystery of the*

*Locks: A Man Story; An Ante Mortem Statement;
The Confession of John Whitlock; Lay Sermons; Paris
and the Exposition; Daily Notes of a Trip Around
the World, 2 Vols; Country Town Sayings; The Trip
to the West Indies; Travel Letters from New
Zealand, Australia and Africa; The Hundred
Stories of a Country Town; Preaching of a Poor
Pagan; Success Easier than Failure; The Blessing of
Business; Ventures in Common Sense; The Anthology
of Another Town.*

WILLIAM DEAN HOWELLS

Though in his life time Mr. Howells was invariably referred to as the Dean of American Letters, now that he is dead it is the fashion to belabor him and to disparage his various works. His (we are told) was an enslaving philosophy, compact of don'ts, filled with negation. Go slow, he said; use caution. Indeed caution played so large a part in his valor that running away became a habit and his first thought in a fight was that, at all costs, he must live another day. Only fools lost their heads—and Mr. Howells was never foolish. He liked a dignified mien, a calm and judicial air; he affected the traditions that had become tongue-tied in Boston; he aped the speech of the Brahmins and lisped in platitudes.

There is some truth, of course, in all this. Warm-hearted as he was and kindly, he did try to pretend that his spirit could feed and grow fat on the sparse fare of the Cabots, the Lodges, the Lowells and their God.

But that, according to our younger critics, was not the worst of his offense. Having been shorn himself of all unrighteousness he tried, like the fox in the fable, to get his friends to submit to the sheers. He wanted them to conform. There must be no rebellion. The village blacksmith was the only proper hero and the skipper's daughter the one woman in the world. The scene of every romance must be some quiet village in the hills of New England. Cities were dens of iniquity—And as editor of the *Atlantic* he came within an ace of enforcing his rule.

II

Like most literary fashions this side the waters the pummeling of Mr. Howells can be directly traced to the hard facetiousness of Mr. Mencken and his little group of mercurial thinkers. It is due to what they consider Mr. Howells' cold-blanketing of the more Rabelaisian outbursts of the Olympian Twain. They blame Mr. Howells for the failure of Mark Twain because Twain never became all that he might have been.

The discovery that Twain was a failure came like a bolt from the blue to most of them. They had gone about praising *What is Man?* as an epoch-making pamphlet—it was greater than anything Voltaire had ever attempted. And every spring they read (and rejoiced in) *Huckleberry Finn.* Then Van Wyck Brooks wrote a book which he called *The Ordeal of Mark Twain;* and in it he proved, to their entire dissatisfaction, that the author of *A Tramp Abroad,* etc., was anything but happy. Why wasn't he happy? He was starving to death—metaphorically speaking. His soul was too weak for utterance. He had been dosed with aphorisms from Boston and similes from Concord until he scarcely knew his own mind. The excellent jests he had contrived to put his fellows in their places all fell flat. It was impossible for so ravenous a brain to live on the thin twaddle of the Back Bay.

Why, then, did he try it? Because Howells told him he must; because Howells, gaining a peculiar ascendency (on account of his superior education) over

Twain's weak will, persuaded him that, if he ever expected to write, it was the thing to do—he must be nice.

III

All this strikes me as a little far-fetched.   If Twain
was a failure, he failed through faults of his own—
because he was over-impressed by the solid worth of
Howells, because he was not critical of the claims of
publishers, because he never learned self-reliance.   He
was humble, too humble.   He lacked guts.   The
good rebel confesses and glories in his revolt.   Only
the weak, as Harvey Fergusson has said, stew in the
juices of remorse.   Twain accepted Boston because
he could think of no substitute that was preferable.

IV

But what did Howells have to do with all this?
The blasphemies of Mark Twain sounded harsh to his
ears.   He begged Twain to go a little easy—and for
his sake, Twain was willing to interpolate a few dashes
where before there had been nothing but damns.
Was Howells in this going beyond his province as a
friend?   He spoke only for himself.   Who knows
but what Twain, who did at any rate write some quite
unapproachable satire, might have done nothing had not
Howells insisted that discipline was necessary if he was
to consort with the more respectable members of the
writing profession in his generation?

I am not at all sure that Howells' influence was an
evil one.   Twain never said so; and Twain was well
able to speak for himself—did speak for himself, and
is on record as having said that for forty years the

English of William Dean Howells was to him a continual delight and astonishment.

"In the sustained exhibition of certain qualities," he says "—clearness, compression, verbal exactness, and unforced and seemingly unconscious felicity of phrasing—he is, in my belief, without a peer in the English-writing world. *Sustained*—I entrench myself behind that protecting word. There are others who exhibit these great qualities as greatly as does he, but only by intervalled distribution of moonlight, with stretches of veiled and dimmer landscape between; whereas Howells' moon sails cloudless skies all night, and all the nights.

"There is another thing," he continues, "which is contentingly noticeable in Mr. Howells' books—his stage directions. Some authors overdo the stage directions. Other authors have nothing in stock but a cigar, a laugh, a blush, and a bursting into tears. They say:

" '. . . replied Alfred, flipping the ash from his cigar.' (This explains nothing; it only wastes space.)

" '. . . responded Richard with a laugh.' (There is nothing to laugh at; there never is. The writer puts it in from force of habit—automatically; he is paying no attention to his work or he would see there is nothing to laugh at.)

" '. . . murmured Gladys, blushing!' (This poor old shopworn blush is a tiresome thing. We get so we would rather Gladys would fall out of the book and break her neck than do it again. In a little while we hate her, just as we do Richard.)

"But I am friendly to Mr. Howells' stage directions,

more friendly than to anyone's, I think.   They are
done with a competent and discriminating art, are
faithful to the requirements of a stage direction's
proper and lawful office which is to inform.   Sometimes they convey a scene and its conditions so well
that I believe I could see the scene and get the spirit
and meaning of the accompanying dialogue if some
one would read merely the stage directions to me and
leave out all the talk.   For instance, a scene like this,
from *The Undiscovered Country:*—

"'. . . And she laid her arms with a beseeching
gesture on her father's shoulder.
"'. . . she answered, following his gesture with a
glance.
"'. . . she asked, laughing nervously.
"'. . . she asked, turning swiftly upon him that
strange, searching glance.
"'. . . she reluctantly admitted.
"'. . . But her voice died wearily away, and she
stood looking into his face with puzzled entreaty.'

"Mr. Howells does not repeat his forms and does
not need to; he can invent fresh ones without limit."

V

This is praise from Sir Hubert, and, without comment of mine, you know that it is well deserved.

VI

Nevertheless, for all his great talents, there was, as
Francis Hackett has pointed out, particularly in his
early days and towards Bostonians, a deference in Mr.
Howells which fairly makes you ache for him.   He

listened to advice and trimmed his sails until it is a
wonder he did not run aground in some back-water of
stupidity. How he ever got to sea and steered his
course, almost unerringly, toward the Islands of the
Blessed where all good writers go to muse, remains an
everlasting mystery.

Yet he got there just the same. Wishing no peace
to the tormented souls of our young Sainte Beuves,
I'll say he did. He is still, in the now ages-old
words of Lowell, one of the chief honors of our liter-
ature—*A Modern Instance* is a book one interested in
American letters cannot afford to miss; *The Rise of
Silas Lapham* ranks with the best of Flaubert and
Meredith.

VII

Yet I cannot get over his timidity. Why should a
'good woman' seem to him a fine phrase, or anything
but buncombe? He must have known 'good women'
who were simply awful, 'good women' who were mean,
penurious and hard. Yet 'good woman' was the highest praise he ever had to offer. He could divide the
sex just by making physical examinations, the virgins to
one side; the rest in Tophet—and the hell of his
Tophet was that he insisted upon pitying the rest.

VIII

He had a notion that second thoughts were best and
that all such wise young fellows as the Kipling of
the '90s were upstarts. Children, he was quite sure,
for all their visibility, should not be audible. He
would have nodded 'serves him right' above the grave

of Chatterton; he might even have joined with the
Edinburgh Reviewers in the hounding of Keats.   It
was a fixed belief of his that whiskers made for
wisdom.

"It is good for the literary aspirant," he said, about
midway of his career, in that quaint volume *A Boy's
Town*, "to realize very early that he is but one of
many, for the vice of our comparatively virtuous craft
is that it tends to make each of us imagine himself
central, if not sole."

As though each one were not the center of his own
universe—and rightly so.   We must make the world
go round us or we will go round the world begging for
a place to lay our heads.   Why must diffident old
men, out of the years that have brought them all too
little, repeat Browning's sneer at Byron—a man talking to a mountain.   Can't they ever realize that if the
man is Byron he can talk, and quite comfortably, to
mountains or, for that matter, to God?

IX

But to continue with my quotation:—

"As a matter of fact the universe does not revolve
around any one of us; we make our circuit of the sun
along with the other inhabitants of the earth, a planet
of inferior magnitude."

You can see how beside the point all this is.   True
enough; but surely our whole mission is not to go revolving, monotonously and complacently, round the sun
with the other inhabitants of the earth.   Though made

of clay we are not necessarily clods. And what difference does it make anyway how small the earth is? Have not good things come out of Nazareth?

"The thing we strive for," says Mr. Howells, "is recognition, but when it comes it is apt to turn our heads. I should say, then, that it was better it should not come in a great glare and a loud shout all at once, but should steal slowly upon us, ray by ray, breath by breath."

You see? He would even apportion the praise a man is to receive for good work. What, then, of those who die young? Or of Bambino whose days are so soon over?

X

But Mr. Howells was always too reticent. And for this reason American criticism has never been rightly focused upon him. He has been neglected and misunderstood. He has been, except to the student, well-nigh lost. There has been no school following his fine example. Far from denouncing him, if they really wanted to render a service to American readers, our young radicals would beat the drum and sound the loud fanfare for Mr. Howells—his instant sympathy for Ed Howe, his understanding of Harry Leon Wilson, his everlasting patience and good cheer.

XI

Mr. Howells was born at Martins Ferry, Ohio, March 1, 1837, the son of William Cooper Howells, a country printer and editor, with, for that time, a large and well chosen library. In this library the young Howells obtained most of his education—beyond the meager three R's of a small town country schoolhouse. He read almost anything and everything that came to hand, specializing in poetry, even going so far as to write a little poetry and set it up in type for his father's paper.

In 1851, the family fortunes went to smash and Mr. Howells was sent away to work as a compositor on the *Ohio State Journal* in Columbus, for $4 a week, a while later graduating into journalism and at twenty-two becoming news editor.

His first published work, *Poems of Two Friends,* written with John J. Platt, appeared in 1860; and about the same time he began to contribute to the *Atlantic Monthly,* which had just been started in Boston. The same year he also wrote a campaign biography for the Republican presidential nominee, Abraham Lincoln. The biography was evidently a success; Lincoln was elected; and as a part of his reward, Howells was made American consul at Venice, remaining there until 1865, studying the Italian language and reading Italian literature.

On his return to America, he wrote for the New York *Tribune* and for the *Nation.* Then in 1866, he was made assistant editor of the *Atlantic,* becoming editor six years later. For a while he contributed to *Harper's,* was editor of the *Cosmopolitan,* returned to *Harper's,* and in 1900 took over the *Editor's Easy Chair.*

He was the author of something over a hundred volumes, thirty odd novels, a few farces, comedies, several volumes of criticism, verse and a series of autobiographies. His early novels were scarcely more than travel sketches. *The Undiscovered Country* is the first book by the real Howells.

JAY WILLIAM HUDSON

Jay William Hudson, the author of *Abbe Pierre* and *Nowhere Else in the World,* was born in Cleveland, Ohio, March 12, 1874. His family came from Connecticut, and settled early in Ohio. His father had been a lawyer in Cleveland; and his mother was Emma Pratt, of Solon, Ohio.

When Mr. Hudson was a boy of seven, his parents moved to Chicago, where he attended the public schools. At the age of thirteen, he started out to earn his living, taking the first job handy, that of errand boy. After several jobs as office boy and file clerk he was able to prepare for college. At seventeen he entered the preparatory department of Hiram College—the school made famous by Garfield. His father had graduated there in 1837. At Hiram he remained until he was twenty-one, except for a term at Oberlin. As an undergraduate he was best known as a writer for the college papers.

In 1896 he removed to California, making his home in Oakland and San Francisco, then in Santa Rosa. In California he became well known as a writer on current issues, and as a lecturer. He finally decided to make a more special study of philosophy, and in 1901 entered the University of California, studying with George Holmes Howison, eminent as the teacher of many men who have since attained distinction. Hudson soon became one of his favorite pupils, and was invited to teach in the department of philosophy as an assistant. He took his Bachelor's degree in 1905, and his Master's degree in 1906.

Hudson had often thought of Harvard, because of its noted faculty in the department of philosophy, including at that time William James, Josiah Royce, George Santayana, Hugo Munsterberg, and George Herbert Palmer. In 1906 Hudson went East, earning his way by public lectures, and arriving at Cambridge with ten dollars in his pocket and a much prized letter of introduction from Professor Howison to his Harvard colleagues. He spent two years at Harvard, studying chiefly with Royce, Palmer and Munsterberg, receiving his Doctorate in Philosophy at the end of that time, during which he was assistant in Philosophy. Immediately upon receiving his degree, he was called to the chair of Philosophy in the University of Missouri, which position he now occupies. During the World War, he served with the American Red Cross in France as an inspector, with the rank of Captain.

Hudson spends much of his time in literary work. One of his most recent books is *The College and New America,* concerning which President Burton of the University of Michigan lately said, "I wish that every professor in America might read at least this one book bearing upon the problems of education in general and especially as they affect the college." Last year appeared *The Truths We Live By,* giving the author's philosophy of life, highly praised by his old teacher, Professor Palmer of Harvard, who remarks "the style alone might give the book currency, but thousands of people are in the perplexity which the book meets." Hudson's favorite recreations are tennis, billiards and walking.   So far as possible, he spends his summers in southern France, where he has made an intimate study of the Gascon county, in which the scenes of *Abbe Pierre* are placed.

Nowhere Else in the World is a story of a dreamer in Chicago.

II

In personal appearance he is short, with dark hair, brown eyes that seem to be dreaming, except when they light up, as they often do at some ready jest.   His face is as smooth as a boy's.   He is quick and alert, so that people guess his age all the way from thirty to forty-five.   He smokes a good cigar with a relish, wears fashionable clothes and talks simply, without any affectations of scholarship.

III

Although a professor of philosophy, and author of a number of technical articles that have gained wide recognition, Mr. Hudson's first interest is literature. At college he was class poet.   Indeed, it is said by his close friends that he has written a volume of poems, which, however, he cannot be persuaded to publish. He says he writes poetry only to keep himself constantly in tune with the beauty of things.   When he lived in California, he was a warm and intimate friend of Edwin Markham and Joaquin Miller, both of whom vainly urged him to publish some of his verse.   When asked recently why he did not teach English literature instead of philosophy, Mr. Hudson said: "Literature is indeed my vocation and philosophy only my avocation; but I have a theory that if one's vocation is an art, he had better not earn his bread and butter by it— the commercial note should never corrupt one's artistic motives. When we conform art to some utility, we lower it. It is all sufficient in itself. Every art is the creation of some new expression of the Ideal; therefore, it is forever it's own excuse or end."

IV

Mr. Hudson does all his writing in the morning, on an old home-made desk, in a little, simple room, his walls covered with the scenes he is writing about. His favorite novelist is Thomas Hardy. He reads detective stories for relaxation; recently Will Irwin remarked that one of his most vivid recollections of a visit to the University of Missouri was Jay William Hudson and his intense interest in detective stories. He is an enthusiastic Rotarian, a member of the Chamber of Commerce, an active member of the national secret music fraternity, Phi Mu Alpha, and an authority on international politics, often asked to speak before clubs and conventions, among others, the Fourth American Peace Congress.

V

When recently asked how he would express his life-creed Mr. Hudson answered in the words of his own *Abbe Pierre:* "I would like to become the dream of my boyhood's heart—which is the inner dream of the world."

RUPERT HUGHES

In *Contemporary American Novelists, 1900–1920*, Carl Van Doren, after lumping Rupert Hughes with Owen Johnson, Gouverneur Morris and George Barr McCutcheon, remarks upon the Major's total lack of true distinction.

Is this fair? Is it fair to dismiss the relentless author of *Empty Pockets* with a conscientious shrug, the intrepid compiler of a *Music Lovers' Cyclopedia* with faint damns? Major Hughes has done his darnedest. Is this the way to treat him?

I need pause no longer for a reply. It is manifestly fair and right since the Major has not long since risen to his full height of 5′ 7″ to denounce Van Doren and call him negligent.

Major Hughes delights in pointing to the folly of critics. He has tried criticism himself at various times and he knows that it is easier to praise than to blame. He cannot see why all critics do not take the easy way. If you point to the flaws in a man's work, you are almost certain to alienate him—why not make friends? Why bother with theories, with standards, with sincerity? Major Hughes never bothers in his criticisms.

This is not to say that he is without his own ideas of what's what. Witness his essays on the introversions of Mr. Harding. Here, he tells us, circumlocution has been raised to a fine art; here is honest-to-goodness phraseology—founding fathers, normalcy

and the rest. Or his continual hurrahing for Mr.
Robert W. Chambers.—

"Sunlight and satin, wealth, success, laughter, love
are quite as important in life and as artistic in art and
as difficult to paint with truth or put into vivid works
as gloom, flannel, poverty, failure, tears, senescence,
and incompatibility. Robert W. Chambers, like Van
Dyck, Gainsborough, Watteau, Monet, Sorolla, and
other painters, and like Mozart, Gluck, Chopin, Wagner, Debussy, d'Indy, and other composers, revels in
luxurious scenes, glittering companions of gentle folk,"
etc. etc.

It follows that Mr. Chambers (with Van Dyck and
the other painters, with Mozart and his fellow-
composers) is a very great man. He is probably even
greater than Major Hughes guesses. He may eat—
just as Homer did. Or sleep—somewhat after the
manner of DaVinci. Or drink as I have been told
was Ben Jonson's custom.

II

Major Hughes has a notion that critics are men and
women who have failed in the arts—as though success
in the arts were the *summum bonum*. He is very
severe on critics. In the ever memorable punctuating
of the incomparable Max, doubtless they themselves
tried to be writers, once.

But there is no comma in the comments of Major
Hughes. He means what he says and he says it—in
five thousand words or so—right out. He wants to
get done. And this getting-done of his results in
letters to almost every one of his reviewers. He is

the terror of the press.   No occasion is too small for him to jump in and have his say or so.

He has argued spiritualism with Ted Robinson and obstetrics with F. P. A.   He defended the movies against Burton Rascoe and the theater from within. He has studied sculpture and botany and numismatics. He knows what there is to know about music.   He is indefatigable, ubiquitous, omniscient—more or less.

I remember that when he returned from his first trip to Hollywood he was enflamed against Lenin. He had been in conversation with Bob Wagner and he had found out that Lenin was a dangerous radical. It seemed that Lenin desired a more equitable distribution of property—and by what right did Lenin express any such desire?   Lenin was a despot.

A while later he kept me standing all one afternoon in a doorway on 42nd street while he put me right about Aristophanes.   Most people who talk about Aristophanes do not trouble (he says), to read him; but the Major had read him—and it is the rough humor, the common talk of common people, that gives the comedies their claim to immortality.   The Major says so.   Not a word about the beauty of the phrasing, the gorgeous imagination that attacked Euripides, the fancy that is repeated in little in Jurgen.   Just slang.   It is for slang that we still read the Athenian Cabell.

III

But it is their preoccupation with the dead—to the neglect of the living—that gives Major Hughes his best opening with the critics.   Let me quote from an earlier edition of this (as Mr. Cabell has said) invaluable work, page 41, Major Hughes speaking:—

"Henry Fielding would have sat up in his grave with a gasp if he had been able to see in one of our strictest weeklies a recent article called The Noblest Novelist of Them All, reviewing a three volume *History of Henry Fielding,* written by a professor, and published by the Yale University Press."

Why? Why should Fielding gasp because there are still some, a professor among them, to recognize his nobility? He was not given to gasping when the Great Cham, Dr. Johnson, defended him against the attacks of Smollet—why should he gasp now that he has been so long dead? The Major knows the answer.

Because "he was a tireless portrayer of the fast set in town and country, among the squalid and the gorgeous, in the attics, palaces, inns and highways"; because though "he filled his books full of scholarship and toyed with Latin, he terrified many of his contemporaries by his vulgar realism."

I must confess that this is fine reasoning, too fine for me. Since when have we been so squeamish that we cannot, in books published by the Yale University Press, refer to the fast set in town and country? Is not Congreve frequently mentioned? Are we not all of us enthusiastic about Falstaff and Sykes and Moll Flanders? I have known more than one professor with a good word for Voltaire—ladies still speak highly of Byron.

At what then is Major Hughes driving? At the critics. He must have at the critics at all costs.

In his life (he says) Fielding was read as "a mere entertainer; and now he is a classic!" (That incredulous exclamation mark is the Major's.)

But this will be good news to Mr. Hergesheimer who believes that it is the business of literature to be entertaining; it was a surprise to Major Hughes only because he has an idea that novels are "a form of social history"—"accuracy of dialogue" he says, "is a mania with me."

But that is not all. He goes on to tell us that "most of Fielding's contemptuous critics are forgotten."

There is much virtue in the Major's phrasing, for had he said Fielding's most contemptuous critic he would have pointed straight at the one man whose fame will endure as long as Fielding's—Samuel Richardson, the first of all the sentimentalists, the father of James Lane Allen and Mrs. Porter and Hall Caine. It was Richardson who confessed that he was unable to read further than the first volume of *Amelia*, Richardson who as early as 1750 prophesied that the run of *Tom Jones* was over.

IV

However, it is best to let the Major tell his story in his own words:—

"The reading of Fielding in my post graduate days had an immense influence on my literary program. I had planned to be a professor of English literature and write a bit of fiction, verse and drama on the side. I came gradually to desire to do for New York a little

of what Fielding did for London. My first long
poem, however, was a blank verse dramatic monologue
of Greek Life called *Gyges' Ring*. It was published
in a volume that had some superlative praise and sold
a few hundred copies. As a counterweight, I wrote a
long irregularly rhymed and rythmed poem describing
the then new diversion, the Serpentine Dance, and trying to catch some of its color and swirl.

"I left Yale without taking the Ph.D. I had
planned to earn, accepted an M.A., 1899, and gave
up professorial ambitions for what I called creative
work.

"My first theatrical production was a terrific failure,
lasting one night in New York. I was twenty-two at
the time. My next production, several years later,
was a second and last try at comic opera, the libretto
again concerning contemporary people. It also
failed. The same year I collaborated on a Greek
melodrama, *Alexander the Great,* which played a season on the road but never reached New York—thank
heaven!

"After many failures, I got a success with *The
Bridge,* which ran three years as *The Man Between,*
a capital and labor play with the hero a bridge-builder,
who stands between the two forces, suffering from the
excesses of both in his frenzy to get things built. This
was produced some years before Mr. Galsworthy's
Strife.

"My farce *Excuse Me* had an immense success.
Other plays succeeded or failed as luck would have it.

"On leaving Yale, I spent a few months as a reporter on a New York daily paper and learned a good
deal about the city, became an ardent lover of it, and
a defender of it against the cheap slanders of those
who call it Babylon or Nineveh or heartless, vile or

anything else but a very large group of assorted people.

"I have been able to love New York without ceasing to love the small town life of my childhood or the London, Paris and other cities of my later residence. I love realism without ceasing to love romance, native and foreign literature, science and fairy stories, classics and newspapers, history and vaudeville. In fact I love everything and everybody, and my whole effort at self-education has been to avoid condemnations, contempts, snobberies and cheap scholasticisms or modernisms.

"I was born in Lancaster, a Missouri village, January 31, 1872, whence my parents moved to Keokuk, Iowa, on the Mississippi River in whose waters I spent a large part of my boyhood.

"My ancestors on both sides came to America early in the seventeenth century, settling in Virginia and North Carolina. My mother's grandfather was a soldier in the Revolution. Her father kept slaves. My father's father was a Kentuckian. As a lieutenant in the Black Hawk War he received a grant of land in Illinois where my father was born.

"My father became a lawyer and played a strenuous part in railroad development in the midwest. He became later a railroad president. As a lawyer he has been concerned in many very famous suits; the Scotland County Bond cases began the year I was born and ran up and down the supreme, district, state and county courts until I was 26 when he finally won it. His analytical mind and grasp of evidence had a great influence on my development.

"My mother is one of the most artistic souls I ever met, with as great a love for art and romance as my father for law. I was brought up on Greek sculpture and Italian art at her knee. My sister and one brother took up music, and another is an inventor of distinction.

"My first published works were sonnets and essays and musical and art criticism. I spent years in offices as an assistant editor of weekly and monthly magazines and of a world's history—Godey's, Current Literature and the Criterion. I have composed a good deal of music, edited a musical cyclopedia, written on American composers—all together a vast amount of stuff on nearly every kind of topic. The only claim a good deal of this has on tolerance is its spontaneous sympathy, its earnest effort at accuracy and its expression of my philosophy of art and life.

"My first serials were the *Lakerim Athletic Club* stories, studies of real boys in the midwest, and these were my first books, 1898. Otherwise I was rather slow about getting started in fiction. I could sell articles and essays and books on almost any subject, but nobody cared for my stories.

"Gradually my short stories began to be accepted and to win increasing favor. Then *The Red Book* in 1914 took me up as a serial writer with *What Will People Say?* and my subsequent success, such as it is, has been a constant surprise to me.

"The next novel, *Empty Pockets,* was an experiment in the mystery story. I began with the usual dead body and then instead of working backward to the solution, I turned time a whole year back and started with the dead man alive drifting toward his doom. I make no apologies for the mystery element for I have a profound respect for the arts of entertainment, even of clowning.

"In a general way, my novels have concerned city life and its more exciting phases, though I keep emphasizing the human, the village side of the metropolis. Some critics praise them as veracious, some assail them as sensational. But I write them with all the earnestness and fidelity of the historian. Accuracy of dialogue is a mania with me. I believe that everybody has a personal dialect.

"Realistic dialogue is a matter of intense scientific research and nothing pains me more in many novelists of eminence than the absolutely impossible bookish talk they put in the mouths of their characters.

"What the people I know actually say and do and wear and spend—all these details of our immediate American life are matters that I approach with the reverence of a witness of sacred gospel.

"While I strive to despise nothing human, I come nearest to hating the sneerers at our own time, the sophomoric satirists of the American present and the pretty misrepresenters of ancient or medieval realities. Five years work as assistant editor of a history of the world taught me the essential unity of human nature. I consider scorn to be a proof of ignorance and I pity the poor critics who pity Americans."

V

Major Hughes is becoming the least bit involved. When he refers to scorn as ignorance, he is referring to the contempt of the Nazarene for the scribes and pharisees of long ago, to Dean Swift's *Gulliver's Travels* and to George Ade's first *Fables in Slang*. The sophomoric satirists whom he pillories are George Kaufmann and Mark Connolly, the authors of *Dulcy,*

To the Ladies and *The Beggar on Horseback*. He makes no mention of *Babbitt* but I doubt not it curdled his blood.

VI

This is not intended as a parting shot. I have the highest regard for Major Hughes. He is at once the most generous and the most energetic person I have ever known. I believe him when he says that he hates to go to sleep. He is literally tireless, into everything, wishing he could live to be a hundred and write a hundred times as many novels, plays, movies, stories as he has already written.

Major Hughes served from private to captain, New York National Guard, 1897–1908; captain Mexican Border service, 1916; assistant to adjutant general, N. Y. 1917; captain of infantry, January 7, 1918; major, September 4, 1918; honorably discharged, January 15, 1919. An impairment of hearing kept him from serving overseas during the Great War; he belonged, as he says, to the swivel-chair army for over a year while the 69th were in France.

He is the author of the *Lakerim Athletic Club*, 1898; *The Dozen from Lakerim*, 1899; *American Composers*, 1900; *Gyges' Ring* (verse), 1901; *The Whirlwind*, 1902; *The Musical Guide*, 1903; *Love Affairs of Great Musicians*, 1903; *Songs by Thirty Americans*, 1904; *Zal*, 1905; *Colonel Crocket's Co-operative Christmas*, 1906; *The Lakerim Cruise*, 1910; *The Gift Wife*, 1910; *Excuse Me*, 1911; *Miss 318*, 1911; *The Old Nest*, 1912; *The Amiable Crimes of Dirk Memling*, 1913; *The Lady Who Smoked*

Cigars, 1913; *What Will People Say,* 1914; *Music Lovers' Cyclopedia,* 1914; *The Last Rose of Summer,* 1914; *Empty Pockets,* 1915; *Clipped Wings,* 1916; *The Thirteenth Commandment,* 1916; *In a Little Town,* 1917; *We Can't Have Everything,* 1917; *Unpardonable Sin,* 1919; *Long Ever Ago,* 1919; *Cup of Fury,* 1919; *Fairy Detective,* 1919; *What's the World Coming To?* 1920.

GEORGE F. HUMMEL

An Interpolated Chapter by Silas Bent

George Frederick Hummel, author of *After All* and *Subsoil,* has been a cowpuncher, a Wall Street speculator, and has specialized in German and English literature. He was born September 3, 1882, in Southold, at the eastern end of Long Island, and spent his boyhood in the country. His parents, Anna and Gottlieb F. Hummel, had been born in Germany, and were of that sturdy stock which made the backbone of this country in the nineteenth century. The father defended the union in the Civil War.

Young Hummel was thrown out of the public school at Southold, and a sister helped prepare him for college. Another Southold boy had "been to" Williams, and probably that was what determined the Hummel choice. Mr. Hummel was graduated there in 1902, and in the following year took post-graduate work at Columbia, where the A. M. degree was conferred on him.

At Williams Mr. Hummel had been a leader in athletics, and at the same time had made a brilliant record in scholarship. After he had taken his master's degree illness threatened to cut short his life. He underwent a series of operations, and the specialists who were attending him finally gave up hope of saving him; but they reckoned without the patient's indomitable will to live. He made his way West to live in the open, and there regained his health, some-what as Theodore Roosevelt regained his in similar circumstances.   Mr. Hummel spent a year punching cattle in southwestern Texas and Mexico, underwent a severe hazing by the cowboys at the outset, lived their rough life with them, and built for himself a physical constitution of extraordinary toughness and strength.

Returning to Southold, Mr. Hummel gave part of his time to managing a summer hotel and part of it teaching in preparatory schools.   The years 1909 and 1910 were spent rambling about Germany and Italy, and studying at German universities.   In the follow-ing year Mr. Hummel completed his residence work at Columbia University for a doctor's degree in German and English literature.

But after all this scholarly preparation Mr. Hummel turned away from his books to Wall Street.   He was not then and is not now a business man in any Rotarian sense of the word.   He played the exchange as a game. His notion was to get rich quick and quit.   He played it as a speculator and promoter, and in the early months of 1914 was a millionaire on paper.

Then came the war and a smash.   Speculative se-curities and real estate ventures shrank almost over-night next to nothing.   Mr. Hummel went "broke" so far as the Street was concerned.   He pulled out a fragment of what had been a fortune, audited the years he had spent with a smile, and cast about for something else to tackle.

In the meantime, early in 1914, Mr. Hummel had married Mrs. Lillie Conrad Busch of St. Louis.

After the outbreak of the World War Mr. Hummel

took up the organization of industrial education for
the Y. M. C. A.   It was not until 1921 that he cut
loose altogether from the business world and began
writing.   By now he had an immense store of experience and observation, and he had a solid literary
background.   *After All,* his first novel, dealt with
the institution of marriage in a refreshingly sincere
way, and was, for a first novel, an outstanding pe-
cuniary success.   It was published by Boni and Liv-
eright, who are publishers also of *Subsoil.*   The
latter, which is in press as this is written, presents a
certain stratum of American village life.   It is a novel
in a novel form.   Each chapter deals with the fortunes
and the psychology of a certain character, but the same
characters run through all.   Thus it may be regarded
in a sense as reflecting the Russian influence; for the
"theme," if there is one, is village life among a certain
class, rather than the development of a single personality, such as is common in American fiction.

The winter of 1923–4 Mr. and Mrs. Hummel spent
on the island of Capri, and there he wrote a drama.
He has written numerous stories and sketches.   When
he was asked for some statement of his attitude toward life and letters he made this somewhat startling
—and certainly emphatic!—reply: "I have no opinions, no morals, no money, no balance, no brains, no
bottom, no beliefs, no aspirations and a hell of a lot of
friends."

The single affirmative after this extraordinary list
of negations seems somehow not to bear them out.

WALLACE IRWIN

There is a fluttering in the critical dovecotes and a scrambling among the pigeon-holes because Wallace Irwin—who was thought to have (and who had) sold his talents to mammon—has recently come out with two ambitious and really, all things considered, very fair novels. A sinner, it seems, has repented; and there has been, quite naturally, some rejoicing. One who had devoted and debased his undoubted gifts to the uses of the cheap and tawdry has decided that there is honor and some reward in self-respecting labors. More power to him, say the critics—and more power, say I.

But I have small hopes for Mr. Irwin. The *Golden Bed,* as Percy Hutchison has said, is masterly; but it is not a masterpiece. Mr. Irwin has been on the loose so long, he cannot now discipline himself, bring his unruly pen into submission, and so write simply and austerely, beautifully and concisely, with no merely silly digressions for the sake of digressing and being silly.

The fault is not altogether Mr. Irwin's. But evil associations corrupt good manners, and for years now Mr. Irwin has associated with those who had an eye only to the quick return and the sudden profit. Art is long and there are no short cuts. Genius is still concerned with taking pains, with thinking things through, with patience. Mr. Irwin is impatient. It is, as I see it, a tragic situation.

Take the story of *Togo*. Mr. Irwin wrote a letter
in the manner of a Japanese schoolboy and for years
he tried to sell that letter. Then a riot broke out in
British Columbia and *Colliers'*, quick to realize the
opportune moment, bought much the same letter in
the same vein and in the same manner from Mr. Irwin.
And for six months Mr. Irwin appeared weekly in
Collier's. But where is there any chance for growth
or development in such a situation? It is all very well
to say that Mr. Irwin did not have to go back years
and assume a tone and style long since become out-
moded for him. Mr. Irwin felt that he had to live;
and it is no answer to his problem to say, in Voltaire's
words, that you cannot see the necessity. It was a
very real necessity for Mr. Irwin.

II

No one has cared. That is the answer. *The
Golden Bed* and *Lew Tyler's Wives*, even the lightest
of his verses, show Mr. Irwin capable of at least so
much as Belloc, Milne or E. V. Lucas. But was he
given a chance? No. Always he has had to struggle against the deadening stupidity of his editors and
the hail-fellow complacency of his friends. And so,
for the sake of bread and butter, his nose to the grind-
stone, he has gone on, repeating himself over and over
again.

III

Oh, I know that others have not submitted so
meekly to the standards of the shallow-pated. I know
that Louis Bromfield has written nothing merely for

the sake of seeing his name in print, that Dreiser has been always honorable, that McFee is no hack.   But I can still feel pity for the waste of Mr. Irwin.

IV

He is benighted.   All the things he has heard, over and over, in his circle he has learned to accept as gospel.   He believes in the rights of the Nordic to invade the homes and the shrines of the Jap and the Zulu and the Hindu.   They are heathen as the Chinaman is a heathen.   They are our market for a surplus of shoddy goods.   In any argument with any other nation we are right.   We are superior to the Russians. We are cleaner and more decent than the Germans. We are not immoral as the French are.

These are fixed tenets in Mr. Irwin's circle and he can never unlearn them.   But he might have unlearned them had he adventured out into the realms of thought, read Renan and Samuel Butler and Schnitzler and Turgenieff, in the days of his forming judgment.   As it is, he is hopeless for anything but a passing hour and a muddled discussion of Babbitt's problem, in love and business.   He has no wide vision—the artist in conflict with his environment—and that alone is enough to keep him out of Valhalla.   But he is ambitious; that should make us glad for him.

V

I quote in full the outline of his life as he has set it down for me:—

"My paternal grandfather was Admah Irwin, a farmer of Scotch descent who lived near Erie, Penna.

"My maternal grandfather was Charles Chauncey Greene, a descendent of the Founder of Rhode Island. The best known member of his family was Nathaniel Greene, the Quaker general. Charles Chauncey Greene was a friend of Poe and Nathaniel Hawthorne. He was a member of the Brook Farm Experiment, an abolitionist and one of the first American feminists.

"My father was David Irwin, my mother Edith Greene.   I was born in Oneida, New York, but my father's home was at Canandaigua, New York.

"In 1880, when I was 4 years old and my brother, Will Irwin, 6, our parents went to Leadville, Colorado, where my father had ambitions to follow silver mining. Leadville was then a primitive camp of the Bret Harte type.

"I was about 15 when my parents moved to Denver, my father having tried mining, lumber and cattle without success.   Up to then my education had been very sketchy (my mother encouraged me in a taste for reading, but I had gone to school very little).   When I entered the Denver public schools I was put in the third grade, but by the combined efforts of my mother and myself I was admitted to high school the following year.

"After graduating from the West Denver High School (1895) I spent a year in Cripple Creek as assayer in a cyanide mill for the reduction of low-grade ore.   That winter Cripple Creek was burned down and I was one of the deputy sheriffs who patrolled the town until the situation was relieved by State militia.

"I entered Stanford University in the class of 1900. I took a literary prize in my freshman year and wrote the class play in my sophomore year.   Subsequently I held the editorship of my class annual and of the literary magazine.   In my junior year I was expelled on a charge of stealing chickens.   I was not falsely accused.

"I went to San Francisco quite penniless, in search of newspaper work.   After a month of almost literal starvation I made my first dollar writing topical verse at five cents a line for an obscure weekly paper.   I gained a local reputation for light verse.   I did my first reporting for the *Report*, a Scripps-Blade paper which went bankrupt in two months, not through paying extravagant salaries.   I went on the San Francisco *Examiner*, first as a writer of rhymed headlines, then as Chinatown reporter.

"The following year I became editor of the *Overland Monthly*, and during that time I wrote the *Love Sonnets of a Hoodlum*, a cycle of slang-sonnets which were intended as a literary joke, but were praised by Professor Barrett Wendell of Harvard and had a sale of 100,000 copies (the edition was cheap—25¢). Soon afterward I wrote the *Rubaiyat of Omar Khayam Jr.* which was also popular.

"I came to New York about 1901.   The first verse I wrote I sold to *Life*.   For a year or so I was engaged on the *Globe*, writing a topical rhyme a day. At the same time I had a rhyme about every week in *Life* and appeared in a number of other magazines (all verse).

"My first prose was a series of burlesques on Steffins' *Shame of the Cities* which I wrote for the *Saturday Evening Post*.   The series was called *Shame of the Colleges*—it was pretty primitive humor, but quite popular at the time.   On the strength of this popularity I was taken on *Collier's* as a member of the staff.   I started with a series of rhymed lampoons on public

characters called *Who's Zoo in America*—my subjects
were such men as Uncle Joe Cannon, Charles Warren
Fairbanks, Chauncey M. Depew, etc. One on Wm.
Randolph Hearst was used as a campaign verse against
him when he ran for Governor.

"I had always wanted to try a series of letters in
Japanese dialect, but it was not very strongly encouraged—I had learned a great deal about Japanese
letter-writing during student days in California.
However, an occasion arose. This was about 1907.
The British press had been rather scathing on the subject of California's brutal treatment of the Japanese.
Then the Canadian press began criticizing us in the
same tone. In the midst of the dispute an anti-
Japanese riot broke out in British Columbia and several Japs were killed. This was a fine chance, so I
wrote a *Letter of a Japanese Schoolboy,* pretending to
come from a "Japanese Schoolboy enjoying a brickbat
wound in Vancouver Hospital," and "asking to know"
about where international friendship came in. The
letter was so popular that *Collier's* was deluged with
mail, asking for more. For six months I appeared
almost every week in *Collier's* signing myself Hashimura Togo. Almost everybody thought the stuff was
being written by a Jap. Then there was a brisk dispute among correspondents—about a third of them
maintained it was a hoax, cooked up by a white man.
At last *Collier's* came out with the author's real name.

"In the meantime Mark Twain had written a letter
to *Collier's* very warmly praising the Japanese Schoolboy in an imitation Togo letter, as follows:

" 'Hon. Collier Weekly which furnish Japanese
Schoolboy to public not often enough, when is his book

coming out? I shall be obliged if you will send me the earliest copy, or at least the next earliest. That Boy is the dearest and sweetest and funniest and delightfulest and lovablest creation that has been added to our literature for a long time. I think he is a permanency and I hope so too.

S. L. CLEMENS.'

"After a year in *Collier's*, Hashimura Togo went into syndicate for two or three years. Up to 1917 he was a monthly feature in *Good Housekeeping*. He also had been serialized in *Life* for nearly a year.

"When I came to New York in 1901 I had vague ideas of writing fiction and brought with me a manuscript of a short story called *Pelicon Smith*. This I hawked about for years, rewriting time after time. Finally, in a strangely altered shape, it was published in the *Cosmopolitan*. That was my first attempt at fiction.

"I did not write another story until about 1909, when *Everybody's* printed a Christmas story called *A Transplanted Ghost*. A short time before that I was associated with Richard Harding Davis in a comic opera called *The Yankee Tourist*, and from my own experience I got material for several theatrical stories which appeared in *Everybody's*.

"I did not attempt fiction again until about 1912 when I had a monthly agreement with *McClure's* Magazine and wrote eight or ten stories, among which were *The Highest—What Became of Deegan Folk?* and *He Shot the Bird of Paradise*. I wrote a great many stories for various publications after that.

"My first serial (it wasn't exactly a novel) I finished just before we entered the War. It was called

Venus in the East and appeared in the *Saturday Evening Post* which was then using all my short fiction. —*The Blooming Angel* appeared subsequently in the same periodical and *Trimmed with Red* followed.

"In 1919, I went to California to study the Japanese situation with a novel in view. After a year of writing and investigating I finished *Seed of the Sun* in which I attempted to tell the story of the Japanese farmer and the American farmer from both angles. The book was popular and has been considerably used as a text book on the immigration question.

"About 1912 I wrote a comic opera entitled *Dove of Peace* with music by Walter Damrosch. It was a failure. My recent novels are *Lew Tyler's Wives*, 1923, and *The Golden Bed, 1924.*

"In 1915 I was married to Laetitia McDonald, daughter of Donald McDonald of Louisville, Ky. I have two children, both boys, Donald McDonald Irwin and Wallace Irwin, Jr.

"In summer I live in *The Strongbox* at East Setauket, Long Island. The *Strongbox* is a Colonial relic, having been built in 1702 by Seelah Strong, one of Lond Island's pioneers. George Washington visited this house during the last years of his life."

OWEN JOHNSON

If it were possible to batter down the steep sides of Parnassus or with a trumpet blast to cause them to fall, Owen Johnson would long since be standing where, idle in a golden chair, Ovid sits, with Sappho at his feet, discoursing on the arts of love. But since main strength was never yet accounted a virtue by the daughters of memory, Mr. Johnson stands still (where he has stood for twenty years), a little to the right of Rupert Hughes, in the offices of the *Cosmopolitan Magazine*—and no divining rod is needed to prove the *Cosmopolitan* a long, long way from the grooves of Arcady.

You cannot, unless you have drunk of Wotan's wine, take Valhalla by storm. It is true that young Kipling tried it, in *Naulahka,* and more or less succeeded— but Mr. Johnson is not Kipling. And Mr. Johnson cannot, by substituting Kipling's self-assurance for Kipling's conviction, take Kipling's place; and Mr. Johnson, almost invariably, mistakes assurance for conviction. Proud feminine beauty passes muster with him for that beauty which Keats cried up as a joy forever.

No, mere brawn counts for little in the long history of the arts. There were mighty men in Rome and their literature is none the better for it. There are mighty men in Sweden to-day, but it is Selma Lägerlof who is their leader. And this seems a pity since energy is surely a fine thing and worthy of remembrance. But so it is. For all his earnestness, Mr. Johnson somehow misses being convincing. There are quatrains by the leisure-living Omar that are more provocative than his most impassioned diatribe against the secret societies at Yale; DeQuincey's essay on murder as a fine art is more thrilling than a dozen such mysteries as the *Sixty-First Second;* the unspeakable Verlaine in his cups devised phrases that will be potent when Mr. Johnson's *Blue Blood* is no thicker than water. You cannot make up in sound and fury what you lack in patience and understanding.

III

Mr. Johnson was born in New York City, August 27, 1878, the son of Robert Underwood Johnson, a poet, sometime editor of the *Century Magazine,* and soon or late bound to be one of Mr. Wilson's ambassadors carrying our enlightened viewpoint as a candle to dispel the naughtiness of the Old World.

I do not know what sort of youth one might be forced to pass in the home of an incipient ambassador. It may be there was, for Johnson, too much poetry in the air. At any rate, he took to prose, entered Lawrenceville as a prep for Yale, graduated from Yale, wrote (and in 1901, a few months after leaving college, published) the *Arrows of the Almighty;* and four years later, *In the Name of Liberty*—high-sounding titles, if nothing more. Then, having read Balzac, he turned to the seamy side of life, studied New York's shyster-law offices and pictured their infamy in *Max Fargus.*

He has been four times married, was the first **editor**

of the *Lawrenceville Literary Magazine,* chairman of
the *Yale Literary Magazine* in 1900; and in his ma-
turity a member of the National Institute of Arts and
Letters.

IV

When *The Humming Bird* appeared in 1910, (a
jolly and ingenious account of the doings of various
boys at school at Lawrenceville), it became the fashion, so much the creatures of the mode are we, for
those motoring between New York and Philadelphia,
through Princeton, to break the journey at Lawrenceville for the purpose of visiting the Jigger Shop where,
upon a time, to the amazement of the Prodigious
Hickey and the Triumphant Egghead, Hungry Smeed
established the Great Pancake record.   Indeed, with
the appearance of the *Humming Bird,* Lawrenceville
became a place in history.   *The Varmint* and *The
Tennessee Shad* but added to that place.   Mr. Johnson had arrived.   He was the delight of every one
who has ever been away to boarding school and the
envy of those who have not.

But ambition laid hold on him as it has laid hold on
many of us, Macbeth among the rest.   He wanted a
broader field in which to exercise his authority over
words.   Besides he wanted to have his little say about
women.   Women, as you know, do most of the reading and (such is the fancy of authors) women like best
to read about themselves.   He would give them themselves to read about.   And a title to catch the eye—
The Woman Gives.   Then *Virtuous Wives.*   And

The Salamander. Making Money. And *Murder in Any Degree.*

The Salamander had possibilities. It is the tale of a demi-vierge who, living to incite the lusts of men, remains a virgin because, in desperate circumstances, she was always able to summon up before the eyes of her would-be seducer a picture of that seducer's mother. Such a character might serve as the wicker-work woman from which to hang the trappings of a real romance; but for Mr. Johnson she is merely a clothes horse. He does not treat her satirically or with abuse. He is sentimental about her, as much her dupe as the veriest slave in her entourage.

V

In a review of *Babbitt* Mr. Johnson gives us, among other things, an aside concerning the humble qualities of romance—which, he says, simply stated, mean only that the lights and shadows of life are relative and that the compensations of love, ambition, sacrifice and hope are just as active, precious and real under the cloak of vulgarity as where refinement, opportunity and education fashion a society. The secret of the success of Dickens (he says) was not in the pencil of the caricaturist but in his power to draw out of the masses characters that were often lovable and always sympathetically understandable.

VI

Considered as a novel *Babbitt,* Mr. Johnson says, is extremely vulnerable. He analyzes the vulnerability of *Babbitt*. Then he turns over the page and writes *Blue Blood,* a far-fetched best seller doing its best to masquerade as realism.

VII

Mr. Johnson wants to be taken seriously, but since there is nothing under heaven that he will not himself take seriously, since he is credulous of every hyperbole, a fond believer in the G. O. P. and the workers' place at home, I do not very well see how that can be.

BASIL KING

Kipling made a reputation for himself because he wrote in the English of the King James Version of the *Bible*. He was quoted far and wide. There was vigor and conclusion in his writings. You could pick them up anywhere and get a kick out of the style. It was at once the language of thugs and the language of the crusader. It was an inheritance from the days of Raleigh and Drake and Ben Jonson. It spoke of men who drank deep and looted the Spaniard, of pirates and cut-throats, incest and a fine reliance on the mercy of God. It was no uncommon occurrence for a man, in those days, depending upon his dagger, to end up on the gallows, after a night in the taproom; but never a man went to his death without a prayer on his lips. Men were hearty, but they were superstitious and, according to their lights, devout.

If I wanted to knock a man over the head with a sentence I would pick my words out of the *Old Testament*—I would share in the lust of the Elizabethans; there was nothing pretty in their speech.

But Basil King has made it pretty.

He is an Episcopalian and for long he was an Episcopalian minister, the Rector of Christ Church, Cambridge, Mass. I am myself an Episcopalian and the son of an Episcopalian minister; I studied for the church and I know how such things go. It is the

business of the minister to keep the church solvent, and
to do that he must not offend the ladies.   But any
honest reading from the *Bible,* with the right accent
and proper emphasis, will offend a perfect lady—the
Bible is not nice.   It deals with fundamentals; it digs
down; the sinful heart of man is laid bare in the *Bible.*
You are face to face with death and faced with the
glorious women of old Jewry.   You come upon them
bathing Rahab and Bathsheba and Susanna.   Not the
Arabian Nights, that book drunk with the Arab's imaginings, is more sensuous or more lovely and splendid
and awe-ful.

Mr. King was in a quandary.   He had to read the
Bible and he had to read before ladies.   But Mr. King
is a gentleman.   And he is sensible.   He did not hesitate.   He knew that we are not living in the age of
Solomon when a thousand wives was but a quorum.
He chose to compromise.   And through the years, for
the sake of the ladies, to spare their blushes and to
continue their contributions to the church, he has not
ceased to compromise.   He reads from the *Bible* but
only prettily, nicely as in a parlor.

And so it has been with his novels.   His words are
the words of the *Bible,* but the voice is the voice of
compromise.

II

Mr. King is always pretty.   In *The City of Comrades* he tells of bums and burglars, but they all reform—and when they see a little child—well, it is
just like the movies—the innocence of a child can bring
tears to their eyes any day.

III

Mr. King was born in Charlottetown, Prince Edward Island, Canada, February 26, 1859, the son of William and Mary Anne Lucretia King; and in due course he was baptized William Benjamin Basil King, after his father and his mother's father and an uncle. He was educated at St. Peter's School in Charlottetown, and at King's College, Windsor, Canada. On June 23, 1893, he married Esther Manton Foote of Doublin, New Hampshire. He then took up his work as rector in Cambridge, Mass.

In 1900 he commenced as an author with the publication of *Griselda*. *Let Not Man Put Asunder* followed the next year. There has been an average of a novel every other year since. The theme never varies—patience, humility, trust in the infinite goodness of God—always a moral and always one that even the most narrow and circumspect could approve—something pretty.

IV

Mr. King was little known until 1908, although he had already published five novels. But in 1908 *The Inner Shrine* appeared; and Mr. King was made—anonymously.

"*Harper's* wanted my book," he says, "to publish as a serial, but up to that time they had never taken a serial except from the very best authors. After they had taken the works of Thomas Hardy, Gilbert Parker and Mrs. Deland, it can readily be seen that hesitation on their part to feature a serial for the

coming year by a man who was practically unknown
was natural. It was suggested that my novel be run
serially, but anonymously. At that time I was very
ill, I was losing my sight rapidly, and when the publishers suggested that the story should be printed anonymously, I jumped at the idea, for the simple reason
that this would allow me to remain abroad two years.
I was so ill I took no particular interest in the serial
when it was published, and, as a matter of fact, I did
not know at the time that it had aroused any curiosity.
I had very little communication with the United States
during the first year of my story abroad. *The Wild
Olive* and *The Street Called Straight* were published
anonymously, too, though as 'by the author *The
Inner Shrine*'; but now the authorship of them is everybody's secret, in a way. I don't mind. Naturally, it
would be foolish to keep up my anonymity any longer,
though I should have been glad to do so."

v

Mr. King is the author of *Griselda*, 1900, *Let not
Man Put Asunder*, 1901; *In the Garden of Charity*,
1903; *The Steps of Honor*, 1904; *The Giant's
Strength*, 1907; *Inner Shrine*, 1909; *Wild Olive*, 1910;
Street Called Straight, 1912; *The Way Home*, 1913;
The Letter of the Contract, 1914; *The Side of the
Angels*, 1916; *The Lifted Veil*, 1917; *The High
Heart*, 1917; *The City of Comrades*, 1919; *The Abol-
ishing of Death*, 1919; *Happy Isles*, 1923.

PETER B. KYNE

"My alleged literary output," Mr. Kyne says of his writings, in the dedication to *Never the Twain Shall Meet*.

Mr. Kyne knows better than to claim that he is either Turgenieff or Defoe. He is an Irishman with an Irishman's bluff and an Irishman's blarney, but there is no silly pretense about him. He does not say, over and over, that he is saving young girls from the fate of his heroine, that he is anxious about the future of this country, that he knows a lot concerning the nether-depths of life. He frankly confesses that he has made a business of writing, and a business of selling his stories to the magazines and the movies. He's a first-class salesman. It is selling when he tells us his stories. He sells us on his characters, on his situations, on the locale—the mountains, the forests and the seas that are the background for *Cappy Ricks, The Go-Getter* and *The Pride of Palomar*. He makes no claim to being literary.

And his publishers are equally frank. Their reason for saying that *The Pride of Palomar* is worth buying lies in their proof that it has sold 150,000 copies in a few months. *The Go-Getter* sold 100,000 copies; business men bought it in quantities to give to their friends; if you're a business man, buy it. Or buy any one of his books—they are written for business men and the business man's wife.

317

II

All this disarms the critic.   And yet it is possible
to say, with the Brooklyn *Eagle,* that Peter B. Kyne is
dependable—you can depend upon him to turn out a
good workmanlike job, right up to specifications.
Running over the titles in a book store, any readers
might come upon a new book by Kyne with something
of a thrill—you know that though the story may not
be epoch-making, exciting extravagant comment in
literary circles, it will be a good story of its kind and
well told.   He writes only about the life he knows and
understands—the coast-wise trade on the Pacific, real
estate boosters, lumbermen and miners.   And he has
a knack with his characters, an evident liking for canny
business men, Kiwanians and joiners, that makes it
possible for him to get the essential man that is in each
one of them down onto paper in something like flesh
and blood.   They seem real enough, though shallow
and unscrupulous.   And undoubtedly they live in his
pages, as profoundly as in life do most of the men and
women from whom they are copied.

III

Kyne made his first success with *Cappy Ricks,* a retired sea captain, owner of a coastwise navigation
company, in a series of stories that ran in *Saturday
Evening Post.*   He had a meal ticket, good for years,
in *Cappy Ricks;* but the movies killed the captain, so
Kyne had to turn to John Stewart Webster, a mining
engineer who, entangled with South American revolu-
tions, met up with all the adventures necessary to a

thriller—death lurking in the underbrush and a pretty girl around the corner. But *Webster, Man's Man* was not to compare with *Cappy Ricks*. Cappy Ricks had humor—and a fine irascible temper; Webster was just another big, silent fellow, the sort that sets the flapper to wondering—and Kyne could not repeat on him as he had repeated with his skipper.

So Mr. Kyne has been looking around for another Cappy Ricks. He thought, for a while, that he had him in the *Go-Getter*. But the Go-Getter soon ran his course. He hasn't found his paragon yet. When he does he will go on as endlessly as Wallace Irwin with Hashimuro Togo and Roy Octavus Cohen with Florian Slappey and his colored kith—for the way to make money is the way Conan Doyle took with Sherlock Holmes—serialize your hero in short stories.

IV

Peter Bernard Kyne was born in San Francisco, California, October 12, 1880, the son of John and Mary (Gresham) Kyne. He was educated in the public schools and at business college. And in 1910 he married Helene Catherine Johnston, of Des Moines, Iowa.

He began life as a clerk in a general merchandising store, later going into lumber and shipping offices, becoming a lumber broker and then a newspaper man.

In '98 he served in the Philippines with the 14th Infantry; and more recently, during the Great War, in France as a Captain of the 144 Field Artillery.

He is the author of *Three Godfathers*, 1913; *The*

Long Chance, 1914; *Cappy Ricks,* 1916; *Webster, Man's Man,* 1917; *The Valley of the Giants,* 1918; *Kindred of the Dust,* 1919; *The Green Pea Pirates,* 1920; *The Pride of Palomar,* 1921; *The Go-Getter,* 1922; *Cappy Ricks Retires,* 1922; *Never the Twain Shall Meet,* 1923.

His publishers say that he epitomizes the national traits we take pride in—business ability, quick thinking, resourcefulness, energy, integrity and bubbling, infectious humor. These are not, of course, the traits that necessarily make for great literature; but Kyne would rather be American than literary any day.

SINCLAIR LEWIS

On page three of *Our Mr. Wrenn* you can read: "Mrs. Zapp was a fat landlady. When she sat down there was usually a straight line from her chin to her knees. She was usually sitting down. When she moved she groaned, and her apparel creaked. She groaned and creaked from bed to breakfast, and ate five griddle-cakes, two helpings of scrapple, an egg, some rump steak, and three cups of coffee, slowly and resentfully. She creaked and groaned from breakfast to her rocking-chair, and sat about wondering why Providence had afflicted upon her a weak digestion. . . ."

That is Lewis.

Our Mr. Wrenn was published ten years ago and written, I'm sure, under adverse conditions, but there is more than a promise of the later Lewis in it—Lewis the bounder and Lewis the dandy, Lewis the satirist, Lewis the wit.

The Trail of the Hawk followed the next year.

Both *The Trail of the Hawk* and *Our Mr. Wrenn* fell, to all purposes, on deaf ears. Then came *The Job*. *The Job* made something of a stir. I remember myself, in 1918, announcing that Mr. Lewis had arrived. But really he hadn't. He was there, the essential Lewis, in all three of those books. But we didn't know it. Mencken tells a story of Lewis coming in to interrupt a pleasant evening he and Nathan

were spending together. Lewis drank their good
liquor and talked interminably of the great novel he
had written. Neither of them believed him. They
pooh-poohed the idea that anything great could come
out of Lewis. And then they read *Main Street;* and,
by God, it was great.

It was great because Lewis had finally worked himself up into a passion—and because he had found
something very real to write about, the dullness and
contentment of middle-class America. . . .

"It is contentment . . . the contentment of the
quiet dead, who are scornful of the living for their
restless walking. It is negation canonized as the one
positive virtue. It is the prohibition of happiness.
It is slavery self-sought and self-defended. It is dullness made God."

Militant dullness, dullness that is mean and intolerant.

II

I should say (since I must place him) that Red
Lewis is our keenest intelligence. His is the pen that
Upton Sinclair laid down when Sinclair ceased being
apposite and satirical and became merely maudlin
about our miseries, choking over his facts. Lewis is
lithe and athletic. He is pointed, probing like a surgeon, with a sharp knife.

Besides that, he is opportune, as Stuart P. Sherman
has said. He has industriously studied both himself
and his age, like a good humanist, and he knows the

needs and aspirations and powers of both. And he is equal to speaking out for both. There is no clamoring with him. He is direct and to the point. And he has style, the greatest command (I believe) of our modern idiom of any one now writing in and for America.

III

Stuart P. Sherman is stretching a point—as is the way with Stuart P. Sherman—when he says that Lewis is the only successor to Mark Twain and Henry James and W. D. Howells. Mr. Mencken is Mark Twain's successor. Hamlin Garland has written nobly in the tradition of Howells. James was enough of a good thing in himself without more of the same kind. And you cannot—unless you are Stuart P. Sherman—simply ignore Stephen Crane and Ed Howe, referring to Dreiser as a barbarian who has never learned how to write, to Ben Hecht, Waldo Frank *et al.* as the lunatic fringe, and pass on to *Main Street* as the great American novel for which we have all been waiting.

Such idle comparisons do not help Mr. Lewis. *Main Street* is a hodge-podge of invective and scorn. It is great only because Mr. Lewis is so exactly right in his reactions to the deadening monotony and cheap sophistication of American life. As writing—well, I have tried, as writing it is almost unreadable the second time.

IV

"I was born," he writes me, "February 7, 1885, in a Minnesota village, Sauk Center, a genuine prairie town, ringed round with wheat fields broken by slew and oak-rimmed lakes, with the autumn flight of ducks from Canada as its most exotic feature. My boyhood was alarmingly normal, midwestern, American—my father the prosperous pioneer doctor whose diversions were hunting and travel; my school the public school, with no peculiarly inspired teachers; my sports, aside from huge amounts of totally unsystematized reading of everything from dime novels and new books and casual sentimental novels to translations of Homer, were the typical occupations of such a boy: swimming in the creek, hunting rabbits, playing pom-pom-pull-away under the arclight in the evening. There was not much work—a few evening chores, of the woodbox filling sort.

"I don't know how I got the inspiration to go east and become irregular, abnormal, happy, and otherwise literary. But I went to Yale; then for eight years—1907–1915—was a literary jack of all trades: newspaper reporter (on the New Haven *Courier* and *Journal,* San Francisco *Bulletin,* and for the Associated Press) magazine editor (*Transatlantic Tales, Volta Review, Adventure, Publisher's Newspaper Syndicate*), manuscript reader for F. A. Stokes Company and George H. Doran.

"I did get in a few savingly unliterary hikes, however. During college I made two cattle-boat trips to England; on one of them landed in England with only fifteen cents, and stayed alive by borrowing three dollars from a fellow cattleman, which lasted till the boat returned. Again I wandered down to Panama, going steerage, returning stowaway, and in between failing to get a job on the Panama railroad. A year and a half I spent in California, part of it reporting, part trying (vainly) to free lance, sharing a bungalow at Carmel with William Rose Benet. And once Allan Updegraff and I shared miserable rooms on the east side in New York.

"Now, for three years of free lancing as a rather perilously respectable citizen, with a wife and baby, I have combined wandering with being settled down! In Minneapolis, St. Paul, New York, California, Cape Cod, Florida, we rent furnished houses, and regard the curious ways of new people without sacrificing bathtubs—which are, of course, esthetically and economically, the symbols of civilization.

"As to music and pictures, I am altogether naïve. In authors my preferences are: H. G. Wells, Compton Mackenzie, Joseph Hergesheimer, George Moore, Joseph Conrad, Vachel Lindsay, Edgar Lee Masters. I am, I suppose, to be technical, a discoördinated radical in politics. For sport I drive a motor car—a thousand miles at a whack—and work."

v

His methods of work have been described by Dr. Paul H. de Kruif, his collaborator in the latest of his novels—and what promises to be the best, for the hero has genius and the girl (which is rare in Lewis) grace of body and mind—*Dr. Martin Arrowsmith:*

"A passenger ship is plowing along through the smooth, mysteriously weedy waters of the Sargasso Sea in mid-Atlantic. Down below in a snug little stateroom, before a typewriter on a little folding table,

sits Sinclair Lewis, a lank, towsly, red-haired figure in
an impossibly gawdy silk dressing-gown.   Ever and
again with two powerful fingers he makes the flimsy
machine resound with a staccato racket like machine
gun fire.   Now and then he stops to fumble a little
hurriedly and nervously among the confused pile of
maps, huge books, diagrams and papers that litter the
table, the couch on which he sits, the floor, the wash-
stand and the life-preserver-wracks.   Failing to find
what he seeks, he rasps out in no very choice language,
'Paul, what the devil have you done with Manson's
Tropical Medicine?'   A   hot   argument   ensues,
through abusive personalities to religion and philosophy, through science to the arts, dying away at last
amid a renewed clattering of the typewriter."

That, says Dr. Kruif, is Lewis at work—and particularly at work upon his new novel, the story of the
hopes, the struggles, the schooling in love and failure
of a young American from the Minnesota made famous
in *Main Street,* a young American who wants to be
and is a scientist in medicine.

VI

There is a steady and remarkable growth in the
work of Sinclair Lewis.

Our Mr. Wrenn, obviously influenced by the Wells
of *Kipps* and *Mr. Polly,* was the story of an incon-
spicuous, middle-aged sales-entry clerk who, inspired
by Kipling and Jack London, throws up his job and
goes wandering off to England on a cattle-boat, to find
romance incarnate in a red-haired art student who,
for a while, amuses herself with him.

The Trail of the Hawk is more nearly autobiographical, the story of a typical American boy emerging out of the frontier and becoming, as aviator, something of a figure in the world. Ericson, the aviator, shares with Mr. Wrenn (and with Lewis) a love for adventure; but Ericson is not satisfied—rather is his love of glory made a mark of distinction. This is a step forward. Lewis is beginning to see himself in his fellows and to deal more wisely with them. And he is beginning to speak out for some of the things he admires as well as against the things he loathes.

The Trail of the Hawk was written, principally, on commuter's trains while Lewis was rushing in and out of New York on his errands as a magazine editor.

And that summer his first story was accepted by the *Saturday Evening Post*. In three months three more stories were accepted. So Lewis quit his job and set to work on *The Job*.

The Job is a woman's job, Una Golden's, to be exact. Una Golden graduates from a woman's college in Panama, Pennsylvania, becomes a stenographer in New York, works into real estate, becomes assistant manager of a string of hotels, leaves one suitor in Panama, is left by another in New York, and finally marries a fat and voluble commercial traveler. As you can see, all of Una and all of Una's ambitions and Una's compromises with her conscience and with fate are in the book. It is Una's revolt against the humdrum and Una's desire to amount to something. It is Mr. Lewis' own story over again. "Into her working mind," he says, "had come a low light from the fire which was kindling the world." She joins the army of rebels who, if they are not soon ground underheel by the belligerent Dawes and his minute men, will finally make this country a fitting place for sane and respectable people to live in.

Free Air, Mr. Lewis' next novel, was written (quite plainly and quite rightly) for money. He needed money that he might have leisure to write *Main Street.* He got it—at least enough for that superhuman task.

VII

Main Street was no sudden inspiration, flying in the face of the populace who had for so long forced him to adhere to their smug standards of thought and living. Fifteen years before it was actually written the same notion had taken a hold on Lewis, to be roughly sketched with a small town lawyer as the central figure, and titled *The Village Virus.* During the intervening years Lewis started to write the final draft three different times, once actually getting as many as thirty thousand words down on paper. But though he always put it aside he always returned to it. He felt that it would not sell, could not sell, yet he had to write it. It was his book, his scorn and rage and rebellion, accumulated through all his youth and middle years. So with the money from *Free Air* he set to work; and after a year the book was finished in the summer of 1920, to be published in October.

In two months, by Christmas, it had sold 56,000 copies. By the end of 1922 it had reached the enormous sale of 390,000 copies. With this one book Lewis attained the success and popular fame that he had imagined in his most optimistic moments might result from a life time of consistent labor.

VIII

But the success of *Main Street* is not alone a credit to Lewis—it is a further proof, since proof is always needed, of the detachment and vision of a large and increasing body of Americans. For all of Mr. Sherman and others of our damning critical brotherhood, we are the support (and often the sole support) of the best that is available in the literatures of the world. It is America that asks for and receives Shaw and Galsworthy and Conrad, Yeats and Ervine and Lawrence, Tchekoff and Gorky and Artzibazeff, Reinhardt and Balieff and Copeau, Strauss and Cesar Frank and Stravinsky. Here you will find Kreisler and Heiffetz and Kubelik domiciled. Here are the great conductors. Here is Chaplin a cockney and Lubitch the *verfluchte Preuss*.

IX

The success of *Main Street,* its fineness as a novel, is due, according to Professor Sherman, because it is not autobiographical. But that, to my peculiar way of thinking, is exactly where it fails. Mr. Sherman sets it apart because in Gopher Prairie Mr. Lewis has not a single personal representative. His characters are all distinctive individuals, standing on their own feet.

X

I have never been able to understand the touting of impersonal art. To me, as to William Allen

White, an author's characters are so many fascets of his own personality. He must love even the meanest of them, as Sam Merwin has said. He can speak only for and through himself no matter what the disguises he puts on.

In *Main Street* Lewis has failed to recognize this ancient truth. He has tried to pretend that he is not as these others are, Dr. Kennicot and Carol and Guy Pollock and Vida Sherman and Sam Clark, Mrs. Bogart and Fern Mullins and the rest; that they are not Lewis. But they are. And, but for the grace of God, he might still be anyone of them, for in his exasperations, his itch to reform, his veneer of polish, he is as ridiculous as Carol and as pathetic.

The failure of *Main Street* to be for me as fine a book as *The Old Wives' Tale* or even *Riceymans' Steps* is due to Lewis' want of a feeling of common humanity with the people he satirizes. He kicks them and he abuses them, but they are his neighbors, his kind, and he cannot kick them and abuse them with impunity.

XI

And it is right there that *Babbitt* succeeds. Sinclair Lewis recognizes Babbitt as a universal type, and so recognizes himself in Babbitt—and, oh, what a great, what a fine, what a wise and (at bottom) kindly book *Babbitt* is.

XII

Babbitt is at once a person and a symbol. He is America and America's craven fear of failure; and he

is his own hopeful and beaten self. With a forlorn
cheerfulness he says at the end to his son, "Practically
I've never done a single thing I've wanted to in my
whole life." He has been a booster and a Rotarian,
a member of the Athletic club, with a wife, a son, a
home and car of his own in the typical city of three
hundred thousand: yet he has never been happy.
Why? Because he has tried to feed his soul upon
bread alone. He has been without desire for anything but bread, for bread and ease and talking big.
He has been undisciplined. And he has been all his
life haunted, as every American is haunted, with the
fears of a deserted and lonely old age. Read the advertisements of any bank in America, listen to an insurance agent, notice the toothpaste slogans or Feaz-
ley's constant dwelling upon the insidiousness of halitosis. What is the one emotion that all these appeal
to? Fear. Look up and down the faces in the subway, look at Coolidge, at Bryan now that his sun is
setting—what do you read in every line? Fear. And
it is fear that makes Babbitt the brother to us all.
Life is uncertain; and try as we may we can gather few
roses here.

XIII

Yes, *Babbitt* is an immensely better book than *Main
Street* because *Babbitt* is seen with pity.

And *Babbitt* is humorous, a comic masterpiece.
There is the address delivered by George F. Babbitt to
the Real Estate Board of the city of Zenith, the soul-
saving activities of Mr. Drew, the dinner parties, the
clandestine whisperings, Babbitt's affair with Tiris, the

gatherings of the alumni of the State university.   And
the marvelous talk.   It is as though Lewis had listened
to all the conversations in all the pullman cars, in all
the bedrooms, in all the restaurants and offices in
America.   So exactly has he caught the accent of vulgarity and hollow mirth that is our common speech.

XIV

Make no mistake.   *Main Street* was the novel of its
year, but *Babbitt* is more serene and more amusing and
so (for me) less tedious.

And, for me, *Dr. Martin Arrowsmith* is even better.
There is less to prove in *Dr. Martin Arrowsmith* and
more in the young doctor, his tutors, his friends, his
wife, for Lewis to admire.

XV

By way of explanation and as a foreword to *Dr.
Martin Arrowsmith,* Lewis has said:—

"A small boy whose memory is of being awakened
by his father's talking to a patient, down at the door;
of catching 3-A. M. phrases: 'Where is the pain?
Eh? Well, all right, but you ought to have called me
earlier. Peritonitis may have set in.' A small boy
who was permitted to peep at anatomical charts and
ponderous medical books in The Office. Then his
brother going off to medical school—gossip of classes,
of a summer's internship, of surgery versus general
practice. And behind father and brother, a grandfather and uncle who were also doctors.

"With such a background, the work and ideals of
the doctors have always been more familiar to me than
any others, and when I began to write novels (I

started my first one just twenty years ago, and the first that was ever published fourteen years ago) I thought of some day having a doctor hero. Part of that ambition was satisfied in Dr. Kennicot, of *Main Street,* but he was not the chief character, and furthermore I desired to portray a more significant medico than Kennicot—one who could get beneath routine practise into the scientific foundation of medicine— one who should immensely affect all life.

"In the summer of 1922, in Chicago, I was in the office of Dr. Morris Fishbein, of the journal of the American Medical Association. This man Fishbein is a melancholy person for a novelist to meet, because he really knows something—in fact I've never found anything which he did not know. Into the office came a huge young man who might, except for his super-intelligent face, have been a prize-fighter, but was introduced to me as Paul H. de Kruif, Ph. D., formerly assistant professor of bacteriology in the University of Michigan, later a researcher in Rockefeller Institute, and a good bellicose scientific journalist as well.

"The three of us fell to debating. De Kruif and Fishbein hurled ideas about medical education at each other as though they were bricks. We planned to go to dinner together—an early dinner and home at nine—certainly nine, at the latest—lots of work to do.

"At two next morning we were still shouting philosophy.

"All the while I meditated, 'Here's my next novel, now that I've read the proofs on Babbitt.' What protagonist of fiction could be more interesting, more dramatic, and less hackneyed than a doctor who, starting out as a competent general practitioner, emerges as a real scientist, despising ordinary success."

XVI

Then with Kruif he wandered for three months from Barbadoes to Panama to Europe. They saw leper asylums and hospitals and small dispensaries among the Barbadoes canefields. They spent hours in laboratories in Panama, in London, in Paris. And with all their wandering they managed five or six hours of intense work every day, finally rounding out a complete plan for the book in some sixty thousand words.

To produce the actual novel required a year, Lewis working by himself in London and in the country near Fountainebleau.

XVII

And now he is off in Saskatchewan with an official Canadian government party, his brother, a doctor and the official agent.

"It won't be any picnic," he says. "The purpose of the party is to pay off the pensions of the Cree Indians, in right of their land grants and such like, and to give them medical or other help. For me it will be a chance to relax and forget all about writing.

"We won't have any rest houses to reach at the end of the day's march, mind you, where one can get a hot bath and sleep between sheets. We'll pack our own kits and portage our own canoes. We'll pitch camp where night finds us. It's going to be bully."

JOSEPH C. LINCOLN

How many homes are now the brighter, how many hearts have kept those homes and made them bright, all after reading Mr. Lincoln's facile and optimistic tales of Cape Cod, I can not tell you; but I have heard the figures, well up into the tens of thousands, repeated in a hushed awe—for here's the man who has made a business of putting every one's best foot forward, showing that under the weather-beaten tan there's a cheek as soft as a babe's and under the gingham a mother's heart on which to lean.

II

"Cape Cod?" he says.   "Well, I ought to know the folk of Cape Cod.   I was born there,—at Brewster, Mass., February 13, 1870—lived there all my youth, and since leaving I can't remember ever having missed visiting the Cape during the year.   Sometimes I've only gone there for a few days, often for months; but I always go back; I suppose it's the call of the blood.

"My father was a sea captain, so was his father, and his father before him, and all my uncles.   My mother's people all followed the sea.   I suppose that if I had been born a few years earlier, I would have had my own ship.   But when it came time for me to earn a living, the steamship was driving the old square rigger out of existence, and the glorious merchant marine that we had built up in the first part of the nineteenth century was fading into tradition.

"So when my mother and I were left alone in the world, since I was to be a business man, it was decided that I had better not waste time going to college. We went to live in Brooklyn and I entered a broker's office. It was not work to my liking, however, for I wanted to draw, and eventually, under the guidance of Henry Sandham, whose familiar signature was 'HY' I went to Boston. There I took an office with another fellow and we started to do commercial work. We were not overwhelmingly successful, and often, to make the picture sell better, I wrote a verse or joke. Sometimes the verse or joke sold without the drawing. Shortly after this, Sterling Elliott, who was editor of the League of American Bulletin, sent for me and offered me a position as staff illustrator. I accepted. That was in the days when every one rode a bicycle, and the journal had a circulation of over a hundred and twenty-five thousand, so my verses and illustrations became known to a fairly large public.

"In the meantime I was back in Brooklyn, married to a Massachusetts girl, and doing considerable verse for various publications. They were mostly poems in dialect (that is, in the vernacular of the Cape), and I had almost unconsciously turned to the Cape for my inspiration. I sensed the fact that there is a subtle humor in the men and women of my own stock. Then, too, they were unusual characters, and the homes that made a background to their lives were picturesque to a superlative degree.

"It was at about this time that I wrote my first short story. I went again to the Cape for my inspiration, drawing the type of man I know best for my central character, and the story sold to the *Saturday Evening Post*.

"And I have been writing fiction ever since. In 1904 my first novel, *Cap'n Eri*, was published. Other novels have followed with fairly annual regularity. They have all centered about Cape Cod and its people, for having thoroughly mastered the psychology of a type of American that was known, appreciated, though through an economic law, fast becoming extinct, it seems best to keep on picturing these people. I have, of course, taken them away from the Cape, setting their individuality in various phases of life.

"The type of sea captain who figures in my stories has not necessarily an accurately corresponding type in my acquaintance. Going back to the Cape after having lived in New York and Boston, I was able to get varying angles on the lives of men and women I had known in my childhood. The old sea captains that I remembered best as a child were of more than one character classified according to their work. One was the dignified old man who had traveled to some faraway corner of the earth and returned prosperous, to spend the rest of his days as an autocrat among his own people. He had met strange peoples, he had been trusted with a ship, and, as in the days I write of there were no instantaneous means of talking across the oceans, he was shrewd at bargaining, and, being one of the owners of the ship, lost no chance to bring home a cargo that would bring rich returns. In other words, he was a shrewd trader as well as a sailing master. The same dignified bearing that he used in his trade followed him on land, and, though jovial in manner, he was developed in dignity and character.

"The other type of captain was more popular with the youngsters. He may have been as shrewd, and possibly made as much money, but he was filled with a greater sense of humor, and took life as a pastime. Men of this description would gather round the stove and tell wonderful stories, though all sea captains talk *shop* when they get together.

"Then too there was what are termed the 'longshore captains.' These are mostly engaged in fishing, or in trading with coast towns and cities. They were necessarily more limited in their views, for they spent more time ashore, often working a good-sized garden, fishing when the spirit moved, and running a schooner to New York or Boston if the chance came. . . .

"The old captain was a picturesque character, and I wrote of him—the man who sailed the seven seas. In drawing the type, I did not choose one man—the various captains that have figured in my books are entirely fictitious—for it seemed to me that it was hard to find one man who could fulfill all the characteristics of one fictional character. My captains are composites of many men, as I felt that it is hardly fair to accurately describe a living man, when writing fiction. . . .

"The same is true with the other characters of my books. My Cape women are generally true to type—big-hearted, motherly women who loved the sea. My other characters, with the exception of the Portuguese, whom I occasionally mention as Cape dwellers, are obviously drawn from the city types one sees in every-day life. . . .

"After having studied the man, it is not difficult to imagine what he would do in certain society.   In *Cap'n Warren's Wards* I took my Cape Codder to the city and showed that his high sense of what was right and wrong, and his saving sense of humor, were as much in evidence in one place as in another.   In other words, a good man is the same everywhere.   And in *Kent Knowles,* I took my hero to England, and the contrast made the story a revelation of the Cape Cod type."

III

Elsewhere Mr. Lincoln has said: "I know there are people who can turn out a short story in two or three hours and it will be good enough to sell, but I cannot but help feeling it would have been much better if the writer had devoted more time to it.   In my case, doing work that is satisfactory to me in any degree, means that I must fairly sweat it out, if I may use the expression."

And again, in an interview for the Boston *Globe*: "A man writes what he knows.   If he tries anything else it must fall—show hollow.   And I find that it is necessary to write to your audience—that one must consider that a large number of his readers are apt to be women, and he must write things that will appeal to the women of to-day."

And of humor: "Perhaps I could write a story with gloomy situations and an unhappy ending, but I wouldn't like to try it.   I would much rather try to make people cheerful at the same time.   There's enough sorrow in this world without finding it in books."

IV

Mr. Lincoln is cheerful, let who will cry out that (even as he pictures it) life is mean and small and confined. This week's *Judge* or *Life* is preferable, he says, as civilizing tonic to *Lear, The Idiot, War and Peace.* Laughter—that's the stuff our dreams should be made on—something ephemeral, nothing gripping or disturbing or glamorous—the quest of Galahad or the love-life of Parnell—and, above all, no solitude, that sly conducer to thought. Get together like good fellows.

V

Mr. Lincoln lives at Hackensack, N. J., and is a member of the Hackensack Golf Club, and the Union League Club. He attends the Unitarian Church, and for fifteen years (maybe) has been a member of its board of trustees. He has been for several years on the Hackensack board of education. He is, so I hear and am ready to believe, an extremely agreeable person, somewhat after the manner of the justice in Shakespeare's Seven Ages, interlarding his talk with quaint saws, instances from the sea, the proverbial wisdom of men who have learned from taking life easy rather than from the solemn books of philosophers and all such as define our limitations and express our hopes. True to his endeavor, Mr. Lincoln keeps all those about him happy and cheerful.

Mr. Lincoln is the author of *Galusha the Magni-*

ficent, as good a book as any of his to read, *Shavings,*
Mary-'Gusta, Extricating Obadiah, Cap'n Erie, Mr.
Pratt's Patient's, Partners of the Tide, Cap'n Dan's
Daughter, Thankful's Inheritance, Kent Knowles,
The Rise of Roscoe Paine, The Woman Haters, The
Postmaster, Cap'n Warren's Wards, The Depot Mas-
ter, Our Village, Mr. Pratt, Keziah Coffin, Cy Whit-
taker's Place, The Old Home House, Cape Cod Bal-
lads, The Portugee, Doctor Nye.

HUGH LOFTING

Palmer Cox is dead, but—such is the irony of an author's life—the tiny creatures of his fancy, inherited from Scottish and German folklore, live on in ever new editions of the Brownie books. Palmer Cox is dead and Kipling bowed down under the weight of the white man's fallen prestige. There remains then only Hugh Lofting among the chance visitants from that never-never country that was the home of Peter Pan and the goal of Barrie.

There remains Hugh Lofting.

In my first uncritical enthusiasm I hailed his four volumes as the best four in all the boiling of books sent me for review. Such pictures, I said; and such captions; and (every once in a while) such superlative nonsense. It was Edward Lear with a dash of Eugene Field—Oliver Herford, married and raising a family —Belloc with no axe to grind. Yet I was not mad enough, even, then, to follow in Hugh Walpole's phrases and say it was *Alice,* the immortal, ever-young, ever-wise *Alice;* but it was good—good of its kind, most good and better than most.

II

And why not as good as *Alice?*

Because, in the first place, few men can write as Lewis Carroll wrote. Take the *Jabberwocky,* and think of Mr. Lofting attempting anything like it. Or like the *Hunting of the Snark.* Or those gravely serious lines that tell of the old man sitting on the gate, the old man who fired the brooks and mumbled to himself.

There is rhythm to Lewis Carrol's prose as there was rhythm to his verse; and purpose to his books as there is style.

And Carrol was more than a story-teller—he was a great critic of life and of literature. His parodies are exact. They touch the dross in Robert Southey and Isaac Watts—who wrote that drivel about "the voice of the sluggard"—they improve with laughter the solemn platitudes of fools.

Lofting writes facilely of impossible adventures. He does not deal, as Carrol did, in exact images. A good half of his fancy has no counterpart in real life. Should he get his characters into some inescapable dilemma he need merely invent their way out. He does not have to abide by any rules or speak in anything but abstractions.

And so his books lack form; and already I am tired of them. They seem shipshod, written on and on simply because their author has a contract with the newspapers. There was only so much of Alice as there is only so much of Falstaff or Hamlet or you or me. There is a limit even to *Doctor Dolittle*, but Hugh Lofting doesn't know it. He believes the Doctor capable of a thousand incarnations. That's the way with enthusiasts and bores—they never know when a subject is exhausted.

III

Perhaps my weariness is a reaction from the too great expectations I felt on first opening Mr. Lofting's books.   Mr. Lofting is so clever a draughtsman, so frugal and careful, I was certain that he knew that one line too many can spoil a fine picture.

Besides I am not referring to *The Story of Doctor Dolittle,* his first book, but to its endless sequels.   In the first book he really creates a character in the quaint and placid little medico who, for want of other patients, takes to waiting upon the animals and from his parrot learns their language, going later on a journey to Africa to stem an epidemic that has broken out among the monkeys.

IV

However, I must protest against Hugh Walpole's introduction—"Here is the first real children's classic since Alice"—for here is a very poor second to the *Just So Stories.*   Say what you will (and I'll join you) against his politics, Kipling knows English.   There are no such phrases in Doctor Dolittle as occur in every line of the *Just So Stories.*   Nor are there any adventures to compare with the adventures of Mr. Henry Albert Bivvens, A. B., the mariner with his infinite-resource-and-sagacity.   Or any occasions that can make us forget how the camel got his hump.   Or any such curious souls, O Best Beloved, as the bulgy-nosed elephant's child.

V

But most, of course, with me, it is a matter of plain writing, hard down-right writing, common sense writing, every day writing; and there isn't a chance in the world of Mr. Lofting's ever touching, with simple words and few—

"Unless I go to Rio
These wonders to behold—
Roll down—roll down to Rio—
Roll really down to Rio!
Oh, I'd love to roll to Rio
Some day before I'm old!"

Or, in the exaggerated beauties of a familiar prose—

"Once upon a time, on an uninhabited island on the shores of the Red Sea, there lived a Parsee from whose hat the rays of the sun were reflected in more-than-oriental splendor. . . ."

Mr. Lofting hasn't got it in him, that's all—any more than Doctor Dolittle has in him the hearty resignation of G. K. Chesterton's Noah—"I don't care where the water goes so long as it doesn't get into the wine." If we are looking for that sort of exuberance, just that quality of artistic restraint and humorous aptness, this side the Atlantic, we must look to Don Marquis for it—and in prose to Ring Lardner.

VI

Yet it is after all, I presume, a matter of taste. There are those who refer to Charlie Chaplin as common and those who think they can silence Darwin with votes in the Georgia State assembly. But if there be more children to read *Doctor Dolittle* than read the *Just So Stories,* it simply bears out my contention that children are no wiser than their parents.

VII

Mr. Lofting was born in Maidenhead, England, on the Thames, of Anglo-Irish descent, spending his time entirely at home, telling stories to his brother and sister, until he was eight, when he was sent away to a Jesuit school in Derbyshire. As a boy he had no thoughts of becoming anything but a great explorer, traveling over the world, and as a young man (after a short career as an architect), he traveled through Africa, Canada and the West Indies as a civil engineer. The first story he ever wrote had to do with bridges and culverts—though not published until after he had quit engineering and decided to give all his time to writing.

He began with short stories in the magazines.

Now it is a toss-up as to whether Mr. Lofting is not a better illustrator than author, yet he offered no illustrations for his own romances until, in letters home to his children, during his service overseas in the war, he took to making pictures of Doctor Dolittle—amusing and delightful pictures.

VIII

It was Mrs. Lofting who first saw the possibilities in *Doctor Dolittle*. The Doctor had grown enormously in the letters. He had made a name for himself in the family circle. Why not a name (she asked) among strangers? And so in 1919 when the family came back to America, she persuaded the children to release their beloved manuscripts long enough to allow Mr. Lofting to show them to the Frederic A. Stokes Company. The conclusion was foregone. Mr. Morrow is an expert on children's books. He could have told you even then that the *Voyages of Doctor Dolittle* would win the Newberry Prize as "the most distinguished contribution to American literature for children in 1922."

IX

There are, to date, three Dolittle books: *The Story, The Voyages* and *The Post Office* of the quaint little M. D.,—M. D., as Mr. Lofting has explained, means that he was a proper doctor and knew a whole lot. And there is *The Story of Mrs. Tubbs* who was turned out of her farmhouse at the awkward age of a hundred, with her pig and her duck and her dog. The story tells of how these three—the dog, the pig and the duck—managed to eject the usurping owner and install the good lady again in her chair before the fire.

PETER CLARK MACFARLANE

Death is a poor untidy thing, as Synge's Deidre said—
poor and untidy, though it's a queen that dies. I
have no love for death. And it seems especially insane when it comes, as it came in the case of Peter
Clark Macfarlane, self-wrought, after a deal of boast-
ing about courage and a lifetime devoted to telling the
other fellow how to live. . . .

I confess that I object to being told how to live, to being told anything by such men as Peter Clark Macfarlane. He and his kind are, I think, the scourge of
America—petty messiahs, Y. M. C. A. secretaries, professional patriots, temperance unionists, always correcting some one's English, putting us right about religion
and politics, interfering in a thousand and one small
ways with such will as we have towards power and a
good life.

II

The week before he died, by his own hand in the
shadow of the San Francisco morgue, we discussed together his fitness and adequacy as a preacher; and I
told him then that I thought his message a lot of fol-
derol. I saw him—as I see his friend, Sammy Blythe
—bustling about, enamoured of big words, stumbling
over them, bellowing at the top of his lungs, shouting at
his readers as though he thought them all deaf. I
felt pity for him; and I told him so. He had gotten
himself into a mess. He had been whoring after false

gods, the gods of mammon, of the loud-mouthed and self-important. He thought a man had to be 100% American in order to be a good American—whereas, as a matter of fact, the best Americans are first of all good Europeans and good Chinamen and good Japs. The best possible American would approach to the perfections of Christ—and he was a Jew from Nazareth—and had he remained a Jew from Nazareth he would still have been a better American than Peter Clark Macfarlane—simply because he would have been always a better man—as Hauptman is a better man or Antonio Scotti.

Macfarlane could never see that his good intentions, which were always so obtrusive, served only as paving for Hell—for Hell is paved with good intentions and not (as America needs to learn) with bad ones.

III

The good things of life are the simple things—the sound of the sea washing along the beach, the chatter of children at play, the quiet of night and the warmth of the sun. All these were the heritage of Peter Clark Macfarlane; but he chose to exchange them for a big name in the magazines, for a fame he could not possibly deserve, for applause. He was ordinary and he wanted to seem a fine fellow, ranting on the platform as a Chautauqua lecturer, dressed out in the tawdry finery of a stock actor.

But always he was conscious of his own inferiority. He was inferior, third or fourth rate and he knew it. And so he despaired. Had he been content to serve humbly, in some lowly position, he might never have

been aware of his own shortcomings, he might never
have felt himself unequal to the tasks before him.
But no, he must associate with the great—or those he
thought great; and contending with them he despaired
—and blew out his brains.

IV

As his reason for quitting he gave the diabetes from
which he suffered—but my grandfather suffered from
diabetes for twenty-five years and he was no mountain
of courage. He simply went without sugar and tomatoes and what not—and died of pneumonia,
aged 76.

V

When Macfarlane came back from the war where
he had been representing the *Saturday Evening Post* at
Queenstown in Ireland, covering the American de-
stroyer fleet, he announced that there was something
different about American courage, that it was a greater
courage than any other kind of courage. Of course,
he didn't know what he meant by American courage or
why it was greater than Carpentier's; it might be the
courage of Benny Leonard or the courage of some
Italian mother in the slums of New York, a courage
inherited from a German father or a Cardiff tinsmith
—he just knew that it was greater because he was an
American. But if we are going to build our faiths on
any such shaky foundations we are bound to end up
gibbering with fear the first time we encounter reality.
There may be, as one of his friends said to Marlow,
hope while there is life; but as Marlow said, there is

also fear. And we must come, sooner or later, to recognize that courage is an essential, that it is a commonplace, the only thing in life that really matters—and that the poor and miserable have it, the Zulu and and the Senegalese—and only bounders boast because they think they are courageous.

VI

With his extravagant notions about living, Macfarlane could never be satisfied with ordinary men and women and virtues; he must reduce them always to the absurd and ill fitting proportions of the go-getter, the grotesque measurements of the giants of modern industry, the fatuous estate of the paragons of the movies.

He asked more of life than he had any right to expect, and more of his fellows—they could not possibly measure up to his preconceived ideas. And so he was perpetually disappointed in them and in living.

Then he snuffed out the candle.

VII

His end was typical, one of his friends on the San Francisco *Examiner* said. By that, I presume, he meant "not unexpected."

I am not sure that I could have foretold it, for even knowing the emptiness of his philosophy as I did I thought him a better man than he turned out to be.

PERCY MARKS

Mr. Marks, an instructor in English recently fired
from Brown University, is the only man on my lists at
present represented by a best seller. And this is odd,
as Lewis Carroll would say, not only because *The
Plastic Age* is a first novel but because it was turned
down by Alfred Harcourt and Mr. Harcourt has,
among publishers, a reputation for infallibility. If he
says a book won't sell it won't sell; he never pulls a
boner. Or so the legend runs. But evidently the
public does not believe in legends.

II

Mr. Marks was fired from Brown, but not, I am
told, for any of the many reflections upon college
honor contained in his book. He was fired because he
could not see eye to eye with the average college trustee—for which we, his readers, may well be grateful.
His ideas are his own. Roughly speaking, he is a
free-thinker—by that I mean he thinks freely and not
by rule of rote. He can think of almost anything and
of one thing about as quick as of another. Most of
his thinking is destructive. It clears away foregone
conclusions. And, though *The Plastic Age* is to date
our only proof, it is safe to say that he will go far with
his thinking. He may become a sort of Samuel Butler.
He has a quick wit and a lively style; often sweeping

in his generalizations, he is nonetheless observant and a patient worker.

Percy, in the ordinary sense, as a handle does not suit him at all. Percy has been joked about. It is a name by which a rose might well smell sweet. And Mr. Marks is thin, a little stooped, well-dressed in a casual sort of way, with a whiff of tobacco about him. He is the popular prof., the sort the students like, the kind that hates to be called Professor—a pleasant sort, alert and not too oddly scholastic. He is the Jim Henley of Sanford. A guide to English literature, not a dictator. He wants his class to feel at ease with him. There is no necessity laid on them to like George Eliot or dislike Kipling and W. W. Jacobs. They are free to pick and choose. He is not the sort the ordinary trustee would elect as an instructor.

III

The Plastic Age is all about college and college students. It tells of Hugh Carver's four years, from matriculation to graduation, at Sanford. It begins as he hurries up the hill from the station to his dormitory, his two suitcases banging at his knees. It takes him through the hazing and maladjustment of his freshman year, his memories of the last walk with Helen Simpson, her kiss and his roommate's gallery of girls. It tells of chapel and the smut sessions, of booze parties and dancing, of petting and football and track. Young Carver is a runner. And a tenor on the Glee Club. And, as the son of an alumnus, the member of one of the leading fraternities. Good looking and popular.

IV

But if you have pictured the stude as a callow innocent believing all his father has told him and seeking enlightenment concerning the things of the spirit, *The Plastic Age* will give you a jolt.   Our young ideas (if we trust Mr. Marks) are mostly interested in sex. They are Freudians with a vengeance.   It is women, women, women.   Bags, as they call them.   Tarts. And liquor.   And the house parties staged at fraternity houses quite often go the limit, with boys and girls together in bed, while the chaperons are carefully herded in the library.

I am not in a position to say how much of this is true.   It is my impression that *The Plastic Age* is deliberately scandalous.   It was written in part to shock us out of our ignorance.   Youth has problems. Youth is told one thing and going out into the world finds that thing a very small part of the truth—if true at all.   Youth is restless.   And disillusioned.   And Mr. Marks is sympathetic.   He tells us the worst; but he tries to make us see that the worst is the best possible under the circumstances.   Youth needs teachers; and youth is not getting them—at any rate, youth is not getting the right sort.

V

The Plastic Age over-emphasizes youth's interest in sex, but it is well written and unafraid; and in Cynthia it introduces us to a flapper who even though she fails to win Carver's undivided attention is a real person and extremely attractive.

EDGAR LEE MASTERS

Mr. Masters marks an epoch. He marks it not because he came first or foremost, but because he lives in Chicago and all his friends, the frenzied literati of the West, when they went to writing novels took their cue from him. They reviled the village and called it a sink hole, *Main Street* and what not, after the manner of *Spoon River*—which was in the manner of Ed Howe's *Story of a Country Town* and Mark Twain's *The Man Who Corrupted Hadleyburg.* This is not to take any credit from Mr. Masters, but merely to point out that he was in the right tradition. Bucolic innocence is the fat and stupid innocence of the dairy wench who giggles when a kiss is mentioned, who is without that shrewdness and courage that makes the city girl so fine and interesting. Time out of mind, for Menander and Shakespeare and Villon and Chaucer, the country virtues have been a butt for jests.

II

Spoon River needed doing—as now we need a rattling fine yarn to prove the cowboy no better than he ought to be, shying at street cars and gaping open-mouthed at the progress, in thought and invention, made by the rest of us any time this past five hundred years. *Spoon River* was a brave book—though it may have been the scandal, and not the poetry and irony and truth of its matter, that spread its frame.

III

Mr. Masters was born in Garnett, Kansas, August 23, 1868; his father a law partner of Herndon who had been a partner of Lincoln. He spent a typical Middle West boyhood in that "Lincoln country" where Mitch Miller also lived. The legend of Lincoln and the gossip of an every day country neighborhood moulded his youth.

"My grandfather and grandmother," he says, "came from Tennessee and eventually settled, in 1847, on a large farm five and a half miles north of Pottersburg. My grandfather was well acquainted with Lincoln and employed him in some legal business which he once had. This country, though very friendly to Lincoln as a man, did not sympathize with the war. The population was too much made up of Kentuckians and Tennesseeians, who had grown up amidst the institution of slavery and who had definite ideas as to the powers of the States in this and other matters. And one of the results of the war was to fill up these various towns in Central Illinois with various colorful and reckless characters, who had come up from the South, sometimes to escape the war and on errands of adventure and otherwise. In writing the story of Mitch Miller I have used the real names of towns, for example; Petersburg, Havana, Springfield, Bobtown, Oakford, Atterbery, etc., and in a few instances I have used the names of real persons; and I have also drawn upon the knowledge that I have of this part of Illinois and its people as they were when I lived there as a boy. My attempt has been to portray these people, the country and the events used in utmost fidelity and to put into them the feelings of a boy, the knowledge and understanding of a boy, perhaps somewhat emphasized, but through the method of quotation from older people who spoke in the presence of these boys and whose words impressed them."

His reading, he tells us, included "a certain wonderful edition of Grimm's Fairy Tales in a blue binding:" an anthology of poetry edited by Bryant, which led him to Burns, one of his early idols, and later to Poe, first the poems and later the stories. These in turn were followed by metaphysics—Hamilton and Locke —browsing around in libraries, and (after he settled down to reading law) into bypaths of literature, Don Quixote and Calderon, and where not.

IV

Mr. Masters graduated from Knox College at Galesburg, studied law in his father's office, was admitted to the bar in 1891, and married the daughter of Robert E. Jenkins of Chicago in 1896.

V

His first literary essays were lyrics in the conventional Shelleyan poetic manner. Finally, William Marion Reedy, after listening to some of Masters' pungent stories of the people he knew, protested sharply— "Write about what you see and know." It proved the right advice. *Spoon River's* dead were resurrected and published, first in Reedy's *Mirror* and later in book form.

Later he gratified a long-cherished desire to write

a novel, encouraged by a luncheon conversation with the sister of Theodore Roosevelt.   They discussed the immortal fascination of Tom Sawyer and Huck Finn; and Mr. Masters outlined the possibilities of a hero-worship such as that of Mitch and Skeeters Kerby. The idea grew into *Mitch Miller*—as good a boys' story as most.

VI

Mr. Masters is described by one interviewer as "ever so much like Thackeray, with his round face and halo of hair."   He is, however, quite unlike him in his philosophy—quite modern and very detached.

GEORGE BARR McCUTCHEON

The least pretentious of authors, the least auctorial—
those are superlatives and possibly superfluous, but
they apply to Mr. McCutcheon. There is no pose of
the editorial We about him. He does not try to
change your notions of art and literature. He is not
free with glib descriptions of life and the pageantry of
life, its color and movement and wonder. He writes
because he likes writing and because he has found a
market for his stuff. He writes because he needs the
money, because he is incredibly lazy and knows of no
easier way to a good fat living.

I repeat that he is unpretentious, and add that he
is kindly and good, a very decent sort. I might even
add that he likes writing because he likes writers. All
his best friends are writers; and they are good fellows,
great fun, excellent company. They make a full life
for him. He feels that he has chosen well in choosing
them; and he is happy. Not that he is self-satisfied.
He is as humble as they make them. His very real
success is still a surprise and always a surprise whenever his books get into the best seller class. Yet in
reality there is nothing surprising in his success. His
are honest books. He puts into them the very best of
which he is capable. They body forth the fondest of
his dreams, the most beautiful, the most ingenious and
interesting. They interest him; and so, of course,
they interest the thousands who are like him, in fancy
and in fact—the men and women who believe this a

good world, who like suburban architecture, and think Americans top-hole—the millions who insist that any attractive young flapper is certain, soon or late, to meet up with Prince Charming.

II

Mr. McCutcheon was born on a farm near Lafayette, in Tippecanoe County, Indiana, July 26, 1866. His father was a cattle buyer, of Scotch descent, born in Kentucky of parents who had emigrated from Virginia.   His mother, though born in Ohio and raised on a farm in Indiana, was Pennsylvania Dutch.

Certain of Mr. McCutcheon's earliest memories center about the cows and sheep and hogs, bought up in the country round about and waiting shipment in his father's fields.   But, at about ten, he moved, with his family, to Lafayette, a city of thirty thousand, older than Chicago and more romantic; and so his contact with the country ended.   He became a small town boy, in all things thoroughly American.   In Lafayette his father went into the banking and brokerage business, became sheriff, served four years, and died as county treasurer—a Democrat in a three-to one Republican district, and yet (for all that) sure of election whenever he stood for office.   He was a McCutcheon; and they are a family used to success.   Mr. McCutcheon's sister, Mrs. Raleigh, a few years ago began to make Good Fairy statuettes, just a few at a time, selling them where and as she could—now she is the successful head of a huge factory, manufacturing the Raleigh dolls.   One brother, Ben, is a well-known advertising man in Chicago—during the war in charge of publicity for the various Liberty loan drives. Another, John T. McCutcheon, is famous as a war correspondent, as a lion-hunter, an island owner and wit, and (of course) as the most notable of newspaper cartoonists.

III

Mr. McCutcheon was educated at Purdue University.

In the summer of 1882, between his freshman and sophomore years, he joined up with C. P. Hormig's Comedy Company, playing juvenile leads under the name of George M. Clifford. He had been stage-struck from his earliest youth. As a boy he had written plays more awful than the ranting melodramas of which the drunken Pistol made such mock, in Dame Quickly's taproom, when he bade his sword feed and grow fat. These plays young McCutcheon produced in the backyard, with certain of his accomplices as foils for his humor. His bent was toward the theater. Naturally, the chance offering, in his vacation, he made off at the first opportunity to try his hand at make-up and gesturing. But his hopes of a career in the theater were soon blasted. The life of a trouper was anything but what he had in his ambition, expected. And after a summer of tent-storming—for they played under canvas—he was forced to beat his way home, with no money, on foot.

His disillusion with the stage was completed when *Graustark* was dramatized and produced in New York. That was an experience even more terrible than acting had been, for he was the helpless author—than whom there is none on Broadway more helpless. He can tell you many stories of the theater, few of them leading you to believe that the managers are such Argus-eyed genii as their press agents insist.

IV

Graustark, (the title a happy accident), was written between December and March 1898–9, while Mr. McCutcheon was still city editor of the Lafayette *Courier,* a respectable family newspaper in his home town.

Graustark was written because Mr. McCutcheon was already tired of newspaper work and wanted to try his hand at something else. And *Graustark* was sold for $500.

Such are the bargains made by the novice. *Graustark* is the best known of Mr. McCutcheon's books; and the $500 might well have proved a tragedy to Mr. McCutcheon; as a matter of fact, it was an incentive to more and better work. He felt that if he could sell *Graustark* he could sell others—as he could write others, having written *Graustark.* The $500 was all that was needed to give him confidence in his own abilities.

V

Graustark is as full of impossibilities as a fairy-tale and as full of good reading. Swords are carried easily and gracefully; swords are drawn and crossed; step by step the villain is backed to the wall. There is intrigue in the court and loyalty among the guardsman. Beauty is often in distress and as often rescued.

Graustark, in fine, was enough to make the reputation of any young novelist. It made a reputation for Mr. McCutcheon.

Yet Mr. McCutcheon's own favorite among his books is *The Sherrods,* which deals with Indiana farmer folk. Mr. McCutcheon has always liked farmers. He likes rustics. He likes quaint characters, the homely things in life, the humor and patience of the poor. At heart he is a cockney. . . .

I remember how surprised he was when I told him that Harry Leon Wilson was much given to making little of Dickens, calling Dickens a mere caricaturist— as though caricature could not be great art, and even better criticism. Mr. McCutcheon could not understand how any one could feel anything but affection for Dickens, gratitude to him for having discovered so much individuality among so many lowly creatures, such wealth of good nature, such abundance of high spirits.

VI

The Day of the Dog had its beginning in a dream which Mr. McCutcheon recounted to his brother, John, urging the brother to write the story. But the brother's answer, as is the way with the answers of brothers, was simply: Do it yourself. So Mr. McCutcheon was forced to cudgel his brain—for the dream had ended with the young lovers trapped in the barn by a ferocious bull-dog. To free the lovers, marry them in some semblance of leisure, and all the rest of it, took a bit of doing. However, it was at last done when, by good fortune, Mr. McCutcheon thought of the waistcoat, the box stall and a bull-dog's well-known tenacity.

VII

Then came *Brewster's Millions.*

Mr. McCutcheon, no longer a newspaper man, was riding one day in Chicago, on a street car, with his brother Ben when they passed a long row of billboards advertising some brand of ham or soap or cheese. "They're spending millions on that campaign," Ben said.   And they fell to talking of the various ways in which large corporations spend their money.

"Supposing," Mr. McCutcheon said "you had a million, where would you spend it?   And how? Without dissipation and without investing any part of it, how could a fellow go about spending that much money?   And if you could spend it, how long would it take you?   Could you do it in a year?"

There you have the plot of *Brewster's Millions.* But the story was not an easy one to write.   It taxed to the limit Mr. McCutcheon's ingenuity.   To be rid of every last cent of a million in a year, to use it up, to get a million dollar's worth of fun out of it, to live like a millionaire—only Brewster could have done it, inspired as he was by the prodigal imagination of Mr. McCutcheon.

When the book was written it was turned over to Stone in Chicago and brought out by him over the name of Richard Greaves.   There was a reason for this.   Dodd, Mead and Company were to publish another of Mr. McCutcheon's books that same year, and Mr. McCutcheon felt that it would injure his sales if the public knew that he was writing so facilely and so fast. Besides he did not feel that his name as author had any value. People do not remember the author's name, he said. Nobody cares about the author—the book's the thing. He was so sure of this that he wagered a hundred dollars with Mr. Stone that Greaves was as salable a name as McCutcheon. And he won the bet. *Brewster's Millions* outsold any of his other books.

VIII

Then came *Beverly of Graustark, Nedra, The Purple Parasol, Cowardice Court;* books that lent themselves to the illustrations of Harrison Fisher; books about beautiful girls and men and little else.

And *The Rose and the Ring* which expresses Mr. McCutcheon's high regard for circuses and circus people. He had spent a season traveling with Wallace's Circus, as a guest of the manager. The book is his bread and butter letter, an honest and friendly book.

And *The Hollow of Her Hand* which tells of a young girl who, in defense of her honor, kills her would-be seducer and leaves him at the road house to which he had enticed her, wandering out into the night, to be picked up by his wife, taken to her home, and, in vengeance on the man who wronged them both, to be protected by her, etc. A readable book.

And *Mr. Bingle,* who is the child of Mr. McCutcheon's liking for Dickens. *Mr. Bingle* who is out of Dickens, an elderly bank clerk come suddenly into a huge fortune through an irascible old millionaire for whose sake Mr. Bingle played the good Samaritan.

Mr. Bingle who adopts a dozen children and then loses his money, loses his children, but nevertheless ends happily—as Mr. McCutcheon knows is only right.

IX

Mr. McCutcheon is primarily a story-teller, influenced by the great Victorians, and not at all concerned about the other fellow's complexes. A collector of first editions, on his walls you will find an occasional Corot, Ranger and Brangwyn.

WILLIAM McFEE

It may seem incredible—to all who have not suffered in like fashion—but for years McFee's *Casuals* knocked about, from one publisher to another, to be finally published only because Chris Morley refused to let up on Frank Doubleday. At every meeting of the editorial board Morley would get up to begin his little speech. . . . "Now . . . about McFee. . . ." It became an office joke—and jokes are long-lived. When Morley's son was born, that joke popped up: "Congratulations—name him Casuals."

II

McFee has said that he cannot resist a story that begins in the first chapter with a birth. To him *David Copperfield* is the book of a lifetime. On page 1 you will read, "I am born." What more majestic beginning could there be? It is, as McFee has said, a start. One may be starting for the White House or the penitentiary, for Eldorado or the grave—no matter, there is nothing like a start. Later we may grow pessimistic, but at birth all things are probable. A fellow with wit enough to be born is a fellow of infinite possibilities.

III

I shall not longer delay the announcement of McFee's birth. He was born, without mishap, about the time *Copperfield,* a fat and fascinating volume, first is-

sued from the press.   His father, an English sea captain and the son of an English sea captain, had married
a Canadian; and together they voyaged, trading about
the seven seas, in a three-masted square-rigger, *Erin's
Isle*, designed, built and owned by the skipper.   Their
son was born, in 1881, on a voyage homeward-bound
from India.   The family then settled in New South-
gate, a suburb in the North of London.   McFee was
educated in various local schools and finally at Bury
St. Edmunds in Suffolk.   From 1897 to 1900 he was
with McMuirland's Engineering shops at Aldersgate.
His father paid McMuirland's a hundred pounds a
year and McMuirland's in return made an engineer of
young McFee—and, I hear, a damned good engineer.
He holds his Extra Chief's Certificate from the London Board of Trade and a Chief's License in the
United States.   He is probably the best known ship's
engineer in the world to-day—certainly the best known
in England and America.

From McMuirland's he went on a water works job
at Tring, thence back to London and the office of a firm
of Yorkshire engineers.   During these days he was
deep in socialism and Kipling.   He even lectured on
Kipling and wrote Kipling verse.   His evenings he
spent at the Northampton Institute, his Saturday
afternoons in the reading room of the British Museum,
with an occasional cricket match in between.   About
this time he met Arthur Elder; and Elder induced him
to leave his home and move to Chelsea.   But McFee
was twenty-four, and the sea was calling—there was
small chance of his settling in Chelsea,—though Chelsea days are recalled in his latest novel, *Race*.

McFee could see little enough ahead in the engineering works where he was employed. He wanted to be off, adventuring. So he resigned his position and took a berth as junior engineer on one of his uncle's ships, the *Rotherfield*, and sailed for Genoa. With but brief interludes ashore—the longest at Nutley, N. J., with Arthur Elder in 1912—he has been at sea ever since.

IV

I first heard of McFee in 1916 when I came, by what good chance I now forget, upon *Casuals of the Sea*. *Casuals* was the third of McFee's books—*Letters from an Ocean Tramp* having been published in England in 1908, and *Aliens* in 1914—but it was *Casuals* that made the necessary stir. Wilson Follett proclaimed McFee an "artist, if not before everything, then in everything." Mr. Mencken suddenly discovered that "England has discovered suddenly that she is heir to another young man who shows the stuff of which genius is made." But it was Huneker who got the most out of the opportunity *Casuals* presented, to a reviewer. "It reeks with actuality," he said, "for the author's sincerity is a form of his talent. . . . He insists on telling his tale in his own fashion. . . . It is my notion that Flaubert is his major god. . . . He reminds one at times of Dickens, especially in his humorous passages. . . . He has the gift of projecting upon paper vivid images that instantly evoke a character, a place, a situation. . . . His book is suffused with pity. He loves humanity. . . . Best of all, he has genuine power."

V

McFee has, in part, in the preface to *Aliens,* explained his literary credo:

"Of art I never grow weary, but she calls me over the world. I suspect the sedentary art worker. Most of all I suspect the sedentary writer. I divide authors into two classes—genuine artists, and educated men who wish to earn enough to let them live like country gentlemen. With the latter I have no concern. But the artist knows when his time has come. In the same way I turn with irresistible longing to the sea, whereon I have been wont to earn my living. It is a good life and I love it. I love the men and their ships. I find in them a never-ending panorama which illustrates my theme, the problem of human folly."

VI

The problem of human folly! It is a theme that might well engage a benevolent marble-heart, as McFee terms himself. There is no end to it. In old Chaldea men talked, gathered about some sacred stone, in temple yards, of human folly. They talked of it in Romany—and to-day in London, Paris and Vermont. It is a theme for Vesey Street and one for the *Kunstlerkneipe* of Munich and *Alt Wien*. Countless thousands have mourned, thousands have smiled, while contemplating with amazement and chagrin the folly of our kind. It is the gist of Voltaire's demonic essays, the moral of Cervantes and Rabelais, a footnote to La Rochefoucauld, the turning point of that most lamentable comedy enacted before the lords and ladies

of Athens by Bottom and his amateurs. It is all any
one needs in making a novel or a parody. And
McFee has done well by it—if for no other reason,
then because he loves humanity. As Huneker has
said, his books are suffused with pity.

VII

Nonetheless I am yet to be convinced that McFee
has done anything better than *Casuals*—though that is
scarcely the point. The truth about McFee is that he
has done nothing cheap, nothing hurried, nothing
merely for the sake of getting it done. His least ambitious note—a letter to his publishers, a short review
—is stamped inevitably with his high regard for the
writer's calling. He is careful always of the rhythm of
his prose. Always his writing has that charm and flavor that only generosity, a rare tolerance and a fine
tradition can give it. It is McFee's, whether it be
Casuals, that Odyssey of a middle-class boy and Helen
his sister with her world of scarlet, or *Race,* a quiet
and kindly remembering of the people with whom
McFee grew up and worked in London twenty years
ago.

VIII

The sea is in all his books, for the most part a tropic
sea, the Caribbean, or the blue Mediterranean, with
Vesuvius on one side and Egypt on the other, a sea
across which men have trafficked from the very beginnings of history. It is now a sea of Greek merchants
and P & O boats bound through the Suez for India and
Japan. It has been a sea of submarines and Gallipoli,

It was the sea of *Captain Macedoine's Daughter* and *Command.*

IX

In *Captain Macedoine's Daughter* McFee tried to build up such an air of intimacy and wonder as is conveyed, in Conrad, when Marlow talks; but it does not quite come off. As I recall the book, after three or four years, it is all about a junior officer talking, a trifle monotonously, and an island—Crete, perhaps—and the schemes of Captain Macedoine, schemes to make us rich—and little else. I do not remember the daughter at all, except as some sort of governess.

X

But *Command* is vivid. There is the unforgettable Dainopolous in his counting room; there is the silly and fatuous captain, his boat gone from under him, sunk by a submarine, and his correspondence memory courses; and the cat-like Evanthia, the adventurous and provocative, with her young *Herr Leutnant* to pursue, and the Britisher to deceive—and use. A book that stays with you, no matter how impossible its heroisms. It has green waters and white houses with shady gardens, banked about a harbor that is a haven, safe from the ravages of war; and on the evening air there comes a song, a careless song, boyish and impudent, and talk of fidelity and love, whispers from a balcony and dope smuggled aboard ships.

XI

There is a sentence in *Aliens* that I like, a sentence referring to a type that peculiarly fascinates McFee,

the dashing (not too scrupulous) promoter of stock
companies and oil wells— "Ask me how he did it and
all I can say is 'Personality.' He could do anything
with anybody—but the serious business of his life
was girls."

XII

For some years, on and off, Mr. McFee has been in
the employ of the United Fruit Company as ship's engineer. Before the war he was with S. S. *Cartago*.
But in October 1914 he returned to England to enlist
—and to be refused by the army.

(His younger brother who fought with the Cana-
dians was killed in the last two weeks of fighting after
having been overseas for three years.)

McFee himself became an engineer officer in the
transport service and served most of his time on the
Mediterranean. And there he rewrote *Aliens*. "Up
and down the Ægean, past fields of mines and fields of
asphodel, past many an isle familiar in happier days to
me, I took my book and my new convictions about human folly. It was a slow business—but *Aliens* grew."

When the war ended, McFee returned to the United
States. And in 1920 he married Miss Pauline Khon-
doff whom he had met in Budapest while on leave three
years before. She came halfway across the world to
join him.

XIII

Somewhere in *Casuals* McFee has said that "the
world belongs to the enthusiast who keeps cool." And
there is another sentence in *Casuals* that will bear re-

peating; "She considered trouble was a trouble and to be treated as such, instead of snatching the knotted cord from the hands of God and dealing murderous blows."

Mr. McFee is the author of *Letters from an Ocean Tramp*, 1908; *Aliens*, 1914, revised edition, 1918; *Casuals of the Sea*, 1916; *Captain Macedoine's Daughter*, 1920; *Harbours of Memory*, 1921; *An Engineer's Notebook*, 1921; *Command*, 1922; *Race*, 1924.

HAROLD McGRATH

Mr. McGrath was born in Syracuse, N. Y., on September 4, 1871. He was educated there; he still lives there; and there in 1890, as Skinny McGrath, he took up with journalism. Nine years later he published his first book, *Arms and the Woman*. The title has since been used by others; it is apparently a good title; but the book was only moderately successful. However, it was not long—two years, to be exact—before Mr. McGrath, following the lead of Anthony Hope Hawkins, moved into that imaginary central Europe— which lies somewhere east of Dresden, west of Warsaw and north of the Balkans, to achieve financial independence with *The Puppet Crown, The Grey Cloak* and *The Princess Elopes*. Though these stories are not now so well known as is the *Prisoner of Zenda,* they compare favorably with the most of those that have been written since that memorable romance of subterfuge and light adventure. They are light hearted. They have action in plenty. They are told with a rush, with spirit and humor. There is an air of innocence about them that is, even now, disarming of criticism. Mr. Arthur B. Maurice, the learned book reviewer, places them in the front rank of the thousands of stories that, every year, are being written about mythical kings and princesses, sleeping beauties waiting only to be rescued by handsome and dashing young Americans.

And Mr. McGrath has this virtue—he has never

tried to read and propound the riddle of existence in half-baked aphorisms and second-hand fables. He does not pretend to know what is the cause of our modern unrest or whether that unrest be especially modern and not a heritage from the ancient Egyptians. He has not been free with advice to the flapper. These may seem negative values but they are valuable for all that.

And he has ingenuity, a gift for fabricating yarns, an almost inexhaustible energy. He devised the *Perils of Pauline* for the movies; *The Goose Girl, The Carpet of Bagdad* and *The Voice in the Fog*. One of his novels, *The Man on the Box,* in dramatic form, has lasted a decade on the stage.

SAMUEL MERWIN

"Life, as I see it," says Mr. Merwin, "is largely what, in fiction, by parrotty little critics, would be classed as melodrama."

That is an awkward sentence, involved and angular, but it conveys Mr. Merwin's meaning—life is what the newspapers say it is. Life is politics and finance and baseball, war and privation, hatred and jealousy; life is the never-varying surprise of marriage, divorce and murder—life may be blatant and ugly in its make-up, but it deserves an occasional banner spread; it is a stuff for headlines.

Perhaps. I am no authority. Yet, to me, it seems, life can be beautiful. There is life to the moon as it peeps through the trees scattering silver and gold on the lawn, life to the love songs of William Butler Yeats, life to Schnitzler's Anatol. I believe that Thoreau was alive; I know that Sir Horace Plunkett is. Life is not all shrill and deafening. Indeed I should hesitate to describe life as largely anything. It seems, at times, so vast and various; at times drab, but more often just uneventful.

To Mr. Merwin life may seem melodramatic; to Sir Horace Walpole it was a comedy; and (as Sir Horace said) for those who feel it is, all too often, a tragedy.

II

"I saw Walter Hampden play *Hamlet* last week," Mr. Merwin once said, "and was struck again by the

377

fact that *Hamlet* is melodrama seen through a mind."

Well, and what if Hamlet is melodrama? Not even the parrotty little critics so despised of Mr. Merwin (and others) claim for *Hamlet* that it is anything but a play. Hamlet is moving, witty, full of action and color—but is it life? Is life a series of sword thrusts? Is marriage with your brother's wife incest, in life? Do ghosts walk abroad and complain of the fiery furnace where, for want of a priest as they lay dying, they now must expiate the sins of their youth and middle-age?

III

"Henry James knew that life is melodrama. Balzac knew it and de Maupassant and the exuberant but pretty real Dickens."

So Mr. Merwin tries to prove his point. Yet, (though I can forgive him much for his affection for Dickens), I cannot pardon such an outrageous begging of any question. The things that Balzac knew and de Maupassant, Dickens and Henry James, have now, most of them, gone by the board. Had Mr. Merwin said Voltaire I might have listened to him, but as well quote Victor Hugo or Walter Scott, confessed romantics, as Balzac and Henry James, de Maupassant and Dickens. Balzac is all surface detail and Henry James all innuendo; Dickens was real but not profound; de Maupassant—well, de Maupassant was first rate and had reason enough, I presume, for his pessimism. However, de Maupassant never claimed all life for his province. He knew that there was room enough and to spare for the wit and good humor of

Molière, the laughter of Cervantes and the folly of Polichinelle.

IV

But Mr. Merwin is serious. He honestly believes that to be interesting life must be violent. The war, he says, has taught us that life is immensely nearer the primitive than we had dared to think these last few years. Whose life, may I ask? Not the dear queen's, surely.

V

However, Mr. Merwin is not in himself melodramatic. He is round and fat and jolly, the perfect type of genial tradesman, just such a person as the family grocer ought to be, Babbitt in the flesh. You see him by his thousands, of an evening, in his shirt-sleeves, puttering about the lawns of Suburbia. There is nothing threatening or unexpected, nothing of the swashbuckler about him. Behind his horn-rimmed glasses are the mildest eyes; and behind those eyes—well, if his books be a fair sample, behind the eyes are the visions of opium-runners in China, of prize fighters on the boulevards, dancing-girls and stage-struck Johnnies, dreamers and ne'er-do-wells and masters of finance, the whole mad world of the popular imagination.

VI

To say that appearances are deceiving is to say the truth, I doubt not, in half a dozen cases out of ten. Most of us are better than we seem, to some, to be; the average is way above what passes for the average in mankind with statisticians. But to say flatly that you cannot judge a book by its cover is to confess yourself ignorant of books, their covers and contents. All about us able men engage themselves to publishers and make the covers to fit the contents of a book—a passionate linen for Elinor Glyn, delicate grays for Miss Millay, the colors of the rainbow for Rupert Hughes, plushes for Tennyson, the exotic in boards for almost any one of Mr. Knopf's excitable group of earnest stylists.

So, too, with life. If Mr. Merwin looks like Babbitt, be not deceived—the chances are that he is Babbitt. Listen:—

"I wish it were possible to express in a letter something of one's serious philosophy. But of course, it isn't. . . . The life I see about me is bewildering. The only philosophy of life—of personal life, that is —that I have could perhaps be best expressed in this way: that I hope to keep in the rush along what I always think of as a sense of direction. Nothing is fixed to me, nothing settled. In writing I must confess to a love of surface color and contrast. Thus, in *The Charmed Life of Miss Austin,* which was frankly light enough in the subject matter, I loved describing Shanghai at night, and the details of the costume of the Chinese girl 'behind the screen.' I liked the big, dignified Mandarin who had played third base at Yale, yet remained Chinaman. In these recent books I have been doing about the boy, Henry Calverly, I have loved giving, or trying to give, a picture of the old town of the nineties back in Illinois; and I have loved

the people—all the minor characters of those stories—
including all the ones I didn't like. You will understand that."

Of course, I understand—as Babbitt will understand—this business of loving everybody and everything. The chief thing that distinguishes Babbitt (as
it distinguishes Mr. Merwin) is a want of austerity.
They make few choices. They could not have written
Il Penseroso, they give up too easily. They are undisciplined. They do not share the scholar's love for
solitude, his self-immolation, his dedication to one high
aim. They call their all-embracing philosophies tolerant but as a matter of fact they are merely uncritical.

VII

"I am not, except in spots," Mr. Merwin says, "a
Victorian. To me man is not a fallen angel, but a
rising animal. And I find it inspiring to think how
high he has already risen, and how bright his hopes
are for future growth and development."

There, in brief, you have the best of Mr. Merwin.
He has been able to realize that the theory of
evolution is an inspiring and not a degrading theory.
To believe, as Bryan does, that man was once a perfect
creature in a divinely appointed world and that he has
since sunk to his present low estate through meanness
and ignorance is to libel man and God. But to look
back on the savage and know that we have, some of us,
attained, through an effort of the will, through the
good uses of imagination, to a place beside Sir Thomas
Browne and Lincoln, is to have faith in man and God.

VIII

"I have said," Mr. Merwin says, "(I think in *Anthony the Absolute*) that books are pale things. That, of course, is true. Our accepted fiction—our best fiction—tends to the thin, squeamish, upper-class, over-refined."

Reading such dogma one wonders where Mr. Merwin has been keeping himself. Books are anything but pale. I know that Alexander in his teens set out to conquer the world; I know that at twenty-nine he died and that in the ten years intervening he had made himself a world conqueror. How do I know it? I know that Aucassin met with his love in the garden of Beaucaire; I know that Guenevere gave herself to Lancelot, that Paola suffered all the pains of hell, that Odysseus came home to find only a dog ready to make him welcome and all this knowledge (which is very real to me) I owe to books. Books are, as Milton said, the life's blood of master spirits treasured up to a life beyond life and our best books—our best fiction—are anything but thin. Our best fiction happens to be Dreiser; and Dreiser can tear the heart out of you.

IX

Mr. Merwin was born in a frame house on Orrington Avenue in Evanston, Illinois, October 6, 1874; grew up in other houses; went to school, (still in Evanston); and graduated from Northwestern University. In his twenties he decided to make writing his profession and (with Henry Kitchell Webster) he set to work on a series of operas, grand and comic, books of nonsense verse, plays, etc.; and finally, in 1899, still in collaboration with Mr. Webster, produced and published *The Short Line War*, all about the lurid piratical railway days of Jim Fiske, J. Gould, et al. Later he was associate editor of *Success Magazine*, 1905–9, and editor, 1909–11. In 1907 he spent six months in China studying the opium trade as a special investigator for *Success;* writing in 1909 his story, *Drugging A Nation*.

Mr. Merwin is the author of *The Short Line War*, 1899; *Calumet K*, 1901; *The Road to Frontenac*, 1901; *The Whip Hand*, 1903; *His Little World*, 1903; *The Merry Anne*, 1904; *The Road Builders*, 1905; *Comrade John*, (with Mr. Webster), 1907; *Drugging A Nation*, 1908; *The Citadel*, 1912; *The Charmed Life of Miss Austin*, 1914; *Anthony the Absolute*, 1914; *The Honey Bee*, 1915; *The Trufflers*, 1916; *Temperamental Henry*, 1917; *Henry is Twenty*, 1918; *The Passionate Pilgrim*, 1919; *Hills of Han*, 1920; *In Red and Gold*, 1921; *Goldie Green*, 1922.

CHRISTOPHER MORLEY

Since I do not pretend to speak for anyone but myself, there need be no disputing about tastes. I like Morley. He is a friendly soul, famous for his good cheer, for his trick of writing, almost daily, a note, a brief letter, to remind you of his thoughtfulness. He is jovial and generous, without sham and—more important still—without shame. There is nothing simpering or coy or silly about him. He comes out with his predilections. If he believes in a thing, a man or a book, he believes in saying so. And he believes in his friends. Once, when charged with log-rolling, with favoring his friends in his reviews, he answered, quite simply, "Why, of course, I do." Why not? What, in heaven's name, do you find in a friend if not something good, something you can rave about, something to praise? The claims of the self-contained that they view literature with a calm detachment, finding this book good because of the excellence of its construction, that because it is in the right tradition, are nonsense. If I like a book I like it because of something the author has put into it—and nine times out of ten I like the author.

II

Morley is that most horrible example, a good influence. He has brought to American literature something of the sweep and breadth that is in Hilaire Belloc, something of the gusto of George Saintsbury and the catholic simplicity of G. K. Chesterton. He is a mighty reader. He knows the classics and he knows the less conspicuous figures, the ancient worthies in whom Austin Dobson and Augustine Birrell have for so long delighted. He has a good word for Lever and Lover and Godwin, for Locker-Lampson and Christopher Smart, for Mrs. Meynell and Leigh Hunt; he has touted McFee and Don Marquis, George Gissing and the Fielding of *Tom Thumb* and *Joseph Andrews*.

Yet his is by no means exclusively a literary world. Rather is it a domestic one. He lives at home before the fire. He lights a pipe and sits back, with children playing on the hearth rug. He reads. But he is not too busy to talk. He is never too busy to talk. Indeed talk is his chief occupation. It was for the sake of talk that he founded the Three-Hours-For-Lunch Club, that pleasant oasis in a desert of lunch rooms. Morley had grown weary of the hasty greeting and the sandwich gobbled at a counter; he wanted to consort with his cronies. And he has. He always will. He's got to have some one to talk to.

III

A good book, Morley has said, in *Parnassus on Wheels,* should come, like Eve, from somewhere near the third rib—there ought to be a heart vibrating in it, the author's heart.

There is heart in all of Morley's books, heart rather than head. His characters are lovable. This does not mean that they are not wise. You can be heartwise. Indeed, I think the heart-wise, Duse or Ellen Terry, are infinitely preferable to those who merely

calculate their effects, who are all head—as with Bernhardt or George Jean Nathan.   There is nothing calculating about Morley.   He knows, as did his name-
sake the Viscount, that all truly great thoughts spring
from the heart.   They are intuitive.   They strike us
as right because, as in the Sermon on the Mount or the
essays of Charles Lamb, they are emotionally true.
They have a sincerity no mere pondering can ever
have.   They are humane.   They meet the test set by
Anatole France; they combine pity and irony.   They
recognize man for what he is, a wanderer in a dream,
and they honor him because, though he knows not
whence he came nor whither he is bound, he continues
on his way, unabashed and unafraid.

IV

Morley's books are packed with observations which
we believe to be true, even though we know that, driven
into an argument, we could not prove them true.   Take,
as one example, his lines *To A Post Office Inkwell*—

"How many humble hearts have dipped
   In you, and scrawled their manuscript!
   Have shared their secrets, told their cares,
   Their curious and quaint affairs!

"Your pool of ink, your scratchy pen,
   Have moved the lives of unborn men,
   And watched young people, breathing hard,
   Put Heaven on a postal card."

V

Somewhere or other, Morley has described his up-
bringing as an Anglo-American capsule.   He is like

the kitten born in an oven—not exactly a biscuit and yet——

He likes to think of England and America as two halves of the same whole. His sympathies are not divided. They run together and join hands. There are fine things that are English, fine American things—and things not so fine that one might criticize in Englishmen and in Americans.

VI

But I shall not attempt to incorporate the versatile Morley in a sentence. Such sentences as I have read —a latter-day Swift, a modern Cervantes—seem to me beggarly when the question is one of his quality; or if not beggarly, then obscure. He is more than the columnist whose *Bowling Green* was so well conducted and so well-behaved, which is something in this age of bad manners. He is not alone a taster of quaint and curious conceits, a practical paragrapher, the scold of carping obscurantists. There is more to him than in reading *Shandygaff* and *Mince Pie* one might have supposed. He has been compared to Cowper and Crabbe and Herrick; and, by E. V. Lucas, to the Burns who wrote *A Cotter's Saturday Night*—but what have comparisons to do with *Where The Blue Begins?* There is a book that is well nigh perfect in its own right; a book well able to stand alone; a little masterpiece.

VII

Morley was born at Haverford, Pennsylvania, May 5, 1890, and christened Christopher Darlington Morley. Both his parents were English by birth, but

Americans by long residence. His father, Frank Morley, an English Quaker, from Woodbridge in Suffolk (the home of Edward Fitzgerald, the translator of Omar), graduated from Cambridge University and came to America in 1887 to be made professor of mathematics at Haverford College. His mother, Lilian Janet Bird, was from Haywood's Heath in Sussex; she is a gifted musician, a poet, and (as her son invariably adds) a good cook—her father was at one time associated with the well-known London publishing house of Chapman and Hall.

At Haverford young Morley lived until he was ten years old, playing hide-and-seek in and out of the cornfield that stretched away towards the sunset from the old house called Westward Ho, over near the ancient astronomical observatory of the college; and watching the young collegians play cricket.

In 1900 Professor Morley transferred to Johns Hopkins, moving his family to Baltimore; and there young Morley passed through the various trials of his teens, learning to love oysters, practical jokes and the Enoch Pratt Free Library. In 1906 he entered Haverford as an undergraduate, graduating in 1910 and the same year being awarded the Cecil Rhodes Scholarship to Oxford, representing Maryland. The three years at Oxford were spent at New College.

Oxford made a poet of him; and it was there that, in 1912, he made his first appearance in print with *The Eighth Sin,* a book of verse.

In 1913 he returned to America and, after insistent application, got a job with Doubleday, Page and Company at $15 a week. The next year, getting a raise of $10, he married Miss Helen Booth Fairchild, a New York girl whom he had met in England. But $25 a week was not enough; the marriage budget had to be increased and, looking about, he began to bombard the editors with verses, essays, paragraphs and whatnots.

In the summer of 1915 he began his first novel, *Parnassus on Wheels,* finished it the next winter and turned it over to Doubleday, Page. For a year it lay in the manuscript safe; and then just as he was preparing to leave, in 1917, it was taken out and published. But Morley left to become one of the little group of wilful men who edit the *Ladies Home Journal* in Philadelphia; then a vacancy offering, he transferred to the Philadelphia *Evening Ledger;* and, in 1920, to the New York *Evening Post* as a column conductor.

In the summer of '24 he resigned from the *Post* to take his family—a wife and three children—to Europe.

VIII

In about 1921 Morley decided that he had come to the parting of the ways. He had jollied his generation and prodded it gently in a hundred essays. Now he would go further. He would presume upon his acquaintance with his fellows and tell a few homely truths. He had written two or three novels, but they were little more than space-fillers, though amusing and charming. He wanted to do something real. His satire had been whimsical and gentle; he wanted to strike out, to get down in parallel contortions of ink the really heavenly dreams that invaded his skull.

He began with a short story, *Referred to the Author.* But editors are a perverse and conservative

lot. They bade him stick to his last—the last one,
they said, was all right; but this—One and all they refused *Referred to the Author.*

But Morley was not daunted. He collected his
stories and brought them out in book form. *Referred
to the Author* came to the attention of Edward A.
O'Brien; he included it in his anthology and voted it
as one of the finest stories of the year.

Then, in 1922, Morley, published *Where The Blue
Begins;* and even the editors sat up and took notice.
It has sold over 50,000 copies. It is the story of the
dog Gissing's search for God, but it includes the whole
of man's adventures seeking his fortunes in a half-mad
world.

IX

Late of an April evening Gissing goes for a walk.
He is afraid to stay in, lest he be asked to fix the dish-
cloth rack in the kitchen. His man Fuji, a combination butler and cook, has already asked him six times
to fix that rack, but like all people of active mind
Gissing hates to fuss with details. So he pretends to
forget all about it. However, Fuji's insistence has
forced him to write *Fix Dish Cloth Rack* on a piece
of paper and pin the paper to a cushion on his dressing
table—but he pays no attention to the memorandum.

He goes out into the April dusk. Down by the
pond he hears a mysterious piping, shrill and insistent.
It draws him; it troubles him. So he walks that way.
But the nearer he approaches to the heart of the mystery the less shrill the piping becomes. That is worth
noting, he says—if you go straight to the heart of a

thing it ceases to be a mystery and becomes only a
question of drainage.

There, where they have been left to drown, he finds
the puppies and brings them home.   The butler quits.

"I'm sorry, sir," he says, "but when I took this place
there was nothing said about children."

As Gissing remarks, this is unreasonable of Fuji.
Rarely, if ever, can everything be explained before-
hand.   When Adam and Eve were put into Eden, no
mention was made of the serpent.

However, the children prove to be a good deal of a
care, almost too much for Gissing's income.   He loves
them, but if he wants to support them he must go to
work.   So he hires a housekeeper, packs a suitcase and
sets out for New York in search of a job.   He goes to
the maddest city in the world in search of sanity—in
search of a voice to the city that has silenced even the
poets— to a city so tall that even the sky seems to have
lifted in a cautious remove, inconceivably far—so
proud and beautiful that heaven has retreated.

He gets a job as floorwalker in a department store;
and it is there that he learns the intricacies of big
business.   He is borne along on a roaring spate of
conferences, telephone calls, appointments, Rotarian
lunches, Chamber of Commerce dinners, picnics to talk
ariff, house parties to discuss demurrage, tennis tourna-
ments to settle the sales-tax, golf foursomes to regulate
price-maintenance.   All these things have nothing
whatever to do with Beagle and Company for whom
he works, but they are a part of big business so he
attends to them, makes endless speeches and tells
countless jokes.   Then he throws up the job.

In his walks about the city in the evening he finds his first real happiness. He is still searching for God, seeking the place where the blue begins. And there, in the evening, he sees at the foot of every crosstown street a blaze of glory, the bonfire lit by the sinking sun. It is exhilarating, magnificent. He feels as though he had been given the freedom of the city.

X

And so it goes. He joins the church as a lay reader. A charming young lady belonging to the Long Island hunting set falls in love with him. He joins in long theological discussions with the bishop. He gets run out of the church. There is a tremendous scandal; the most marvelous escapade when he steals a road roller and goes touring down leafy lanes, rumbling and bumping in search of peace. Then he escapes to sea as a stowaway, is brought before the captain, involves the captain in arguments about the soul, takes over the running of the ship while the captain tries to unravel some of the philosophical problems proposed by the plausible Gissing. He steers for every patch of sunlight, for weeds, day after peaceful day. When the pasengers grow restless he summons them to fire drill, puts them in life-boats, lowers them to the water and leaves them.

XI

Again, I must repeat, so it goes. A glorious book. A whimsy that has all the depth of Gulliver and none of Swift's bitterness, that is gay and reverent and, like good farce, a roaring comedy. A book to read after

Red Lewis' *Babbitt*.   You may know that we are
dumb and cruel, still you need not despair.   There is
a child to love in the heart of every man.

Mr. Morley is the author of *The Eighth Sin*, 1912;
Parnassus on Wheels, 1917; *Songs for a Little House*,
1917; *Shandygaff*, 1918; *The Rocking Horse*, 1919;
The Haunted Bookshop, 1919; *In the Dry and Dry*
(with Burt Haley) 1919; *Mince Pie*, 1919; *Travels in
Philadelphia*, 1920; *Kathleen*, 1920; *Hide and Seek*,
1920; *Pipefuls*, 1920; *Tales from a Rolltop Desk*,
1921; *Plum Pudding*, 1921; *Chimney-smoke*, 1921;
Thursday Evening, a one act play, 1922; *Translations
from the Chinese*, 1922; *Where The Blue Begins*,
1922; *Rehearsal*, a one act play, 1922; *The Powder of
Sympathy*, 1923; *Pandora Lifts The Lid* (with Don
Marquis), 1923; *Parson's Pleasure*, 1923; *Inward
Ho!* 1924.

ROBERT NATHAN

He moves, reserved and strange, under the quaint disguises of a Persian Prince, through the colorful pages of Elinor Wylie's *Jennifer Lorn.*

But I knew him. "You've been reading Anatole France," I said.

Knowing that denial was useless he confessed—I might almost say, with pride—that he had been reading Anatole France.

"Thank Goodness for that," I said. "It's about time we began to feel the urbane and tolerant influence of Anatole France over here—I'm thoroughly fed with our adolescent obsessions."

II

Anatole France!

France is generally supposed to be the foremost living man of letters. *Autumn,* the first of Robert Nathan's novels, reads like a translation from one of Anatole France's causeries, an essay from *L'Histoire Comique,* where he speaks of the country round about Rouen, the Norman landscape and the Norman peasant. Read the first few sentences:—

"On Sunday the church bells of Hillsboro rang out across the ripening fields, with a grave and holy sound, and again at evening knocked faintly, with quiet sorrow, at doors where children watched for the first stars to make their wishes. Night came, and the croaking of the frogs, the moon rose over Barly Hill . . . the

tranquil voice of Mr. Jeminy disputed with the hum
of bees."

It is pure France, an echo from the *Tales of Jacques
Tournebroche* or the meditations of *Monsieur
Bergeret*. . . .

Listen then to that most inexplicable of the critics,
Walter Pritchard Eaton—"Barrie lost in a fog."
That is Eaton on Nathan.   Yet there is never a sentence, in *Autumn* or *The Puppet Master*, to convince
any one that Nathan had ever heard of Barrie or read
a line of *Sentimental Tommy, Margaret Ogylvie* or a
Window in Thrums. . . .

Eaton—I say it after watching him for years—
doesn't know the half of what he believes he is talking about.   For dismissing *Autumn* as beneath his notice he should be spat upon on the Rialto and made to
lunch with his favorite actress every day for three
consecutive years.

III

The voice of Mr. Jeminy disputes with the hum of
bees. . . .

So begins the story of this quiet and kindly New England schoolmaster, teaching plus and minus to a lot
of country boys and girls, musing on Boetius and
Epictetus, helping Mr. Tompkins with his garden. . . .

"With every toss of his fork he covered with earth
the little piles of straw and ordure which Mr. Tompkins had spread on the ground.   As he advanced in

this manner, small flocks of sparrows rose before him
and flew away with dissatisfied cries. 'Come,' he said
to them, 'the world does not belong to you.   I believe
you have never read the works of Epictetus who says
true education lies in learning to distinguish what is
ours from what does not belong to us.   However, you
have a more modern spirit, for you believe that whatever you see belongs to you, providing you are able to
get hold of it. . . .

"'Thus of old the farmer stopped to refresh himself.   When he was done he gave thanks to the mystic
god, who watched his house and protected his flocks.
They were the best of friends; each was modest and
reasonable.   To-day God is like a dead ancestor;
there is no way to argue with him.'"

IV

Autumn is as quotable as a poem, as lovely, as heart-
felt and thoughtful.

V

At times Mr. Jeminy is impatient with the selfishness, the cruelty and intolerance of the present age—
but he knows that it will pass.

"Let the young be free to build a new world," he
says.   "It will be happier than ours.   It will be a
world of love and candor.   Perhaps it will be also a
world of poverty.   That would not do any harm."

VI

The life in the village about him disturbs Mr.
Jeminy a little—the illicit love affair of Anna and
Thomas, the playing of little Juliet, the loss of his

job, and the death of his housekeeper—but not for long. His spirit is mellow. The stream of his life runs deep and can only be ruffled on the surface.

VII

In 1923, Mr. Nathan published *The Puppet Master*, the story of Papa Jonas and Mrs. Holly and Mrs. Holly's six-year old daughter Amy May, and Amy May's doll, Annabelle Lee, and Mr. Aristotle who is the best clown in all Papa Jonas' collections of puppets. Amy May is determined that Annabelle Lee and Mr. Aristotle shall marry. Mr. Aristotle loathes the very thought of matrimony. But they are married nevertheless——

"The bride-to-be lay on her back and looked at the ceiling. Whatever the future held for her she faced it without alarm. Her gentle nature, composed of rags, did not permit the most outrageous accidents to alter its character. Such souls, made of tatters, are firmer than iron. They can be cut to pieces, but they cannot be broken!"

Annabelle Lee is determined. But the marriage is short-lived. Mr. Aristotle cuts off her one shoe-button eye and flings himself from a window to the gutter below. He is broken in spirit, disillusioned and cynical. . . .

" 'It is difficult to understand the purposes of heaven,' Papa Jonas says, 'they often have an appearance of improvisation. . . . It is absurd to expect them to appear anything but vexatious and mysterious to a doll made of linen and wood.' "

VIII

"After all," Robert Nathan wrote, in my copy of *The Puppet Master,* "I am not adapted to a life like this. I am a philosopher, which is to say that I look on life from a distance and by myself.—For such purposes there is nothing better than a nail in the wall. . . ."

He is quoting, with evident approval, his own Mr. Aristotle. But you must not take him too seriously. Mr. Nathan is well adapted to an age like this. He is a philosopher, true, but he is also a fencer of some skill, a tennis player, a musician—he threatens to write a symphony after he is through with *Jonah,* the novel he is now writing, a novel dealing with Jonah and Nineveh, Jonah the poet and Nineveh that wicked city. . . .

Mr. Nathan is not robust, but beyond that he **can** hold his own with the best of us.

IX

Mr. Nathan was educated in public and private schools, first in New York, then in Switzerland. Later he was sent to Phillips Exeter, where he established a music club, and thereafter to Harvard, where he wrote for the *Harvard Monthly,* made the gym team and became, for a time, a flyweight boxing champion.

"After Harvard," he says, "I came to New York to get a job in an advertising agency with my cousin. Got one account. Wrote some verse and some short stories. Account dwindled. Got no more. Wrote

my first novel, *Peter Kindred,* the scenes of which are
laid in Exeter and Harvard.   Learned to ski.   *Peter*
unsalable.   Advertising account died.   Wrote two
other books which are still apparently unsalable.   Finally found a publisher for *Peter*.   *Peter* published.
Wrote *Autumn*.   Moved to California for good.
Swam with the seals.   Returned from California for
good.   Still writing."

X

In 1922 Mr. Nathan published *Youth Grows Old,* a
sequence of sonnets and lyrics which, in some sort, form
an emotional autobiography.   I like especially :—

> "I am no stranger in the house of pain,
>   I am familiar with its every part,
> From the low stile, then up the crooked lane,
> To the dark doorway, intimate to my heart,
> Here did I sit with grief and eat his bread,
> Here was I welcomed as misfortune's guest,
> And there's no room but where I've laid my head
>   On misery's accommodating breast.

> "So sorrow, does my knocking rouse you up?
>   Open the door, old mother, it is I.
> Bring grief's good goblet out, the sad, sweet cup,
>   Fill it with wine of silence, strong and dry;
> For I've a story to amuse your ears,
> Of youth and hope, of middle age and tears."

Mr. Nathan is the author of *Peter Kindred,* 1919;
Autumn 1921; *Youth Grows Old,* 1922; *The Puppet
Master,* 1923; *and Jonah* (In preparation).

MEREDITH NICHOLSON

The good men, George Ade has said, come from Indiana; and the better they are, the quicker they come. This means (if it means anything) that those who stay home are not to be compared with those who leave in search of greener fields.

Mr. Nicholson is a case in point. He stayed home; and you cannot speak of him and at the same time think of Dreiser. Mr. Nicholson is just Tom or Dick or Harry. Mr. Dreiser is a person of some consequence, a figure in the world of art—Mr. Nicholson is anybody, you or me or that infernal Smith he holds up as the *beau ideal* of a provincial paradise. If you stop the next man you meet and ask him what he thinks of El Dorado or taxes or fame you will have the answer Mr. Nicholson would give to the same questions. Mr. Nicholson is regulation Indiana, pretty and flat and prosperous, without being striking or especially interesting.

II

Mr. Nicholson was recently nominated on the Democratic ticket for state senator in Indiana, to represent Marion County. And once, at Mr. Wilson's hands, he refused the job of Ambassador to Portugal—which caused some to wonder whether the Portuguese had read his books or whether they had not.

III

"When I left school at fifteen," he says, "owing to my inability to master algebra, it was with the fixed purpose of becoming a printer. There had been printers in my mother's family; my grandfather Meredith had been a printer, and a pioneer editor in Indiana. I knew to my youth great numbers of printers, including many of the old *tramp genus;* and I thought them very fine fellows. They knew a lot and I found their cynical philosophy delightful. To know as much as a printer and wander over the world, holding cases in strange cities, struck me as a noble thing—but the gods were against me.

"For a time I was employed in a small job office attached to a news stand. There I had full swing at *Bonner's Ledger* and the latest dime novels; but I was a clerk, not an apprentice, and only on rare occasions did I get a chance to sort pi or otherwise toy with the types. I moved to another and bigger establishment, but there again I was thwarted. I was required to push a wheelbarrow through the streets of Indianapolis, piled high with books and stationery; and at seven every morning I gained strength for this task by sweeping out the counting room and administering to the cuspidors. The performance of these duties had the effect of stimulating my ambition. I resolved to become a stenographer and practiced the pot hooks at night until I found employment in a law office.

"At about seventeen I began to write verse; and wrote a great deal of it. I had been mailing my jingles to all sorts of newspapers and magazines when one day I was highly satisfied by the receipt of a check for three dollars for a poem called *Grape Bloom* which I had sent to the New York *Mercury*. My recollection of the *Mercury* is very indistinct, but I believe it printed fiction against a background of theatrical and sporting news. For about two years I bought the paper regularly but never saw my verses in print.

"At nineteen I was reading law and I learned a great deal about courts, legal forms and procedure. Born far from tidewater, (at Crawfordsville, December 9, 1866), I specialized in admiralty law. The romance of the thing must have caught me, for I ran down all the decisions available in this branch of legal science. With all modesty I assert, pretend and declare that at that period I knew more of the law of the sea than any other Hoosier ever knew.

"At that time James Whitcomb Riley's poems were appearing every Sunday in the Indianapolis *Journal*. I was a stenographer in the law office of William and Lew Wallace, and one of the many fledgling bards whose work was tacked onto the end of Riley's column. One Saturday, Riley, whom I had been worshipping from afar but had never spoken to, appeared suddenly in the law offices carrying a copy of the Cincinnati *Enquirer*. He pointed to a poem of his own and one of mine that were reproduced in adjoining columns and said a friendly word about my work. His invaluable friendship to the end of his days may not be described here, but in those years there was a sweetness in his characteristically shy manifestations of good will that are indelibly associated with my memories of him. The first time I ever ate beefsteak and mush-rooms he spread the banquet for me, the ostensible purpose being to invite my criticism (I was nineteen!) of a new volume he was preparing for the press.

"My rhyming in the law office did not prevent a few attempts at story-writing. The Chicago *Tribune* was offering every week a prize of five dollars for a short story about a column's length. The first one I offered, called *The Tale Of a Postage Stamp*, earned the five. I immediately wrote several others which did not, however, take the prize. The short story didn't interest me particularly and after a second had been printed in the Chicago *Current*, an ambitious literary journal that was braving the airs of Chicago just then, and a third in the *McClure Syndicate*, I didn't write, or even try writing, short stories until about six years ago.

"Having mastered maritime law, I skipped the rest and became a reporter. This was good fun; and I kept at newspaper work for twelve years.

"Then I took a flyer in business and was for three years auditor and treasurer of a coal mining corpora-tion in Colorado. All this time I had been writing something, prose or verse, and in Colorado I wrote a historical book which is my longest seller. I was so elated to find that I had indeed become an author that I chucked the coal business and a very good salary and began to write novels, essays and all sorts of other things. In my experiments with literature I have been both serious and frivolous. The only way to have a good time as a writer is to do the thing that interests you most at the moment. As I have a journalistic sort of mind, I have dropped fiction many times to write an essay on some such subject as Should Smith Go To Church? or the Second-Rate Man in Politics."

IV

Mr. Nicholson is the author of *Short Flights*, poems, 1891; *The Hoosier*, 1900; *The Main Chance*, 1903; *Zelda Dameron*, 1904; *The House of a Thousand Candles*, 1905; *Poems*, 1906; *The Port of Missing Men*, 1907; *Rosalind of Red Gate*, 1907; *The Little Brown Jug at Kildare*, 1908; *The Lords of High Decision*, 1909; *The Siege of the Seven Suitors*, 1910; *A Hoosier Chronicle*, 1912; *The Provincial American*, essays, 1913; *Otherwise Phyllis*, 1913; *The Poet*, 1914; *The Proof of the Pudding*, 1916; *The Madness of May*, 1917; *A Reversible Santa Claus*, 1917; *The Valley of Democracy*, essays, 1918; *Lady Larkspur*, 1919; *Blacksheep! Blacksheep!* 1920; *The Man In The Street*, essays, 1921; *Honor Bright*, a play, 1921.

CHARLES G. NORRIS

His publishers, the Messrs. Dutton, tell me that when
he was ten years old Charles G. Norris began an elaborate historical novel which he called *In The Reign
of the Grand Monarch* and on which he worked seven
years, finally reducing it to the consistency of hash,
a mediocre revamping of all the elder Dumas, with
just enough of Saint Simon to lend flavor to the mess
and make one wonder why Norris ever thought he
could improve upon his models—or why he should
think the book needed doing at all.

II

That is like Norris. All his books are elaborate and
they all give evidence of having been worked over for
years.

III

And it is like his cheek to say, as he does: "My
sole purpose in writing is to make people think."

Hergesheimer writes only to entertain us; Conrad
wants to make us feel and, above all, see; but Norris
is bent upon making us think.

And, Lord, how we hate it! But can you blame
us?

IV

"In *Salt*," he says, "I tried to give a picture of our
national system of education, to show the good and ill

effects of our schools and colleges. In *Brass* I attempted to present different phases of what we understand as marriage, to show some of the reasons why people cannot get along with one another."

V

Is it any wonder we are bored with Mr. Norris?

VI

If I were asked, by some aspiring youngster—don't worry; I never shall be—what not to attempt in writing a novel, in writing anything not intended for the woman's page of one of Mr. Hearst's innumerable newspapers, I should quote the few sentences I have already quoted from Mr. Norris, and say: "My boy, stay away from that sort of blather. Don't let anyone tell you that our national system of education can be pictured by you or any one else. Don't let any one fool you into believing that our colleges and schools affect us one way or another, for good or ill. And don't, for Heaven's sake, refer to wedlock as 'what we understand as marriage.' You will never write anything worth a damn if you fall into that sort of cliché. And remember, always, that people can get along together if only they try. Besides what difference does it make if they don't? And anyway it's none of your business."

VII

Mr. Norris was eleven years the junior of Frank Norris, his brother and the author of *McTeague*, *The Pit* and *The Octopus*. Mr. Norris was just out of the

University of California, with no future ahead of him save the family jewelry business, when Frank was already famous. Mr. Norris felt immensely sorry for himself. He was to be a drudge while his brother enjoyed the plaudits of the critics. This seemed unfair to Mr. Norris. At the University of California he had been told that he was better fitted for rooting at football games than for literature. But he could not think so harshly of himself; and so five years after leaving the university he went to work on the staff of *Country Life*, at five dollars a week, reporting the dog shows and contributing articles on tulips and fire risks in the country home. Two years of this and he left to become circulation manager of *Sunset*, in San Francisco. There he met Kathleen Thompson and decided to make money and get married. He returned to New York. He got a job with the *American Magazine*, persuaded Kathleen Thompson to join him and to marry him. Then they both settled down to write. Her first story was declined by twenty-six magazines before the *Atlantic Monthly* accepted it. Then she wrote *Mother*, sold it to the *American Magazine*, published it as a novel and sold 600,000 copies. Charles G. Norris ceased to be Frank Norris' brother and became the husband of Kathleen Norris.

But Kathleen Norris refused to let him rest upon such ill-gotten laurels, bustled him off to California, sat him down at a typewriter and told him to produce. In three years he had produced *The Amateur*. Three years more and he had produced *Salt*. Another three years and he had added *Brass* to the slow-growing work of his life-time.

You and I might have quit there and gone in for something fresher, gayer, something light and playful. But not so Mr. Norris. There was still the problem of the woman in business. He set to work and in three years he had produced *Bread*. I think that even the peasants who stormed at Marie Antoinette would have asked for cake had they been offered such a morsel of hardtack as this *Bread* of Mr. Norris'.

GRANT OVERTON

"Turning to *The Answerer* by Grant Overton," the *New Republic* says, "we are face to face with an ambitious proceeding that is a failure on two counts—bad writing and bad construction. The novel, fictionally of course, purports to give the story of the early years of Walt Whitman, those years passed on Long Island, the uncertain and unauthenticated love affair in New Orleans, and the Civil War activities. Several historical characters—Abraham Lincoln, Margaret Fuller, Horace Greeley and Herman Melville—are introduced into the narrative. It is quite futile to attempt to pick out historical flaws in the book because the author admits taking large liberties in a prefatory statement. Therefore there is nothing to do but consider it as a novel and, as such, it does not hold up at all. It is loosely constructed—being almost picaresque in form although not picaresque in matter—and the author overwrites considerably."

II

Overton might retort that the chap who speaks of "taking large liberties in a prefatory statement" when he means taking liberties in the book proper and not in the preface at all, is no judge of good writing, or bad either—but alas, the charge is true, for all that. The book was written simply because Overton wanted to write a book; and it is about Whitman not because Overton was interested in Whitman, caring or knowing anything about him, but because Whitman lived on Long Island and Overton wanted to write about Long Island—in the Joseph C. Lincoln and not in the Whitman manner. In short, the book's a jumble. Overton overwrites, he over-emphasises, he draws futile conclusions from half legendary facts; and then he generalizes to prove that this is a very fine world.

Overton is over-nice. By that I don't mean that his books don't go down into the by-ways and alleys—(he was a police reporter for nine years on the New York *Sun* and he shipped, in his sophomore year at Princeton, before the mast around the Horn)—I simply mean that not for worlds would he hurt the feelings of any one of his possible readers. He would not run counter to popular fallacies, as Whitman once did. And so *The Answerer* is not really Whitman at all.

But even so I cannot see why it should not be picaresque in form, if Overton wanted it to be picaresque.

III

There is never a prejudice or a qualm that Overton will not recognize and say, "Well, perhaps you have reason for thinking as you do." I am his friend, but I confess that his anxiety to find some good in everything bores and annoys me. I like gusto and spirit. I want my authors to be up and doing.

IV

I feel that Overton has something to say; and I want him to say it. I want him to out with it, to have done with care and speak his mind. Such tip toeing as

Mark Twain engaged in when he decided not to publish his autobiography until he had been long and safe in his grave, does not become an author in a world where all men must speak their minds lest all men be forever silenced by the pussy-footers.

V

But the *New Republic* has since made amends by saying that *The Thousand and First Night* is such a book of adventure as only Stevenson could have written—and I, for my part, know of a manicurist on 42nd Street who is just crazy about *The Mermaid* because there's no mush in it, or so she says.

VI

An old manor house on Long Island is the scene of Overton's latest novel, *The Thousand and First Night*. Within its walls generation after generation of the Fannings have dwelt. As the story opens only Magellan Fanning and his granddaughter Cynthia are left. Magellan is an old sea captain, worn out, crippled, half mad and desperately poor. He is obsessed with fear lest the estate be taken from him; he is suspicious of all strangers. And so when an airplane crashes near the house, Cynthia keeps the presence of the bruised and weary aviator—a transatlantic flyer whom she takes in—a secret from her grandfather.

Cynthia, her grandfather and Evan Lloyd, (or Evan Owen, the aviator) are the only living characters in the book.

But there are memories of others, legendary figures from the past, ghosts; and Mr. Overton links the past with the present as Cynthia, to amuse her grandfather, tells story after story, for a thousand nights. They have been alone in the house. This is their recreation and delight. Yet even so they have been somewhat bored. But on the thousand and first night, the night of Evan Owen's arrival, she tells the story of the first Cynthia Fanning, the granddaughter of Colonel Charles Fanning of Tangier, and her lover Pedro da Gama, a descendent of the great Vasco da Gama. She believes that she is making the story up, but Magellan Fanning recognizes it as an old family tradition—except that Cynthia makes her story so convincing that he believes that now, at last, he is hearing the true version of what really happened in Tangier long ago, and that it is the spirit of the first Cynthia who has whispered this tragic tale to the last of the Fannings. He even sees, or imagines he sees, the shadowy figure of Cynthia of Tangier standing beside his granddaughter.

Overton's reason for introducing this romance of the past becomes apparent when we see how closely the story of Cynthia and Evan Owen parallels that of the earlier Cynthia and Pedro da Gama. It is as if the seventeenth-century lovers lived again in the persons of the twentieth-century—for Evan Owen has in his veins the blood of the da Gamas. It is the example of his illustrious ancestor, Vasco da Gama, that has inspired him to make a round-the-world flight, the last leg of which he has just completed. And here, at his journey's end, he finds his reward in a love that endures until death and perhaps beyond.

It is a tale of adventure, gaily and gallantly done.

VII

Overton was, at one time, for a year or more, editor of the book review section of the New York *Sun:* and as editor and reviewer he made, and rightly, a name for himself. He edited his reviews and those of his reviewers as book notices should be edited in a newspaper. Names meant nothing to him. It was the book that counted. Was the book of interest? Was it timely? Could it serve to pass an exciting or a pleasant hour?

Never was an editor so much in earnest, so anxious to offer to each one just the book he was looking for.

That was the way he interpreted his job—to find each book its proper audience and then sell them on the book. And, literally, there seemed to be no end to the catholicity of his taste, nothing he could not away with. An invaluable trait in a reviewer.

Books to Overton were news and he wrote them up as news.

VIII

Since then he has gone in for blurbs, making a business—and a very necessary one—of finding readers for all of Mr. Doran's books and most of Mrs. Rhinehart's.

But he is not writing himself any more; and that seems to me a shame since he was in a fair way to finding his own—and he has, I am sure, a story to tell.

IX

Further he is generous and free from all jealousy. I doubt if there be any other in the book business as generous and helpful as he. At times it seems as though he were intent only upon helping others. And, as I have said, this seems to me a sin, for he has understanding and sympathy; and now that his novitiate has been served, he should be ready with his own best book.

X

Mr. Overton was born in Patchogue, out on Long Island, September 19, 1887, the son of Floyd Alward and Ardelia Jarvis (Skidmore) Overton. He attended Blair Academy and, for two years, 1904–06, Princeton University. In 1921 he married Clara Wallace of Mohawk, N. Y.

He is the author of *The Women Who Make Our Novels*, 1918; *Why Authors Go Wrong*, 1919; *The Mermaid*, 1920; *World Without End*, 1921; *The Answerer*, 1921; *When Winter Comes to Main Street*, 1922; *The Island of the Innocent*, 1923; *American Nights Entertainment*, 1923; *The Thousand and First Night*, 1924.

THOMAS NELSON PAGE

Santa Claus was a very real person, Christmas a sacred celebration, to the late Thomas Nelson Page. He believed that good things grew on trees; and that if we waited and were well-behaved they would be given to us. And so he cautioned us to listen for the singing of angels and to watch how the shepherds tend their flocks at night. A star, he said, will guide you; you don't need anything but a star, be patient.

You can imagine the effect of such a philosophy. There we would be, all of us, trusting in God—and doing nothing.

But this simple Christian doctrine was fair enough, for a Virginia gentleman. There was nothing much that he could do anyway—except enter the legal profession or write. Mr. Page did both. And after he had published some twenty odd volumes and faithfully served the law for thirty years, he came into his reward—he was made American Ambassador to Italy by President Wilson, himself a Virginian and naturally well versed in the proper formalities.

II

Loving kindness—that was to be Mr. Page's moral and a motto for his crest. You don't find any of his characters giving their lady-loves a thumping great whack in the belly as do the lovers of Somerset Maugham in *Liza of Lambeth*. They scarcely touch hands. And my word, how gracefully they can grow old! I

remember at school in Alexandria, Va., being especially respectful to an irascible old cavalry officer, who
taught me Homer and had served under Stonewall
Jackson, simply because he looked like Mr. Page's old
gentleman of the Black Stock; and I know I doubted
the thefts of our worthless colored man because Uncle
Billy, the negro of *Mars Chan,* was so good.

III

Yes, sir, a cotton field was a cotton field to Mr.
Page; and the passing of the Old Dominion the greatest calamity that has yet befallen the human race.
There, in old days, according to him, existed the perfect civilization. That it was founded on injustice,
that it flowered in sloth, meant nothing; the men and
women were gracious, their homes were stately, their
friends welcome. And indeed it was lovely. As one
who has dwelt there among the ruins I can bear witness to its beauty. But it was lazy and no account
just the same. It produced nothing and it has left
nothing—if we overlook the embittered memories of
its now impoverished gentry.

IV

Mr. Page was born on the family plantation in Han-
over County, Virginia, April 23, 1853, the son of Major John and Elizabeth Burwell (Nelson) Page. He
descends from two governors—one, Thomas Nelson,
a signer of the Declaration of Independence. He
was, if report speaks true, a rather precocious child,
entering Washington and Lee University at sixteen,
graduating in three years, spending a few months in

Kentucky, and then transferring to the law department of the University of Virginia at Charlottesville. He finished the course in about half the time usually required, and took up the practice of law in Richmond, 1875–93. He was twice married.

V

Mars Chan, the first of Mr. Page's stories, was published in 1884. Of its writing he tells us: "A friend showed me a letter which had been written, by a young girl to her sweetheart in a Georgia regiment, telling him that she had discovered that she loved him, after all, and that if he would get a furlough and come home she would marry him; that she had loved him ever since they had gone to school together in the little schoolhouse in the woods. Then, as if she feared the temptation might be too strong for him, she added a postscript in these words; Don't come without a furlough; for if you don't come honorably I won't marry you. This letter had been taken from the pocket of a private, dead on the battle-field of one of the battles around Richmond, and, as the date was only a week before the battle occurred, its pathos struck me very much. I remember I said: The poor fellow got his furlough through a bullet. The idea remained with me, and I went to my office one morning to write *Mars Chan,* which was finished in about a week."

It won immediate recognition and praise. It is as fine as anything Mr. Page ever did. But it is, of course, sentimental and silly. Instead of being outraged by the organized stupidity that decreed a war to free slaves who, by everything that is decent, should never have been enslaved; instead of crying out against the hopelessness of such a love as that young girl's; or noting how life goes on, with its longing and desire, even in the midst of battle; Mr. Page sat down and grew maudlin over the disappearing South.

VI

There was no growth in Mr. Page's work. *Mars Chan* appeared with other stories, under the general title *In Old Virginia,* in 1887; and Mr. Page was through. He could only repeat himself endlessly. When it wasn't Virginia, it was Santa Claus or Robert E. Lee or Jefferson.

Mr. Page is the author of *In Old Virginia,* 1887; *Two Little Confederates,* 1888; *On Newfound River,* 1891; *The Old South,* 1891; *Among the Camps,* 1891; *Elsket and Other Stories,* 1892; *Befo' the War,* (with Armistead C. Gordon), 1894; *Pastime Stories,* 1894; *The Burial of the Guns,* 1894; *Meh Lady,* 1896; *Social Life in Old Virginia,* 1896; *The Old Gentleman of the Black Stock,* 1896; *Two Prisoners,* 1897; *Red Rock,* 1898; *Santa Claus' Partner,* 1899; *A Captured Santa Claus,* 1902; *Gordon Keith,* 1903; *The Negro —The Southerner's Problem,* 1904; *Bred in the Bone,* 1905; *The Coast of Bohemia,* poems, 1906; *Under the Crust,* 1907; *The Old Dominion,* 1908; *Robert E. Lee, Southerner,* 1908; *Tommy Trot's Visit to Santa Claus,* 1908; *John Marvel, Assistant,* 1909; *Robert E. Lee,* 1912; *The Land of the Spirit,* 1913; *Thomas Jefferson,* 1918; *Italy's Relation to the War,* 1920.

ELLIOT H. PAUL

There came running to Diderot in all haste one day a man who had been reading Diderot's reviews. The man was excited. He was angry, almost. "Look here," he said—in French of course—"I've been reading your stuff and on the strength of it, advised by you, I bought So and So's book; and none of the things you mention in your reviews, are in the book." "Well, they ought to be," was all the satisfaction he got out of Diderot. . . .

And that's the way I feel about Elliot Paul. None of the things I want to put into this review are in his books—but, I am sure, they all ought to be. Here it is Sunday, the world fliers just hopping off from Iceland, Miss Wills again a victor over Molla Mallory, the Yankees in the lead and Bambino batting .406—yet Mr. Paul expects me to weep over I don't know how many inverse ratios.

I feel like crying, really I do. I've suffered so much I'm getting tired of it. I've agonized with every heroine in every book published in America any time this last thirty years. I've been so tormented that just the color of one of Mr. Knopf's jackets will cause me to break down and sob like a child. I've got to call a halt. Whenever babes and sucklings get to appearing on my desk with unnameable diseases and one inferiority complex piled on top of another, I quit. There must be balm somewhere for some of these miserable wretches. Why don't they go get it

before begging a dole at my door? I'm no physician.
I'm just an ordinary fellow in search of recreation. I
asked for spiritual sustenance and they give me pain,
thinking it is bread—but I'm not French for all my
references to Diderot.

II

There is a line in Masefield that is one of the great
lines in English verse, something about following some
Helen for her gift of grief. It is a line that Mr. Paul
might read with profit. He would be less confused by
the miseries of his lovers. They come together in-
articulate and strange, and they remain strangers to
the end. It is because they lack the insight their author cannot give them. They do not understand because he does not understand. He sees a little tiny
corner of the world, an attic in Boston, with only a
half-light peering through the windows—and in that
half-light his characters are born. They live obscurely and they die obscurely, only half-realized by
their readers and by Mr. Paul. . . .

The scene is reminiscent. It is the room of Char-
lotte, the mistress of Wilhelm Meister, but the mood
has changed. There reigns no longer the serenity of
Goethe, but in its stead the confusion of Mr. Elliot
Paul. . . .

This is not to say that Mr. Paul, is not, comparatively speaking, a very fine writer. He has been
ranked ahead of Dos Passos by Heywood Broun. He
is exactly to the taste of our sensation-loving reviewers
out in Chicago. But Lester Davis, his latest hero, is
Mr. Paul. He envies those—men, plants and animals

—who seem to have evolved some plan, some philosophy, whereby they may direct their lives,

III

It is a return to *Man and Superman.*

In the best known of the notes to that gorgeous triumph over the lures of the flesh—where, embracing, Tanner cries out to the shameless Ann, "I hate you!" —Shaw has said that this is the true joy of living: to be used for a purpose which you yourself believe to be a great purpose and not to be thrown on the dust heap until you are thoroughly worn out.

These characters of Elliot Paul's know no purpose, great or little; and they believe in none. They go aimless through life, and they are miserable. Of course, they are miserable. They are selfish. They know not, in the Shavian sense, the true joy of living. They are utterly without joy. They are clods, complaining that the world will not devote itself to looking after them.

IV

But Mr. Paul is interesting. He has a thousand innuendoes and a thousand phrases. He is devoted to a search for beauty. He has his peculiarities, but they make him all the more striking; they set him apart and give him reason for speaking out. He, at any rate, is not parroting the fashions, repeating over and over the story of young lovers who, on page 346, will marry happily for all that the girl is an orphan and the man a fellow who speaks hastily.

V

Mr. Paul was born in Malden, Mass.; lived there most of his youth; studied engineering at the University of Maine; spent six years in construction work in the northwest; served in the war with the 37th Field Signal Battalion; became interested in writing after he read Dostoievski's *Poor People;* wrote *Indelible,* 1922; *Impromptu,* 1923; and *Imperturbe,* 1924.

Mr. Paul lives in Boston at the present time, earning his livelihood by doing manual labor. He follows literature as a profession. His avocations are music and painting.

DAVID GRAHAM PHILLIPS

David Graham Phillips was born in Madison, Ind., in 1868. He attended Depauw University, transferred to Princeton and graduated there in 1890. He did some writing at college, but his first real work was as a reporter on the *Cincinnati Times-Star* and, later, on the *Cincinnati Tribune*.

Late in the nineties he moved to New York, continuing in newspaper work, and after a few weeks on the *Tribune*, joined the city staff of the New York *Sun*. In those days the *Sun* had a great reputation as the revealer of talent. It seems that all, or almost all, of our better known journalists worked on the *Sun* at one time or another. It was the *Sun* that gave Phillips his chance. He converted a simple news story of a child lost in the Adirondacks into a news classic.

From the *Sun* he went to the *World*, took the fancy of Joseph Pulitzer and was soon transferred to London as special correspondent. There one of his outstanding beats was his exclusive account of the sinking of H. M. S. *Camperdown*. Returning to New York he was made a member of the *World's* editorial staff.

Now came the first evidence of his amazing energy and industry. While still a member of the editorial staff, every day at his desk, reading, reading, reading, he wrote his first novel, *The Great God Success,* and

423

published it in 1901 over the pen-name of John Graham. It was instantly successful and has been mentioned as one of the best of newspaper novels.

The success of *The Great God Success* emboldened Phillips to cut loose from daily journalism and become a free lance. He contributed to *McClure's, Munsey's, Everybody's, Success, Harper's Weekly,* the *Delineator* and many another weekly and monthly magazine.

In 1902, this time over his own signature, he brought out his second novel, *A Woman's Ventures;* and, the same year, *Her Serene Highness.* The next year he produced *The Golden Fleece* and *The Master Rogue.* In 1902 *The Cost.* And in 1906, *The Plum Tree, The Social Secretary, The Deluge* and the *Reign of Guilt*—so maintaining an average of something better than two novels a year.

But he had not given up journalism, for all the time he was making ready for the *Treason of the Senate,* as scathing a series of muck-raking articles as any yet written. Business and politics. That was the tune he played. The oil trust and the steel trust; and the politicians who were and are their hirelings. It was the same old story that is being repeated to-day, but he gave a new twist to it—because he was so much in earnest. However, nothing came of his earnestness. Publicity is apparently powerless to rouse so self-satisfied a people as we Americans to a proper sense of our civic duties. We are not even surprised when we read of Coolidge's wires to McLean; and the cunning Slemp is but another wise one to us.

II

Between 1906 and 1917, when he was murdered, Phillips wrote eighteen novels, six of which were published posthumously—*The Grain of Dust, Degarmo's Wife, The Price She Paid, The Conflict, George Helm* and *Susan Lenox*. Of these only *Susan Lenox* need detain us. Indeed it is for *Susan Lenox* and for *Susan Lenox* alone that Phillips is remembered. He put everything he had into *Susan Lenox*. Years before, while on a visit home, to Madison, he had seen a young girl sitting in a farm wagon alongside a country lout. They were married. They had been forced to marry. And she became for Phillips the symbol of unhappy womanhood. For nine years he worked over her story. A dozen other books were written in the meantime, but always he returned to *Susan Lenox*. As finally published the book contains 400,000 words, but that did not deter him. Four different times he went through those 400,000 words, from beginning to end, writing always with a soft lead pencil on half-sheets torn from a yellow pad.

Yet all his work came within an ace of going for nothing when the editor, who, after Phillips' death, had bought the serial rights to the story, read of *Susan Lenox* and blushed, fearful lest such frankness imperil the sales of his magazine. But four years gave him courage; and four years later the story began. Immediately the magazine's circulation increased by leaps and bounds. You could not get a copy high or low. *Susan* became as much a topic of conversation as in her greater day *Clarissa Harlowe* had been with the beaux and bells of a century gone.

III

It was so with Phillips always. He was topical. He wrote as one in the know. And he made news of his stories. They always seemed important. In *Light Fingered Gentry* he anticipated the insurance scandals that once were a nine day's horror to New York. With *The Cost* and *The Deluge* he introduced Wall Street to fiction. And he was passionately in earnest. He believed sincerely in freedom of expression, in democracy and in his fellows. He gave great promise of some day, at his leisure, writing something fine. And he was, from all accounts, a likable chap.

ERNEST POOLE

I know that I am expected to cry over Ernest Poole's characters, but somehow I never do. Yet my heart is like paint, almost always wet—at any rate, when there is a sign upon it—and surely it is the author's business to put a sign upon the heart of his reader—a sign of the cross or the sign for laughter. . . .

It must be that Poole is solemn rather than serious, industrious rather than inspired—it may be that he has no gleam of humor.

II

Long ago, I said of him that he was being acclaimed beyond his just deserts, that he was not a great novelist —as Dreiser is great. He writes well and thoughtfully of certain troubled old men, and with interest of a certain type of restless and ambitious woman. But I am inclined to agree with him that his best work is in *The Village,* a book of Russian impressions—*The Village* is journalism, pure and simple, and, for our purpose, not a proper test of the novelist.

III

He began with *The Harbor* in which he personified a certain picturesque corner of New York, making his characters subordinate to their environment. As the note-book of an intelligent observer the matter is significant; but the manner grows tiresome, over and over the leit-motif, without poetry or passion.

He followed *The Harbor* with *His Family;* and
won the Pulitzer Prize—as who hasn't?

(The Pulitzer Prize is awarded every year to the
one who best represents the wholesome atmosphere of
American life and best upholds the high standards of
American manners. It might best be awarded to
Matt McGrath, the shot-putting traffic cop, or to the
Boy Scouts to build themselves a rest camp. It has
nothing whatsoever to do with literature. It would
certainly have been withheld from Poe and from Mark
Twain, that chief of the barbarians.)

His Family tells of Roger Gale and his trials and
tribulations as his daughters grow up, one to become a
mother, the second a nun, and the third a fancy-woman.
It has, as Carl Van Doren has said, more kindliness
than criticism. It is an antique fable dressed out to
represent these modern times.

Then came *His Second Wife;* and we knew that Mr.
Poole had been cast in a mould he could not break.
He will go on, like a hurdy-gurdy, playing the same old
tune until he breaks down—a little mechanical, a
trifle tin-panny, but music of a sort, played where music
seldom comes.

IV

Mr. Poole feels that we have fallen upon desperate
times, that life is uncertain and men bemused. Something (he knows) will happen, soon or late, to shatter
this sorry scheme of things. But what? He cannot
tell. Ah, me, how should he know? And so he tem-
porizes.

I feel that if he had more spirit he might some day

reach a conclusion. He might, but he never will. He
is indecisive. He is the Hamlet of our latter-day realists, and only a voice from the grave can force him to
strike home—home to the heart of an intolerant and
selfish age, an age in which, later by almost ten years
to the day, Mr. Hughes follows Austria's insolent note
to Serbia with our insulting demands upon Persia, the
excuse this time being the death of Major Imbrie, as
in the first case it was the death of the Arch Duke
Ferdinand.

v

Mr. Poole was born in Chicago, January 23, 1880,
in an old-fashioned red brick house over on the North
Side. When about seven or eight years of age, growing adventurous, he joined a gang of boys and played
at various war-games about the lumber yards near the
mouth of the river. Later he was sent to a private
school and took some part in athletics. Meanwhile
he had taken up the violin and had begun to hope that
some day he might become a great musician—being
prepared for college a year ahead of schedule, he devoted that year to the study of music.

Then he went to Princeton. "It got a tremendous
grip on me," he says, "the more so because in my freshman year I was not only for a time on the Mandolin
Club, rehearsing, making short trips, etc., but because
I also tried out for the daily paper, scouring the college
for news of all kinds. I spent about six hours a day
on these two essential parts of a college education—
and failed in both. I was dropped from the Mandolin Club before the Xmas trip and was not elected

an editor.   I doubt if I shall ever forget the night on the campus when a friend going by on a bicycle told me of that failure."

Later, however, he was busy in other college activities, stood fairly well in his studies and graduated as an honor man.   He spent a great part of his time reading—long afternoons in the quiet old Princeton Library, rummaging through books of all sorts—and some time writing: the libretto of a light opera refused by The Dramatic Club, a play that received rather more than passing attention from the English profs. He belonged to one of the famous eating clubs, and with his mates took long tramps through the country round about.

"On the whole, I had a wonderful time," he says, "and should not like to have missed it—though I realize how many other things I might have learned in those four years."

VI

In 1902 he went to live in the University Settlement on New York's East Side—simply because he wanted to write about life in the crowded ·tenement sections and wanted to see it all at first hand.   He spent two or three years down there, doing little or no settlement work, giving his days and nights to digging into the ways of existence, the terrors, the celebrations of the poor—writing short stories and news articles for various magazines.

In this way he was drawn more and more into the labor and radical movements of the times.   Some sort

of revolt seemed the only way out of the terrible poverty everywhere, the want that degraded even the most
courageous, the misery that cried out to be comforted.

He began to write articles inspired by his interest in
the development and reorganization of the labor
unions.

And then, as the *Outlook* correspondent covering
the strike in the Chicago stockyards, he lived for six
weeks in the stock yards and gradually became a sort
of volunteer press agent for the union; and in that
capacity was allowed to sit in on the meetings of the
Strike Committee. A part of the knowledge so gained
he used, years later, in the latter part of *The Harbor*.

VII

Meanwhile he had learned something of the radical
movement abroad, especially in Russia; and during the
revolution of 1905 he went over to Russia for the
Outlook, remaining several months, traveling all the
way from Leningrad to the Caucasus—an exciting
journey.

He was then twenty-four years old.

VIII

Shortly thereafter he married, and during the next
few years he lived in a small house near Washington
Square, devoting his time to the writing of plays.
About a dozen in all were written, though only six
were submitted, and of those six only three produced—
two in New York and one on the road. From a financial point of view they were all failures, for the longest

run was less than three months; but they attracted some notice and—more than that—helped him to learn how to write.

IX

About ten years ago he turned to the making of novels, and wrote *The Harbor, His Family* and *His Second Wife*.   On each he spent something like eighteen months, rewriting them eight or nine times—a task that, though it sounds hard, is easier far than the construction of the first rough draft.

X

During the war Mr. Poole went to Germany as a special war-correspondent, spending some months on the Western Front.   After President Wilson announced that this country, too, was at war, Mr. Poole entered the Foreign Press Bureau of the Committee on Public Safety—and shortly after left for Russia, again as correspondent.

Since the war he has been whole-heartedly occupied as a novelist.

Mr. Poole is the author of *The Harbor*, 1915; *His Family*, 1917; *His Second Wife*, 1918; *The Dark People*, 1918; *The Village*, 1919; *Blind*, 1920; *Beggar's Gold*, 1921; *Millions*, 1922; *Avalanche*, 1924.

EDWIN MEADE ROBINSON

Ted has his enemies.

I would not say that that is, by any means, the most notable thing about him; but it takes my errant fancy captive.

"Shaw," said the sardonic Oscar, "has no enemies—and none of his friends like him." Though such an epigram is a base libel—no harm is done to Shaw, considering the source: I know a many who love Shaw devotedly: the late John Butler Yeats and his two sons, George Russell and Sir Horace Plunkett—yet there is force to such placing of your words. He has no enemies! How many times we have heard that said; and how weak the man of whom it can be said, how colorless, how anemic.

Ted is not colorless. And though he is the soul of generosity, he is not weak. He can stand out for an opinion until relief seems hopeless—and he can give ground as graciously as a courtier.

II

Ted is the author of one novel, *Enter Jerry,* the story of a boyhood spent in a small American city in the Middle West. It lacks, I think, the verve that is Ted's chief charm. It lacks the ready turn of phrase that so distinguishes his verses—notably in *Piping and*

Panning. But it is honest history, thorough and truthful. . . .

If this reads like faint praise it is only because *Enter Jerry* is not for me. Yet there are many who praised it heartily, among them the not easily pleased F. P. A., Ted's fellow in column-conducting.

III

What about a sequel to *Enter Jerry?* I asked.

"It was finished a year ago," Ted said. "Then I started the third one. I found that my plot necessitated a rewriting of a large part of the second. I recalled the book from the publisher. I haven't had time to write a line since. I was in Europe all last summer; when I came back I had a lot of extra work to do. I hope to get at the novel again this summer, when I shall be in the West."

IV

Ted is the editor of a column in the Cleveland *Plain Dealer;* and a fellow-member of mine in the Colophon Club, that recently put out *A Round Table in Poictesme*—a volume that, undoubtedly to his delight, extolled Mr. Cabell to the skies.

The only fault I can find with Ted's column is with Ted's prose—and with his too exacting demands. He expects his contributors to be as wise as Lucifer and as sane as Anatole France. Most of his time he seems to devote to proving that they are neither the one nor the other. However, the column is like a green bay tree flourishing above the plain and uninteresting levels of Cleveland journalism.

v

And now to the bare outlines of his career:—

Born in Lima (now Howe) Indiana. Grew up there (with summer intervals in the old New England homestead of his ancestors) and received his early education at Howe School—the peculiar institution described in *Enter Jerry* under another name: Osborne Academy. Went to Wabash College, Crawfordsville, Ind., A. B., 1900. Member Phi Kappa Psi Fraternity. Instructor in English, Attica (Ind.) High School, 1900. Reporter, Indianapolis *Sentinel,* 1901–2; Denver *Republican,* 1902; staff correspondent, telegraph editor, chief editorial writer, Indianapolis *Sentinel,* 1902–3; editorial paragrapher, column conductor, Indianapolis *Journal,* 1903–4; feature editor, column conductor, Cleveland *Leader,* 1904–11; column conductor, literary editor, Cleveland *Plain Dealer,* 1911. . . .

Married, Martha M. Coon, Cleveland, 1909. One son, born 1910. President American Press Humorists' Association, 1914. President Cleveland Association of Wabash Men, 1923. President The Rhymers' Club, 1923–24. Member of the City Club, The Playhouse, The Rhymers' Club, The Colophon Club, (Cleveland), and the Beachcombers' Club (Provincetown). Politics—independent; religion—ditto.

Author, *The Firstborn,* 1899, (out of print), *Mere Melodies,* 1918; *Piping and Panning,* 1921; *Enter Jerry,* 1922. Contributor for many years to *Puck* (deceased), *Judge, Life, Saturday Evening Post,* miscellaneous periodicals. Sequel to *Enter Jerry* still un-

published.   Two volumes of verse ready for the press.
Co-author of *The Book of the Rhymers' Club,* (Cleveland: three numbers now issued).   Co-author of *A Round Table in Poictesme,* (Cleveland 1924; limited edition already exhausted.   Collector's item—see catalogues of Janvier, Drake, et al).

In the fall of 1922, opened Ted Robinson's Book Shop, in the Fine Arts Building, Cleveland.   Had a good time, but found it too hard to be a bookseller and columnist at the same time.   In the summer of 1922, moved the stock to Provincetown, Mass.   Immense success.   Shop very popular—stories and pictures in all New York and Boston papers; made money.   By fall, had no books left.   Closed up, satisfied.   Only man on record who ever went into the book business, lasted only nine months, and came out ahead of the game; but if it hadn't been for Mrs. Robinson, there might have been another and a sadder story to tell. She was the business end of the venture.

Father a native of Connecticut; direct male line from John Robinson, Pastor of the Pilgrims, the John Robinson of Leyden, of Oliver Wendell Holmes' poem.   Line   goes: John—Issac—Jacob—Peter— Peter II—Vine—Edwin—William Edwin (the father)—Edwin Meade, (Ted himself)—Edwin (his son).

Mother a native of Ohio; daughter of the Rev. J. Meade Drake.

Father and mother living; residents of Portland, Oregon.   The father has been working westward from Connecticut ever since he was 21; now he has gone as far as he can and he intends to stay there.   In politics, religion and art, he is Republican, Episcopalian and Victorian, as is right and fitting; if Ted is otherwise, it is a fault of the times. Father taught Ted to love books, bass fishing and theological disputations; and Ted inherits from him a conviction that Dickens is a better novelist than Thackeray and Tennyson a better poet than Browning.

VI

Ted's first literary enthusiasm was for Dickens; *Bleak House* was the first novel he ever read. "And such," he says, "is the force of first impressions, I have read it eight times since. I was eight years old the first time.

"I discovered Kipling early and thought him the greatest of living writers. I had a Swinburne-madness at eighteen, and a Fitzgerald-Omar madness a year later. And once (about the same time) I caught a bad case of Mysticism, read many theosophical tomes and pinned much faith to the Blavatsky—Besant—Olcott—Judge delirium. I got over it."

VII

"I have learned what I know about writing," Ted says, "by writing. I have never earned my living in any other way—which means that I have turned out at least a column a day for the last twenty-four years. I seldom revise; my first copy is my last. *Enter Jerry* was copied by a stenographer from my original copy (the first draught) without change. This may be thought to be laziness; and indeed I am lazy. But I complete my sentences before I start them, and it is useless to try to improve them. They are (as none knows better than I) susceptible to improvement, but not by me. I retouch nothing that I do not ruin. I write all my verses on the typewriter and send 'em to the printer. If any bulls creep in, I know it the next day when I read the papers."

VIII

"I love Chaucer," Ted says, "Rabelais, Villon, Pepys, Cabell and other such sturdy rogues. I love Lamb, Montaigne, Sir Thomas Browne, Walter Pater, Anatole France, Austin Dobson, Max Beerbohm, C. E. Montague, Ibsen, Edna St. Vincent Millay, Franklin P. Adams, Don Marquis, Jake Falstaff, Wilbur Daniel Steele, Ring Lardner, Krazy Kat, Thomas Hardy, Henry Harland, Maurice Hewlett, Hillaire Belloc, G. K. Chesterton, Harry Leon Wilson, et. al.

"I hate Maxwell Bodenheim, Waldo Frank, *Broom* and that sort of stuff. I like Joyce's *Portrait of the Artist as a Young Man,* but I cannot tell whether I like *Ulysses* or not because I haven't read it.

"I am not a Conrad fan. I read Conrad with pleasure but without enthusiasm. I cannot read Theodore Dreiser at all; his awkward and blundering style and his total humorlessness make it impossible for me to appreciate or acknowledge his literary power."

IX

Ted says that he has never had any literary theories that he did not discard, after playing with them for a while. And he has no theories about life that are hard and fast. He is an adventurer and to be with him is an adventure. The sun comes up and the sun goes down, the wind whispers in the trees or a girl sends a glance over her shoulder—and it is all so new, so worthy of note.

Ted is alive.

ROBERT SIMPSON

If I remember rightly, long ago when some one or other, bewailing the fallen state of the nation, moaned that poor old England was lost, Dr. Johnson, his eye on Boswell, roared down the length of the table: "It is not so much, sir, that England is lost as that the Scotch have found her." Nor was it. The Scotch are a thrifty folk; and in the hundred and fifty years that have elapsed since then they have about decided that findings are keepings. What with McKenna, Mac Donald, Haldane and Balfour, England is theirs, more or less.

Mind you, I do not say that this is a calamity. It was a toss-up between Lady Astor, the Irish and the Scotch—the Scotch won. But it should be warning to us. Young Simpson hails from Scotland.

II

Young Simpson is already the author of twenty serials and four novels. He may be the author of much more before he is through, for he seems to have the energy of Dumas added to that of E. Phillips Oppenheim. And he has skill. His work improves. The latest of his novels, *Eight Panes of Glass,* while not so exciting as some of his African adventure stories, has a whimsical charm that, to say the least, to a reader of *The Bite of Benin* and the *Gray Charteris,* was wholly unexpected and quite delightful. It will not be long now before he takes his place in our affections beside the author of the *Stickit Minister*—he has already been compared to the Barrie of *A Window in Thrums*.

III

"My father," he says, "was a Scots schoolmaster of the old school, and his business in life, when I was born, was that of teaching the young idea in the vicinity of Strathy, Sutherlandshire, everything from the alphabet to Latin and Greek conjugations. A considerable part of his reward for doing this was the privilege of living rent free in the schoolhouse, which bore the same relation to the school as the manse did to the kirk. The schoolhouse at Strathy—one of the three slated-roofed houses in that meager, thatch-roofed Highland parish—stood upon the edge of a low bluff or brae overlooking the stormy Pentland Firth, and in this house, which is still twenty-one miles beyond the railway's end, I was born on October 12, 1885.

"My mother, a gentle little woman, who had been educated in an Elgin seminary and was the daughter of a small town provost, informed me afterward that the day was Friday and Melvich Market Day—an event of no little importance in those parts. That the date was also the anniversary of Columbus' discovery of America did not achieve any significance until about twenty-one years later when I began to discover America on my own account.

"I was the ninth child and, after some six months hesitation, was named for my father who had thus far resolutely refused to inflict the name of Robert upon any of my older brothers; and being registrar for the parish, his decision was made only when he was threatened by the annual visit from the inspector of registers. However, having finally and officially vested me with his own name, he seemed rather to like the idea, and thereafter paid me more attention than he had ever accorded to any of his other numerous children. I have my mother's word for this over and over again, and though he died in 1893, shortly before my seventh birthday, my memory of him is altogether one of kindness to me—this, in contradiction to memories held by my brothers and sisters that are not quite so kind.

"My father's death automatically ousted us from the schoolhouse, and the succeeding few years are best remembered by me as the meal-bag period. With her large family and painfully little money my mother moved to Thurso, the nearest railway town, and it was in this place I earned the sobriquet of Meal-bags, principally because my mother, not being a particularly good tailor, made my knickers after an all too generous pattern.

"There were about two years of Thurso, and then, in 1895, we took the longer leap to Glasgow. There I continued my schooling and held odd jobs, before and after school hours, delivering milk and newspapers and groceries in a very serious way until, at the age of thirteen, I left school behind me and went to business.

"My first job was in the offices of a political organization. And in this office, and later in the offices of the legal secretary of the organization, I came in contact with some of the biggest guns in British public life at that time. Joseph Chamberlain, Lord Kelvin,

Lord Roseberry, A. J. Balfour, Bonar Law and a host of lesser lights, helped me to form, quite early, certain fairly definite notions about the great and near-great, which may find their way into print some time. It was at this time, too, that I first turned my attention toward writing stories of my own instead of reading the other fellow's. The secretary of the political organization was Robert Bird, senior partner of the law firm of David Bird & Son. In his spare time, however, he was one of Scotland's minor poets, and the author of one or two novels, and though he had no direct influence upon my decision to write—because we never discussed the subject at all—the fact remains that I wrote my first stories while employed as a clerk in his office. Also, he was my only contact with literature in the making until I began to sell stories in New York in 1909; and even after that, until 1916, when I deserted writing for editing, I did not number among my friends a single writing man. This does not, of course, include the editors to whom I sold my stories. And at that, I had to wait seven years before I met my first editor, and he told me I couldn't write, and that I'd better stop right there. Sometimes——

"But to get back to 1902. I had been attending various night classes for English, Latin, French and a business course, and, inspired by my respect for Mr. Bird, I decided I'd become a lawyer. This decision, however, did not live longer than the first examination for at this stage of the journey toward law, I came to the conclusion that the years of preparation were going to be altogether too lean for comfort. So I secured a job as bookkeeper and cashier with a wholesale

grocer and, from this new start in life, drifted out to
West Africa two years later. This was in 1905; and
I was now eighteen, and, as the junior assistant on
a trading station on the Niger River, absorbed most
of my material for my Nigerian novels and short
stories, some of which I wrote at that time and later
sold in New York.

"My West African experience was, in the main, just
a youthful episode, but there was a great deal of writing material in it, and in this particular it was invaluable to me inasmuch as it gave me something definite
and unusual to write about. And for the man with an
ambition to write, nothing is more essential and helpful than this.

"Leaving West Africa after two years of absorbing
about as much fever and local color as I could stand,
I returned to Glasgow; and a few months later—in
August, 1907—set sail for New York. I arrived at
23rd Street on August 13, and have been in or around
Manhattan ever since.

"I celebrated my twenty-first birthday in Harlem,
was married before my twenty-second rolled around,
and sold my first stories just a jump ahead of the doctor's and nurse's bills incident upon the birth of my
first-born. The succeeding five years, until 1914,
were exclusively devoted to babies—four of them, one
of which died in infancy—to the writing of magazine
serials and short stories and to the frequently necessary business of securing a job when the returns from
writing thinned off to vanishing point.

"Fortunately, as far as writing was concerned, I
knew I was only an infant, and being lucky enough to

interest one of the Munsey Company editors—
Thomas Newall Metcalf—in my work, I sat at his feet
for three or four years, listening and learning and
profiting accordingly. And through the medium of
some twenty odd serials and numerous short stories,
which I sold to various magazines of the old time Munsey group, I began to understand something of technique and to feel that I was getting ready to stop
crawling on all fours and really begin to walk a little
bit.

"So, early in 1914, I decided to write my first book.
This was *The Bite of Benin,* a story of West African
adventure. But, though I sold it serially to Bob
Davis, who had given me an invaluable suggestion
anent the handling of the principal character in it, the
book had to wait five years to find a publisher in the
shape of James A. McCann who, in 1919, was just
starting up in business. Mr. McCann's acceptance of
the book brought about its publication by Hodder &
Stoughton, in London, and on both sides of the water
—for a first book—it was a flatteringly conspicuous
success.

"By that time, however, as previously intimated, I
had temporarily deserted the pen for the blue pencil
and was then buying fiction for the *Argosy*—a job I
was closely engaged in from 1917 to 1920. I found
that buying fiction was much easier than selling it; and
I also found, to my great profit, that it was a compelling way to learn how the other fellow went about the
business of writing; more particularly the young writer
who, though prone to mistakes and crudity, was constantly bringing to my attention some semblance of

originality.   Also, analysing 'bad ones' to find out just
why they were bad was excellent mental calisthenics;
and when I resigned my editorial chair in 1920, I
found myself in possession of a great deal of useful
information on the subject of construction which I at
once tried to put into practise.

"So much for my history.

"My early enthusiasm for writing began with plays
rather than with books.   In the beginning I was instinctively drawn toward the stage, making my first
public appearance at the age of seven in the Thurso
Artillery Hall in a version of *The Sleeping Beauty!*
From then on, almost every year until I left Scotland
for West Africa, I was mixed up in amateur dramatics
of some sort; and at the time of my departure for
West Africa I was an active member of no fewer than
four of the best dramatic clubs in the City of Glasgow.
I cannot say that any one guided me in this, any more
than in my reading or my writing.   I just wanted to
do these things and did 'em, pretty much in my own
way.

"My reading, ever since I got *Robinson Crusoe* as
a school prize at the age of six, has been ceaseless and
omnivorous.   I'll confess there was not much direction
to it for a long time, but having waded through most of
the classical and otherwise novelists from Boccacio to
Kipling, I tackled the essayists, the dramatists and the
epic poets, dabbling a little in each until I found what
I thought I liked best.   And just to indicate a few
likes and dislikes, without any profession of being anything of an authority on the subject: I like Homer

and Dante and the sagas of the north, and do not care particularly for Vergil or Milton or Ariosto. I prefer Shakespeare's comedies and his poetry to his tragedies—with the exceptions of *Hamlet* and *Macbeth*—and do not care for the Elizabethan drama as a whole. I like what I've read of Keats and Shelley and Burns and Coleridge and Pope but do not care particularly for Byron or Wordsworth or Tennyson or Scott as a poet. I like Lamb, Addison, Swift, Newman, Emerson, Carlyle, Irving, Taine and Renan, and do not care for Macauley, Bacon, Rousseau, Montaigne or Voltaire. I like Poe and Hawthorne and Scott and Dumas and Hugo and Thackeray and some of Dickens, and do not care for Fielding, Richardson, Smollett, Jane Austin, Trollope or Bulwer Lytton.

"Of modern, or near modern writers, some of those who have influenced me most have been Kipling, Barrie, Henry Seton Merriman, O. Henry, Galsworthy, George Eliot, Stevenson, Mark Twain and Bret Harte. For some reason or other, Hardy and Meredith have escaped me completely. I have not read a line of either of them!

"But of all books, as a molder of style and from a purely literary standpoint, my favorite is the *Bible*.

"My present way of life is simple in the extreme. With my wife and family I live in Sheepshead Bay, and if I have any hobbies at all, walking and reading are the sum of them. Every seven years or so I stumble upon a golf course and play something approximating a game of golf. The last time this happened was in Atlanta; and the time before that at Pelham Bay.

The next time it may be in Oshkosh or Tobermory. And yet, in my youth, I was the captain of an athletic club.

"My present plans are to write another Scottish Highland novel to succeed *Eight Panes of Glass,* to be finished sometime in the Fall. As an indication of what is possibly my only literary prejudice, I shall try to make it as different from *Eight Panes of Glass* as I possibly can. For, in fiction, there is nothing I dislike more than the string of novels, each and all of them built to a pattern and cut from the same piece of cloth.

"As for my 'literary passions,' I am pretty intense on the importance of the study of construction, and equally intense on the subject of the crying need for simplicity in an appalling number of our present day novels. Only by studying construction—technique—and making oneself the master of every trick of the trade, can one possibly cut loose from the necessity of following a formula. The really good cook never bothers with a cook book. She cooks by instinct because she has, by dint of long and understandingly acquired experience, thoroughly assimilated the technique of her business. It is the same with writing. Unfortunately the 'formula' is the shortest road to the check; and that, for too many writers who could do much better work, is that.

"And speaking of simplicity: almost any novel of four hundred pages or over is at least one hundred pages too long, and most of them could quite readily be cut in half and leave nothing out. These novels are also the result of poor construction, for simplicity is merely a matter of reducing to the fewest number of simple words the story one has to tell. Before a writer can do this successfully he must learn to the marrow of his bones the meaning of the words 'restraint' and 'elimination' and 'suggestion' so that he can restrain and eliminate and suggest, without making his story read like a synopsis. And that means the study of construction. It means work that is not paid for; not for a long time; and as far as magazine sales are concerned, it means working very hard to cut the check in half!"

IV

Mr. Simpson is the author of *The Bite of Benin* (1919), the story of a young and beautiful woman on her journey through the fever-ridden dangers of the Black Lands; *Swamp Breath* (1921), another West African adventure story; *The Gray Charteris* (1922), in which, in the person of the white-haired though still young Charteris, the author tries to picture the very spirit of adventure itself, while two rival chieftains, on the Niger, bring their feud to a close; and *Eight Panes of Glass,* a thoroughly convincing account of life in a little town in the Scottish Highlands, where a bedridden but indomitable old lady through her tact and patience straightens out the rough course of four pairs of lovers—it comes within an ace of being a really beautiful book.

UPTON SINCLAIR

Here is proof of our greatness—There is scarce a reviewer, scarce a clubmember, never a Tory in these United States who cannot (if he would) improve upon the work of Mr. Upton Sinclair—and this despite the fact that our clubmembers and Tories spend all of their time in thinking of themselves, while Mr. Sinclair devotes his enormous energies to puzzling out the problems they dismiss so glibly—despite the fact that Mr. Sinclair is highly regarded in Europe, where they are unknown.

II

They think well of Mr. Sinclair in Europe. He is, with Jack London, in France, our most popular novelist. In Denmark, Georg Brandes, the most renowned of the Danes, sings continually in praise of Mr. Sinclair. He is the only American whom Maxim Gorky reads—and Gorky is the only Russian with a world reputation, the only Russian capable of viewing with an impartial eye the whole literature of the world today—Gorky, a butcher's boy, who has made himself a formidable and a tragic figure, a figure of romance, in a series of autobiographical novels that must finally take rank with the confessions of Rousseau and St. Augustine, the memoirs of Cellini and Casanova. . . .

Mr. Sinclair has more than a touch of genius. He has something of the divine impatience of St. Francis,

the rebellious lyric quality that is the revealing spirit
of Shelley. . . .

Right or wrong—and he is often hasty, over-
shooting his mark, making an ass of himself—Mr.
Sinclair is superb, as all the ragged philosophers, since
crusading began, have been superb. . . .

But for us, alas, Mr. Sinclair is something of a fool.

III

Alas for us!

Yesterday—wasn't it?—one judge welcoming another to the bench to the oldest criminal court in
America, the county court of New York, said, "You
take your place at a time when America must answer
guilty to the charge of being the most lawless of the
civilized nations, the most degraded of the peoples of
this earth."

And to-day—twenty-four murders in the New York
papers, a running fight at sea between federal advent-
urers and rum pirates, a prize fighter on the rampage
in Los Angeles, a state's attorney in Chicago bawling
that he will be satisfied with nothing less than hanging, jury-bribing and stock-swindling, a dozen young
thugs setting upon a lone girl in the New Jersey
suburbs, a drunken prohibition agent stabbed by his
wife, a Follies girl dead in the bathtub, bathing
beauties disputing in Rye as to which has the better
turned leg, the Klan in Virginia threatening Harry
Thaw and our State Department threatening Persia,
in every line of every comment on the Ruhr a callous
unconcern for the miseries of the harried poor of
Europe—and through it all, to top it all, droning over

the radio, the blameless self-satisfaction of Mr. Coolidge, the blameless cheering of Hughes and Mondell and Butler.

IV

This is a violent and terrible country, ruled by anarchy—though supposedly governed by the most inept gang of professional office-seekers ever assembled under one banner in the cruel history of man's futile attempts to legislate his neighbor into righteousness.

V

It has been Mr. Sinclair's business to point accusingly to proofs of our depravity, our selfishness, our chicanery and meanness. We are miserable sinners. You know it and I know it. We depart from Mr. Sinclair only because we do not agree with him in the matter of emphasis. He sees in all this lust of ours, our abuses of power, a conspiracy against the weaker members of society. We are aware of no conspiracy. We believe—and I think rightly—that Mr. Sinclair in dramatizing his materials has exaggerated folly into evil. We are the most lawless nation in the world because we are the most negligent, not, as Mr. Sinclair believes, because we are the most evil. Mr. Sinclair sees evil where you and I see only indifference—among the young bloods who play polo out on Long Island, in the tennis galleries at Forest Hills, on the bleachers, along Fifth Avenue where wealth and beauty is on show. These people that are his villains are no more villainous than he who is the villain of their threatening deluge. They are the state as they see the state

—and as he sees the state, they are the shameless courtiers of Marie Antoinette. . . .

Mr. Sinclair may be all wrong, but, I repeat, he is superb nevertheless.

VI

He has no humor.

Well, who has? I have gone diligently through the novels of a generation and, on my honor, the faces are as straight as a plumb line. I would not have believed it possible that so many men through so many books for so many years could have kept such glum expressions. Almost without exception they never smile. . . .

" 'Jesus wept,' " Victor Hugo said, unveiling a statue to the old invalid of Ferney, "and Voltaire smiled. On that divine tear and human smile hangs all the sweetness of our present civilization. . . ."

Hugo, of course, was extravagant—he always was, fine ranter of hyperbole and splendor—but a smile (such as Voltaire's) would do more for us in our present slough of despond than all the analyses of all the psychiatrists sprung, like Minerva, full-grown from the brain of Freud.

VII

That is the most serious of the accusations to be brought against Mr. Sinclair—he too seldom smiles. But he does smile; and that is more than can be said for ninety-nine out of a hundred of our novelists.

VIII

He comes of fighting stock. His immediate ancestors served in the United States Navy—their fathers were with the British. It was war, the Civil War that swept away the family fortune. . . .

Into a somewhat empty house in Baltimore, into a family of no money—though of fine old traditions, the traditions of Maryland before the war—Mr. Sinclair was born on September 20, 1878. He emerged slowly, rising out of the despairing poverty of his environment, doing hack-fiction to pay his way through the College of the City of New York, graduating in 1897, and post-graduating for four years at Columbia. Before he was twenty-one (he has often said) his work bulked as large as a complete set of the Waverley novels.

His first novel, *Spring and Harvest,* appeared when he was twenty-three; and his second, *The Journal of Arthur Sterling,* two years later. In these two books he has told what, at that time, he thought was the story of his youth, the story of a young poet neglected and allowed to die by a stupid and selfish world. Already, so young, he had a personal grievance against society, for allowing him to live and almost perish in obscurity. It was, he says, an outrage.

IX

Prince Hagen, a fairy tale in the manner of Wilde's *Birthday of the Infanta,* a legend of the gold and money mad world, appeared the same year, to be later dramatized and included among Mr. Sinclair's *Plays of Protest.*

Then came *Manassas,* one of Mr. Sinclair's best books and one of the best novels dealing with the Civil War, that war of enthusiasms and bitter hatreds. It is a story repeated in *Jimmy Higgins,* a story of splendid heroisms and fearful hopes, of a new world to be shaped on the iron anvils of conflict—so Mr. Sinclair hoped in *Manassas,* so Mr. Sinclair knows was impossible in *Jimmie Higgins.* He sees more clearly now. He is less the poet and more the historian. He is less lyrical and more ironic. But he is no less moved by the magnificient courage of his fellows, no less amazed and horrified by their slaughter.

X

The Jungle appeared in 1906. For most of us *The Jungle* is Mr. Sinclair at his best, but it is really Mr. Sinclair at his most leisurely. *100%* is as good a book. The four volumes to be published under the single title of *The Dead Hand* are certainly as astounding, if not so popular in appeal. *The Jungle* had to do with the poison that is fed into our tummies by the meat barons of Chicago. *The Dead Hand* has only to do with the poisons that feed our minds, the poison of the newspapers, the schools and organized sectarianism.

XI

Mr. Sinclair had hired out in 1906 to assist in the Government investigation of the Chicago stockyards.

Packing-town was his home. He lived among the workers and got at first hand (to use the words of Clement Wood) the sordid bloodiness, the sorrowful filth, the torturing toil that ground down the hapless serfs of our modern overlords to pile up dividends for the fifth and sixth generation of them that deserve them not. . . .

Read to-day the pages of *The Jungle* wring the heart. Such brutality seems incredible. The faith of the Armours in their rights to the labor of others. The faith of Judge Gary in himself as a superman. One turns away sickened. God, what a country (you say)—no wonder the poor are at last in revolt and LaFollette raging like a lion to tax the rich out of their unearned increments.

XII

To quote from Mr. Wood again—

"Book after book followed, each laying open one of the fester spots of a moribund capitalistic society. *The Industrial Republic* is a study of ten years hence. *The Overman* pictures the higher possibilities of the spirit. *The Metropolis* uncovered the decay in the New York smart set; *The Money Changers* attacked the financial powers of the country; *The Machine* is a withering indictment of the vicious alliance between politics, finance and commercialized vice; *Samuel the Seeker* is a fictional explanation of Socialism; *Love's Pilgrimage* another of Mr. Sinclair's finer books, a treatment of love and the home relationships, with a caustic understanding; *Sylvia* continued this; and *King Coal* seeks to do for the despotic feudalism of the

Western mining camps what *The Jungle* did for the packing hells."

XIII

It may seem to some that Mr. Sinclair does nothing but complain, that he is a fault-finder—and he is— a prophet wailing in Old Testament style, Repent! Repent!

But you must not forget that, though he leaves out of his calculations much that is good, all that he puts in of brutality and sorrow is there ready to his hand. He has simply obeyed the dictum of Bernard Shaw— "If people are rotting and starving in all directions, and nobody else has the heart or brains to make a disturbance about it, the great writers must."

XIV

For making a disturbance, commend me to Mr. Upton Sinclair. . . .

As I have said our reviewers and clubmembers and Tories scorn him, but there isn't a one of them that can answer the damming accusations he brings against them and all their works.

Where are the clubs of Nineveh, the politicians, the poets and singers? And wnere—you know as well as I do—is Jonah? At the top of the pile—*n'est-ce pas?* Well, that is where Mr. Sinclair will be sitting when our social butterflies have gone down with the elite of Russia to join the washerwomen of Paris and the nurse-maids of Switzerland.

You cannot much longer put off a decent distribution of the good things of this earth. The dis-

inherited are not asking for charity but for an end of
such monopoly as our present systems of economy
encourage.

XV

"I have been supporting myself," Mr. Sinclair says,
"since I was fifteen, and always with my pen. Since
the age of twenty I have written exclusively in the
cause of human welfare, nearly all my writing being
part of the class war. I was able to say to a newspaper man the other day that in those years I have
never written a line I did not believe. I have written
many lines which were beneath my best from a literary
standpoint, for I have been ill part of the time, and
poor most of time; but I have stood by my faith such
as it was and is. I have won much notoriety and
possibly a little fame; also I have made a good deal
of money. I made thirty thousand dollars out of one
book, and proceeded to invest it at once in a socialist
colony, so organized I had no possibility of making
money out of it, it burned down, and I lost nearly
everything and started again. The next time I got
on my feet, I launched here in California" (he lives
in Pasadena) "a Socialist dramatic enterprise, again
without possibility of profit; and when I had got out
of debt from that, I went in a third time, trying to get
justice, or a tiny modicum of it, for the slaves of the
Colorado coal mines. . . .

"Before my literary success I lived in New York on
four dollars and a half a week, and later I supported
a wife and child on thirty a month. Since my success
I have taken a living out of my work; but the taking

has generally been behind the living—that is to say, I have spent more on causes than I had at the time. I have never owned an automobile—not even a Ford. I once owned a saddle horse, as a matter of health; but at present I ride a bicycle, for which I paid ten dollars second-hand. . . .

"So here, behold me, a bug impaled on a pin for study; a specimen of the agitator auriferens, popularly described as parlor socialist."

XVI

Mr. Sinclair's latest diatribe is dubbed *The Goslings,* a continuation of *The Goose-step,* and a delightfully furious assault upon our present ideas of higher and lower education and the administration of those ideas by as fancy a lot of hand-picked ignoramuses as it is possible, in four or five crowded years of research, for Mr. Sinclair to find among our professors and high school instructors.

Read it—you will be vastly entertained and no end the wiser when you are through.

JULIAN STREET

By making himself ridiculous, Mr. Street manages, in *The Need of Change,* to squeeze some fun out of the motor, the butler, the valet, the maid, the host and hostess of an English country house. He goes there with his wife over a week-end, but the forms of that polite society drive him frantic and he runs away with little ado, leaving his wife to make apology.

Ship-Bored is in much the same strain, a thing of quips and idle fancy. And *Welcome To Our City.* But in 1913 *Collier's* commissioned Mr. Street to travel from city to city through this broad land, in company with Wallace Morgan, and to write for that national institution a series of articles. That series appeared later as *Abroad at Home;* and Mr. Street had found his forte and settled down to the pleasant life of a traveling journalist, a Vigilante and one of Roosevelt's most tireless admirers.

II

Street is a nice feilow, a good mixer, one of Booth Tarkington's innumerable collaborators, a playwright, and now, with *Rita Coventry,* a novelist. For those who want their authors to treat them respectfully, he's the man. He will never bludgeon you with his prejudices; and he has made even so sour a person as I chuckle no end.

He has very kindly written an essay on himself to be included, among other things, in my book—

460

JULIAN STREET

By Himself

"My earliest memories are of my grandfather's house in an outlying part of Chicago called Oakland, which was pleasanter then than it is now. The street was called Lake Avenue, being near Lake Michigan; later it became Lake Park Avenue, a doubtful improvement, since there is about it nothing parklike.

"There I passed my early childhood, going to public school, digging caves and building shanties on the ground and in the trees. It was a simple American neighborhood, free from scandal and sophistication; most of the families on our block were old friends and almost all of them owned their houses, each with its little lawn. Those who kept horses drove them to fringe-topped surries, several neighborhood cows grazed in the vacant lots and altogether the atmosphere was not unlike that of a small town, though Chicago was then, in fact, a large city.

"At twelve I went away to boarding school (Ridley College, St. Catharines, Ontario), became interested in the school paper, and thereafter wished to be a paper man; and it was to become a reporter in New York that I left Chicago at nineteen.

"After two or three years of newspaper work, including a season of dramatic reviewing for which I was ill-equipped, I was told my services were no longer required, whereupon I joined another young newspaper man in founding an advertising agency which somehow managed to survive, though its first years were precarious. Presently I sold out to my partner and began to write for magazines.

"As a writer my difficulty has always been in the department of production. I am now (1924) forty-four years old, but with the years ease has not come to me as I hoped it would.

"In my early twenties I wrote some light verse, and later short stories and articles. I have published three large books of travel, *American Adventures, Abroad at Home* and *Mysterious Japan*. My 'best-seller' is a small book called *The Need of Change,* and other short stories of mine are assembled under the general title *Cross-Sections*. I collaborated with Booth Tarkington on a comedy, *The Country Cousin,* and my novel, *Rita Coventry,* first published in the *Saturday Evening Post,* was dramatized by Hubert Osborne and was also movieized under an alias.

"I have a wife and two children and we live in an old house in Princeton, New Jersey—a pleasant change after more than twenty years of New York. In a modest way I collect old mahogany and first editions.

"Of American literary figures of the past, Mark Twain seems to me the greatest; I have in mind particularly his *Life on the Mississippi* and his *Joan of Arc*. Of living American novelists my preference is for Booth Tarkington, Harry Leon Wilson, Edith Wharton and (since her *So Big*) Edna Ferber. *Madame Bovary* is, I think, my favorite novel, but this opinion may be colored by my sympathy for the struggles of Flaubert, and is in any case subject to change without notice. Among the short stories I most admire, aside from short stories by the novelists already mentioned, are those of Harvey O'Higgins, Thyra Samter Winslow and—to include an Englishman—Leonard Merrick. Merrick I prefer, on the whole, to O. Henry, and both I admire in spite of a

conviction that stories depending upon structural
tricks are generally inferior to stories, equally well
done, which develop out of character."

III

Mr. Street is the author of *My Enemy the Motor*,
1908; *The Need of Change*, 1909; *Paris á la Carte*,
1911; *Ship-Bored*, 1911; *The Goldfish*, a child's story,
1912; *Welcome to Our City*, 1913; *Abroad at Home*,
1914; *The Most Interesting American*, 1915; *American Adventures*, 1917; *After Thirty*, 1919; *Sunbeams,
Inc.*, 1920; *Mysterious Japan*, 1921; *Rita Coventry*,
1923.

T. S. STRIBLING

When Mr. Stribling published *Birthright,* those who think literature should be a true expression of the possibilities of life were at once surprised, delighted and a little shocked—here was a book that went to the heart of the negro's problem; and it was written by a Southerner.

If you are of the North, with time on your hands and a liking for superior airs, mention the Negro to the Southerner; say you think that something should be done for the negro; that after all he too is man and cannot be expected to drag out his life like a beast, confined to the cotton fields, employed in road-work, with no chance to give his wonder-working imagination play, no opportunity for singing and dancing—the negro who is, incarnate, the spirit of melody. Say what you will and you will have some notion, in the harassed words that greet you, of the diatribes that greeted *Birthright.* It was, according to some, a revelation; and, to others, the dastardly mouthings of a sinner seven times deadlier than the female and more original than the cynic who first bore witness against his neighbor. It was a book for those who like their books pointed and pathetic and barbed.

II

And this book Mr. Stribling followed with *Fom-bombo,* a romantic and fearful tale of Venezuela,

464

a book in the never-forgotten tradition of Marion
Crawford, with nuns and plagues and runaway
matches.

Then came *Red Sand,* sun-baked and lazy, with
bursts of temper and passion, revolution, love, the
scheming of toreadors, the machinations of big business—and a panorama of impossibilities, set down
under the tropic skies of Central America.

III

These three books have set Mr. Stribling apart,
with a name of his own, and a place that, were he a
Spaniard, would be second only to that earned by
Blasco Ibañez among those who do not like their
heroes to take "no" as an answer from women.

IV

Mr. Stribling has gone to some pains to give me the
story of his life. I shall not alter so much as a
comma:—

"The 'T. S.' in T. S. Stribling, stands for Thomas
Sigismund, both of which are old names in my family.
The Striblings were in this country before the Revolution, and my father's uncle had an old flint lock and a
canteen which had seen service in the Revolutionary
War. The family of my father, C. C. Stribling, came
from North Carolina to Lawrence County, Tennessee,
where my father was born. When he was sixteen years
of age the Civil War broke out and he immediately
joined the Union Army, was captured at Shiloh and was
confined for about a year in the confederate prison at
Tuscaloosa, Alabama. Later, in the years 1904–5,

I taught school at Tuscaloosa and saw the old prison where my boyish father had been imprisoned. He was eventually exchanged, returned to the Union Army and fought through the remainder of the war.

"My mother was Amelia Waits before her marriage. The Waits family immigrated from South Carolina to North Alabama where my mother was born. All of my mother's brothers fought in the Confederate Army, my Uncle Lee Waits being wounded in the Battle of the Wilderness. My mother taught school in Waynesboro, Tenn., where she met my father. When they married they settled at Clifton, Tennessee, where father ran a country newspaper. He and mother did all the work of typesetting, proofreading, themselves. In the midst of this atmosphere of printer's ink, I was born on March 4th, 1881.

"I suppose I inherited the taste because I never in my life wanted to do anything but write stories. As early as I can remember I have been trying to write. Also, when I was much younger, I was obsessed with the idea that not only would I write, but I would become a very great author.—I didn't know just when. I never mentioned this faith except twice in my life. My original name was not Thomas Sigismund, but Thomas Hughes Stribling. My father named me for a friend named Hughes. The daughter of this friend once reproved me for throwing stones at her pigs, and said she was ashamed for a boy who bore her father's name to be throwing stones at pigs. I said, 'All right, I'll change my name to something else, but that is your father's last chance ever to get his name in history.'

"About this time my own father had sold his newspaper and was running a village store. It was a typical village store, a dark jumbled place with plows, tobacco, bacon and hardware, cheek by jowl. He put me in as a very little fellow to clerk. I was small enough to sit down behind a counter and be perfectly concealed. I took the wrapping paper for a pad, hid behind the counter and started stories while the trade passed in and out. Father warned me a number of times that he would surely whip me if I didn't quit hiding, but trading was such a bore and writing so pleasant, I overstepped the limit. So father took me and a strap to the hardware room. I can recall now my mental writhings for a word fitly chosen to get me out of my dilemma. Just as he was about to strike I gasped out,

" 'Wait! Wait, Papa, do—do you want to go down in history as a man who beat your little boy for learning to write?'

"He didn't whip me but gave me a severe lecture, and later told the incident to mother as a great joke.

"I never would clerk, nor indeed do any other sort of work because I wasn't interested in it, and money, *per se,* never had any especial attractions for me. When I was a boy I looked over my home village, of Clifton, and saw a few wealthy men and many poor ones, but they all appeared to be getting an equal lot of fun out of life, with the preference, if any, going to the poor; and I acquired a disrespect for money, which I think I still have. Money is nice enough, but it's no use bothering your head about it. Moreover I am convinced that few men are in business for the money. The only service brute money performs is to act as a barometer of their success or failure. One likes to make money because one feels one is getting on, but beyond a fairly low point, no person can spend money on himself without becoming absurd; and I have noticed successful men do not make themselves absurd.

A man with brains enough to succeed, usually has brains enough to live afterward.

"However, what I wanted to do was to write, and according to the belief of my family and my village, writing was a direct road to pauperism. I was always afraid of my father, but I would go around to my mother and beg naïvely, 'Mamma, let me be a writer.' And she would say sadly, 'You can't make a living, just writing, Tom.' Once I asked one of my teachers to go to my parents and beg them to let me be a writer. He did so, assuring my parents I had talent. But what was the use of having talent when writers starved either with or without.

"In the interim I went on keeping diaries, going out into the woods and trying to write down how the trees looked. One of my sharpest recollections is walking in an old corn field among dead corn stalks in a drizzling rain, and wondering just what I could write to catch that gray veil of rain and the soaked melancholy field.

"First Dickens and then Tolstoy acted as models for me to judge my writing ability. I would write a story or a page or paragraph, and then read a page or two out of *The Resurrection* and I could feel how much solider and more intense was the work of the great Russian than what I had done. I would puzzle and fret over it. What in the world had Tolstoy done that I couldn't do? It eluded my childish analysis, but I felt my lack as a painful thing, and I would try to describe something else, a crowd, a building, the river on which I lived, anything, but somehow or other, the Russian always managed to stay a lap or two ahead.

"I cannot remember when I was not sending stories to magazines. My first acceptance came from a little magazine in Louisville, Ky., called the *Illustrated*

South.   A month later the editor accepted another; both gratis.   Those were the last stories I had accepted until a period of about six more years had passed, during which I continued to write assiduously.

"At last I came to the conclusion that I would never be printed at all; that it was impossible for me ever to earn my living at such work, but nevertheless I continued.   I did not keep on through any strength of purpose or of character; there was no grim determination or anything like that about me.   I kept on because it amused me to write and all work bored me.   I kept on because I wasn't very keen about money anyway, and was bent on having a good time while I could.

"One day my father told me I would have to choose a profession.   He said I wouldn't work so he thought I would better go to school and become a lawyer, which was sort of like writing—only different.

"I was bundled off to Florence, Alabama, to live with my mother's brother, Uncle Lee Waits.   My uncle got me a place in the law office of George Jones, who was one of the finest lawyers in Alabama.   Mr. Jones had a huge legal library with a few good books of fiction stuck in it here and there, and above all he had a typewriter.

"It had always seemed to me if I had a typewriter I could write my stories neatly and perhaps sell them.

"Now I seized on Mr. Jones' typewriter with a hunger of years standing, and I kept it going constantly all summer long.   Mr. Jones, who was in his office only semi-occasionally, reported my doings to my uncle.   He said, 'For the last month or so I have been thinking that boy was the most assiduous law student I ever saw.   I thought he was making notes on my whole library.   He worked all day long like a slave. Yesterday I glanced over some of his notes, and it is some sort of tomfoolery about how a boy loved a girl, and that's what he's been sweating over for months.'

"But my uncle did not take me out as Mr. Jones perhaps implied, but he gave me a talking over and told me I'd better get down to brass tacks.   Mr. Jones did not turn me out on his own account because he was a friend of my uncle's, and he had plenty of stationery and typewriter ribbons.

"The following autumn I entered the Normal College in Florence, Alabama, and finished in two years. Then I took a somewhat more serious law course in Tuscaloosa, Alabama, where I was graduated in 1904. Again I went to Florence and started practicing law with a Mr. John Ashcraft, but again I slumped into stories and became the merest hanger-on.   By this time I had it drummed into my head that it really was necessary to make some money even if I did not respect it deeply.   Just when my legal career was fizzling out through inertia, I received a letter from the editor of a small magazine in Nashville to come up and go to work on his magazine.   I did so and was put in the subscription department—keeping the lists straight for the printer.   This in turn languished because I didn't care anything about lists.   In the meantime I had borrowed an old typewriter from the office and wrote every night in my bedroom until I went to sleep.   I turned out reams of unsalable stuff.   I wrote novels, short stories, all sorts of things.

"Then into my subscription department one day walked a well dressed boy of about my age.   He had a story he wanted to sell to the magazine.   We got to talking and he said he made his living regularly by writing stories.   I asked him what did he use in making a sale, the sand bag or automatic.   He said neither, he sold to the Sunday school magazines.   That was the first time I had ever heard of a Sunday school magazine. I had never haunted Sunday schools to any great extent. But this young fellow gave me a list of these little periodicals, and also explained the idea of a Sunday school story—just any little adventure with a sort of moral twist to it.

"I went home that night and wrote two Sunday school stories. I sent them to the address and next Friday I received five dollars for the two.

"The next month I parted with my subscription lists. I won't say I resigned, for the satisfaction at parting was mutual, but I quit on the strength of my five dollar check and went to New Orleans where I lived in an attic in an unsavory part of town and wrote seven Sunday school stories a day regularly. I had at last gone to work at something I liked and I worked terrifically. No, that isn't a good word, I worked beatifically, rapturously.

"I can say this about Sunday school stories, and I am sure I have written ten thousand, they allow a far wider latitude of thought and philosophy than any one dreams of who has not followed that market. I have had stories rejected by the *Youth's Companion* as too risky, and not sufficiently moral and had them accepted by these little magazines. Their pay, of course, is slight, but you can live on it, and after all what more than life can one want, if one is doing what one loves to do.

"I wrote Sunday school stories steadily for about ten years, then suddenly I balked. My ideas became too complicated and too undecided for Sunday school consumption. I began to perceive that heroes were not always right nor villains always vile. Also my style had expanded from the abridgement of a short story to the detail of a novel.

"And still I could not write for the regular magazines.

"That was just about the time America entered the World War and everyone was experiencing a material and mental upheaval. I decided I needed to see a little of life, which it seemed to me I had somehow entirely avoided meeting. So I went to work on the Chattanooga *News;* then I went to Washington and worked as a stenographer in the aviation bureau, and still somehow I slid around life.

"In Washington I exhausted myself typing all day, but at night I would dig out a few pages of copy and finally had a story which I sent to *Adventure Magazine.* I received two hundred and fifty dollars for it, the first check of any size I ever received.

"That was the last of the Sunday school stories with me. I came home and went to work on grown up fiction. At first I stuck to the usual rather impossible stuff the American magazines somehow prefer, then I tried my hand on a novel that not only was possible but that was palpably true. My friends in New York telegraphed me it was a great book but that I could never hope to get it printed. However, it did get printed and was discussed to some extent, and this book, *Birthright,* made it fairly easy for me to get an editorial hearing in any American magazine or book publishing house. I don't mean to say any magazine will take anything I write, far from it, but they will read what I have written and consider it, which is something.

"If I should revert to my early Sunday school training and draw a moral from this tale, I suppose it would be: Do what you like without regard to consequences. I should say that if most Americans were not so anxious about the physical setting of their lives they would have a better time. However I would not press my particular philosophy on any other person, for philosophies are all tailor-made and fit nobody except their owners.

"I have a few hobbies. I like golf and bull fights. I play one badly and the other not at all. I like the Russian novelists best of all, but I think *The Forsyte Saga* one of the greatest novels I ever read, although I don't care much for anything else Galsworthy ever wrote.

"On the whole I have ceased to enjoy fiction and seldom read it, but I do get a great thrill out of writing it.

"It may just be possible that my method of writing fiction is unique in America. I write in an invalid's chair, and vary my writing with numberless naps. I sleep a little while, write a little while, sleep again, write again, and so on. I never cudgel my brain for the solution of a situation, I sleep. When I wake up if I haven't got it I sleep again. Finally I have it—without labor. I never did like work."

Mr. Stribling is the author of *Birthright, Fombombo* and *Red Sand*.

BOOTH TARKINGTON

Mr. Tarkington is that most incorrigible person, the parsons's next of kin; and it follows that his sins are many. He is, for one thing, our most consummate liar; and—but that should suffice as a first count.

II

Take the end tacked onto *The Magnificent Ambersons.*

The Magnificent Ambersons retells the story of *The Egoist* in terms of a fast-growing city in our own Middle-West; and up to a certain point the retelling is admirable. Mr. Tarkington's hero is despicable: and Mr. Tarkington knows it. No pains are spared to deal out to him a fair and even justice. He is the gilded calf; but his feet are clay and Mr. Tarkington wastes no time in idle worship. Mr. Tarkington is fair—up to a certain point. . . .

The magnificence of the Ambersons began in 1873 when Major Amberson made a fortune; and the book tells of the blaze of glory in which his daughter marries, of the devotion with which she spoils her son and the arrogance in which that son grows up. He rides roughshod over friend and foe; and we wait, with his distracted neighbors, while fate (in the person of Mr. Tarkington) plays out to him the rope with which, soon or late, he must hang himself. We can bide our wrath, for time is with us. The world moves and he will be left standing, alone and forlorn, in his

distorted attitude of graceless nobility. He is in the
wrong tradition and he will be deserted. The world
moves; and the world will move despite his prejudices,
in ignorance of them and in defiance of his family.

But he will not care. He has an almost illimitable
contempt for the world. Riffraff, he calls the struggling men and women all about him. He is a gentleman; he will not associate with them; he will retire
from the world and dwell in the ivory towers of his
pride, in the security of his mother's love.

Yet the world moves. The automobile is invented.
Git a horse! he shouts after it as it goes lumbering
down the street. The automobile is brought to a
comparative perfection; but still he is unable to understand the necessity for such contraptions. Over and
over he proves incapable of meeting and adjusting
himself to the changing conditions of life. And the
boy is father to the man. He goes away to college
and returns unchanged—the Ambersons are still the
Ambersons and the people of the town are, as always
to him, riffraff.

So far so good. Mr. Tarkington proves equal to
a difficult task. His hero is utterly incompetent and
Mr. Tarkington has made no bones about saying so.
And then the hero's mother dies; his grandfather dies;
the family disperses; their fortune is gone; George is
thrown out onto the world, friendless, without talents,
with no money. We know, of course, what his end
must be. We may feel pity for him now, but the
world is no more selfish than he was in the days of his
easy, second-hand triumphs. The world is about business of its own. It will ignore him—as once he chose

to ignore the world—and it will soon forget. He will become a laborer, a tramp or a suicide. That's the way with life—you sow tares and reap a harvest of weeds.

We have Mr. Tarkington's word for all this. It is the old story of King Robert of Sicily—the mighty shall be cast down from their seats. We need no monks chanting the *Magnificat* to point the moral. We know. As I have said, we have Mr. Tarkington's word for it.

But have we? And even though that word be given can we rely upon it? Apparently not. George marries an heiress.

III

In a letter to Julian Street, written in 1917 when *The Magnificent Ambersons* was nearing completion, Mr. Tarkington tells of the hectic winter he has been passing through, constantly interrupted what with meetings of one kind and another and even (heaven save the mark!) with pleas for speeches. "It is no time," he says, "for a novel, yet somehow I am writing —digging a little deeper than before, but the action is so slow that there appears to be none at all, and people may not read the book."

People—but somehow they must be made to read it. Oh how? how? how?

And Mr. Tarkington begins to wrack his brain.

"It is my usual later plan," he says, "a slowly intensifying situation—developed a little further—the hero an overbearing important-family-in-Midland-town boy—begin before his birth and combine his life with the life of an epoch in the town's life—the town's change is the jugernaut that goes over him."

Can you think of a more ambitious plan or a worthier one? Mr. Tarkington has turned honest at last. He has given up romancing and sugar-coating life.

But has he? In that letter to Julian Street there is yet another phrase to be quoted—the jugernaut goes over him, but "of course that's not all."

No, of course not.

His hero is in City Hospital, with both legs broken and innummerable internal pains; he may die; but he is not beyond hope so long as Mr. Tarkington can worry about his readers. Mr. Tarkington can save him—and what's more, Mr. Tarkington will. Mr. Tarkington has had an heiress up his sleeve all the time.

IV

The Magnificent Ambersons was awarded the Pulitzer Prize of $1000 in 1918 because *The Magnificent Ambersons* is a "wholesome picture of American life." Wholesome pictures are a business with Mr. Tarkington. He is adept in their presentation. So it need surprise no one that again, in 1921, he should receive the Pulitzer Prize, this time for *Alice Adams*.

Alice Adams purports to be the true story of a true girl growing up in a pinched and stupid family, pretending to be at least as good as she is, making a friend and becoming engaged to him only to have the engagement broken when he meets the family.

As you can see, an ambitious plan carried (this

time) to a fitting climax. It is perhaps a little too
sentimental in its avowed sympathy for Alice; it may
be less lively than is usual with Mr. Tarkington; it
is certainly not the flawless novel Julian Street thinks
it. But it is good. The only fault that I can find
is that again Mr. Tarkington has allowed his readers
to do the writing for him. *Alice Adams* is every
girl's idea of her own superiority to her miserable
family. Mr. Tarkington shows us what she could
have been, what she hoped to be, and then excuses her
for not being all that one might expect because—well,
look at the family!

Nor is Alice a tragic figure. All this pother is
about nothing very much—except, of course, that she
would rather marry than go to work. But desire, in
any real sense, she never feels. It is not Russell that
she loves but his assured prosperity and the assured
position a marriage with him would give her. Indeed,
her queer efforts to enchant her lover are of the stuff
from which countless farces have been made. But
that stuff is never farcical in the hands of Mr. Tarkington. And that is the true significance of *Alice
Adams*. After so many years spent in laughing at
and with adolescence, Mr. Tarkington has at last come
to an understanding of the essential pathos of youth
in a world dedicated to the pursuit of power and
wealth.

v

It is a step forward. But Mr. Tarkington steps
right back again in the latest of his offerings, *The
Midlander*. *The Midlander*—if we are to believe

Robert Morse Lovett; and I do believe him—is a
feeble presentation of the Indiana superman, by conventional methods from material which has become
trite.

VI

Mr. Tarkington does not change. Indiana super-
men, conventional methods, material that has become
trite—these are his humanity, his wit and wisdom.
For twenty-five years he has been writing about the
Midlands and for twenty-five years, with one benign
smile or another, he has murmured, with Harkless in
The Gentleman from Indiana, "the dear, good
people." The dear people, the good people—that,
and that alone, is his comment on the emptiness and
loneliness of life in the Middle-West, the futility of it,
the shallow pretence, crowding together in hail-fellow
clubs, bargaining with bootleggers, smirking when
graver passions are mentioned, corrupting the language
in feeble imitations of vaudeville actors doing the more
expensive movie theaters. It may sicken his heroes;
they may rebel; but it does not sicken Mr. Tarkington. You can always climb out of it, he says—always,
mind you, and especially when Tarkington is your
creator—and seen from above it's not so bad. . . .

That is the moral of *The Turmoil.* And the wind-
up of *The Turmoil* is Bibbs Sheridan, an ugly duckling,
with wasted years of dreaming behind him, suddenly,
over night, to leave a good taste in the reader's mouth,
become a master of capital and the lord of beauty.

But the city of *The Turmoil,* though unnamed by
Mr. Tarkington, is Zenith, Babbitt's Zenith; and it

is high time that Mr. Tarkington found it out.
These, his characters, are the men and women whose
governor is doing time in Atlanta for using the mails
to defraud, who vote for Jim Watson and are terrorized into joining the Klan, who realize their greatest
happiness in getting down to the office bright and early
and home in time for Mah Jong at night.　Penrod is
Babbitt's son; and Penrod's future is Babbitt's past—
football leading to a sports roadster, petting climaxed
in a loveless marriage, the fraternity exchanged for a
so-called athletic club.　Not—it needs no saying—bad
in themselves, but utterly hopeless and soul-destroying
when they are all there is and all there can be to life,
when they are life, its pleasures and ambitions, its joys
and reward.

VII

Mr. Tarkington has, of course, come out as a realist
now that realism is the fashion.　But he has dawdled
so long, toying with his readers, musing upon the
rewards of virtue, that Red Lewis, exasperated, in two
books, was able to remake his entire world, rechristen-
ing the *Midlands* Main Street.　Every house in Tark-
ingtonia has heard of Lewis, his name is used to con-
jure there; and the scandal of Carol Kennicot's rebellion has become fireside gossip.　When one author
allows another to invade his kingdom and with an air
of finality, brush its significance aside, that author's
measure has been taken. . . .

There is, of course, truth to Mr. Tarkington's as-
sumptions—not all Mid-Westerners are fools, as *The
Green Bay Tree* proves.　But Mr. Tarkington has

never produced a book as good as *The Green Bay Tree*. His has been a house of cards—and now that the winds of controversy blow about it, it is tumbled, scattered, gone into the discard.

VIII

Perhaps Mr. Tarkington feels, as did the elder sons of Noah, that it would be disloyal to expose his father's nakedness, for he is himself a Midlander and the son of Midlanders. For three generations the family has been prominent in the affairs of Indiana. Mr. Tarkington's father John Stevenson Tarkington, (died 1922, aged ninety), was captain of the 132nd Indiana Infantry during the Civil War, a member of the State legislature and a judge of the circuit bench —the last few years of his life he devoted to literature, publishing two books. Mr. Tarkington's mother was Elizabeth Booth; and he was christened for an uncle, Newton Booth, who had at one time been Governor of California and at another a senator from that State. He was himself born in Indianapolis, July 29, 1869.

Before he could write, Mr. Tarkington began to dictate stories to a long suffering sister. These stories bodied forth his two principal heroes, Jesse James the outlaw and G. P. R. James the novelist. They always began at dusk and usually four horsemen could be seen crossing the brow of a hill. Later they were dramatized and enacted as desperate robber plays out in the barn.

It was the youth of Penrod, a town boy's youth, for Indianapolis was neither city nor country but just a town in those days—and a near neighbor was James Whitcomb Riley.

The poet and the boy became fast friends and they remained friends up until the time of Riley's death. They used to take long walks together and wind up with midnight suppers of pie, watermelon, strong coffee and Welsh rarebit.   Meredith Nicholson was another of Mr. Tarkington's boyhood friends.

IX

When it came time for the boy to go away to school, he was entered at Phillips Exeter Academy.   From there he entered college at Purdue, transferring to Princeton as a Junior.   At Princeton he helped to revive, and was for a time editor of *The Tiger;* he contributed essays to *The Lit;* he wrote a play for the Triangle Club, made Ivy, and, on graduation, was voted the most popular and the most promising member of the class of '93—his singing of *Danny Deever* is still remembered and has become something of a legend.

X

On leaving Princeton, Mr. Tarkington returned to Indianapolis and set himself up as a writer.   He began to read a great deal and (in Stevenson's famous phrase) to play the sedulous ape to such writers as he admired.   But, as Overton has remarked, the unusual and interesting part of all this is that the beginner kept his activities strictly to himself.   He was a little ashamed of them; he has always been ashamed of fussing, as he puts it, with litrachoor; he does not "want to be caught writing prose." So he pretends that he is a social lion; he gives himself over to the appearances of being a good fellow—and he is a good fellow. There is no more charming host, no more tactful friend. Everywhere Tark is popular.

But this sort of thing exacts its price. His writing has suffered.

Nor would this matter were Mr. Tarkington— Harold Bell Wright or Henry Sydnor Harrison. It is no crime to suit the fancy of good fellows. But Mr. Tarkington had genius; and that, as James Branch Cabell has remarked, is even more tragic than the pleasant wind-up of *The Magnificent Ambersons*.

XI

Mr. Tarkington is generally considered our most fortunate writer. He has the ear of the public, the good-will of the booksellers and the respect (so far as anyone knows) of the reviewers. Yet the first five years of his writing life netted him just $22.50.

In '95 he got a pen drawing into *Life* and thought his start had come. *Life* then proceeded to reject 31 additional drawings and Mr. Tarkington quit—that is, he quit drawing and proceeded to bombard the editors with *Cherry* and *Monsieur Beaucaire*. *Cherry* was accepted for *Harper's* (and paid for); but Mr. Alen had not the courage of his convictions, so *Cherry* was put away in a desk drawer. And then *Monsieur Beaucaire* got around to S. S. McClure; and Mr. McClure not only accepted it, but published it in his magazine—and Mr. Tarkington was made.

XII

Monsieur Beaucaire tells of how Prince Louis-Phillipe de Valois masquerades as a barber in the train of the French Ambassador to England; and then, thinking better of it changes his mind and becomes a fop and gambler at Bath.   He is misjudged on the evidence of his own disguises, just escapes catastrophe when the French ambassador, arriving in the nick of time, reveals his true identity—and, then, in honest Tarkington fashion, Beaucaire graciously forgives the beaux and belles who had so cruelly doubted him—why not?

XIII

Monsieur Beaucaire was followed almost immediately by *The Gentlemen from Indiana,* through which drifts the melancholy Harkless, seven years out of college and not yet a howling success.   But he rises because there must be some compensation for the bitter years spent in struggling up out of the commonplace life of a small midland town—he rises to Congress, the consummation of all his splendid dreams.

XIV

The Conquest of Canaan (1905) is played through to much the same tune—Lowden, the associate of rowdies, wins the mayoralty with a rush once he is ready.

Indeed, Mr. Tarkington has only one or two plots —in that being about three ahead of Mark Twain. "Don't worry about plot," Tarkington says. "The characters make their own plot—all the plot they should have. Think of them in their relation to one another and they will make your story. Your struggle should be against everything extraneous. It is unusual poignancy that makes a book unusual, not unusual plot. Treatment is the big thing."

And it has been the big thing with Mr. Tarkington. Take his attitude towards the young lovers in *The Magnificent Ambersons*. They are sitting out a dance; the steps are narrow and uncomfortable; moreover they are strangers to each other; they had met for the first time that night and neither had said anything in which the other might discover matter for profound thought; there had not arisen between them the beginnings of congeniality—but stairways, as Mr. Tarkington points out, have much to answer for, more perhaps than moonlit lakes or mountain sunsets—and he muses upon the laws of glamour—he comes right out and says that the world would be wiser if Sir Isaac Newton had been hit on the head, not by an apple, but by a young lady—because the laws of glamour must be discovered and (evidently) only a Newton can discover them.

Of course, this is superficial stuff, but it is none the less delightful.

XV

Then there is *Seventeen*.

Seventeen is Mr. Tarkington's high water mark. It is farce, without passion, without poetry, palpably insincere and shallow—but it is hilarious. The fool in every boy is made a hero and offers himself up as another Sidney Carton to the implacable stupidity of the world.   Baxter never comes alive, but he is nonetheless a creation with his calf-love, his sighs, his fastidious scorn for the mere business of living; and I should no more think of criticizing him than I shall think of criticizing *Bunker Bean*.

XVI

Indeed it is folly to criticize Mr. Tarkington or to expect great things of him.   Books are written to be read; and that would be his answer, as it was Dr. Johnson's long ago—the answer to a thousand cavils. There remains only a doubt as to whether it be answer enough.   Dr. Johnson, at any rate, did not always truckle to the prejudices of his readers.

FREEMAN TILDEN

Every once in so often something or other in the daily round reminds some reviewer or other of Mr. Freeman Tilden and the worth of Mr. Tilden's works. Then we are told that we should read Mr. Tilden, that we must read him, that he will amuse us—not to have read *Mr. Podd* and *Khaki* argues a lack etc. in us. Always the assumption seems to be that we have not read *Khaki* or *Mr. Podd*. Why? No one would think of advising us to read *Main Street;* no one offers advice concerning Conrad or Bennett or Wells; we are not taken aside, openly, and held, with bold faced type, amazed, to listen to the merits of *Cranford* or *Kipps* or *Love Among the Artists*. Why, then, should *Mr. Podd,* that is scarcely a year old, be held up to our belated attention? Who told the reviewers—for, as a rule, they are told the things they know—that Mr. Tilden, along with Amrose Bierce and Leonard Merrick, belongs to that great company of the unread which includes Firdusi and Lucian and Lao Tze? What are the merits of Mr. Tilden's books that they should be ignored, as for so long Dreiser was ignored, as Cabell might be but for *Jurgen?* Who is Mr. Tilden anyway and what are his peculiar virtues?

II

Mr. Tilden is a writer of magazine articles on farming, an upholder of the home, a tourist recently returned from Europe and now busy recounting (with what humor he can) his adventures among the strange and alien peoples of the continent—backward peoples who have none of our decisive love of order and action, lackadaisical folk whose trains are so quaint, to whom a bath is a luxury, to whom English is almost an unknown tongue. Mr. Tilden is a kindly critic of this whirling globe, with a notion that haste makes waste.

III

Few and far are the lands where the jumblies live; and far and few are the masters of humor. Nothing is so rare, even in June, as perfect nonsense. Yet Mr. Tilden aspires to be nonsensical, Mr. Tilden wants to be funny, tries to be funny, and, at times, succeeds in being funny. *Mr. Podd* is funny.

Mr. Podd was inspired by the mirth-provoking slogan of the Oscar II—Get the boys out of the trenches by Christmas! Mr. Podd, as Mr. Tilden reveals him to us, hopes to bring about a reign of enduring peace on earth. And so he outfits a peace ship. With a cargo of peace-makers he sets sail from New York. Over the bounding waves he sails and all about him peace-makers argue their various panaceas, their plans for world peace. There shall be an end to war, and an end to race prejudice and hatred. But how to consummate so dear a dream? No two plans agree. No two peace-makers agree or can be made to agree by the ineffectual and idealistic Mr. Podd. Hate is engendered; trouble brews; there is intrigue and backbiting and gossip aboard ship. Then the ship is

grounded, the party wrecked, on an island in mid-seas.
Here is Mr. Podd's opportunity and an opportunity for
those who have accompanied him to prove the infinite
possibilities of pacificism. Here, far from outside
interference, a kingdom can be set up, a heavenly kingdom, law-abiding and just. But is it? Foolish question number I know not what. Of course, it isn't.
Pacificists are only human, vaguely human, errantly so.
They criticize the shibboleths one of the other. They
waste time in debate that might better be used in practical experiments with governing. Mr. Podd has
more trouble than ever Charles Livermore will have,
at great expense in time, patience and money.

Mr. Podd and Mr. Bok and Mr. Ford—a trio of
dreamers—fit butts for the paragraphs of columnists!

IV

So ends for Mr. Tilden a chronicle of vain endeavor. But Mr. Tilden forgets that dreaming is not
necessarily ridiculous simply because dreams are sometimes impossible of realization. The unselfish St.
Francis, renouncing the world, took poverty as a bride
and left (as his heritage to mankind) a plague of
gray friars, begging at every door in Christendom.
The austerity of Cromwell's puritans ushered in the
license of the Restoration. So it is with hope again
and again.

No, though *Mr. Podd* makes us laugh at the folly of
the pacificists, it is not a good or a fine or a fortunate
book. We may decide, with the reviewers, that it is
funny, but (alas for human decisions) a book must be
more than that. It should be profound and wise

and witty; and it should run counter to our unreasoning complacencies.

V

Mr. Tilden is always like that. He seizes upon the prejudices of the crowd, their know-nothingness, and exalts them into criteria. He is the first to laugh at misadventures. But that sort of humor is all too easy. It cannot be compared to the understanding raillery of Ring Lardner or the apt articles of George Ade. Cervantes was gentle with Don Quixote and loved him.

VI

I recently came upon three paragraphs by Mr. Tilden, under the caption *Man Proposes,* comparing Fielding and Dickens to their hurt with the mode of proposal now in good form.

Says Fielding: "O my Sophia, do not doubt the purest passion that ever inflamed a human breast." And so on, for three pages, in this strain, according to Mr. Tilden.

And Dickens, in *David Copperfield:* "Dearest Agnes! Whom I so respect and honor—whom I so devotedly love!"

Lastly: "Listen, Ethel!" etc., so unaffected and to the point.

The purpose of Mr. Tilden is plain. We are to consider the out-worn styles of Fielding and Dickens and rejoice that we, at any rate, do not engage in any such ridiculous talk.

Now I ask you—do we need to think ourselves

superior to Dickens and Fielding? Are we so fine
that we can afford to look down on them? Is our
speech so refined, so true and clean and honorable that
we can find no good in the men and the women of gone
days? And is it fair to us to so mislead us concerning
Fielding and Dickens that we assume this to be a fair
sample of the best they have to offer? Are we to believe ourselves well rid of any necessity for reading
their books? Are we the better for not reading them?

VII

"It is not often that I write about myself," Mr. Tilden says, in reply to a letter of mine. "I think the
only other time I ever told the story of my life was
when I made out my questionnaire during the draft——

"I was born in Malden, Mass., (near Boston),
August 22, 1883. My paternal ancestors were English; they came from Tenterden, England, in 1628,
eight years after the *Mayflower*. Maternal ancestry
is English-Irish. So far as I know, the Tildens, in
that two hundred and fifty odd years in America, were
never engaged in purely intellectual occupation until
my father, Samuel Tilden, became a newspaper editor,
after having been a master printer. They had been
ship-builders for the most part.

"As I grew up in the atmosphere of newspaper offices, it was not unnatural that I should follow in that
business. My newspaper apprenticeship was at the
Boston *Globe*. Afterwards I was with the *News and
Courier* of Charleston, S. C., and then came to the
New York *Evening Post,* where I did my last newspaper work. To say truth, the newspaper work never
enthralled me. I regard it as a superior training

school; but, the everlasting ineffectuality and 'dailiness' of it wore on me.   I was not a good newspaper man. I could write entertainingly, but I never acquired the facility for intrusiveness which is the reporter's stock in trade.   After that, (after the newspaper training), I traveled a good deal in Europe and South America. By this, I do not mean that I went a-foot or adventurously.   My notion of wild adventure would not lead me, at farthest, to do more than spend a night in a third rate hotel.   I marvel at those who tramp abroad.   To make a journey through Siam on foot is, to be sure, a novel experience, but I think as preparation for fiction one would do better to cultivate meetings of the Plumbers' Union or the Longshoreman's Literary Society or Grocers' Picnics.   That is my notion; I claim no merit or originality for it."

VIII

Having entertained few illusions concerning life, Mr. Tilden has had few disappointments.   When his first volume of fiction, *The Night and Other Stories,* was a *succes d'estime* and not another *Soldiers Three* he was not disappointed.   He had wanted to find out if there was a public for satirical sketches; and he found out.   For such sketches as he wrote there is not.   So Mr. Tilden switched to the popular magazines, wrote deliberately for the *Saturday Evening Post,* sold his writings, and made money.

IX

He lives on a small farm in the Berkshires, and writes at length on farming for the press.   In the winter he plans what he will do when spring comes round again; but in the summer his plans amount to little or nothing, for in the summer he is tired—so he sits on the porch and reads books published prior to 1870.

X

"Neither my philosophy," he tells me, "nor my position in life or literature are at all fixed. They are notably fluid. I try to maintain a policy of benevolent indifference—or, if that sounds paradoxical, you might call it static good-will. My own notion is that if you attend to your own moral and spiritual growth and improvement, other people will thrive better. I would as lief knock a man down and trample on him as prod him with unasked assistance. But if he be mentally sick, I will, if he seems to want it, practice any sort of buffoonery to laugh him into a better mood.

"I used to write for *Puck* in the old days when it was a humorous paper published by Keppler and Schwartzman. So I passed, and do pass, for a humorist. But that I am surely not—at least, not in the common acceptation."

XI

What remains? Mr. Tilden is very successfully and wholly married to a Vermont girl whose name was Mabel Martin. They have three children—two girls and a boy—and are, he declares, quite domestic and happy.

ELIAS TOBENKIN

The pessimist who gave us Ecclesiastes—as fine a reader as ever lived—used to complain of the books that, in his day, tumbled from the tables of the scribes. They were ephemeral, he said, food for flappers and fat women; they made life seem a vain and fleeting show. And he was especially disturbed because he could forsee no end to this nuisance.

There has been no end to it. Only the other day the American Booksellers' Association, meeting in convention in New York, reiterated the complaint of the prophet—there are too many books, they said. For all I know they may have said the same thing before; yet nothing is done about it. The publishers promise us fewer and better books—and then go out and drum up trade for Mrs. Porter and Harold Bell Wright, for the speeches of Mr. Coolidge and the seductions of the Sheik. Fewer and better books for whom? Not for me, I can assure you; and not, I hope, gentle reader, for you. Perhaps for themselves. Indeed, I've a sneaking suspicion that they are thinking, first off, of themselves. Despite their slogan I am not convinced that they are the pious and self-sacrificing vestals, dedicated to the muse, that they would have us believe.

Yet am I grateful to the publishers. They have kept Mr. Mencken in groceries; they supply Sherwood Anderson's mischievous hands with something to do; they import Bennett and Yeats and Hamsun. In fact

they save us from a devil of a lot of ennui; and every
so often they uncover something worth while.   It was
a publisher who produced *David Harum*.   After nine
refusals it came to the attention of Mr. Ripley Hitch-
cock, to be rewritten on his recommendation and accepted by D. Appleton and Company, to sell 12,000
copies the first year and 382,665 the second.   You
see, good deeds have their reward.

II

And it was a good deed that held out to Mr. Elias
Tobenkin a home in these United States.   Soon or
late we will reap a harvest from his work—it may be
in journalism or social service and not in the novel, but
it is as sure as shooting.

III

He hails from Russia and is of Jewish extraction,
but he is not sure whether he was born on the 4th or
11th of February, 1882—the family Bible was lost
somewhere in the family's travels and with it the
records of about half the family's history.   Of one
thing, however, he is pretty sure and that is that he was
born prematurely and in haste.

IV

"Whenever I think of my childhood," he says, "two
landscapes invariably seem to flow into each other.
I begin my recollections with the monotonous plains of
White Russia, where I was born, the infrequent and
gray peasant villages, the huge century-old forests.
And then, quite imperceptibly, I find myself ruminating

about Wisconsin, its green hills and many lakes, where, after emigrating to America, I experienced a sort of rebirth.

"It is the same with my education. I recall the private school in a thatched hut in Russia, fifteen or twenty children sitting about a table, learning to read and write and figure, with very little system and no program. And then this picture becomes somehow fused with the American high school, with its dignified assembly and spacious class rooms, the music, orderliness and rhythm with which we marched to and from classes.

"I recall something else, something unforgettable. I was twelve years old and I found that for two years I had been repeating the same arithmetical problems, the same reading lessons. The private tutor of the village had nothing further to give me. I talked it over with another boy, two years older than myself. It was spring and we decided to put in the summer preparing for a regular school of which there was one in the capital of the province twenty-five miles away.

"After considerable scheming and planning both of us finally raised the necessary amount for books. In order to save every possible expense, my friend decided that we should walk to the capital on foot. We started about two o'clock one morning. We reached the city about three that afternoon. In a half hour we had secured our text books. We looked about the town for a while and then, in order to save the expense of paying for a night's lodging, we started for home again before sundown. Outside the town we met a band of peasants and beggars going our way to a fair.

We joined them, walking, with brief intervals for rest by the wayside, all through the night. About nine o'clock the next morning we reached home. We could not move a limb for several days after. But we did prepare for the accredited school that summer."

V

Mr. Tobenkin believes that one should be fond of one's birth place and say nice things about it; and yet there was a time when he would not speak of the city of his birth, and this merely because the Germans had over-run that part of Russia—so the compulsion is not binding under any and all circumstances. I do not well see how it could be. They are selling corsets where I was born and—but corsets have been practically discontinued—and I, for one, think the house should be torn down.

VI

Mr. Tobenkin was for a long time an only child and his father's hopes and ambitions centered in him. They were inseparable, taking long walks together, through the fields or up into the forest that skirted the edge of town, and as they walked the father, with many a sweep of the hand, recited heroic tales out of the Old Testament. In this way the child became familiar with the Bible before he could read or write. Kings and prophets were his constant companions.

His mother, too, played a great part in his education, singing him songs in Russian and Ukrainian, the yearning melancholy songs of the peasant. Wonderful songs they were and unforgettable; and sometimes

even now, as he walks on Broadway, something that he
hears recalls the past and the present fades away, the
noise dies down, the sky-scrapers disappear, and before him he seems to see the face of his dead mother
and to hear her voice singing the old sad songs of
Russia.

VII

"When and how did the thought of writing come to
me?" he asks.

"Well—somewhere about the age of thirteen a boy
companion in the Russian school where I was studying
informed me one day very solemnly that he had concluded that there was no God and could be no hereafter. I looked up to this boy in everything; his
father was a military doctor and a very important
person in the capital, and, though I was not so convinced, I embraced his conclusions.

"For months I was profoundly miserable. It
seemed to shatter the foundation under me. Life
without a hereafter seemed scarcely worth living. It
was so full of trouble. Certainly mine was. My al-
lowance from home was very meager and, in order
that I might keep up my schooling, I had been forced
to give lessons at very miserable prices. I seldom
got to bed before twelve or one at night and at seven
I had to be up, ready for school.

"It was in the weeks and months following my
friend's startling declaration that the idea of writing
came to me. There seemed to be no point in living a
life of suffering and privation and then getting off the
scene without a trace. There had to be some com-

pensation. Writing was to be the compensation in
my case. Writers were not utterly forgotten after
they were dead. Not only were such writers as Push-
kin and Lermontov, Koltsov and Aksakov (whose
works we were studying) not forgotten, but even the
writers of Greece and Rome continued to live. Our
teachers spoke of them with reverence."

VIII

Why should one write? That has been a question
down the ages; and yet I am afraid that Mr. Tobenkin's dreams of immortality are doomed to disappoint-
ment. What if his teachers did speak of Lermontov
with reverence, Mr. Tobenkin is neither one of the
great Russians nor a lesser Greek. He has not the
stuff of genius in him; and even genius can be forgotten. The name of Keats, you will remember, was
writ on water.

But what of it? Mr. Tobenkin is a first class journalist and *Witte Arrives* still sells. Besides there is
a present need for writing, our own immediate need,
that takes no thought of immortality—that, without
waiting on posterity, also serves.

IX

Witte Arrives is Mr. Tobenkin's first novel. It
was published in 1916 and deals with a family of
Russian Jews, emigrated from the Pale and settled in
a small town in the Middle-West. It is autobiographical. When Mr. Tobenkin says, "I report life in my
novels," he means that he is reporting his own life.
He is Emil, his father a peddler, held, on account of

his strict orthodoxy and stern honesty, in high esteem by their neighbors; and the problem that faces Emil (as it faces Mr. Tobenkin) is the everlasting problem of bread and contentment.   His characters try to adjust themselves to life and at the same time to wrest from each fleeting moment some of the happiness which they believe to be their due.   They have their disappointments; they have their hopes and their despairs; but in the end they find peace of a sort.

Emil graduates from the university and gets a job in a nearby city, reporting obituaries and the doings of labor.   He writes sympathetically of the people of the tenements and gradually makes a place for himself in the newspaper world.   Then he meets his desire and marries young.   Mr. Tobenkin understands the hopes and the failures of that harassed home.   The wife dies in childbirth.   Emil is desperate.   Broken in body and soul he returns to his father and the old man nurses him back to a belief in his own destiny.   During a long convalescence he writes the novel that, after various adventures, is to signal his arrival.

X

Mr. Tobenkin insists that we are all of us entitled to happiness.

Perhaps I am cynical, but I have no interest in Mr. Tobenkin's frantic efforts to force the world to devote itself to making his people happy.   Why should they be happy?   And even if they were what business would it be of ours?   Besides there is no fun in his books and, as I understand it, no beauty.   I love the pomp of kings and the carnivals of Nice and Munich;

I love tulips bordering a garden walk. To Mr. Tobenkin all these things are vanity. He is in deadly earnest. He is not going to waste his time considering the lilies. He's going to uplift and instruct us. He is St. Paul and he has no patience with those whose afternoons are given over to playing with little children. Life is a serious business: the things that are worth while can only be come by after a deal of sweating. They do not grow on thorn bushes or thistles. So says Tobenkin—but I would not give a fig for such a philosophy.

XI

Though *The House of Conrad* (1918) is now out of print I think it a vastly better novel than *Witte Arrives*. It is more mature and less concerned with the ache of the dissatisfied. It opens in the spring of 1866 when Gottfried Conradi arrives in New York from Germany, one of the first of the followers of Ferdinand LaSalle to come to America. In the Old World he had been a bookbinder but the Germans he meets in New York are cigarmakers and he sets about learning the new trade. Within a year he has saved passage for Annchen and sent for her. They settle in Kleindeutschland on the East Side. He dedicates himself and the house of Conrad (which has come into existence with the birth of his son) to the service of humanity; and it is the history of that service through three generations that Mr. Tobenkin outlines for us with sympathy and understanding.

But again all is somber as the grave. It is this business of being unable to write without a purpose—to

which Mr. Tobenkin pleads guilty—that makes even
the purpose of writing as he understands it seem dull.
There is nothing accidental or haphazard, nothing
spontaneous in Mr. Tobenkin's world.   It is very well
ordered, full of restrictions and a heavy gravity.   But
it is honest.   And Mr. Tobenkin is honest.   You can
take his word for it; the immigrant has an unneces-
sarily hard time of it—yet man for man the immigrant
is as fine a fellow as either you or I.

Mr. Tobenkin is the author of *Witte Arrives*, 1916;
The House of Conrad, 1918; *The Road*, 1920; and
(just finished) *The God of Might.*

ARTHUR TRAIN

Grant Overton, in his fulsome capacity as press agent
extraordinary for American Literature—American
Literature as contrasted with European and, of course,
as vastly to be preferred—says of *His Children's
Children* that it represents Mr. Arthur Train's most
serious work to date.

This, first off, like the general run of Grant's dicta,
seems a harmless statement of undisputed fact—as
who should say, Bobbie's had his hair cut or Hylan's a
loud bassoon. But I am a quarrelsome stickler for
proof.

How does Grant know that Mr. Train was never
more serious than when he sat down to write *His
Children's Children?* Grant himself has said that
Mr. Train's novels and stories are the work of Mr.
Train's leisure, the product of an active imagination.
Is Mr. Train, then, one of those terrible pre-historians
who are serious even in their leisure? Does he never
take life lightly, come and go, and with the rabble hear
the chimes ring out the midnight hour? Besides,
why should anyone want to be serious about the
younger generation? Youth's a stuff that can't endure; 'tis but a passing phase—why grow solemn about
its fancies lightly turning to thoughts of love? Can
we never learn, with Shaw, to make merry over Dar-
ling Dora; or, with Fanny, for a lark, so construct

Act I that the heroine shall kick off the policeman's hat and land, as a suffragette, in jail?

II

Can we? Never?

Echo is a long time answering, but I'm sure the answer will be, We never can! We are adolescent and we are trivial.

Coningsby Dawson, for instance, got all het up about Dos Passos' *Three Soldiers*. *Three Soldiers* was a libel upon the A. E. F. The A. E. F., without exception, was made up of men who thought of war as a chance to exhibit such guts as they might have; death was a great adventure; and dying for ideals the ambition of every Yank—except Dos Passos. Dawson went around for days pointing a finger of shame at Dos Passos. Then Dawson settled down to the serious business of his life. And what do you suppose that serious business was? Writing for the *Cosmopolitan Magazine* stories that should serve as a warning to young girls! Young girls were to know that if they kissed, the odds were on that those whom they kissed would try, with all their might and main, to father a lot of unexpected babies upon them.

I digress in this fashion only to express the hope that Mr. Train is not like that, that Mr. Train does not consider *His Children's Children* anything more than a rattling good story, made to slightly horrify fat women and greatly amuse such cynical souls as your humble critic.

III

Mr. Train is a person of parts. Mr. Train is well informed and, as they say of country gentlemen in England, to the manor born. He has played, in his time, the schoolboy, the lawyer, the lover, and the poet; and he has played each rôle with success. I trust that Grant errs when he tells me that Mr. Train is concerned over the future of American Society simply because Mr. Train knows that money is lost and made on Wall Street only by gamblers and that some of our oldest families are in the bootlegging business. Lord, it is but a change in metaphor that makes of the Four Hundred either the cream or the scum of civilization—the good stout broth is stewing all the time in the center of the melting-pot.

IV

Though it is beside my point a little, Mr. Train is the author of *Tutt and Mr. Tutt;* and *Tutt and Mr. Tutt* are very fine fellows indeed. Their reputation has travelled overseas and my friend Sir Horace Plunkett speaks of them, without hesitation, as of excellent company who can always be sure of a welcome.

V

Mr. Train wrote *The "Goldfish,"* which caused a stir when it ran serially in the *Saturday Evening Post*— it seemed so perfect a satire on the emptiness of upper-class society, the futile rebellion of a moneyed man against the empty existence forced upon him by his wife's social ambitions.

VI

Mr. Train was born in Boston, Mass., September 6, 1875, the son of Charles Russell Train and Sarah M. (Cheney) Train—he was christened Arthur Cheney Train.

His father was Attorney-General of Massachusetts from 1873 to 1880.

Mr. Train was graduated from Harvard, (A.B.), in 1896 and received his law degree three years later.

In 1897 he married Ethel Kissam, daughter of Benjamin P. Kissam of New York. Mrs. Train died in 1923. She was the author of *"Son" and Other Stories of Childhood and Age,* which was published posthumously.

VII

Almost immediately upon graduation, Mr. Train entered the District Attorney's office in New York, remaining there, in more or less close connection with the District Attorney, until 1916 when he became a member of the law firm of Perkins and Train.

As a special deputy Attorney-General of New York in 1910, he brought about the indictment of some hundred and odd persons, charged as political offenders, in Queens County, New York.

Mr. Train is the author of *McAllister and His Double,* 1905; *The Prisoner at the Bar,* 1906; *True Stories of Crime,* 1908; *The Butler's Story,* 1909; *Mortmain,* 1909; *Confessions of Artemus Quibble,*

1909; *C. Q. or In the Wireless House*, 1910; *Courts, Criminals and the Camorra*, 1911; *The "Goldfish"*, 1914; *The Man Who Rocked the Earth*, (with R. W. Wood), 1915; *The World and Thomas Kelly*, 1917; *The Earthquake*, 1918, *Tutt and Mr. Tutt*, 1920; *By Advice of Counsel*, 1921; *His Children's Children*, 1923; *Tut, Tut! Mr. Tutt*, 1923.

ALLAN UPDEGRAFF

It may be that in the years to come Updegraff will be best remembered as one in the group of optimistic young rebels with whom Sinclair Lewis lunched and to whom, in part, *The Trail of the Hawk* is dedicated; but if so the fault will be with memory—Updegraff is well able to stand on his own feet. He is a poet of parts and has been quoted again and again, by Professor Phelps and others, in anthologies and histories of modern English verse. He is the author of two novels. He should be the author of much more. He isn't. But that doesn't make him any the less memorable to those who know him, for he has a Rabelaisian wit and a way with the world that is all his own. He is, in short, a lulu.

But memory is a treacherous thing. We can never tell for what it is that we will be remembered. Laurence Sterne (I think it was) chiefly regretted, at his death, a certain Robert who had been Bishop of Ely because the Bishop had been valuable for hallooing at elections. And Macbeth who was one of the greatest of Scottish kings, freeing commerce from the lawless tyranny of the barons, is to-day known only for the murder of sleep and the sudden and inexplicable taking-off of Duncan, and, later, of Banquo—Macbeth who murdered no one. It would be just like the luck that is forever pursuing Updegraff if he should go down in history as the author of the worst movie that was ever made—

Second Youth, with Lynn Fontanne and Alfred
Lunt in the cast.

II

Updegraff, a huge ungainly person, is the snake editor of the *Literary Digest,* the man who prepares all
the jokes and personal glimpses that wind in and out
among the advertisements on the back pages; but, so
far as I can make out, he spends most of his time on
vacation.   This he can do because, as he says, he has
his work well organized.   He has a system of some
sort; and since his is usually the best part of the magazine, it must be a good system.   Only recently it allowed him to spend a full—I think that's the right
word—and glorious three months or so in Europe,
with beer in Nuremburg and some delicate sort of wine
on the Piazza San Marco in Venice.   He traveled
from Frankfort by Zeppelin and by aëroplane from
Paris.   He wasted no time, as you can see, in the open
and lonely country.   His route lay from principal
point of interest to crowded café in public square and
thence directly to the hotel.   As a consequence, he is
thoroughly disgusted with all this talk about suffering
in Europe.   "Why I had a glorious time!" he says.

III

As you can see, I like him.   And I like his books.
If I had my way he would be kept busy writing satirical
burlesques on the folly of human pretensions.   To
hear him talk of Hutchins Hapgood and Emma Gold-
man, of the poets and painters around Woodstock, of
the men and women who frequent the studios in Green-

wich Village, is a thousand times better than any of the parties staged by the ultra-artistic. He spares no feelings; and he draws back from the sundering of no veils. In all their nakedness his characters strut upon a stage that is like the carnival at Nice or the most perverse of Diaglieff's ballets. And the best of these desecrations is that Updegraff himself enjoys them.

IV

He was born on a farm near Grinnell, Iowa, February 24th, 1883; his father, a high-class farmer who had been intended for the ministry; his mother a painter of landscapes and the author of children's stories, of French descent. Of pioneering stock, of men and women to whom the fields seemed greener further off, there is the beat of gypsy music in his veins; and at eighteen he escaped from Springfield, Missouri, where he had just finished high school, going to Chicago in search of such good things as fortune might offer. He got a job reporting on the South Chicago *Daily Calumet,* became city editor, but almost immediately, chance offering, left to enter Yale. At Yale, he worked up until he became editor-in-chief of the *Monthly Magazine.* But his funds ran out and he was forced to go to New York to earn a living. It was not too easy. He tried clerking for Siegel-Cooper's, living with Sinclair Lewis in a bare rented room on Avenue B; occasionally he sold a rhyme or two; he got a job in a bookstore; he worked in factories. Then, facing consumption, he was ordered West by a doctor to whom a chance friend had sent him. He started for California with a borrowed twenty dollars. He got as far as Ogden, Utah, broke, skin and bones, talking to himself, the *Oxford Book of English Verse* in his pocket. He went to work "mucking" for the Northern Pacific Railroad, contracted in a small way, went broke again. But all the time he was writing; and his verse and short stories were beginning to attract attention. It wasn't long before he returned to New York, with a strengthened physique and the least bit of a literary reputation, to edit *Transatlantic Tales*. Then, for a brief period, he was editor of the *Publishers' Newspaper Syndicate;* and just now, as I have said, he is one of the editors of the *Literary Digest*. For the most part, he lives at Woodstock, in the Catskills.

v

If he could only get mad, really excited, and shout out, as Lewis has done, that life is literally a ridiculous farce, a meaningless pantomime, with stuffed and foolish puppets going through unexacting gestures, there is no telling what Updegraff could not do, for he has read Trugenieff to good purpose and he knows America and Americans as few of us do. But he is inconceivably lazy and puts off until even I have begun to despair. Yet his books are at least as good as most; and his impudence is unequaled.

In *Second Youth* he tells how the eyes of the virginal (if middle-aged) Mr. Roland Francis were opened to the sensual charm of the vivacious Mrs. Adelaide Winton Twombly and what happened to him in consequence; and in *Strayed Revellers* he describes the revolt of an extremely modern young lady against the conspiracy of silence that would foist her mother's husband on her as a father when she knows very well that she is the child of a midsummer flirtation.   Both books have the gaiety, the knowingness, the detachment that distinguishes the best of Continental fiction.   They are closely related to the novels of Marcel Prevost, the tom-foolery of Collette Willy and Otto Julius Bierbaum or Ludwig Thoma's rhymed romances of the Bal Parè.   They have something of the cynic wisdom of de Maupassant.

VI

Mrs. Twombly, grown contemptuous of the claims of passion, sure that there is no beauty in love, still smarting from the brutal frankness of a too insistent husband, enters McDavitt's Department Store ostensibly to buy silks but in reality to seduce the heart of the handsome and very proper Mr. Francis behind the counter.   She knows that he has been waiting through unadvancing years for the coming of the true romance.   He is the sort that would dedicate himself to dreams of the perfect mate.

She catches his interest with talk of philosophy, pointing out the earthiness of worms, silk and otherwise, dwelling upon the loneliness of human-kind. She wins him and they make a date.

Her mind is made up.   To her he is no more than is the salesgirl to the young gallant who hangs around the aisles looking for someone with whom he may have what he calls a good time.   She will turn the tables on the male; and in vengeance on the sex which, represented by her husband, disillusioned and degraded her, she will drag the fancies of this lordly creature in the mire—she will make a sordid and fleshly reality of his high-prized dreams.

She fails, of course. When, in the hotel room, lip should meet with lip to seal in fact the vain hopes of an impossible bliss, her courage fails her; and she sends him away, without explanations, to wander home alone through the night, strangely troubled by a love he cannot understand.

Then follow still other adventures. He encounters the various hazards that beset the path of an un-attached bachelor suddenly promoted to the buying staff of a vast retail business—the interested friendship of his widowed landlady, the dinners of his chief, the fluttering smiles of marriageable daughters. But he comes at last, as is fitting, to a quiet place beneath a tree where he can sit with one beside him, singing and drinking—a wilderness, perhaps, to you or me, but for him paradise enow.

VII

Strayed Revellers is another story. Here there is no shy peeping at the mysteries of nature, no hesitation, no dream of exalted purity—just the riotous life of a summer colony of artists; and, in Hen Hoot, the portrait of a farmer who, in a moment of moon-madness, joins with a New York girl to create Clothilde. The book revolves around Clothilde and the embarrassment consequent upon her claiming Hoot, now luckily married, for a father, repudiating the preacher who had so magnanimously saved her mother, marrying her shortly after she had embarked upon what he maintained must be a life of shame.

VIII

Mr. Updegraff is no untraveled Ulysses coming suddenly upon Circe at the bend of a river, nor is he a neuropath. His people are naïve and charming, with the directness of children; and their talk has all the simplicity and all the unexpectedness of real life. While fanciful, his books are realistic—by that I mean they read as though, in any properly organized society, the various accidents recorded in them should have happened, actually.

LOUIS JOSEPH VANCE

I am told that what distinguishes Mr. Louis Joseph
Vance, setting him apart from the ordinary writer of
the usual crook story, is not so much his selection of
wildly exciting plots as his honest effort at genuine
characterization. He attempts to invest his somewhat over-dressed and always high-class criminals with
an air of seeming reality. A line or two of explanation here and there, a few deft strokes of interjection,
and he has succeeded, more or less, in making flesh and
blood of his otherwise impossible heroes and heroines.
So too with the lesser characters—the widows with an
unaccountable weakness for denizens of the lower
depths, the adroit and knowing Parisian cocottes and
demimondaines, the thousand and one waiters, butlers,
detectives, soldiers and travelers who make up the cast.
Which is well enough. But when I read about
bandits, I prefer the real thing, the story of some less
happy criminal as reported to the court by a properly
advised probation officer—Miss Mahon, for instance,
when she recounts for us the tragic youth of the lonely
and courageous Cecilia Cooney. Here, for once in a
long long time, we have a tale to touch the heart.
Here is a damning and unanswerable indictment of our
present way with the world, our selfishness and the failure of our good intentions, the half-hearted efforts of
the church and charity to aid those who cannot aid
themselves.

Cecilia Cooney was born in a basement on the lower
East Side in New York, of shiftless and drunken
parents.   She was the youngest of eight children; and
since her father refused to work, she was sent out
early to beg on the streets.   She was never properly
clothed, properly fed, never clean and she slept as a
rule in coal bins.   When she was four, she was taken,
for six months, by the Children's Society, and then, on
the recommendation of the Department of Public
Charity, turned back to her mother, who promptly
deserted her.   Next she was taken to Brooklyn to an
aunt's and, for ten years or so, attended a parochial
school.   At fourteen, her mother brought her back to
New York, stole her clothes and again deserted her.
At fifteen, she became a child laborer in a brush factory in Brooklyn, associating at night with sailors
picked up on the water front.   A year later, she was
back in New York, living with her mother, and working, for a few months at a stretch, in various laundries.
At twenty she was married, had borne a child, had
terrorized a city of four millions by a series of dashing
and impudent hold-ups, and was condemned to spend
the rest of her youth in prison.

It is not at all a pleasant tale.   It is not made up
of deft and seemingly careless strokes of interjection;
it is not romantic or gay; it has the remorseless and
terrible inevitability of truth.   It begins in misery and
ends in jail.   Yet it is none the less a gallant attempt
to have something out of that society which neglects
its manifest duties to read the melodramas of Mr.
Louis Joseph Vance.

Mr. Vance, of course, is not to blame for this.   But

Mr. Vance has brains; he has wit, he has leisure. It seems to me that he is wasting his gifts. I would have him employ his undoubted talents to some better purpose than this everlasting rehashing of the utterly trivial adventures of the Lone Wolf. The Lone Wolf may be a good meal ticket, but Mr. Vance is a citizen of New York and as such he is responsible, in part, for the misery of Cecilia Cooney, the luckless bobbed hair bandit.

II

I do not say that Mr. Vance's stories are not thrilling; simply, in Rube Goldberg's phrase, that they don't mean anything. In this they are all alike. He has been writing for twenty years and still aspires to meet Marie Corelli on neutral ground and have it out with her. He wants to imitate and improve upon her most ornate passages. "Pensive rains" take his fancy, and "misty mirks," and even (at times) "pulsing gold streaks." And he has contracted the not unusual habit of rounding out his paragraphs with a long line of dots. He wants to be a real honest-to-goodness writer—but, apparently, he reads the wrong books. Hall Caine crossed by E. Phillips Oppenheim, with a dash of Curwood and Chambers, would seem to be his ideal.

Take *The Lone Wolf Returns,* the latest of his novels. The story opens in New York, with Michael Lanyard, the Wolf, arriving from Paris, supposedly cured of his miserable trick of stealing million dollar necklaces, and madly in love with a rich widow— widows are a weakness with Mr. Vance. In chapter

two, affairs begin to pick up and from then on to the
end of the book, Monsieur Lanyard is beset by sin,
tried and threatened with everything from blackmail
to murder, hurried from one escapade to another with
scarce pause enough to allow the reader to catch his
breath.   It is all like a madly revolving stage on which
some grotesque melodrama is being played out to a
false conclusion; and high over all, inscrutable and
sinister, the cloaked figure of Lanyard the crook.

Or take *False Faces,* which had to do with the War.
We first encounter Lanyard, new-risen from an untimely grave, in No Man's Land, the pock-marked
world that lies between the trenches, and thence we
travel with him, always in haste, across the feverish
seas to a New York cabaret where we watch German
spies as they plot their meanness.   The Lone Wolf is
now active for the Allies.   A grave and reckless believer in democracy, he takes his cue from Napoleon,
and muses upon the advantage that lies with those who
fight upon the offensive.   He decides to attack; and he
is so furious in his attack that (so his publishers assure
me) the mere record of his doings is "one of the most
vivid, realistic and timely pieces of war fiction that has
yet been written—an amazingly convincing account of
the activities of the Prussian spy systems."

III

All this, of course, is nonsense; but that is not the
point.   The point is that Mr. Vance is really a very
decent sort and should be roughly handled for capitu-
lating so completely to the magazines, for surrender-

ing without a struggle to the lure of the almighty
dollar.

IV

Yes, I like Mr. Vance. He has an engaging humility. There are no fictitious airs about him. He
is simple and honest and direct. But we fall out just
the same. He is taking too easy a road. Let him observe the diligent and far wiser Mr. Wallace Irwin.
Let him give a year of his inexhaustible time to something better worth our while and his than this everlasting money-grubbing. Let him study Mrs. Cooney
and show us, in a feminine counter-part of *Haunch,
Paunch and Jowl,* how those who climb up on the
benches climb across the bodies of fallen women, in
their cupidity depriving of food and shelter the little
children who should be our hope and are our constant
despair.

V

Mr. Vance professes to find any sort of autobiography a task well-nigh beyond his means. He believes
that once an author begins to prattle about himself he
must, in the end, stand self-revealed as an insufferable
ass.

This, I think, is too wide and general an assertion.
It depends upon the author. Certainly Mr. Shaw
does very well when his subject is Shaw; and Joseph
Conrad was never more Conrad or ever more suffer-
able than in *A Personal Record.*

But Mr. Vance says that "the ego, being mildly pe-

titioned to lay aside some of the vestments of its
proper privacy, seems unable to refrain from stripping
itself naked and running wild, with uncouth shouts."

Mr. Vance is too self-conscious.   There are no uncouth shouts in F. P. A.'s column and the bewildering
Broun is modesty itself.   Indeed, I think you will go
far to find better poised writing than occurs day after
day over their signatures.   Mr. Adams' Pepy's Diary
is a thing of rare and lasting joy; Broun's confessions
are truly soul-shaking.

VI

But Mr. Vance continues his short-sighted and ob-
stinate way.

"If I like an author or his work," he says, "I never
read the stuff he writes about himself for publication;
otherwise I gloat over it.   My own impression is that
authors as a class are rather dull people who lead
rather dull lives; a few, very few, are either offensively
or pleasingly otherwise, depending on whether they
know it or not.   I believe their work should be judged
and written about, not their personalities, providing
they have anything of the sort."   And Mr. Vance
means it.

It is easy enough to say that he ought to know—but
does he?   Wasn't *Babbitt* a drab and colorless creature until Sinclair Lewis got a hold of him?   Isn't
Bottom exciting—and yet we all know that he was an
illiterate Athenian weaver?   So it is with authors.
If they are Mr. Vance they may seem dull, even to
themselves; if they are Ed Howe they will be exciting
to every one.

VII

Mr. Vance was born in Washington D. C., September 19, 1879; and he has been writing more than less steadily and voluminously since he was twenty. He comes of a normal middle class family and his boyhood was normal. His schooling at Poly Prep in Brooklyn, while satisfactory, made no great impression upon his mind, leaving his imagination free to concoct the most dangerous and terrible yarns. His first effort, sustained to a fitting climax, was what might (perhaps) be termed a sex-story—but its author has forgotten its contents and I could not jog his memory. He travels—when he can afford it—and he likes to travel because when away from everyday surroundings, he finds it difficult to work and that gives him a good and reasonable excuse for not working, which is what, at times, he is after. He has had a wide and extensive experience with the movies, profitable but otherwise enervating. He gets along comfortably with the magazines and has never yet published anything in book form without first selling the magazine serial rights. His first novel was written in sixty days at the rate of fifteen hundred words a day, appearing serially in *Munsey's Magazine* and never anywhere else—it was a tale of adventure but what form of adventure, Mr. Vance neglected to tell me. He has few literary passions; indeed his passions are mostly prejudices. He loathes people who talk to him sympathetically about his books, calling them all the while, "detective stories"; and he gives as his reason for this loathing, the fact that detectives seldom appear in any of them.

Having written, as he says, the other sort, the sort admired by these simple souls, he knows that detective stories are the most difficult of all stories to write; and he would rather write five so-called psychological or social studies than one story of mystery and adventure —the mystery story takes it out of you; *Esther Waters* is child's play.   He hasn't any hobbies that he knows of or any special interests in art or life.   He just spreads himself.   He's catholic and comprehensive, but not exactly concentrated.   He likes dogs, cats, horses, boats and people so long as they are able to make him forget himself and his job of writing.   He doesn't write verse and, though he is addicted to them, he doesn't believe that there is any special magic in a title that contains a double B.   In short, he is quite normal when he might and ought to be so much more.

Mr. Vance is the author of *Terence O'Rouke, Gentleman Adventurer*, 1905; *The Private War*, 1906; *The Brass Bowl*, 1907; *The Black Bag*, 1908; *The Bronze Bell*, 1909; *The Pool of Flame*, 1909; *The Fortune Hunter*, 1910; *No Man's Land*, 1910; *Cynthia-of-the-Minute*, 1911; *The Band Box*, 1912; *The Destroying Angel*, 1912; *The Day of Days*, 1913; *Joan Thursday*, 1913; *The Lone Wolf*, 1914; *Sheep's Clothing*, 1915; *Nobody*, 1915; *The False Faces*, 1917; *Beau Revel*, 1919; *The Dark Mirror*, 1919; *The Lone Wolf Returns*, 1924.

CARL VAN VECHTEN

In *Peter Whiffle*—than which there is nothing of its kind more engaging—Mr. Van Vechten allows Peter to tell of his theory of the novel:—

"Life is made up of a collection of objects, and the mere citation of them is sufficient to give the reader a sense of form and color, atmosphere and style. And form, style, manner in literature are everything; subject is nothing. . . . It is not range of information, nor mastery of some little known branch of science, nor yet novelty of matter that will insure immortality. Recall the great writers, Théophile Gautier, Jules Barbey d'Aurevilly, Joris Huysmans, Oscar Wilde: they all used this method, catalogues, catalogues, catalogues! All great art is a matter of cataloguing life, summing it up in a list of objects."

Peter Whiffle was published in April, 1922.

In November, 1917, Van Vechten, speaking for himself, while reviewing that unparalleled dance-operetta, the Spanish *Land of Joy,* said, after making some mention of George M. Cohan, a Mozart finale, Manet pictures, Manila shawls, prehistoric roses and Robert W. Chambers: "I cannot resist further cataloguing." Whereupon he rapidly runs through the intricate rhythms of Valverde, the utter absence of tangoes and habaneras, two-four and three-four time, a dozen Zuloaga paintings, the apparently inexhaustible skill of the dancers, what Richard Ford saw and wrote down in 1846, what Aristotle, Havelock Ellis and Louis Sherwin have taught us of the theater, and something about an outlet for suppressed desires and an exit onto Columbus Circle.

II

It's all one with Van Vechten, novel or review—and, as you have guessed, it's all cataloguing.

Take *The Tattooed Countess*—that is the latest of his *tours de force*. He tells us that the Countess is just recovering from an affair with Tony, a rough and uncouth barn-stormer. But recovered or not, before she is through with Van Vechten he has thrown her into the arms of yet another and younger lover. The Countess is fifty—if she's a day, as the village gossips have it—Tony was twenty-three. But Gareth Johns is seventeen. Here is a nymphomaniac, then, if ever there was one—here is Louis Bromfield's Lily made ridiculous and reduced to begging for a kiss. But is there any glamour about her or passion? Has she the ways of a woman used to abandon? Is she charming? Or wanton? Or gay? She may be—but not from anything Van Vechten makes you feel will you know that there is aught but a printer's ink in her veins. Van Vechten gossips about his characters, catalogues their amours, knows about them; but since he does not understand them he never makes them live.

III

Don't mistake me. *The Tattooed Countess* is worth your time and mine. The title alone is priceless. And the scheme of the book, done, as it might be, by some master satirist, would bring our ponderous civilization up with a start, making us see ourselves, a divine occasion, as now only the gods can see us.

IV

I shall soon find myself defending Van Vechten, for I hear on all sides a faint murmur of praise that makes me believe our readers, even the gentlest of them, are aware of the incontrovertible fact of his having nothing to say.

But why must a writer have something to say? Surely the jolliest hours are spent with those friends who are merely amusing or charming or wise in an unprovocative way? What, as Mr. Shaw has repeatedly pointed out, did Shakespeare ever say—and even if he had said anything would it not now, after three hundred years, be stale news indeed? It is the manner, as Peter Whiffle maintained, that matters.

V

Speaking for himself, in *Peter Whiffle,* Van Vechten has said that things rather than people awaken whatever sympathy and sentiment is latent in his heart.

And on the same page, to show that he can be right and humane even so, he notes a Chinese woman holding in her arms an exquisite Chinese baby, and adds: "All Chinese babies, with their flat porcelain faces, their straight black hair, and their ivory hands, are exquisite."

Was truer word ever spoken by the most besotted humanitarian?

I myself must admire any author who admires

Chinese babies—and love the quixotic Peter who asks:
"Don't you think Chinese babies are the kind to have,
if you are going to become a father at all?"

VI

This interest of Van Vechten's in things rather than
people leads him to some queer dilemmas, so that at
the sight of Peter in rags, he feels himself choking with
an emotion which he usually reserves for the sight of
old theaters.

It also limits his allusions, for people are more various and more interesting than things—and there are
more people.   I can quote you easily a thousand authors and each will be a distinct personality.   You will
have your troubles quoting me a thousand door-knobs,
nails, books, rails, pins, spoons, motors, trees, rugs,
fences, fires, rakes, canes, teapots, etc.

Van Vechten, by his preferences, forces himself to
repeat—and repetition of Van Vechten is not exactly
a startling business.

He quotes George Moore; and then he quotes
George Moore again; and names the cat George
Moore and quotes George Moore; and speaks of
Manon, and again *Manon,* and *Manon* in *Peter Whif-
fle, Manon* in *The Tattooed Countess.*

VII

No two people should be more unlike than Peter
Whiffle and the Gareth Johns who, when she leaves
us, is the latest of the Countess Nattatorrini's loves—
but Van Vechten tells us that they both desired, when
young, above all books the somewhat thin and not too

moving *Chevalier of Pensieri-Vani* by H. B. Fuller—
it is apparently the book Van Vechten read when himself a boy and is the only book he can think of a boy's
reading.

VIII

As a boy, Peter liked to talk to older people and
found special pleasure in the company of the Reverend
Horatio Wallace, a clergyman who had visited New
York.   This reverend doctor was violently opposed
to art museums, novels and symphony orchestras, but
he talked about them—and he was the only person in
Toledo, so far as Peter knew, who did.   He railed
against the sins and vices of New York and Paris, but
he described them and——

There you have the Van Vechten touch at its best—
there and in the picture of Peter playing the piano as
"professor" of a bawdy house—and in Campaspe
Lorillard who is the best excuse for *The Blind Bow-
Boy,* its heroine and villain all at once, and very good
company, I can assure you.

IX

Of course Van Vechten does not want to be taken
seriously—except as a poseur.   With him, as with
Oscar, in Huneker's words, it is always attitudes.   But
he is not, as Wilde was, as Arthur Symons knows
Wilde was, an artist in his attitudes.   He is too self-
conscious and he began too late (in Cedar Rapids,
Iowa) to take notice of blue china and what-nots.
Say "Paris" to Van Vechten and he carries on with no
more reserve than a sophomore.   To him the name

has such magic as only wines should have—or a woman's lips.   After all, Paris is, as time passes, a rather shallow city by the Seine, with too many flunkeys and too many palms out and not enough humor in the right Falstaffian manner.   It lacks heartiness— besides, the beer, as even Van Vechten admits, is rotten.

X

Van Vechten, Burton Rascoe tells me, has a bland and saturnine countenance which lights up into a grimace of merriment now and then, showing widely separated teeth.   He is tall, white-haired, youngish, with a head that inclines forward from erect shoulders, and a nervous way of moving his head in intermittent, slight jerks when he is talking.   He looks intently at you in a disconcerting sort of way, then asks some unexpected question for which there is no ready answer.   He is deliberate; and witty or somber, acid or unctuous with his moods as they vary.   He is unaware, he says, of the people against whom Mencken howls; and even if he were aware of them he would not howl against them—he would merely avoid them. He is without rancor and without the messianic urge. He would change nothing, uplift no one, interfere with no one.   In fact, he is very well satisfied with himself, his life, his friends and his country.   I am not sure that he is likable.   He may be.   He is (at any rate) the author of three finely finished novels, vastly amusing, strange, entirely his own—and if not such books as Aldous Huxley writes and Wilde was in the habit of writing, still the best of their kind produced, as yet, over here.

Mr. Van Vechten is the author of *Why and What,* 1914; *Music After the Great War,* 1915; *Music and Bad Manners,* 1916; *Interpreters and Interpretations,* 1917; *The Merry-Go-Round,* 1918; *The Music of Spain,* 1918; *In the Garret,* 1920; *Marguerite D'Alvarez, A Broadsheet,* 1920; *Interpreters,* 1920; *The Tiger in the House,* 1920; *Peter Whiffle, His Life and Works,* 1922; *The Blind Bow-Boy* 1923; *The Tattooed Countess,* 1924.

Mr. Van Vechten has written prefaces for *Sophie,* by Phillip Moeller, 1919; *A Letter Written in 1837* by Morgan Lewis Fitch, 1919; *Lords of the House-tops,* 1921; *Kittens,* By Svend Fleuron, 1922; *In a Winter City,* by Ouida, 1923; *My Musical Life,* by N. A. Rimsky-Korsakoff, 1923; *Prancing Nigger,* by Ronald Firbank, 1924; *The Lord of the Sea,* by M. P. Shiel, 1924.

Mr. Van Vechten is the composer of *Five Old English Ditties,* 1904.

WEBB WALDRON: AUTO-PHOTO

(By Himself, of Course)

One of my first memories is of sitting by a narrow rushing river in the north woods, watching my mother paint. Painting was her passion; whenever she could steal away from housework she was at her easel along the tawny-banked river or at the old sawmill or in some nook in the woods. The names of paints and brushes were familiar to me, the methods of sketching outlines, of mixing colors; and the natural desire of any child to draw pictures of things was accentuated in me to a passion equal to my mother's. My father was a school teacher. He had come West to Michigan from Pennsylvania when a young man. The family was English via Holland—the first of the line in America that Resolvert Waldron, my great-great-great-great-great-grandfather, who accompanied Peter Stuyvesant to New Amsterdam in 1647. My father taught school in villages at north woods cross-roads, and finally in a grade school in Bay City, Michigan. All through my childhood the idea that I was to be an artist wavered before me. How I could become one I had no notion, and actually, I believe, my talent was very small. But the constant practice with pencil and pen kept alive and emphasized a habit of visualizing, a natural fascination in the shapes of things, colors, visual appearance. Even now in imagining the thought and emotion of a character, I find myself squinting to catch his facial expression, the light in his eyes, the movement of his lips, and from all that deducing his inner self.

My first literary venture was a serial story produced at the age of twelve or thirteen, in the manner of some juvenile writer I then adored. Its instant rejection by our best magazines lowered my spirits somewhat, but later at high school and at a Michigan fresh-water college I acquired local fame by a series of poems and short stories of outlandish theme, in the usual false adolescent style. At the University of Michigan I wrote incessantly, always in imitation of some idol of the moment and occasionally sold a story to a New York magazine for ten or fifteen dollars. I even sold to a southern periodical for four dollars a translation of a Maupassant tale, rendered in the best sophomore French fluidity.

After graduation I drifted West, in poor health, worked in a hardware store on the prairies, taught country school, toted shingles in a lumber yard, mucked in a sewer gang in Denver, rustled baggage in the Denver Union Depot, got a high school teaching job and got fired, tutored an insane man, clerked in the U. S. Indian Agency at Santa Fé, and finally taught English two years at the University of Arizona. Through these mischances the hope of becoming a writer often was completely submerged. I wrote short stories intermittently, but after my first juvenile successes I never could sell anything.

The attempt to write fiction persisted through a newspaper career in Detroit and four years of advertising-writing in New York. Oddly, I was

rather successful at advertising-writing, while never
becoming really interested in it, actually at times hating it and maintaining a certain pride in my ignorance
of the articles whose qualities it was my job to parade.
My own writing was still cursed by imitativeness, and
by a curious preoccupation with certain narrow phases
of radical life—the stale hang-over from the jag into
which my first contact with the anarchist world of New
York had projected me.

The stimulus to genuine writing came during the
war, or rather just after it.   I had been assistant editor of *Collier's Weekly,* later acting managing editor,
and I had the chance to go to France as war correspondent.   By luck, my wife, Marion Patton Waldron,
was able to go with me—one of the only women correspondents in France.   In France, again, I had difficulty in writing, but just after the armistice, by great
fortune, I got to Berlin ahead of all other American
correspondents, went through the German Revolution.
When I got back to Paris, for the first time in my life
I forgot to ask myself how to write.   I was full of
gorgeous exclusive stuff and I simply *wrote*.   That
experience broke down the barrier that had always
held me from genuine writing, the puzzle about form,
the aimless groping for phrases, the inevitable refuge
in some other writer's style.   No, it is not true to say
it broke the barrier down, but it did a great deal toward it.

When my wife and I came back from France, sickened by the noise, dirt and expense of New York, we
wandered out here into the Connecticut hills and found
an old farmhouse—with a brook, a river and a cliff

attached—that has been our *pied à terre* ever since. Here, in 1921, I wrote my first novel, *The Road to the World*. Of all comment that book received, the most precious reward was a letter from Joseph Conrad. In 1922 my wife and I took a loaf through the Great Lakes country and produced that curious work "We Explore the Great Lakes," whose greatest virtue is the drawings she made for it. I am now at work on another novel, laid in New York and Paris, to be published in 1925. Three other novels clamor to be written—a realistic story of the north woods; the drama of two aged sisters in a Michigan village; and the story of a town in the Southwestern desert.

I am fortunate in an utterly happy marriage and in the fact that my wife, a writer herself, has an uncommon insight into the writing art. Ruthless genial criticism of each other's work, dishwashing and D. H. Lawrence, Conrad and carpentry, pruning and Proust, are all in the day's program in this neck of the woods.

.   .   .   .

P. S. by C. C. B.

There is little to add. Like Samuel Butler, Webb Waldron is a writer to be discovered only after long years of neglect. Like Ambrose Bierce, there is something uncompromising in his style and in his matter that frightens our happy-go-lucky borrowers from the library. He is of the tribe of Stephen Crane; and when he has finished the four novels of which he makes mention; some valiant soul—Waldo Frank or J. J. Smertenko, H. L. Mencken or Professor Sherman—will come out with a magazine article on him; and then the coteries will take him up.   By that time he will have grown a little weary;—but he will have made for himself a philosophy to shock and horrify his young discoverers—and be their inspiration.   Here's to him—and the best of luck!

HENRY KITCHELL WEBSTER

No bourne need be set for Mr. Webster. Like Tennyson's futile and fatuous brook, he can go on forever. *The Whispering Man—The King in Kahki —The Girl in the Other Seat*—who shall say him nay? *Real Life,* his latest, or *The Short Line War,* his first, separated by twenty-three years, but not divided by so much as varies the conjugation of one French verb from another—twenty-three years, beginning with the end of the Spanish Empire and ending with the beginning of a new era in world power, all but wasted on Mr. Webster. He wanted to write when he was young; he still wants to write.

II

Born in Evanston, Illinois, September 7, 1875, he married an Evanston girl in 1901, and still lives in Evanston. He is a member of the Cliff Dwellers Club in Chicago and of the Players in New York. He graduated from Hamilton College in 1897, and instructed in rhetoric at Union until '98.

Such, in great detail, is the simple story of his life.

For the rest he has written. He has written for all the magazines and always about some girl or other. Nothing so interests him as girls—and men—and their ways together. Can a girl who goes on the stage remain chaste? Can a man remain honest in business? When you speak of a girl as a thoroughbred—ah, when you do—when you can—a thoroughbred! Is there anything more attractive than a girl who can be spoken of as a thoroughbred? And isn't life interesting? Don't you find it so? So many different sorts of people. You know I think that life, just as it is lived, all about you, is a proper subject for discussion in books. Don't you? I have no patience with people who want to change life, who want to vote. Why should any one want to vote? Politics are so ephemeral. What difference will it make two years from now who was elected three years ago? The world goes on just the same—the enduring things of the world—love!

Love! That's the name they give to the chance embrace that, once three hundred pages have been passed over, closes the chapter—love for which Anthony thought the world well lost—love that made a fool of Touchstone the moment he had been lured into the forest by the scheming Rosalind.

III

Mr. Webster stands, of course, in no need of criticism. He does not ask to be criticized. He is not himself critical. "Things as they are" is his motto. He measures his success by the size of the check that buys the serial rights to his novels as one by one they go to press. He does not venture within the charmed circle that girdles those tormented souls who find life a chaos. He does not dispute philosophies with Mr. Mencken or grope with Sherwood Anderson towards the light. He is regular. He is charming and kindly, happy and contented. He sees no reason for getting wrought up about life or vainly trying to change it with the written word.

IV

Mr. Webster is the author of the *Short Line War*, (with Samuel Merwin), 1899; *The Banker and the Bear, The story of a corner in land*, 1900; *Calumet K* (with Samuel Merwin), 1901; *Roger Drake*, Captain in Industry, 1903; *The Duke of Cameron Avenue*, 1904; *Traitor and Loyalist*, 1909; *Comrade John* (with Samuel Merwin), 1907; *The Whispering Man*, 1908; *A King in Khaki*, 1909; *The Sky Man*, 1910; *The Girl in the Other Seat*, 1911; *June Madness*, a play, 1912; *The Ghost Girl*, 1915; *The Butterfly*, 1914; *The Real Adventure*, 1916; *The Painted Scene*, 1916; *The Thoroughbred*, 1917; *An American Family*, 1918; *Mary Wollaston*, 1920; *Real Life*, 1921.

EDWARD LUCAS WHITE

How authors come by their notions remains one of the minor mysteries of existence. Take Mr. Edward Lucas White—since he is there for the taking. In the preface to *El Supremo* Mr. White tells us—and mind, he's telling us; he is not arguing or debating or wasting any time—that Dr. Jose Gasper Rodriguez de Francia, his hero was "indubitably one of the greatest men this world has ever produced, without question, the most wonderful man ever born in either North or South America."

Indubitably and without question! There seems to have been no doubt about it. But who cares? Mr. White is writing a romance of South America—Paraguay, to be exact—and what his hero was in the flesh is no never mind and ne'er a promise of what he will be in fiction. Cæsar was a noble Roman, certainly as noble as Brutus, but in Shakespeare's play he's a broomhandle.

II

Who said that the way to write a good book was the way Mr. White has taken—pick out the most wonderful man and go to it. Is there anything wonderful about Lord Jim—except, of course, Conrad's understanding of him? Would you say that Long John Silver was wonderful? A book about Bonaparte is not (necessarily) either great or wonderful or even interesting. Why, then, should Mr. White think it a

part of his business as romancer to assay all the men
ever born in North and South America, weigh them
and find them wanting when compared with this prodigious favorite of his?   What has Lincoln earned
that, without question, he should be passed over slur-
ringly for this amazing freebooter of the Andes?
How set Steinmetz or Hamilton or Paul Jones side
by side with this Spaniard and choose between them?

I am back to my first sentence—where on earth does
Mr. White get his ideas?

III

And now to find the answer. . . .

"A literarian can be understood," says Mr. White,
"only through a knowledge of his origin; of the circumstances, influences and training which shaped his
character; of the enthusiasms which inspire and the
theories which control his writings; and of his methods
and aims.

"I am a genuine American, since, before the Declaration of Independence, all my ancestors except one were
in the thirteen colonies, and he, Major Florant Meline,
came over with Lafayette, fought through the Revolutionary War, married here and settled in Albany.   I
am also a genuine Marylander and Baltimorean.   My
great-grandfather, John White (1779–1854), was a
local merchant of some prominence and prospered
sufficiently to retire and live on his investments.   Another Baltimore great-grandfather, Gielding Lucas,
Jr. (1781–1854), was in his time one of the most
prominent publishers in the United States.   I was born
in Bergen, New Jersey, on May 18th, 1866, my father

being in business in New York for some years before
and after his marriage. My earliest recollections are
of Brooklyn, where my parents lived from 1868 to
1872. Later I spent some years with my grandmother on her farm on the eastern shore of Lake
Seneca, in Ovid Township, Seneca County, N. Y. In
1877 my parents returned to Baltimore and I have
been ever since a Baltimorean. I have spent little
time outside of Maryland. In 1885 I went by sailing
ship to Rio de Janeiro, spent the summer of 1889 touring in Europe and for the first half of 1892 was a
temporary, stopgap teacher of freshman Latin at
Dartmouth College.

"In my teens, besides history, poetry and fiction, my
favorite reading was about science; astronomy, geol-
ogy, biology, paleontology and primitive man; Darwin, Huxley and Kingdon Clifford and such writers.
I expected to be a biologist and public lecturer. At
college I quickly realized that my interest in science
was all in its result and that I had no special faculties
for inference and almost none of observation.

"While at sea, in the company of the firmament and
the ocean and their surges and stars, fifty-four days
out to Rio and thirty-five back, I had the leisure to
evaluate my character. I discerned that I was most
positively a poet and planned my life accordingly. I
had to make a living and considered my ambitions,
tastes and powers. Longfellow appeared the best
model. It seemed to me that, as long as I lived, there
would be a good demand for professors of Romance
Languages in American Colleges and universities; that
mastering the Romance Languages would conduce

to development as a literarian, and that teaching them would not be destructive of creative literary powers. I continued my studies with all that in view. After making myself familiar with Old High-German, Middle High-German, Anglo-Saxon, Middle-English, Old French, Old Spanish, Early Italian and what was best in their literatures and in the more modern literatures of those times, I realized with a shock that everything admirable in those literatures is either a reminiscence, an echo or an imitation of something in the literatures of Rome and Greece; that an aspirant for success in creative literary effort should go straight to the sources; that no one ever really comprehends modern literatures without knowing the classics; that no one can be a capable teacher of modern language linguistics without the linguistics of Latin and Greek. I went back to the classical tongues and literatures to put in a foundation on which I could hope to be a really good professor of Romance Languages and literatures and might become a real poet. Before I had completed that foundation, before the superstructure was more than begun, my health broke down. I could study no more and must make a living at once. I was master of merely mediocre attainments in Latin and Greek. School teaching in these was my only resource. A teacher of Greek and Latin in private schools in Baltimore I have been ever since 1892.

"As with my education, so with my literary output; the course of my life has been determined by my bad health. Since nine years of age I have been subject to sudden and unpredictable sick-headaches, which lay me up, abed and fasting in the dark, for from one to three days and after which I dare not look at print or writing more than momentarily for days or maybe weeks. Even when at my best I must be wary and cautious in the use of my eyes; reading or writing too continuously or too long always brings on a visitation. Thus I have been able to do only a small fraction of what I might. I can never work by artificial light, seldom by the waning light of late afternoon, mostly only in the morning.

"My tastes in literature were early dominated by my passion for the writings of Edgar Allen Poe. I fuddled my brain reading and rereading him till I had to banish from my home everything of his, if I was to read anything else. Later Swinburne led me not only to intensive study of prosody, but to the knowledge of some of the authors I love best: Sappho, Catullus, Dante, Victor Hugo, Villon, Baudelaire, Rossetti, and others.

"Besides my dominating interest in literature I have always had others. In Europe I managed to see some hundreds of thousands of paintings in three months and have ever since possessed vague approximations to connoisseurship in paintings. I take a similar interest in sculpture and architecture. I read much about international politics, geography and the inhabitants, products and manufactures of all parts of the world. My chief pleasures are writing and reading. All other occupations are merely interruptions to or postponements of these.

"I early recognized that anything I wrote in verse assumed at once a final form and had a sort of merit: the rhythm was never despicable, nor was any violence

done either to the sense or the meter in fitting each
to the other. On the other hand I might rewrite an
essay or story any number of times and still find it as
contemptible as in its first draft. When, after my
sea-voyage, I reconsidered my manuscripts, I judged
all my prose worthless even as practice-work and my
hundreds of attempts at poems no more than passable
experiments; I burnt them all. Thereafter I soon
acquired the power to write poems by no means beneath notice both in ideas and in expression, but I
toiled on doggedly at prose without ever seeming any
nearer a prose style. Not until August of 1903 did
I write a tale which my critical faculties approved as
not bad enough to burn.

"As time went on my bread-winning and other duties
used up more nearly all my daily energy and my surplus
for creative writing dwindled steadily. I realized
that I could seldom attain that detachment, serenity
and elevation of mood in which alone poetry can be
produced. I was unwilling to waste time on writing
such mediocre verse as might be written by a man tired,
worried and distracted; I turned more and more to
prose, which can be turned out in any mood in any
brief interval of leisure. My one volume of poems
attracted little notice.

"From 1904 on I had some meager success both at
writing short stories and at selling them to magazines.
By 1909 I felt myself capable of a romance. My rash
impulse was to emulate Sienkiewicz's *The Deluge,*
which I rate as the greatest historical romance ever
written; for, when I became fascinated with Francia,
the Dictator of Paraguay, and read up on him, I re-

alized that I had blundered on an unworked Golconda of literary material. I attacked my task with ardor, elated at my great opportunity and wrote my *El Supremo* in the summers of 1910, 1911 and 1912, with some little work in the winters between. I write my tales in a large free hand in lead-pencil on small sheets of paper. My wife typewrites them from cruelly illegible draft. The chief event in my life has been a singularly happy marriage.

"Having meditated for years a picaresque adventure-romance of the days Commodus I was saturated with the spiritual and social atmosphere of that period, and, when, after the completion of *El Supremo,* I considered which of the plots in my notebooks seemed most tempting, I pitched on that of *The Unwilling Vestal* as being of that same period. I had long had an ambition to write a romance of classic times in which the characters would be depicted as talking as the Romans talked, rather than according to the absurd conventions of English literary tradition for classic conversation. The result, while satisfactory to me, has not won the critics or the public.

"In all I have written I have always asked myself how the poem or tale would read a hundred years from now. If, on examination, it seemed of merely ephemeral interest, I have almost always destroyed what I have written.

"My literary creed is that no one should write unless in possession of an idea of theme or plot original and worth writing about; nor unless writing lucidly and agreeably."

Mr. White is the author of *Narrative Lyrics,* 1908; *El Supremo,* 1916; *The Unwilling Vestal,* 1918; *The Song of the Sirens,* short stories, 1919; *Andivius Hedulio,* adventures of a Roman nobleman in the days of the empire, 1921.

STEWART EDWARD WHITE

"The Glory Hole," Mr. White says, speaking of his latest novel, "is something out of the line of what I usually write about. I wrote it because I was interested in the particular problem it covers, just as I have always written anything else because it happened to interest me. When I first began to write and had made a success of *The Blazed Trail,* I went back west to *Arizona Nights.* The publishers raised a mighty howl of protest, saying that I had created a field for myself in the Michigan Northwoods and that if I scattered myself all over the map I would certainly die the ignoble death of all literary favorites. I told them that they were mistaken, that the Michigan woods was not the field I had tried to appropriate for what I need in it. My field was the whole outdoors and Arizona fell in that category. I might extend that argument, and say that the field of any man's writing is the world by which he is surrounded. *The Glory Hole,* is simply another portion of that same field."

"Glory hole" is defined, in the *Standard Dictionary,* as an opening through which to observe the interior of a furnace; and, further, as a place for concealing articles of value; hence, humorously a cupboard for domestic utensils.

The book taking its title from all these various meanings is, Samuel Hopkins Adams tells me, the most ambitious of Mr. White's many novels. It touches upon mysticism, spiritualism, **labor** and dreams and ambitions. As originally written it ran into hundreds of thousands of words—Mr. White is never chary of his words.

II

Mr. White is a voluminous writer. The author of twenty-eight volumes, most of them massive tomes, in less than twenty-three years—twenty-eight volumes covering a wide range, stretching from the coast-wise currents of the Pacific to Nairobi, touching on the Zulu and the prospector, Indians, artists, sailors and lumbermen, squaws and sub-debs.

III

Mr. White writes out of a vast self-made experience, drawing his characters and his situations from a wide acquaintance with men. In his boyhood he spent a great part of each year in the lumber-camps of Michigan, and on the river with the loggers. Later he traveled and camped and hunted all over the West, in Wyoming, in the Sierras, in Arizona and California. Then he made two trips to Africa in search of big game. And always, I think, he has found what he has sought—a broader and more tolerant view of the world, men at their natural best and animals in their haunts, a target for his rifle and occupation for his mind. He has been, I am sure, happy in his adventures. And this happiness is reflected in his books. He does not, as so many of our writers of the out-of-doors do, exaggerate the attributes of man and beast in order to find them worthy of record—good, in the simpler sense of that meaningful

word.   He likes things as they are.   He is a naturalist—not exactly a realist and not especially romantic,
certainly not (as Conrad was) a pessimist—a photographer rather, or an historian.

IV

"As for my methods of writing," he says, "I have
a nice glazed bond paper and six newly sharpened
medium grade pencils situated at my right hand.   Seiz-
ing one of the pencils I wear it down to the place where
the point begins to get rounded, then throw it to one
side and take another.   After I have finished the six
pencils I quit. . . .

"Seriously, I do most of my writing away from my
desk.   When I sit down I know pretty well what I
want to put down and it is a mere matter of transcrip-
tion.   Therefore, I generally work at the desk only
in the mornings.   The afternoons I put in on miscellaneous pursuits.   I do not, as a usual thing, do
much revision or rewriting on this account, though
occasionally a big piece of work has to be visualized
on paper before its construction becomes apparent.
Then I have to pull it to pieces and put it together
again."

V

Mr. White was born at Grand Rapids, Michigan,
March 12, 1873, the son of Stewart and Mary E.
(Daniell) White.   Grand Rapids was at that time a
city of some thirty thousand, but (as I have said)
most of young White's time was spent in his father's
lumber-camps in the Michigan woods.   He did not

attend any formal school until he was sixteen, but studied, at home or traveling, with tutors. Finally he entered the junior class at high school, graduating at eighteen, president of his class. He won and still holds the five mile running record for the school. In 1893 he graduated from the University of Michigan, attending the Columbia Law School, 1896–7, and receiving the M.A. degree from Michigan in 1903.

From 1884–88, from eleven to fifteen, he lived in California. It was there that he was given his first gun, a Flobert .22, the gun afterwards written up as Bobby Orde's in *The Adventures of Bobby Orde.* But his first real gun was a Scott 16 gauge. At sight of this, the cynical men on the Pacific Coast, used to blunderbusses, would follow the boy out into the fields, just to see (as they said) if that pop-gun would really kill anything.

From 1888–91 he spent most of his time in the woods, studying bird life. Six or seven hundred bird skins are now preserved in the Kent Scientific Museum at Grand Rapids as a record of those years. But the most important record, of course, is his first book *The Birds of Mackinac Island,* a pamphlet published by the Ornithologists Union.

VI

While at college his summers were spent cruising on the Great Lakes in a 28 foot cutter sloop. Upon graduation he got a job in a packing house at six dollars a week. He lasted six months. Then he followed the gold rush to the Black Hills of the Dakotas—and came back broke, but with the materials later to be worked over in the *The Claim Jumpers* and *The Westerners,* his first real books.

VII

At Columbia, as a part of his class work under Brander Matthews, he wrote *A Man and His Dog,* which, at Professor Matthews' suggestion, he submitted to the magazines and sold to *Short Stories* for $15.00—his first check for a story. Others were sold to *Lippincott's* and *The Argonaut*—"But I did not get rich at it," Mr. White says. "Thirty-five dollars was the high water mark."

VIII

Then with some notion of learning the book business, he secured a position at nine dollars a week with A. C. McClurg, booksellers, in Chicago. But he quickly decided that that was no way to become a successful author—so he set out for the Hudson Bay country, having first finished and sold *The Claim Jumpers* to Appleton's (published 1901), and *The Westerners* as a serial to *Munsey's* for $500.

IX

"My earliest authors in childhood," he tells me, "were mainly historical writers. Then followed the historical novelists. I read Dickens' *Child's History of England,* and a prose version of Sir Thomas Mallory's called *The Boy's King Arthur, Ivanhoe* and all that group. Cooper came in for his share next. Then I plunged pretty deep on the Emerson type of philosophy, going through all the group and the allied group in England.   That landed me about three-quarters of the way through college, and brought me out of the channel into the broad general sea of literature, where I have sailed according to the winds of caprice, rather than to any definite compass bearing. . . .

"I do not think that I have a predominating affection for any particular one of my books.   Each expresses a different part of the life I have myself lived, and when I feel particularly sentimentally reminiscent of that kind of life, the book that represents it naturally comes in for sentimental attachment.   Take it, all in all, I believe that I would agree with Sam Adams that *The Silent Places* was the most coherent single piece of work, although I like *The Rawhide* in my *Arizona Nights* as an example of my best narrative in compressed form."

X

I have a notion that *The Blazed Trail* where Henry Thorpe meets his April Lady, is the most popular of Mr. White's books.   It has that epic quality, a thousand and one details, sketches of forest and lake and mountain, throngs of rivermen and clerks, a party of campers, the problem of success, that makes *Gold,* with it panoramas of the California of the forty-niners, as history, the best of Mr. White's books.

XI

But it's hard to pick and choose.   Perhaps not a one of Mr. White's books will live after our day is done.   Mr. White was never an artist.   But he is honest and he has an eye for rough and ready honesty, for courage, for patience in victory and defeat. You will not be brought up suddenly by some phrase that will stick in your mind as just the right phrase, but you will not be disappointed. Again and again you will be surprised by the truth and aptness of some observation. And you will hurry on to learn the aftermath of the story he is telling. . . .

There's *The Westerners,* with Jim Buckley and Alfred and Billy Knapp and the wagon train they convoy through the Black Hills, and the breed Michael Lafond who is so thoroughly revenged upon them for excluding him from their party. There's *The Riverman* and *Bobby Orde* roaring Dick Darrell and the scaler Fitzpatrick, log jams and jamborees in town. *The Leopard Woman* and the first rumblings of the great war in Africa; Kingozi, mightiest of Nimrod's successors; Winckelman, the German explorer and spy; *Simba* and the agony, the danger, the wonder of hunting and camping along the Congo or on the plains west of Zanzibar. And then there's that trilogy of the old and new San Francisco, *The Gray Dawn, Gold,* and the *Rose Dawn*—and the philosophical Chink, best of celestials, cook, bottle-washer and grave maker of cakes.

XII

"My family," Mr. White says, "consisted of one wife who goes wherever I go, even into Africa, and two dogs who would like to go wherever I do, but I sternly command them back at times, and friends who dolefully predict that we are coming to a catastrophic end every time we start out. My way of life is to come home to my place in Burlingame, work a while, and then depart for almost anywhere. Just at present we are cruising in a gas boat, ourselves as the only crew, from British Columbia to Alaska. We have done this for the last three years and have not yet drowned ourselves or run upon any sunken rocks."

XIII

"As to my indignation at the present state of the nation," Mr. White says, in reply to a question you may be sure I asked, "I have not the capacity for indignation that Sam Adams has, but have a large capacity for a rather cynical amusement at the show. In the first place I do not think that the government is as important as people imagine. The development of he individual is the important thing. The less government that one can have and still allow the individual to develop the better. Let them orate and legislate and howl their heads off as much as they please. It is not an edifying spectacle and does not make for progress. I repeat, it is not as serious as people imagine. By that I do not mean to imply that it is not serious. It is. But there are other things more serious."

Mr. White is the author of *The Westerners*, 1901; *The Claim Jumpers*, 1901; *The Blazed Trail*, 1902; *The Conjuror's House*, 1903; *The Forest*, 1903; *The Magic Forest*, 1903; *The Silent Places*, 1904; *The Mountains*, 1904; *Blazed Trail Stories*, 1904; *The Pass*, 1906, *The Mystery* (with Samuel Hopkins Adams), 1907; *Arizona Nights*, 1907; *Camp and Trail*, 1907; *The Rivermen*, 1908; *The Rules of the*

Game, 1909; *The Cabin,* 1910; *The Adventures of Bobby Orde,* 1911; *The Land of Footprints,* 1912; *African Camp Fires,* 1913; *Gold,* 1913; *The Rediscovered Country,* 1915; *The Gray Dawn,* 1915; *The Leopard Woman,* 1916; *Simba,* 1918; *The Forty Niners,* 1918; *The Rose Dawn,* 1920; *Daniel Boone,* 1922; *The Glory Hole,* in preparation.

WILLIAM ALLEN WHITE

When a new reporter is engaged for the *Emporia Gazette,* of which Mr. White is editor, he (the reporter) is told that should a story beginning "there was a" appear in the *Gazette,* Mr. White's orders are that he (the reporter again) must be taken out and shot at sunrise. . . .

Long ago and, for most of us, far away, in the early nineties, the vain and lively G. B. S. used to complain of the acting of Sir Henry Irving. It was stilted, angular and awkward; it wasn't acting at all, but merely the posturings of a senile clown—if we (and why not?) believe G. B. S. But even so G. B. S. did not, so long ago as the nineties, say that Sir Henry should be taken out and shot. He merely pleaded that some one gently lead the venerable mime from the stage and, without undue fuss, have him guillotined. . . .

G. B. S. was leagues ahead of White, then and now and always, in such important trifles as concern the meting out of proper punishment to those who transgress the quiet and joy of a somewhat carelessly assembled Christendom.

II

I wish Mr. White were not so scornful of Mr. Mencken. He (Mr. White) could learn a trick worth an odd dozen of those he employs if only he would listen to the dire cursings of Mencken when

Mencken is roused—and Mencken is easily roused. He is like a lion that has had, in his youth perhaps, his fill of sleeping. . . .

When Mencken calls the gods to witness, they come scurrying from all sides, from the dim groves of Arcady and the wide plains of Mongolia, obscene and livid ghosts of a lewd and lusty past—Priapus and Circe, Astarte, Diana and Lingum. They come from the isles of the Pacific and the timbers Wotan frequents; and they bring with them, captives of their triumph, quaint devices of torture that make the wrackrooms of the Inquisition seem as out-moded as (thank heaven) they are.

III

But gods (and even green fish) are a little beyond Mr. White's ken. Mr. White is a provincial with a provincial's prejudices and a provincial's qualms.

In *In Our Town,* for instance, he tells of a girl named Maybelle who came to him in Emporia, saying that she would "accept a position" on the *Gazette.* Just from his way of describing her in the opening sentences, we realize how little she, with her aspirations, could fit into his scheme of things—and how little Bernhardt would have fitted into it—or Duse—or Shaw's Great Catherine—or Meredith's Diana—or any one of the great women of the world. Not that Maybelle was great, but that she was in revolt against Kansas and Mr. White is Kansas. He is Kansas City and Dubuque, points east, points west and most of the people in between. His are the virtues and vices of

common men; his the common man's distrust of
vanity. . . .

Mr. White tells us that Maybelle was as sympathetic
and as intelligent as a collie, and that, in answer to his
various questions, she murmured, "Oh, Yes," passionately. . . .

This same Mr. White, towards the close of this
same book, declares that every human life, if we could
know it well and translate it into language, has in it
the makings of a great story—It is only because we are
blind, Mr. White says, that we pass the men and
women about us, heedless of the tragic quality of their
lives. . . .

IV

Mr. White is undoubtedly blind—for it is vain to
ask him about the tragedy of Maybelle, who thought
in terms of "accepting a position" yet had to beg for
a job on the *Emporia Gazette*.

V

But it is this slipshod method of tying his conclusions together, without thinking anything through,
that is Mr. White's failure as critic and artist. . . .

Now I do not believe that Maybelle murmured
passionately when told of the exigencies of newspaper
work; I doubt if she was, no more, no less, as intelligent and sympathetic as a collie; but I cannot, for all
that, laugh with Mr. White when, to raise a laugh in
his readers, at that time readers of the *Saturday
Evening Post,* he goes to such lengths to prove himself
superior to her.

VI

But that is only the half of it, dearie—that is but
an exhibition of pharisaical bad manners.   What shall
we say to the intolerable condescension that speaks of
the tragic quality of our lives, that refers to those who
pass us, heedless of the great story we might make, as
blind?   My life is no more tragic than Mr. White's.
Why should we pretend that our frustrated passions
are comparable to the broken dreams of Lancelot
or the fallen fancies of Hurstwood and Lear and
Orestes?   Mr. White has accomplished his various
simple ambitions—he has money, friends and an easy
life in a pleasant place—he has his boisterous cam-
paigning, his chances of election, and the Ku Klux
Klan to berate—what more could any man want?
Perhaps he has a great story in him.   But to say that
there is a great story in all of us . . .

Tosh—great stories are not made, haphazard, of
every Jack and Jill.   The simple annals of the girl
across the court, getting breakfast and dinner, making
the bed, for a piano-tuner, have about them neither
wit nor wantonness nor tears.   They are ordinary.
She knows it and we know it.   God himself has made
nothing much of her—and we are not yet gods.

VII

But it is like Mr. White to think that this is the best
of all possible worlds and, with his next breath, to
point out that there are at least a hundred odd million tragedies in this country alone—to say nothing of
the Scandinavian.

VIII

Yet I do not want to give you a false impression of Mr. White. He is only human. . . .

He is only human, vastly human, engagingly so. He may weep upon the shoulders of a crossing-sweeper, bemoaning the furrowed lines on that battered face, or scoff at the harmless vanities of a young girl—but he is good, unquestionably good, meaning everything for the best.

And he is far from ordinary. There is an epic quality, a sweep, to his two novels, *In the Heart of a Fool* and *A Certain Rich Man,* that lifts them, and lifts us with them, far above the humdrum levels of the world they body forth. The whole history of an era is in them; and such boys as only Mr. White can depict. They may teach us to abide by the simple rules of the copy-books, but they teach and preach with gusto, with energy, with an optimism that is truly winning and wholly American. . . .

American—that is what they are.

And make no mistake—the best of Mr. White is the best of America. Not the best of which certain rarely gifted individuals are capable, but the best of the common man, the genius of the common man, his more generous impulses and his better judgment.

IX

In *The Editor and His People,* a collection of editorials from the *Emporia Gazette,* Mr. White tells his own story, the story of the changes that have come over the spirit of his thought in twenty years of newspaper editing.

One editorial in especial takes my fancy. Commenting on a negro golf club, recently organized at Westfield, N. J., Mr. White asks why such a club, such an organization, should make the white man laugh:—

"The reason for this risibility of the white man at the black man's human activities is obvious and is no credit to the white man. He thinks it is funny to see the black man doing things that normal human beings do, because the white man does not think of his dark-skinned fellow traveler on the planet as a human companion. The white man considers any colored man,— black, brown, yellow or maroon—as an animal. The anthropological conceit of the white man is ponderous, unbelievable, vastly amusing to the gods. Why should not the black man play golf if his economic status gives him leisure for golf. Why should he not have a motor car if he can afford it? Why giggle at the normal activities of men whose skins differ from our own?

"Something of the same psychological reason is behind the fact that we middle-class people make merry over the fact that the worker in the mines and shops and furnaces wears a silk shirt or rents a house with a bath or drives to work in a car. Why shouldn't he? Is he an elephant doing stunts? Is he a horse playing a piano? What's the joke if he develops the same desires and aspirations that we do, and who in God's name are we anyway?"

There you have White, the editor and the man, with his long words and his easy conclusions—but, oh, how the things he says, to our shame, needed and need saying.

X

Mr. White is the conscience of the middle west and its hospitality—he is the editorial page of a country weekly and its best advertisements. He rises above his fellows—but not too far, for his faith is in them and not in their leaders. Indeed, he is more than a little suspicious of the man who dares to claim for himself the privileges and the powers of leadership—such a man must be self-seeking.

XI

Mr. White has kindly supplied me with an autobiographical sketch of himself:—

"I was born in Emporia, Kansas, February 10, 1868, when Emporia was a pioneer village a hundred miles from a railroad. My father came to Emporia in 1859 and my mother in 1855. She was a pioneer school teacher and he a pioneer doctor. She was pure bred Irish, and he of Yankee lineage since 1639. When I was a year old, Emporia became too effete for my parents, and they moved to El Dorado, Kansas. There I grew up. El Dorado was a town of a dozen houses, located on the banks of the Walnut, a sluggish, but a clear and beautiful prairie stream, rock bottom, and spring fed. I grew up in El Dorado, a prairie village boy; went to the large stone school house that 'reared its awful form' on the hill above the town before there were any two story buildings in the place.

"In 1884, I was graduated from the town high school, and went to the College of Emporia for a year; worked a year as a printer's devil; learned something of the printer's trade; went to school for another year, working in the afternoons and Saturdays at the printer's case; became a reporter on the *Emporia News;* later went to the State University for three years, and more or less studying and working on the Lawrence papers. I went back to El Dorado as a Manager of the *El Dorado Republican* for State Senator T. B. Murdock.

"From the *El Dorado Republican,* I went to Kansas City, to work for the *Kansas City Journal* and at 24 became an editorial writer on the *Kansas City Star.* For three years I worked on the *Star* during which time I married Miss Sallie Lindsay, a Kansas City school teacher; and in 1895 I bought the *Emporia Gazette* on credit, without a cent in money, and chiefly with the audacity and impudence of youth. It was then a little paper; I paid three thousand dollars for it, and I have lived in Emporia ever since.

"In 1896, I published a book of short stories called *The Real Issue.* In 1899, another book of short stories called, *The Court of Boyville.* In 1901, I published another book of short stories called *Strategem and Spoils.* In 1906 *In Our Town* in 1909, I published my first novel, *The Certain Rich Man.* In 1910, I published a book of political essays called *The Old Order Changeth.* In 1916, a volume of short stories entitled, *God's Puppets.* A volume, half novel and half travel sketches, called *The Martial Adventures of Henry and Me* filled the gap between my two novels; and the second novel *In the Heart of a Fool* was published in 1916.

"I am a member of the National Institute of Arts and Letters; the Short Ballot Association; the International Peace Society; National Civic Federation; National Academy of Political Sciences; have honorary degrees from the College of Emporia, Baker Uni-

versity, and Columbia University from 1905–1913.
Politically I am a Republican and was elected National
Republican Committeeman from Kansas this year.   I
am a member of the Republican National Committee
on platforms and also a member of the sub-committee
of nine that drafted the Republican platform this year.
I am trustee of the College of Emporia; a director of
the Rockefeller Foundation; a member of the Congregational Church, and of the Elks Lodge; Rotarians
and of no other organization."

XII

But that is a mere skeleton of the man.   I wanted
more, and finally prevailed upon the Hon. Victor Murdock of Kansas to tell something of White in his
ordinary habits:—

"A visitor to Emporia," says Murdock, "is apt to
find William Allen White in one of four activities—
political, commercial, literary or domestic.   These activities are unlike.   But in them White remains the
same—that is White.

"Beginning with the last—his home life.   He gives
himself up to the solid comforts of domestic happiness.   There is nothing about him to indicate that he
has a commercial care or a political interest or a literary design.   He takes full liberty with his library,
pulling down Kipling or Wells and scanning a sentence or two at random and then replacing the book
with no sign that he has taken anything out of it.   He
turns on the talking-machine and plants himself
squarely in front of it—going strong for the *Valkyrie*,
Rheingold and Schubert's *Unfinished Symphony* and
plunking the needle back on some particularly favored

phrase. He wanders forth with his family into the garden and notes, without particular enthusiasm, the progress of wistaria, lilac and iris. Back again at the house, he edges over onto the piano seat and tries very softly and quite beautifully *Genevieve* with minor improvisations. He has an eye to the kitchen and an adolescent demand as to the nature of the dessert. He rises a degree in enthusiasm over the business of salad-fabrication, and wanders back into the library when it has been disposed of. Now all this is William Allen White at home—but it is without the identifying characteristic which marks him everywhere. That identifying characteristic is the appearance of mental detachment while he is at it. One cannot too surely charge that he does not know he is looking at the iris, or listening to the *Valkyrie* or gloating over the salad, but one carries away the impression that he is doing these things somewhat mechanically and that his real occupation at the moment is some tremendous thinking in the center of an isolated mental area, safe against all manner of outside invasion. It is not phlegm. It is never mistaken for phlegm in White. His quiescence is plainly the envelope of a prodigious energy. What is true in his home life is true in his other activities—the abstraction carries through and marks him in each.

"He loves politics. The public interest is his passion. Men and their ambitions, in the RAW, fascinate him. But he is never a spectator. He is always a participant. He has an eager hand for the battle-ax, and his voice is clarion with a battle-cry. Always prominent in affairs and at times controlling, there is no question of economics that does not hold him and no infinitesimal detail of personal maneuver that calls in vain on his attention. Like almost all Kansas politicians of this generation, he banks on the long-distance telephone. Over this he consults and is consulted. He is decisive in his counsels, quick and certain in his opinions, and wise in his deductions. And yet when he turns away from the telephone, you are quite sure that even in this instant action and alertness, he has been thinking of something else—and something else of greater moment. In another man, you might say that he was one who was keeping rein on his own enthusiams, and guarding against self-deception. But White's detachment is not that. It is something else—as though he were fitting passing detail into a bigger future, which he is painting for himself and not exhibiting.

"Commercially White has a good head. He knows costs in his own establishment—a newspaper office. He can talk depreciation, overhead, indirect labor. Profit and loss and what can and cannot be done with it, as an accounting device, is known to him as to a bang-up book-keeper. Around his shop he knows the newsprint on hand, whether the quality of ink is keeping up and whether Grocer Jones has left his advertisement out and why. He is a busy, bustling, belligerent solicitor for business about town, an absolutely consistent assailant on bills payable and an enthusiastic enemy of overdrafts. Commercially he carries on well. When he is at it you might say he is a born business genius—except that he here again shows the same detachment.

"Is this detachment his literary side, which is whirring away in his mind when he is busy in other activities? Are the things he sees at home, in business and in politics grist to his literary mill and therefore incidental to his chief mental activity—the writing of books? I do not think so. White writes his books by burning the kilowatt hours. He is infinitely painstaking. He believes in the men and women he depicts. But in the midst of it he remains the artist. He knows when the footlights are acting up and the backdrop is askew. His creations are characters—but they are creations and so are their environments. But when White has been face to face with them in all the tender love that an author must have for his own, he turns away with the old detachment intact and unbetrayed.

"There is no particular psychology to be read into all this. It may or it may not yield anything to analysis. But as I have studied him, it is White."

BRAND WHITLOCK

I would be inclined to like Mr. Whitlock—as I am inclined to like the heathen Chinee, the quaint and self-contained Ras Tafiri, or any one else who does not interfere in any way with me. But when I get to reading Mr. Whitlock's books, I find him too sentimental and too easily horrified and superior. I find him forever, in public, washing his hands of this or that—than which there is no gesture more silly, unless it be a mob howling in the square.

Let me tell you a story that I have from Mr. Judson D. Stewart, in the words of Mr. Stewart. I repeat, in Mr. Stewart's words, for I cannot do much for Mr. Stewart's ways of telling a story. It seems to me the whole thing is botched and sicklied o'er with the pale cast of hero-worship. To me Mr. Whitlock was merely silly and ponderous no end for a lad of eighteen. He was about as natural and human then, apparently, as he is now. . . .

"Say, Whitlock, how'd you like to do police?" the city editor of the *Toledo Bee* asked.

"Thank you, I'll think it over," answered the cub.

For a cub reporter who, only three years before, had come from a little country village, to be offered what so many reporters consider the best job on the staff, was a big achievement in the minds of all the other reporters.

For any live, sane young reporter to hesitate a single moment about accepting such a chance seemed

567

unbelievable to the other reporters; and when, the next day, young Brand Whitlock told the city editor that he did not think he cared for murders but preferred to get a chance at writing politics, his fellow reporters plainly told him that he was "a fool."

"Skinny, you're plumb crazy," one of his friends on the paper told him. They all called him "Skinny" because he was tall, lank and decidedly rangy as to legs.

"I don't think so," young Whitlock told him. "I've thought it all over and I believe I am right about it. You see this police job doesn't lead to anywhere in particular. You cover police for years and years and get to be an expert in writing about fires and murders. But murders do not interest me. I like politics better because it leads somewhere. I've noticed that a good many successful men got a good start through their knowledge of politics and their acquaintance with big men."

"But politics is the dryest sort of stuff to write. Think of the fun there is in covering police," urged his friend.

"If I wanted fun I'd get a job with a circus," laughed young Whitlock.

He was then only eighteen years old. He used his brains at exactly the right time. He did not jump at the assignment of covering police headquarters. He went home and thought it over. If he had not given this extra thought, if he had not used his brains, he might be writing all the big murder and fire stories in Toledo to-day or perhaps he might be city editor of the paper, as that job frequently leads there.

But instead of that he is a diplomat in the service

of the United States—and one of our biggest diplo-
mats. Ask anyone in Belgium, ask any one from Belgium, what they think of Brand Whitlock and tears of
gratitude fill their eyes as they struggle to find words
to sufficiently express their admiration for him. . . .

II

So far Mr. Stewart—but I'm a hard nut, I am, and
I can't do much for that stuff about tears of gratitude welling, filling, flooding the eyes, anywhere and
everywhere in Belgium, at the mere mention of Mr.
Whitlock's name. . . . What if the man in Belgium
happens to be a German? Or a Russian? Or some
self-contained Britisher? Do they too weep at the
mention of that magic name? Or are we to believe
that there are no travelers from other worlds in Belgium, but only lachrymose Belgians?

III

However, Mr. Stewart, misguided though he be, is
not alone to blame. He has taken his cue from his
master, Brand Whitlock. Whitlock encourages just
that sort of nonsense—he even writes about himself in
the same vein. . . .

"I can recall a day," he says, "a sinister one in the
history of this world—when for a moment I was called
back rudely to the realities of an existence that those
days of blue and gold had removed far from my
thought. I was sitting at my table, and through the
open window there came the soft air of the late June
morning, with the odors and the sounds of the country.
I had the manuscript of my novel before me and I

was far away, over seas and in the distant past, in a little Ohio town that was for the moment far more real to me than Brussels, and I was trying to make it as real to those who perhaps some day might idly pursue, on some summer day as that, the book of which I was not yet sure.   And yet it was somehow just beginning to form, beginning to show signs of life; at times some of the characters in it gave evidence of being human and alive; and they were beginning to act now and then spontaneously, beginning to say and to do things after the manner of human beings.   The long vista before me, the months of laborious drudging toil and pain, the long agony of effort necessary to write any book, even a poor one, were beginning to appear less weary, less futile; and there was the first faint glow of the joy of creative work."

IV

The book of which Mr. Whitlock speaks thus caressingly is *J. Hardin and Son,* a quite ordinary and routine novel in the tradition of Mrs. Gaskell and the manner of Mrs. Humphrey Ward.   If you like your Ohio diluted, if you believe that Harding was a real and a good American, you will like *J. Hardin and Son.*

V

Then suddenly a bell rang out and the calm of Mr. Whitlock (as he sat meditating his novel) was shattered.

The Crown Prince of Austria had been murdered! Says Mr. Whitlock:—

"And the Crown Prince of Austria was to me a most immaterial person—a kind of wraith wandering there in those nether regions to which have gone so many of that House of Hapsburg which seems to have suffered in itself as much evil as it has caused others to suffer in this world. I confess that it seemed a rather unwarranted intrusion on that morning. It meant for me putting aside Masochee and going to town at once."

Can you beat it? Mr. Whitlock was actually expected to work, to wait on bells and pay attention to murders in the House of Austria. Really ridiculous, isn't it? He wanted to write a novel. He didn't expect to have to give anything in return for the honors of ambassador, the honors that sat so lightly on his lifted shoulders. He certainly never thought that he would be expected to earn the salary that jingled so nicely in his pockets. But you can never tell. Immaterial though they may seem, the suffering wraiths of the House of Hapsburg wander where they will and they sometimes interrupt the calm waters on which, from one social function to another, American ambassadors bob like corks.

VI

"On Saturday morning, July 25th," Mr. Whitlock goes on. "I had just seated myself at my table and was yielding to all those trifling temptations by which the indolent will postpone the task of composition—sharpening lead-pencils, aligning them on the desk, arranging notes on paper, looking out the window at the summer day—and the golf-links, nearby:—and at

last, having exhausted all the possibilities of petty occupations which by a trick of the lazy mind might
serve as excuses for procrastination, I was about to go
to work when the morning papers were sent up. I
would glance over the report of the Caillaux case, at
any rate, though the full reports were in the Paris
papers which Omer would bring out at noon. I
picked up *L'Etoile Belge* and there was the ultimatum
which the Austrian Government had sent to Serbia
on Thursday evening."

War's hell, isn't it?

JOHN WILEY

The Education of Peter is a first novel and it is all about Peter Carey who spent four years at Yale—where Mr. Wiley graduated in 1921—yet the best that Billy Phelps (of the English Department at Yale) can find to say about it is that, as a first novel, it has decidedly unusual merit.

I mention this not because I want you to take Billy Phelps' word for it—you will be off on some rather wild goose chases if you do—but because I want you to know that their minds run in channels at Yale and the wonder of Wiley's escaping conformity is all the more remarkable. Imagine a review of *The Ordeal of Richard Feveral* that said no more of that devastating and beautiful romance than that it had unusual merit as a first novel—and you have some idea of what I mean. It happens that the story of Gargantua is a first novel; and that *Pickwick* is the first continued story by Dickens. Who said that a first novel must necessarily be weak and wishy-washy? *Joseph Vance* is a first novel and to my notion the best thing De Morgan ever did. Surely it is high time we judged a book on its merits and not on the strength of its being a first, second or third novel.

II

The Education of Peter is exciting. I don't as a rule spend my evenings speculating as to what the young men at Yale may be thinking or doing. I confess the whole subject bores me. How many wait-resses they may have kissed, how many drinks go round to a party, what fraternity they make is matter of no great moment. I can't keep up with the endless procession of Clio's neophytes. But I was genuinely interested in Peter. It seemed to me that he might be any boy starting out to catch up with the past and so fit himself for the future. And after the first few chapters the book became remarkably easy reading.

And as seen with Mr. Wiley Yale is all that its most fervent admirers say for it—a college that helps a fellow a lot in shedding the thin skin of adolescence. I came almost to regret my one short year at Cornell.

III

Mr. Wiley is a native New Yorker, born twenty-four years ago not ten miles from where, about two hundred years earlier, his original Dutch ancestors settled down to till the soil and make ready for Manhattan. His earliest recollections are of a rambling, old-fashioned frame house uptown near Mount Morris Park; and it was there, in the park, that he first knew the grief of disillusion when a burly policeman refused the turtle he proferred as a gift. He was four at the time but the memory sticks and haunts him still. About that time his mother used to take him driving behind the family mare through Central Park, but he invariably slept through these excursions and so nothing of moment now remains from them. His summers were spent at his grandmother's home in Stamford, Connecticut. Then for four years he traveled with his father and mother, through the Yellowstone where he lost his teddy-bear, to Estes Park where he first experienced the pangs of love, to Glenwood, Cal., where he assisted in the christening of a train of donkeys.

IV

"Almost as soon as I could hold a pencil," he says, "I began to write. My first story was entitled *The Princess Burland and the Page*——

Once upon a time there was a king who had twelve daughters. Each was more beautiful than the last. None had ever married. There the story ended. Whether I ran out of material or whether I was not enough of a realist to do justice to the story of a man with twelve unmarried daughters, I don't know."

V

When he was eight the family returned to New York and moved into a house on Seventy-fifth Street. His games were the usual games of city children— roller-skating up and down the block, playing hide-and-seek along the neighboring porches, climbing back fences, marbles and tops. He went to school two or three blocks from home.

At school he had the luck to meet up with a boy who shared his passion for Dumas; and together they wrote whole blank books full of highly colored historical romance. No period later than 1830 would do and the characters must all be of noble birth. Dukes were as plentiful as butlers and there was always at least one queen. Then there was a toy theater; and they took turns as audience and playwright.

VI

"When I was twelve," he says, "my father failed in business and we moved to Stamford.   It was a period of my life when I was both lonely and unhappy. While we were only there three years, life in that small New England City was so strongly etched on my mind that I find it creeping into all my writings.   While I had always been fond of reading, in those years I was insatiable, Scott, Dickens, Thackeray, Bronte, Bulwer Lytton, George Eliot, those grand old reliables which if not tackled with the enthusiasm of fifteen will never be read later.   Of these Dickens was and still is, my favorite.   I re-read him every year in the same stodgy brown volumes, heavy and with very fine print. While that first glorious, uncritical enjoyment is gone, I still love that admirer of Mrs. Nickelby's who threw the cucumbers over the garden wall and Sarah Gamp's handleless bureau, which had to be pried open with a knife or tilted forward so that all the drawers fell out on the floor at once.

"I was seventeen, when we entered the World War. My brother was a captain of infantry at the front, but I never got any further than training camp."

VII

Mr. Wiley entered Yale at the average age, but without the preparatory experience of one of the big prep schools, so he seems to himself to have been unusually young at the time.   The story of his adjustment to the fellows and conditions there is the theme of *The Education of Peter.*

At Yale he was editor of the *Literary Magazine*, a member of the Elizabethan Club and an active participant in dramatics.

VIII

On graduating he immediately started out as a writer, doing Sunday supplement articles for the New York *World* and later joining the staff as a regular reporter. There for a time he was on the editorial staff of a publishing house. Just now he is with an advertising agency.

The Education of Peter is his only book.

BEN AMES WILLIAMS

We live and learn, we do; and there's no place for learning like an American college. Take Dartmouth —if you can. When Ben Ames Williams entered Dartmouth in 1906 he was told that he had no faintest conception of what good English was or ought to be. Four years later, on graduation, the same prof—remembered as the caster of that first slur—openly hailed Mr. Williams as one of only two men in his class capable of producing true literary English.

However, true literary English is a drug on the market; and Williams' learning brought him little or nothing. During six years as reporter (and latterly as a re-write man) on the Boston *American,* eighty-two short stories by Mr. Williams were refused before one, in 1914, was accepted—and in 1912 he had married an old sweetheart, the daughter of a long line of sea-captains familiar with the China trade. It was a desperate business, but it explains, in part, Mr. Williams' austerity. It proves his courage, if proof were necessary. It attests the hard discipline he underwent before winning to his present success.

There is in every line he writes a history of that long bout with the editors. Soon or late he would force them to accept him. But the ordeal made him old as it made him impatient of irrelevance. He has none of the amateur knowingness of Chambers or Vance and none of the sheer fatuity of Arthur Stringer. He is a magazine author, true; but with Hergesheimer, he always gives of his best—he is serious. He writes because he is a born writer, and not because some editor or other has taken a fancy to his writings.

II

Though born in Macon, Mississippi, March 7, 1889, Mr. Williams spent his youth in Jackson, Ohio, where his father was (and is) the editor of a country weekly, one of the most amusing and likable of Ohio's thousand and one editors, recently a candidate for governor in the primaries, running against Donahey.

William Dean Howells was the son of an Ohio editor; and Howells got his learning (what little it was) of Latin and Greek from browsing among his father's books. So too, with Williams. The house was like a library; and until he went East to school, at fifteen, his chief delight had been in listening to his mother read from one or another of his father's books. Indeed, until he entered Dartmouth, he had little formal education, for he had scarcely begun at his Eastern preparatory school when his father was made consul at Cardiff, in Wales, and the family transferred to Britain. There he studied Latin with a tutor until he found himself reading it for pleasure; from then on most of his preparation for college was done alone.

III

It was in 1916 that Mr. Williams was discovered by Bob Davis of *Munsey's,* the most enterprising and generous editor in America—possibly (now) excepting H. L. Mencken. Encouraged by Mr. Davis, Williams resigned from the Boston *American* and settled down

to an author's life.   He took a house at Newtonville
in Massachusetts and spent his summers at a camp
near Belfast in Maine.   One place or the other he
works, fishes, shoots, plays with his two growing boys,
and drives a Ford station-wagon, locally known as the
Yellow Peril.

IV

Mr. Williams is first, last and all the time a story-
teller.   It is the story that matters to him.   And so
his characters are forced, are created and designed, to
fit the patterns of his plots.   Yet because his plots
have something of the diffuseness, the irony and inevitability of life, his characters, at times, grip the
heart.   I say "at times" because I am more often
amazed by the skill of Mr. Williams than touched by
the humanness of his people.   It is the sorry scheme
of things rather than the sorry plight of men and
women caught in the tangle of that scheme that is
brought out and emphasized in Mr. Williams' books.
   Evered is a case in point.   Evered is a farmer in
New England, morose and lonely, with a great reputation for temper and strength.   There is a tale of his
having killed a neighbor, in self-defense, when that
neighbor disputed his way of slaughtering hogs.
Evered marries (for his second wife) a Mary whom
he loves.   She knows he loves her and he knows it;
yet such is his inability, his want of understanding, his
alone-ness, he cannot express that love and so assure
her (and himself) of it.   Evered is the owner of a
huge red bull, a bull gone wild, a bull that is the cen-

tral character of the story, the peg from which everything hangs. This bull breaks loose from the bullpen, to go on a rampage. Evered takes his gun and starts out in search of the bull. In the pasture he comes upon his wife in whispered conversation with a man, in intimate conversation. He stops. He watches them. He notes the way they lean together, how considerate they are, one of the other. He is certain that they are lovers. The world goes black before him. He is consumed with rage and jealousy, his lips are hot with hate. Just then the bull comes into the pasture.

It is a fault (I am sure) in this type of story that you know that Evered, in his madness, allows the bull to kill his wife; and that later, repenting of his folly, coming to see that he has been an idle accomplice in murder, he will go out and with his bare hands duel with that bull, under a clear moon, to the death. It is a fault that is ever-present in the too careful plotting of romance. It may be like life but it is not fine art. Here we scheme our ways or drift to our conclusions; but in art there is a wider vision, more of the divinely unexpected, less of calculation.

V

Black Pawl is like *Evered* in its slow moving toward an appointed goal. It has the directness and simplicity of Greek tragedy, the pity and the irony of the Greeks. You realize that these people cannot escape their fate. But in that realization you lose something of the joy of surprise. You feel that there is no help for them and so you sit back; you do not join with them in their adventures; you are the audience pure and simple, an onlooker.

Black Pawl is the name of a whaling captain, so named to distinguish him from his son, Red Pawl—the one having black and the other a pawl of red hair. The mother of Red had deserted them, running away with a seaman while the boy was on his first voyage to the South Pacific with his father; and Black Pawl raises his son in hatred of all love, of all gentle and good and lovely things. It is the consumation of that hate, its final flowering and destruction, when the good that is in the Captain comes to death grips with the evil in the son, that makes the book.

Not that this is all the good that is in the story. There is the sea—and the clear stars of a tropic night —a missionary—and the captain's daughter who had been born to the runaway wife eight months after Black Pawl set out on the whaling expedition that was to separate them forever. There is talk of God and a man's way with his woman, of murder and vengeance and retribution. There are three or four titanic battles. And there is death to top it all.

VI

Mr. Williams is not an easy writer; he is not facile or slipshod or merely sensational. Again and again his sentences come like periods to a full stop, ending all debate in the just and only appropriate word. They have finality. They are convincing. Indeed I believe that Mr. Williams will take that place in our literature that should have been Hergesheimer's—had Mr.

Hergesheimer been a little less anxious to see his name in print and a little more honest with his readers, giving us something for nothing, life in the trappings of a dream.

Mr. Williams is the author of *All the Brothers Were Valiant,* 1919; *The Sea Bride,* 1919; *The Great Accident,* 1920; *Evered,* 1921; *Black Pawl,* 1922; *Audacity,* 1923; *Thrifty Stock* and other stories, 1923.

HARRY LEON WILSON

There is something good, something lovable, something enduring in the heart of Mr. Harry Leon Wilson. It is fair enough to complain because he is no better than he is, to point out that he can never hope to rival the H. G. Wells of *Kipps* and *Mr. Polly*, to regret that there is no wise and patient smile behind the broad grin of his books; but it is more comfortable to accept him, for *Bunker Bean* and *Merton of the Movies,* and be glad. He may seem the least bit preposterous, fighting out some fancied wrong on the lawns of California country clubs; he may be given to punning; he may drag out his jokes in the all too ordinary American fashion; yet he can make you cry— and that is something in a professional humorist. And he is (when he might have been a Russian) wholly and unaffectedly American. There is, for proof, his comment on the baseball fan in *Bunker Bean:—*

"It is a phenomenon familiar to most of us. The sons of men, under the magic of that living diamond, are no longer little units of souls jealously on guard. Heart speaks to heart, naked and unashamed; they fraternize across deeps that are commonly impassable, thrilling as one man to the genius of the double-play or with one voice hurling merited insults at a remote and contemptuous umpire. It is only there, on earth, that they love their neighbors. There they are fused and welded into that perfect whole which is perhaps the only colorable imitation ever to be had on earth of the democracy said to prevail in Heaven."

Of an absent player, Breede said that he was too old—all of thirty-five. He'd never come back.

"They come back when they learn to play ball above the ears," retorted Bean. "How about old Cy Young? How about old Callahan of the Sox? How about Wagner out there—think he's only nineteen— hey?"

II

There is (too) his way of putting a character before you, in the flesh as it were:—

"The professor was a mere sketch of a man, random, rakish, with head aslant and shifty eyes forever dropping away from a questioner's face. He abounded in inhuman angles and impossible lines. It seemed that he must have been rather dashingly done in the first place, then half obliterated and badly mended with fumbling, indecisive touches. His restless hands ceaselessly wrung each other as if he had that moment made his own acquaintance and was trying to infuse a false geniality into the meeting."

Only Sinclair Lewis, so far as I know, can better that this side of the seas; and Lewis is better only because he means what he says. Mr. Wilson, of course, is talking for effect: he is not, in any real sense, writing criticism. And, after all, to be important art must be critical. It is because *Merton of the Movies* is so much a criticism of things as they are supposed to be, in the human heart and in Hollywood, that *Merton* easily tops his list of books.

III

Mr. Wilson knows the value of appearances. He
has read *Cinderella* to better purpose than most. He
understands that it was the clothes she wore and not
the sweetness of her disposition that made the cinder-
wench, that fateful night, the belle of the ball.

"In a beggar's rags," he says, "few men could be
more than beggars. In kingly robes, most men could
be kings; could achieve the finished and fearless be-
havior that is said to distinguish kings."

Of course, there is nothing especially original in this
—Mark Twain, in an after-dinner speech, once took
off the Czar of all the Russians addressing his royal
regalia as the real ruler of Russia—but it bears repeating. Take away our prestige and you have little
enough left, scarce enough surely to make men of most
of us.

IV

I think that Mr. Wilson is better able to speak for
himself than I for him; and so I will quote him
again :—

"Bean had once attended a magician's entertainment
and there suffered vicariously the agony endured by
one of his volunteer assistants. Suavely the entertainer begged the help of 'some kind gentleman from
the audience.' He was insistent, exerting upon the
reluctant ones the pressure of his best platform
manner.

"When the pause had grown embarrassing a shamed
looking man slouched forward from an aisle amid

hearty cheers. He ascended the carpeted runway
from aisle to stage, stumbled over the foot-lights and
dropped his hat. Then the magician harried him to
the malicious glee of the audience. He removed
playing-cards, white rabbits and articles of feminine
apparel from beneath the coat of his victim. He
seated him on a chair that collapsed. He gave him
a box to hold and shocked him electrically. He missed
his watch and discovered it in the abused man's
pocket. And when the ordeal was over the recovered
hat was found to contain guinea-pigs. The kind
gentleman from the audience had been shown to be
transcendently awkward, brainless and to have a mania
for petty thieving. With burning face and falling
glance, he had stumbled back to his seat, where a
lady who had before exhibited the public manner
of wife to husband toward him, now pretended that
he was an utter and offensive stranger.

"Bean suffered vicariously with this altruistic dolt."

v

However, there is no need for taking Mr. Wilson
too seriously. He is funny but he is (and, I think,
invariably) trivial. Take, as but one example, the
opening of his latest, *Adventures in Geography:*—

" 'Came a day when Ralph Royce found himself
on the West Coast of China.' So flashed the moving
sub-title, and one more educational triumph was scored
for the photo-drama. How few of us, even if came
a day, could find ourselves on the West Coast of China?
Try it on your map."

All that, as you have guessed, because China has no
West Coast and——

But if Mr. Wilson must make fun of the movies, he should go deeper. They are far from perfect. Why, then, pick on the geography of sub-title writers? Why not an adversary worthy of Mr. Wilson's wit? Perhaps because (as seems likely) the sub-title writer is just such an adversary. Water, as you know, seeks its own level.

Mr. Wilson could not have written Arnold Bennett's, *The Great Adventure;* or any of Shaw; or the *Tales of Jaques Tournebroche* as they are retold by Anatole France—and the reason is plain: his are passing fancies and he tries altogether too hard. He belabors his wit and cudgels his humor. He cannot even, in *Somewhere in Red Gap,* cross a field without noting that the white-faced Herefords are putting on flesh to their ruin. The gate he passes through, he says, could be handled ideally only by a retired weight lifter in a barbed-wire-proof armor and is, facetiously perhaps, named the Armstrong. He calculates the inconvenience, the cost in time and energy wasted, in the operation of such a gate. Twenty-eight and a half cents per diem per gate. Say a hundred gates on the ranch $28.50. And so on and so on.

There need be, literally, no end to that sort of funniness. And in *Oh Doctor* there is almost no end to it. 400 pages. You have to be hard put to it for something at which to laugh before tackling *Oh Doctor,* knowing that through the length of it there will be not so much thought and philosophy as goes to the making up of a single chapter in Rabelais.

VI

Mr. Wilson was born in Oregon, Illinois, May 1, 1867. In 1902 he married Rose Cecil Latham, better known as Rose O'Neill, the artist. They were divorced. He has since married again.

From 1896–1902 he was editor of *Puck*, a now long since defunct humorous weekly.

He is the author of *Zigzag Tales* (1896); *The Spenders*, 1902; *The Lions of the Lord*, 1903; *The Seekers*, 1904; *The Boss of Little Arcady*, 1905 (Samuel Hopkins Adams' favorite among his books); *Ewing's Lady*, 1907; *The Man From Home*, 1908 (with Booth Tarkington); *Bunker Bean*, 1912; *Ruggles of Red Gap*, 1915; *Somewhere in Red Gap*, 1916; *Ma Pettingill*, 1919 (my choice among his character creations); *Merton of the Movies*, 1921; *The Wrong Twin*, 1922; *Oh, Doctor*, 1923; *Adventures in Geography*, 1924; and (just announced) *Professor, How Could You!*

OWEN WISTER

The author of the *Virginian* will always be simply that —the author of the *Virginian*. He has published thirteen other volumes, but the *Virginian* (published in April, 1902) is still the best he has to offer—and comes near to being the best of its kind. It carries on a noble tradition, the tradition of the West. It is in line with Mark Twain's Mississippi stories and the understanding tales of Bret Harte. It has charm. It is without melodrama. It tells the story of one cowboy and it tells that story in detail, with sympathy, almost with beauty. The *Virginian* lives—and after twenty-two years that is high praise.

But it is marred by Mr. Wister's passion for irrelevance. He is not content with his cowboy; he must lambaste Wall Street and the politicians; he must extol the horseman of the plains by making odious comparisons with the acquisitive folk back East in Washington and New York.

This sort of thing is forever cropping out in Mr. Wister's books. I am on record as having said that *Philosophy 4* is delightful; but I take it all back. I re-read *Philosophy 4* last night. The book should be a masterpiece. It tells of two young undergrads at Harvard who with the aid of a fellow-classman are cramming for a final exam in Philosophy 4. They have to do with Absolute Intelligence, with Plato and Hobbes and Berkeley and (as they call it) the hard-boiled ego. To them it seems the most tremendous nonsense; but for the sake of their parents they must pass the exam. So there they are, sitting up night after night with Oscar Maironi who pays a part of his way through college by tutoring the less diligent sons of the wealthy at $5 an hour. It is this Maironi who aggravates Mr. Wister. Mr. Wister is all sympathy for Bertie and Billie. They are generous, Careless, happy-go-lucky. But he cannot abide the pedantry and poverty of Maironi.

"Money filled the pockets of Bertie and Billie; therefore were their heads empty of money and full of less cramping thoughts. Oscar had fallen upon the reverse of this fate. Calculation was his second nature."

But are the poor always calculating? And is it true that those who have plenty of money never think of money? Do not they all too often accept money as the measure of everything?

He goes on to say that Maironi's "young days had been dedicated to getting the better of his neighbor because otherwise his neighbor would get the better of him." But can Maironi be held responsible for this sad state of things? We live in an acquisitive society. Does it become us to abuse those who would starve to death unless they kept a weather-eye peeled to the main chance?

II

The *Virginian* is dedicated to Mr. Theodore Roosevelt; and all through the *Virginian,* like a swollen vein, runs the Colonel's indignation against the passing of the frontier and the coming of a more complex and difficult civilization. Nothing to make that coming more easy; just a constant rebuking of the inevitable.

Nor are these rebukes well timed or to the point. In the two prefaces to the later editions much space is devoted to the evils practised in Wall Street and to praise of the common people. But the common people have just such masters as they are willing to serve; the common people are ignorant and selfish; they are content. No good purpose is served by lavishing praise on them and condemning their duly elected governors. It is the common people who have repudiated Pinchot, the common people who join the Ku Klux Klan and read the *New York American*. The powers that be were placed in power by the common people. They voted for Harding because they wanted the sort of cabinet Harding would give them—and they got that sort of cabinet. As Ed Howe says, the man who first called them the Common People was very nearly right.

III

But at bottom the *Virginian* has nothing to do with politics. At bottom it is the work of an artist. Not a very great artist perhaps, but an artist nonetheless— with the first page we are back in the Wyoming of the nineties.

With the first page we move to the car-window with the other passengers and look out on a corral, surrounded by laughing men, inside a whirl of dust, and in the dust a lot of plunging, huddled, dodging horses.

No Western story opens with more of wonder and romance. No Western story figures so fine a rustler

as Trampas, so likable a drawler as the Virginian himself, so eloquent a bishop as was the Talbot of those
earlier days.

I have ridden in the West and it was with the surprise of recognition that I recently re-read *The Virginian*. Mr. Wister has caught the tone and color
of that now passed phase of American life. That I
never myself met the Virginian may be a fault in me.
At any rate, I know the plains are there, the buttes,
the dust and alkali of the desert—and the great good
humor of the men who did the riding.

Perhaps the story is told with a little too much of
sentiment and sweetness.—I know that I can take
my romance with more salt; death is the end of all our
dreaming; even to the cowboy life was not all cakes
and ale.—But this is not to condemn the book. As
books go, it is really very fine.

IV

It is by all odds the best thing that Mr. Wister has
done. For the rest he is rather petulant. He is
afraid of change. The sight of blood nauseates him.
And yet he has his aspirations.

On page 3 of the *Seven Ages of Washington,* he
tells us that Washington, in one of his letters, wrote:
"Our rascally privateersman go on at the old rate";
and that the word "rascally" was taken out as in-
decorous in the first printing of the letters.

Again—"such a dearth of spirit pray God I may
never witness again" becomes "such a dearth of spirit
pray God's mercy I may never witness again."

"One hundred thousand dollars is but a fleabite" is

changed to "one hundred thousand dollars will be totally inadequate."

With a fine show of indignation Mr. Wister cries out against such editing. It makes of Washington a "frozen image, rigid with congealed virtue, ungenial, unreal." We must have the whole truth, he says, or nothing. And then he gives us the better part of valor.

Rascally, fleabite, pray God, we can away with. But in certain of his letters to his mother, always begining Honored Madam as was the custom of their day, Washington's language contains (and does not wholly conceal—even from Mr. Wister) the struggle between the man's displeasure and the son's natural respect and affection. (In later years his mother's conduct with regard to money matters was wont to pain and mortify her son.) Mr. Wister tells us that certain paragraphs in those letters make distressing reading—and so he turns away, leaving them unquoted.

In a word, his courage is not equal to his creed.

v

In 1915, while we were still all of us neutral, Mr. Wister wrote a book (*The Pentecost of Calamity*) to show that though Germany had been at one time a remarkable and beautiful country, the incorrigible Germans, through their habit of obedience, were bound sooner or later to end up badly. They were trained to war and would when chance offered start some sort of fracas,—because a man always does the thing that he is trained for—which simply means that I'm a civil engineer.

The book is nonsense; and has been proved nonsense again and again by after-war confession and by most of the figures available to Mr. Wister when he sat down to write. France had a larger army than Germany's and an alliance with Russia that made the elimination of Germany a logical necessity—yet neither France nor Germany can be held solely responsible for the war. Wars don't just happen because we love music (as Mr. Wister thinks) or because we inherit the wrong sort of emperor. Wars are a part of our way of living.

VI

A convalescing Highlander told my friend Jimmy Purdy in Bombay that when he enlisted in Glasgow he believed that he was going to fight for his king and country but in the trenches he soon discovered that he was fighting for his bloody life. And after all that is what we fight for—our bloody lives. We are moral cowards and haven't the nerve to say so and so we mumble something about honor; but in our hearts we know that we are concerned with food and drink and with food and drink alone.

VII

Mr. Wister was born in Philadelphia, July 14, 1860, of a family that had been writing for four generations —the famous Kemble family of actors to which Mrs. Siddons belonged.

"The first ten years of my life," he says, "were spent in that part of the city known·as Germantown. The Civil War furnished the first picture in my memory. Various of my relations would appear in uniform. The Great Sanitary Fair makes another picture in which the most vivid detail is a model of the ship that went to the Arctic with Dr. Kane. In connection with the War, too, I remember very distinctly going to rooms where my mother worked with other ladies over what must have been bandages or clothing. At any rate, men in uniform fill these extremely early days, and made an impression which lasts. In the same way, I recall the morning when the news of the assassination of Lincoln arrived. I was not quite five years old, but I remember sitting at a table and knowing that something terrible had happened because of the grief of my parents.

"I had a pony very soon in life, and learned to ride bareback on him. Riding has been my favorite exercise always. I went to various schools and was a somewhat troublesome boy, I believe. I never played games very well. The game that is now called hockey, and was then called shinney, was my favorite and the only one in which I could hold my own. I also learned to skate and was very fond of this. I acquired the power and the desire to read to myself before I was six. The first book I remember so reading was *Grimm's Household Tales.* Soon after this, I remember *Alice in Wonderland,* but by the time this came out, I could read fluently.

"From ten to thirteen I was in Europe, first in school in Switzerland where I had a very bad time, and then

in school in England where I had a very good time.
The third year of this journey, I traveled with my
parents and passed the winter in Rome. At the
school in Switzerland, I began to learn music, which
has been my favorite interest ever since, far surpassing
that of literature. There is no book in the world,
with the exception of certain works by Shakespeare
and Scott, of which I am so fond as I am of quite a
few pieces of music. In Switzerland, I did some
mountain climbing and in England I played cricket,
but never well. The school was at Kenilworth and my
memories of the castle are very vivid. I had relations
in the neighborhood and saw a good deal, as a small
boy, of the very best kind of English people.

"In 1873 I went to St. Paul's School, Concord,
N. H., and was there for five years. I then went to
Harvard College. Through these years my chief interest was the study of music and my chief pleasure in
out-of-doors exercise, horse riding, but the winter
sports at St. Paul's School I enjoyed extremely. I
also rowed on a crew and played cricket on a team at
St. Paul's School, but I never did either of these things
well. About this time, I began to be interested in the
West, and was very proud of owning moccasins and
going about the woods in them. I had a gun and
learned how to shoot it. I never shot particularly well
with a shotgun and could always do better with a rifle.

"During these years, I had very excellent training
in English. I have seen no training since that equaled
it or came near equaling it. The teaching of English
to-day is distinctly inferior to the manner in which I
was taught. The classics also were made very inter-

esting to me, both Greek and Latin, and these also I was well taught, especially at St. Paul's School. I do not think the teaching at Harvard College equaled that I had at St. Paul's School, either in English or in the classics. My reading was quite desultory and I never cared for it so much as I did for music. Graduating in 1882, with highest honors in music and the *summa cum laude* degree, I went to Europe, where I passed a year and a half. I was advised by Franz Liszt to become a composer, and I studied under Guiraud in Paris. Circumstances made this impossible, and I came home and had a position in a bank. At this time my health broke down and I spent my first summer, namely 1885, in Wyoming.

"I entered the Harvard Law School in 1885, graduating there in 1888. During this time I had been to Wyoming twice again, camping, fishing and hunting big game, as well as to other parts of the West, and this had become my chief interest. During these and following years, I spent much time at Western military posts. In 1889 I entered the Bar at Philadelphia and practiced for a short time, but soon took to writing stories. How I came to do this, I have told in the preface to one of my books, viz: *Members of the Family*. I devoted my attention more and more to writing stories and gradually ceased to be anything but an official lawyer, having no practice and wishing none.

"My first books were jocose affairs—a three act comic opera for the Harvard Hasty Pudding Club, entitled *Dido and Æneas;* a parody of the *Swiss Family Robinson;* and a burlesque romance, entitled *The Dragon of Wantley*."

VIII

In the preface to *Members of the Family*, Mr. Wister tells how writing had been a pastime of his since first he joined the board of the school paper at St. Paul's.

And then in 1884 Mr. Howells, the patient counsellor of so many, felt his literary pulse and pronounced it promising. A quickening came from the pages of Stevenson. A far stronger shove from the Kipling who wrote *Plain Tales from the Hills*. Then, during prolonged wanderings through Wyoming and Montana, the final push was given by Proper Merimee— and he was launched upon a literary career.

Mr. Wister is a man who believes in playing favorites—if he favors anything he says so. And it was his favorite among short stories, *Carmen*, that made an author of him, that inspired the traveler's tale that was to be sent off with a second to Franklin Square and accepted by Mr. Alden for *Harper's*.

In 1896 Henry James sat up all one night and patiently, carefully, went through Mr. Wister's first book, making a suggestion here, offering a phrase to be substituted there. Mr. Wister had arrived.

Mr. Wister is the author of *The Dragon of Wantley—His Tail*, 1892; *Red Men and White*, 1896; *Lin McLean*, 1898; *The Jimmy John Boss*, 1900; *U. S. Grant, a Biography*, 1900; *The Virginian*, 1902; *Philosophy 4*, 1903; *Journey in Search of Christmas*, 1904; *Lady Baltimore*, 1906; *The Simple Spelling Bee*, 1907; *Mother*, 1907; *The Seven Ages of Wash-*

ington, 1907; *Members of the Family,* 1911; *The Pentecost of Calamity,* 1915.

He has been a contributor of prose and verse to various magazines; and of articles on Musk-ox, Bison, Sheep and Goats to Whitney's *American Sportsman's Library.*

He is a member of the Societé des Gens de Lettres de France and a fellow of the American Academy of Arts and Sciences.

HAROLD BELL WRIGHT

I call him rational, says Anatole France, who, observing human folly and disorder, is not so stubborn as to insist that they are order and wisdom.

By any such criterion Mr. Harold Bell Wright is hopelessly mad, out of his head and raving—for whatever is, is divinely right to him. Someone or other, quoting Browning, has told him that God is in his heaven; and Mr. Wright has accepted the statement as gospel. All's well with his world.

All's well; and we are to smile benignly as Fall loots the national reserves, cheer when Daugherty asks a stay of judgment, shout for the post office jobs given out on the recommendation of Slemp.

II

The business of leaving stones unturned, Mr. Wright's business, is an old one and comparatively simple—you merely sit tight, ruffle no feelings, start no train of thought. But it is nonetheless a damnable business; and it is damnable largely because it is so unintelligent. It would enshrine the shibboleths and superstitions of our fathers, making old creeds and antique fables sacred in the eyes of all. There could be no further questioning of established customs, no seeking after further truths. The truth, we would be told, was in the beginning with God.

Now that may well be, but all things that were with God in the beginning are not now present upon this earth. We are far from perfection. Millions are

601

dying, millions have died in ignorance and neglect. It is not ours to sit back and watch our arteries harden or try, as some do, to stave off fat with hot sulphur baths. There is work to be done. We are being ruled by morons and lectured by swine to whom the wonders of procreation are a secret shame. The code of the intemperate is our law. The lust for power, for ruling the other fellow governs our every action. To us a glass of beer in some garden overlooking the Thames or the Isar is sinful; and those who engage in drinking anything stronger than water are sinners. We pray for them. . . . And we pretend to other than a common humanity with the Tartar, the Mongol and the Jap. . . . And yet, but for the great mercy of God, Mr. Wright himself might have been born in an African Kraal or of peasants in Bessarabia.

III

That young genius Otto Braun, untimely killed in the War, realized, in his teens, that the lot of the workers is a hard one; they live, as though they had been transgressors against some consecrated law, in hovels, in poverty and filth; they exist under conditions unworthy of human beings, embittered or (what is even worse) contented with their lot. And he knew, though little more than a boy, that this apathy, while one of the cornerstones of our modern industrial civilization, is also its most unforgivable crime. He had a social conscience.

But Mr. Wright has no conscience and no concern in the happiness or good health of the other fellow.

He is not a member of society but an individualist growing rich through the sale of tenth rate novels. And the end of his *Helen of the Old House* is defeat for the strikers—a sop has been thrown to them and they are sent back to their tools, their unrest stilled, their search for a better life ended. . . . "And I'd like to see Jake Vodell or any other foreign agitator try, etc., etc." says Mr. Wright's heroic mill owner. Mr. Wright, you see, forgets that the Christ whose name he so often invokes was a foreigner and, if ever there lived one, an agitator who brought not peace but the sword. The only advice he could have given to Mr. Wright's so certain rich man he gave to another who came long ago seeking salvation for his soul— Go, sell all that thou hast and distribute to the poor.

IV

Mr. Wright's publishers may acclaim him an artist with a clean box of colors but to me he is a bigot standing directly in the path of progress. He and his kind, in their exalted manhood, have cried down Darwin. They are the rank and file of the Ku Klux Klan. To them the pope is anathema, the scientist a fool. And they have but one weapon—when they don't agree with you they overwhelm you with numbers.

V

Listen to Mr. Wright fomenting hatred. His subject is professors; and his example, in *When A Man's A Man,* is Professor Parkhill whom he dubs, as though there were such a person, 'the famous professor of æsthetics.'

This is the way the professor talks, according to Kitty, Mr. Wright's 100% heroine; "He says that in the crude and uncultivated mentalities of our, etc., etc."

Now does any professor talk that way, except in anger to his class? And could he be famous if he did? And wouldn't you, if you were inoffensively native to Kansas or New Mexico, resent such talk if you were given the words of someone like Mr. Wright, in whom you believed, that that was the way eastern professors referred to your powers of thought? You might be crude and your mind uncultivated but that is no reason anyone should refer to you with such sarcastic scorn.

But Kitty is interrupted when Patches, the rosy-cheeked cowboy, shouts out, "Here he comes."

And so he does. And he looks, says Mr. Wright, the part—the part to which, according to Mr. Wright, he has been assigned from birth by his over-cultured parents.

I hate to keep breaking in, but I want to know what "over-cultured parents" are. Is a man over-cultured if he can read Sanskrit? Does a knowledge of the sources of Mr. Wells' History make us over-cultured? Is Einstein over-cultured? Was President Wilson? And just how do you go about it to assign a part, at birth, to your son? I have a son; and I'll be blamed if I can make out any of the various parts he plays. Last night, in a high backed chair, he told me that he was in jail; and this morning at breakfast he bit me, explaining that he was a bear. I'd like to assign some more useful rôle to him.

But to continue—and don't forget that Mr. Wright's

publishers insist that his is the spirit that calls to the best in men; so read attentively. . . .

"His slender body, with its narrow shoulders and sunken chest, frail as it was, seemed almost too heavy for his feeble legs. His thin face, bloodless and sallow, with a sparse, daintily trimmed beard and weak watery eyes, was characterized by a solemn and portentous gravity, as though, realizing fully the profound importance of his mission in life, he could permit no trivial thought to enter his bald, domelike head. One knew instinctively that in all the forty-five years of his little life no happiness or joy that had not been scientifically sterilized and certified had ever been permitted to stain his superæsthetic soul."

VI

This is picked at random, but it is typical. Mr. Wright has all the ear-marks of the irreverent. Can't you hear him as he contemplates Steinmetz, his full-throated scorn at that mis-shapen body? And doesn't he know that self-importance was never yet adjudged a crime? Mr. Roosevelt had plenty of self-importance; Lincoln had a high regard for the office he occupied; God has not been dwelling all these millions of years in ignorance of the fact that he is God. But that stuff about instinctively knowing that all the professor's joys are sterilized is what takes the cake. Imagine my saying that I know instinctively and all the rest of it about George Santayana—for I presume that Santayana comes as near to being a "famous professor of æsthetics" as anyone you or I can think of. Imagine saying it about the charwoman—or instinctively know-

ing that Senator Brookhart has had no evil thoughts.
In short, I don't believe we do know that sort of
thing instinctively.   There's blamed little any of us
know instinctively—and what Mr. Wright knows is a
damned sight less, even though most of it be instinct
or hearsay.

VII

But do not, in your laughter, forget that this is
dangerous propaganda, broadcasted by an irrespon-
sible, for it is the cowboy who reads Mr. Wright.
And in the cowboy, through ignorance, by a constant
repetition of just slanderous talk, Mr. Wright has
bred a contempt for those whose interest is in æsthetics
—for John Singer Sargent, Mary Garden, A. E., and
you and me.   He has set the cowboy off by himself.
He has made a division in our fellowship.   Yet surely
we have no quarrel with the cowboy.   I punched cows
myself for three years, in Montana and Eastern Oregon, for the Circle Diamond and the Bell A, but I
love the verses of Miss Millay and the *Shropshire Lad*
of that excellent Latinist, Professor Housmann.

VIII

Along about the middle of *The Winning of Barbara
Worth,* Barbara's mother is sitting on the porch, darn-
ing her husband's socks—the husband is a country
banker.   I'll give you one guess.   What is Mr.
Wright's comment on such doings?
Of course—"Maybe bankers do not usually wear
socks that have been darned."
What else could Mr. Wright say?   To him

"banker" means just one thing—a rich man—J. P. Morgan or little Billie Ladd of Portland.   He never heard of the negro bankers of the south, the bankers in the foothills of Vermont, the bankers who are going broke by their hundreds in the grain states of the West. Say "Banker" and he has his full description, for he is the slave of words.   In any encounter with a word Mr. Wright always comes off second best.   Say "cow" to him and he can think of just one cow.   He is in- curious.   He would not inquire as to whether it was a Jersey, a Holstein, beef, milk or dual purpose.   And so it is with bankers.   It is not the individual banker that excites his interest.   Mr. Worth, simply because he is a banker and can be ticketed, loses all personal traits and becomes one with the sharks of Wall Street.

Mr. Wright is never specific.

IX

Then there is Harold's philosopher in *Helen of the Old House*.   A queer bird, he has a grin that is a blend of admiration, envy and contempt.

I tried all night before last to manage that grin. I stood before the mirror.   I took it slowly.   I began with a look of wonder as I glimpsed the interest in my eyes.   I switched to pride as I noted the fit of my pajamas.   But the best I could do was a worried con- sternation at the faces I was making and a hope my mouth would not grow that way.

But how do we know this chap is a philosopher? First off, of course, because Mr. Wright tells us so; and then because of the added proof he puts into the words his sage lets fall—"You can't think of Mills-

burgh without thinkin' mills; an' you can't think mills
without thinkin' the Mill."

Now the fact that you can doesn't make any difference, of course.   The point is—a philosopher is one
who, dropping his d's and g's, talks portentous twaddle
with a fatuously grave air.

How is that mighty word, lover of wisdom, grown
senile since first it was used by the Greeks!

x

"Suppose," says Grant Overton in his essay on
Harold Bell Wright in *American Nights Entertainment,* "that instead of audibly deploring Mr. Wright
and uttering in their assaults upon him an unconscion-
able amount of twaddle, the literary critics were to
transform themselves into students of popular psychology."

Well, suppose they did?

"In such case," says Grant, "they would see at once
how the usual person proceeds unsentimentally through
life with the assistance of attainable ideals."

Would they?   I doubt it.   But if they did?   What
if we agreed that the "usual person" is the proper
study of literary critics and that ideals are attainable?
Grant does not tell us.   He hurries on to explain that
"Of course, definitions of sentimentality may and do
differ."   He skips the most important part of his argument which is Harold Bell Wright.   And why?   Because he can't think of a darned thing to say about him
—and he has forty pages to fill.   So he drags in a lot
of anonymous literary critics and lectures them on the
definitions of sentimentality.

XI

Overton was in a quandary. I am the only critic that has ever bothered to 'assault' Mr. Wright, but I scarcely seemed important enough for a forty page essay. So he created for me a lot of confreres. I wish I could discover them. I would use them now in my return to the charge.

All literary critics either frankly confess that they have no time for Mr. Wright or, with Overton, praise him because his books sell by the carload. I am the only one whom he enrages. Grant knows this, of course. So he quotes me at length but never by name. One-half of his essay is devoted to me, but his publishers would think him mad if he came out and said so. He is supposed to be writing about Harold Bell Wright—and can't—no one can. There's nothing to write.

This proves the point that I have been trying to make. Wright is empty and shallow and inconsequential when he isn't vicious. I wrote four pages on him in 1919; Grant expanded them into twenty. Wright has written eleven novels and, except for a quotation lifted from my essay, there isn't a sentence in all those eleven novels that Grant could find worthy of quotation. Among all Mr. Wright's ten million readers there isn't a one—except me—who can put his finger on a sentence and say, "That's Mr. Wright's."

XII

Literary critics, as Grant would know if he read them, always ignore Mr. Wright. "How shall we dispose of such beguilers of the millions?" wails Van

Doren.   And they don't try to dispose of him.   They
simply dismiss him as unreadable—as Heywood Broun
does.

Since I need an ally in my controversy with Overton
I shall quote Broun, from a recent issue of the New
York *World*:—

"As a rule, the newspaper book reviewer avoids
saying much about Harold Bell Wright because he
doesn't find Mr. Wright interesting.   Certainly he is
a difficult subject for the critic.   I have read just one
Wright novel, and if I were condemned to remain in
jail until I had composed a column review of the book,
I might well languish for life.   I can't see what there
is to say about it.   Everything I felt could be written
in a paragraph.

" 'This,' I might say, 'is a bad novel.   At least it
is of no use to me.   It is bad from my point of view
because it is not interesting.   The story follows a familiar formula.   There is no quality of surprise
and excitement.   Beyond that I think it is a bad book,
because as far as I can see it falsifies life.'

"After writing that much it would be necessary for
me to ponder and ponder before I could go farther.
The question of the popularity of a novel is a little outside the true function of any sort of critic, but if I
understood the reasons for the success of Harold
Bell Wright, I would be glad to make that part of the
review.   But I can no more explain it than I can explain the long run of *Abie's Irish Rose*.   For that
matter, I have yet to read any illuminating discourse
on the fundamental appeal of a number of American
literary and dramatic successes.

"I doubt very much whether Harold Bell Wright
himself comprehends the psychology of his success.

There is little deliberate forethought in his writing, I think. He just has the good fortune to be internally tuned up in harmony with the minds of many. He has neither invented moral earnestness nor assumed that quality. It just happened to grow in him wild and uncultivated. This natural growth he cuts now and again and markets for profits."

XIII

Mr. Wright's way of work deserves a paragraph.

"The system I use," he says, "may have been used for centuries, or it may be no one else has ever used it. I have wondered whether it is old or new. Whichever it may be here it is; When I start to write a novel, the first thing I do is to figure out why I am going to write it. Not what is the story, but why? I mull this over a while,.and when it is pretty straight in my mind, I write out an argument. No suggestion of plot, you see. No incidents, scenes, location, nothing done at first except the argument, but it is the heart and soul of the novel. The novel is merely this argument presented through the medium of the characters, plots, incidents, and the other properties of the story. Next come the characters, each standing for some element or faction in the argument. Up to the last copying of the *Eyes of the World,* not a character had been named. They were called in the copy, Greed, Ambition, Youth, or whatever they represented to me in the writing of the story."

In short, Mr. Wright tries to prove some mulled-over argument of his own in his novels; and his characters are the personification of Greed, Ambition, and Youth. Overton makes the mistake, in quoting me and quoting Wright's system from me, of insisting, as I had once, that this was Bunyan's method in *Pilgrim's Progress*. But Bunyan's characters, like Shakespeare's, are extra-human while Wright's are less than men and women. Bunyan had a well-stored mind. When he thought of Greed, he thought as the Greeks did of King Midas. When Wright thinks of Greed, his conceptions are mean and uninspiring. Besides Bunyan never said that Prefessor Parkhill was incarnate Ambition or that Kitty was Youth itself. Any such assumption would have seemed as ridiculous to Bunyan as it does to me.

XIV

And now for the bare outlines of Mr. Wright's life.

He was born near Rome, New York, May 4, 1872; for two years a student in the preparatory department of Hiram College, Ohio; successively sign-painter, decorator, landscape painter and pastor of various churches in Kansas, Missouri and California. He retired, in ill-health from the ministry in 1908. In Arizona and Southern California he has, for the past fifteen years, made a persistent and resolute fight for life against the onrush of tuberculosis. He is now a rancher near Tucson.

Mr. Wright is the author of *That Printer of Udell's*, 1903; *The Shepherd of the Hills*, 1907; *The Calling of Dan Matthews*, 1909; *The Uncrowned King*, 1910; *The Winning of Barbara Worth*, 1911; *Their Yesterdays*, 1912; *The Eyes of the World*, 1914; *When a Man's a Man*, 1916; *The Re-Creation of Brian Kent*, 1919; *Helen of the Old House*, 1921; *The Mine With the Iron Door*, 1923.